Experience, Culture and Religion in Systematic Theology

D1496208

Experience, Culture and Religion in Systematic Theology

An Integrative and Pluriform Methodology

Edmond Zi-Kang Chua

James Clarke & Co.

JAMES CLARKE & CO.

P.O. Box 60
Cambridge
CB1 2NT
United Kingdom

www.jamesclarke.co
publishing@jamesclarke.co

Hardback ISBN: 978 0 227 17049 9
Paperback ISBN: 978 0 227 17948 2
PDF ISBN: 978 0 227 17950 5
ePub ISBN: 978 0 227 17951 2

British Library Cataloguing in Publication Data
A record is available from the British Library

First published by James Clarke & Co., 2023

To the Father, my origin, my present and my eternity

Thank you for having been in the thick of all that I have gone through

You are truly a God who sees me and through whom I can hope to see

Contents

Foreword

Experience, Culture and Religion in Systematic Theology is the work of an up-and-coming, emerging Asian theologian that is significant and wide-ranging, bold in its scope and aims. Impressive for its depth and erudition, this is no superficial 'overview' of its subject matter. Rather, it tackles some key doctrines and beliefs from a broadly critical evangelical perspective, informed by the author's own context and experience. This book is not the product of an armchair ruminant. It is the result of someone grappling with very real existential-theological questions and issues. The work is marked by deep intentionality and integrity.

Edmond Chua, a convert to Christianity from his familial Chinese religious upbringing, is acutely sensitive to the question of theology and other faiths and especially how Christian theology views other religions. He is sensitively alert to what salvation means in regard to those who remain faithful to their own and who see no need to embrace Christianity. Does God spurn or abandon them? Coming out of the stable of conversion, Chua's view may surprise some; it will be welcomed by others.

Chua's work is marked by deep Christian engagement with uncomfortable perennial matters, bringing to bear novel and creatively complex perspectives. Theology is not reduced to simplistic aphorisms; it fronts up to demanding questions with challenging answers. A careful reading – this is not a work for the theologically faint-hearted – will be amply repaid.

Chua clearly believes theology should not, indeed cannot be done in a cultural or religious vacuum: theology is not an other-worldly enterprise. It is an intellectual task of marrying the intentions, aspirations and visions of faith with the realities of the world in which the faithful are engaged. It is rooted in the existential realities of human diversity – cultural, contextual, religious, gender – to name but a few that fall into the horizon of Chua's purview.

The first three of the book's seven chapters dive into an exploration of the foundations of theology, aptly identifying a mix of experience, culture and world religions as one contributing matrix, alongside a quadrilateral of faith, scripture, tradition and reason. Chua's discussion of the multi-religious context for doing theology is particularly important, especially in the way he integrates elements of the biblical narratives into his argument, along with references to early Christian doctrine and interpretation.

Together with useful introductions to Buddhism, Hinduism and Islam, Chua also provides succinct overviews of the Bahai, Zoroastrian, Taoist and Sikh faiths, as well as a useful discussion of Shintoism and traditional or tribal religion, together with 'Non-Theisms', all in order to provide necessary background and context for exploring the topic of Christian engagement with world religions.

There is also a penetrating discussion proposing a 'Christian Global Systematic Theology', which Chua speaks of as 'recognising the legitimacy of other faiths and studying their doctrine to see how our own might be enhanced, deepened, or made more comprehensive in its scope'. This is a high ideal, but one which is undoubtedly necessary especially in our time. His methodology section is particularly useful and helpful and shows the extent to which Chua is deeply engaged with the historic Christian theological tradition as well as contemporary perspectives and thought.

Following the first three chapters, the four doctrinal chapters address, respectively, the Trinity, Christology, Theodicy and Sin and Salvation. Each follows a novel scholastic structural schema that provides definition; location in the field of systematic theology; strengths and weaknesses of current conceptions; a proposition with advantages and prolepses outlined; and a conclusion. Each is a very competent, thorough, challenging and penetrating presentation and discussion. Many pertinent questions are raised and addressed.

Not everyone will concur with all of Chua's perspectives and suggestions – but they are worthwhile nevertheless, and very much grist to the ongoing theological mill. Many readers will undoubtedly find themselves challenged, encouraged by and agreeing with much of Chua's thought and ideas. In any event, Chua offers a stimulating combination of a solid grasp of the Christian tradition with a capacity to proffer novel ideas that may yet resolve theological conundrums, or at least open up the possibility of fresh theological thinking actually making a difference.

This is an exciting, must-have book. There is much here for a hungry student to digest and learn from and for the mature scholar to appreciate and be challenged by.

Douglas Pratt, FRHistS
The University of Auckland, New Zealand
26 January 2023

Acknowledgements

Almost every book is a product of collective effort, and this is no exception. Many books contain an imprint of their author's personal history, and there is much to say about those who have come and gone in my life and who have left a mark in some way on it.

Foremost among them is my father, now deceased, whose lovingkindness spurred me to imagine what an empyrean Father could be. I am grateful to my mother for her unstinting care and support; to my spouse for being a comforting oasis; and for my children, beacons of unending joy and hope.

This is a suitable setting to recognise my theological dependence upon the ideas of Professor Jung Young Lee, a prolific Korean-American systematic theologian of the last century. I will always fondly remember the kindness of Professor Douglas Pratt in writing a Foreword, as well as providing a positive assessment of my book. I am also appreciative to Professor Paul Hedges for his timely and useful feedback.

Many thanks are due to Samuel Fitzgerald, editor at James Clarke & Co., for taking on my book and seeing it through to publication, and Dorothy Luckhurst, copy-editor, for her meticulous work.

Above all, I will not fail to extol the supreme benefits I have received from my God, for and about whom this work is written. In a world of ever-contested truths, this book stands as an expression of my experiential understanding of God, the Father, and the Son, and the Holy Spirit, whose name is unalloyed love, supplying the moral nature of all established creeds and human communities and favouring all in any place and time who choose to do that which we reasonably know to be humane and right.

Edmond Zi-Kang Chua
Singapore
14 July 2023

Abbreviations

AT	*Acta Theologica*
BW	*The Biblical World* (1893-1920), University of Chicago Press
CD	*Church Dogmatics* (English translation of Karl Barth's *Die Kirchliche Dogmatik*)
CGR	*The Conrad Grebel Review*, University of Waterloo, ON
CHALOT	*A Concise Hebrew and Aramaic Lexicon of the Old Testament*
Chr. Trad.	*The Christian Tradition: A History of the Development of Doctrine*, Jaroslav Pelikan (1923-2006)
Civ.	*De civitate Dei* (*The City of God*), St Augustine of Hippo (354-430)
Conf.	*Confessiones* (*Confessions*), St Augustine of Hippo
Conf. fid.	*Praelectiones in confessionem fidei* (*Truth's Victory Over Error: A Commentary on the Westminster Confession of Faith*), David Dickson (1583-1663)
Const. Chr.	*De constitutione Christi ontologica et psychologica* (*The Ontological and Psychological Constitution of Christ*), Bernard Lonergan (1904-84)
Contr. Ar.	*Orationes contra Arianos* (*Against the Arians*), St Athanasius of Alexandria (293-373)
CSJ	*Concordia Student Journal* (1978-2007), Concordia Seminary, St Louis, MO
CT	*Christian Theology*, Millard J. Erickson (b. 1932)
DCD	*An Essay on the Development of Christian Doctrine*, John H. Newman (1801-1890)
De Trin.	*De Trinitate* (*On the Trinity*), Richard of Saint-Victor (d. 1173)

DG	*Discovering God: The Origins of the Great Religions and the Evolution of Belief,* Rodney Stark (b. 1934)
DI	*Divine Immutability: A Critical Reconsideration,* Isaak A. Dorner (1809-84) (original title, 'Über die richtige Fassung des dogmatischen Begriffs der Unveränderlichkeit Gottes, mit besonderer Beziehung auf das gegenseitige Verhältniss zwischen Gottes übergeschichlichem und geschichtlichem Leben')
Div.	*De diversis quaestionibus octoginta tribus* (*On Eighty-Three Various Questions*), St Augustine of Hippo
ESV	English Standard Version, Crossway
GDT	*Global Dictionary of Theology*
Impass.	*The Impassibility of God: A Survey of Christian Thought,* John K. Mozley (1883-1946)
Inst.	*Institutio Christianae religionis* (*Institutes of the Christian Religion*), John Calvin (1509-64)
KD	*Die Kirchliche Dogmatik* (English translation, *Church Dogmatics*), Karl Barth (1886-1968)
MaB	*The Message and the Book: Sacred Texts of the World's Religions,* John Bowker (b. 1935)
MNT	*Medical News Today*
NDPR	*Notre Dame Philosophical Reviews,* University of Notre Dame, Notre Dame, IN
NDT	*New Dictionary of Theology*
NTDNTW	*The NIV Theological Dictionary of New Testament Words*
NPNF[2]	A Select Library of Nicene and Post-Nicene Fathers of the Christian Church: Second Series
OT	*Open Theology*
PGWR	*Pocket Guide to World Religions,* Winfried Corduan
PNTC	The Pillar New Testament Commentary, Donald A. Carson (ed.)
REP Online	*Routledge Encyclopedia of Philosophy Online*
RFIA	*The Review of Faith & International Affairs*
SCG	*Summa contra gentiles* (*On the Truth of the Catholic Faith*), St Thomas Aquinas (1224/5-74)
SEP	*The Stanford Encyclopedia of Philosophy*
SLGNT	*Shorter Lexicon of the Greek New Testament,* 2nd edn, F. Wilbur Gingrich and Frederick W. Danker (eds)
Spir./OHS	*De Spiritu Sancto* (*On the Holy Spirit*), St Basil of Caesarea (*c.* 330-379)

ST	*Systematische Theologie* (*Systematic Theology*), Wolfhart Pannenberg (1928-2014)
STK	*Svensk Teologisk Kvartalskrift*
Summa	*Summa Theologiae* (*Summary of Theology*), St Thomas Aquinas
TGC	*The Gospel Coalition*
Tim.	*Timaeus*, Plato (428/7-348/7 BC)
Trin.	*De Trinitate* (*The Trinity*), St Augustine of Hippo
TiAP	*The Trinity in Asian Perspective*, Jung Young Lee (1935-96)
Ver.	*De vera religione* (*On True Religion*), St Augustine of Hippo
WBC	Word Biblical Commentary
WCF	The Westminster Confession of Faith (1647), The Westminster Assembly (1643-52)
WIC	*What is Christianity? Sixteen Lectures delivered in the University of Berlin 1899-1900*, Adolf Harnack (1851-1930)
WSA	Works of Saint Augustine: A Translation for the 21st Century, John E. Rotelle (ed.)
WTJ	*Wesleyan Theological Journal*

Introduction:

Experience, Culture and Religion in Systematic Theology

This book and its distinctive methodology arise from an intensely personal concern. During the last decade of his life, I recall a question my father posed me, 'If we need to accept Jesus in order to go to heaven, where is my father now?' When I heard the question, my heart broke, because I knew how dear my grandfather was to my father, as dear as my own father was to me. I couldn't bring myself to utter that, based on my convictions then, my grandfather was probably somewhere in hell because he failed to become a Christian during his lifetime.[1]

---

1. Writers such as John Piper and R.C. Sproul hold the view that all who have not heard and received the gospel of Jesus Christ, whatever the circumstances for not hearing or receiving it, are righteously condemned to hell because it is only through personal faith in Christ that anyone can be saved and even those who have not had occasion to receive or reject Christ are held to the condition of belief in God, since sufficient witness to the existence of the God proclaimed in the Bible has been given in nature as a portrait of God's glory. Other thinkers, among them, Gavin D'Costa, consider that the lack of explicit biblical statement concerning those who were not aware of the gospel through no fault of their own does not preclude the possibility that a merciful God, who seeks to save all who are lost, might extend a personal invitation through some special means, post mortem, to such individuals to receive salvation. R. Chia, 'Question 11: What about Those Who Have Never Heard about Jesus? Are They Going to Hell?', in R. Chen (ed.), *Honest Questions; Honest Answers: 20 Tough Questions on Issues of Life & Eternity* (Singapore: St Andrew's

Since then, I have found myself wondering about the extent to which it is helpful to say that God discriminates on the basis of religion. Is God inactive in non-Christian parts of society and the world? The question of conversion seems to involve much logical difficulty. If a person has had no real opportunity to accept Christianity, will God judge the person for not having become a believer? If a person refuses to become Christian due to misunderstanding, will God punish him by consigning him to hell? If a person does not wish to embrace the Christian faith because he is already committed to a religion or philosophy of his own choosing or belonging, is this sufficient ground for divine judgement?

The idea that God will judge anyone who fails to become a Christian appears to fly in the face of the nature of religious conversion. The decision to become a Christian believer is a deeply personal one often coupled with communal implications. Furthermore, as with any other personal relationship, conversion entails voluntarily embracing a mutually respectful and loving orientation towards another person; in the case of Christianity, a divine entity, in fact, three, each with personal qualities. If so, any suggestion that this God, who desires a relationship of affection with human persons, is willing to punish any individual who fails to enter into such a bond with God rings very odd indeed. Perhaps a better alternative to such a religious philosophy exists in a Christian theology which seeks to be faithful to all that the Christian Scriptures record of God's nature and purposes for humanity and the world. My firm belief is that the Bible proposes an inclusive trinitarian monotheism that has

---

Cathedral, 2011), pp. 52-55; J.J. Thatamanil, *Circling the Elephant: A Comparative Theology of Religious Diversity*, Comparative Theology: Thinking Across Traditions (New York: Fordham University Press, 2020), pp. 51-55. The idea here seems to be that each person has an implicit and insuperable awareness of God's existence through the majestic orderliness of creation, and yet many choose, for no reason other than a sinful nature, not to nurture that knowledge but instead reject that knowledge and live as though there were no God. However, this is neither a realistic nor historically engaged interpretation of such a passage as Romans 1:19-20, in that few would reject God without sufficient reason and all individuals believe in some ultimate principle; and, insofar as this scripture were resorted to, the writer's meaning is not that some people reject an inherent knowledge of God out of sheer wilfulness, but rather that, in face of the patent inaccuracies and dishonourable nature of extant conceptions of the divine as immoral and indecent deities (see Augustine, *Civ.*, I-X), people failed to challenge those ideas in order to attain to a more palatable and acceptable understanding of God.

by and large not been unearthed until the present time and that is not only capable of promoting a willingness to peacefully coexist with the myriad world cultures and religious traditions, but ready and delighted to enter into dialogue with and learn from them, and even integrate all that is good and valuable from them as the sources of greater theological specificity they have always been.[2]

Accordingly, this book formulates a modern, culturally, religiously and scientifically integrative and religiously pluriform Christian systematic theological method grounded in the Christian Scriptures, Christian tradition and reason, on the foundation of a human experiential context involving psychology, cultural diversity and religious pluralism.

This is a theological exercise which is, in its nature and orientation, culturally, religiously and scientifically integrative in recognising the inspirational role of culture and religion, and the benefits of empirical studies. It is also religiously pluriform, in viewing all religions as presenting distinctive hierarchies of emphasis as well as content which, though differing between religious traditions, is unified via a common pivoting on some sense of a universal moral responsibility and capable of being metaphorically harmonised within each religious tradition.[3] Not a complete work of systematic theology, this book functions instead as a prolegomenon to a more developed, integrated and pluriform Christian systematic theology.

---

2. As a case in point, in a concession made in light of the undeniable fact of religious pluralism in the world, the *Nostra Aetate* of the Roman Catholic Church, a declaration on the relationship between the Church and other religious faiths by the Second Vatican Council (1962-65), pronounces of non-Christian faiths that, while they might be capable of diffusing a single beam of a universal light of truth, Christ remains the whole truth, the consummation of religious existence. Such a declaration implicitly validates an ecclesial mission to turn, as much as possible, non-Christians to the Christian persuasion. *Nostra Aetate: Declaration on the Relation of the Church to Non-Christian Religions*, The Holy See, 28 October 1965, https://www.vatican.va/archive/hist_councils/ii_vatican_council/docume nts/vat-ii_decl_19651028_nostra-aetate_en.html.

3. This is not to be conflated with a pluralist view which may preclude the possibility of human knowledge of the divine. Consider, for instance, the pluralist theology of religions developed by John Hick. See Thatamanil, *Circling the Elephant*, p. 246; S.M. Heim, *The Depth of the Riches: A Trinitarian Theology of Religious Ends* (Grand Rapids, MI: Eerdmans, 2001), pp. 129-30.

In the following sections, I shall discuss the essence of each chapter of this book.

Foundations: Experience, Culture and World Religions

Traditionally, the Christian Scriptures form a primary and fundamental basis for a systematic Christian theology. In placing a discussion of the experiential, cultural and religious underpinnings of a systematic theology prior to that of the Scriptures, this book makes no attempt to contest that viewpoint. Rather, it seeks only to draw attention to the oft-neglected role of the human experience and cultural and religious worldviews or frameworks in the theological interpretation of the Christian Scriptures, all too frequently regarded as they are, in some circles, as a timeless collection of dogmatic teachings and ethical injunctions.

Before embarking on that discussion, this chapter considers the possibility of reformulating the biblical teaching of monotheism and salvation through Christ in non-religiously exclusive terms as a historically and communally conditioned presentation of divine truth. This is achieved through a theology of world religions based on a theory of a perichoretic constitution of the Christian Trinity in which the single divine being exists in three personal presentations. In such a theology, the Trinity constitutes the source of religious knowledge for every religious community by disclosing historically and communally adapted truth about God, the gods and ultimate things. This is followed by an appreciative survey of key tenets of various world religious and philosophical traditions and ideologies such as Buddhism, Hinduism, Islam, Taoism, Confucianism, Zoroastrianism, Sikhism, the Bahá'í Faith and atheism. The theology of God proposed in this monograph is an inclusive monotheistic one based on a trinitarian framework.

Method: Towards a Christian Global Systematic Theology

If the Bible itself provides the raw material from which theology formulates ideas, notions and concepts pertaining to the biblical teaching about God's nature, character, and purposes for humanity and the world, this material does not always settle theological inquiries to the desired level of specificity. Supporting greater lucidity on these issues are ways of thinking about metaphysical questions and ways of perceiving truths of ultimate concern and significance afforded by cultural and religious modalities; that is, the most deeply held philosophical sensibilities of a culture or religious tradition.

Case Study: A Classical Theology of God and Its Philosophical Debt

With the classical and historical Western conception of God as simple, immutable and impassible as a case study, this chapter discusses the probable and potential impact of culture and religion on Christian theology in the form of cultural and religious-guided theological modalities, suggests a method for Christian theologians to engage in such an enterprise, and anticipates systematic theological efforts on the part of non-Christian religions and philosophies.

The cultural and religious-contingent relativity of a systematic Christian theology desacralises the core affirmations of a dominant Western-centric theological system and legitimises the venture to achieve a more reasonable and moderate understanding of Christian theology, one which is concretised and enacted in the doctrinal engagements of the book.

Systematic theological work on the part of the various world religions is given a basis in the manner in which different religions or philosophies tend to emphasise or understate certain facets of divinity or ultimacy, and a purpose in that it is critical for each group to endeavour to arrive at a more holistic formulation through learning from each other and being willing to prune less effective aspects or adopt more profitable dimensions.[4]

Foundations: Faith, Scripture, Tradition and Reason

No work of systematic theology is complete without a discussion of the foci of Christianity, not just as an academic discipline or theological system but as an institution which invites individual persons into a distinctive manner of believing shaped by the testimony of the Christian Scriptures.

Subsequently, the subject of these Scriptures is brought in at this relatively late stage because the actual content of the Scriptures is not primarily in view, but rather the doctrine or conception of the biblical writings espoused in the theological system proposed by this work.

The purport of a following engagement with the Christian tradition is to outline some of the ways in which the theological interpretation of the canonical biblical writings evolved in response to major historical

---

4. P. Hedges, *Controversies in Interreligious Dialogue and the Theology of Religions*, Controversies in Contextual Theology (London: SCM, 2010), pp. 250-51.

factors throughout the timeline of the Christian Church. Reason as a source of a systematic Christian theology addressed in this chapter is understood in a twofold sense of an intellectual conceptualisation and the moderating effect of a rational human contemplation which reins in possible excesses on the part of the theological enterprise.

Doctrines: The Trinity

The discussion of the Christian doctrine of the Trinity inaugurates a new section in the book characterised by a concern to expound, in an integrative and pluriform manner, a number of pre-eminent dogmatic theories maintained by the universal Christian Church. Each of the chapters on doctrine will discuss a definition of a theologically relevant subject matter, lay out its place in a systematic theology, survey the strengths and weaknesses of existing conceptions, and propose a way forward with a consideration of its advantages and prolepses.

The lineaments of trinitarian doctrine as thrown into stark relief by historical controversies and more recent engagements are adumbrated in this chapter, which is dedicated to an exposition of the unity of the Godhead in keeping with the triple personhood of God in a Christian theological conception. Importantly, a theory of the Christian doctrine of the Trinity known as perichoretic constitution, which draws attention to an ontological interdependence on the part of the divine persons, is delineated and explained as a conceptual cornerstone undergirding a solidly Christian theological endeavour to study and appreciate non-Christian religious and philosophical systems, and integrate insights from them.

Doctrines: Christology

A chapter on the doctrine of Christ places a premium on attempts, both ancient and modern, to elaborate on and explicate the nature of his divinity and humanity in relation to each other. Building on the theory of a perichoretic constitution of the Trinity, the Christological doctrine introduced by this work articulates a way of thinking about the divine humanity of the incarnate Son of God as revolving around the idea of an embodied identity. God being defined as essence without body is capable of assuming a human nature through becoming incarnate without ontological dilution in either direction so long as God's authority, role, character and identity are preserved.

A middle road is taken between natural and supernatural theology in relation to the question of the possibility of knowledge concerning the divine in postulating a pre-earthly existence of human beings in angelic forms characterised by a beholding of the divine splendour which moulds an emotional predisposition to the truth. In this way, human thought is oriented towards the divine, ultimate or truly significant; in aid of this process, intrinsic norms and intuition are provided for determining truth and morality, along with the recognition that there is no higher court of appeal beyond an internal and innate human moral sensibility.

Doctrines: Theodicy

Front and centre at this point in the book is the internally varied Christian understanding of what it means to say that God is powerful and yet to continue to experience and see violations of goodness and betrayals of humanity. The moral dilemma is averted by deploying an angelological doctrine of divine providence which posits God as devoid of all direct power and compulsive force, relying instead on angelic representatives to execute the divine will in a comprehensive scope beginning with the creation and development of the material principles of the universe.

Furthermore, God is reconceived as assuming a dual mode as, on the one hand, a functional framework which can be designated a Divine Nature underlying all aspects of reality, promoting its moral, emotional, intellectual and physical wellbeing, and positing the existence of such things as the Trinity and all sentient souls capable of being embodied in angelic, human and animal frames, and, on the other, the Trinity itself. God's relation to the created order is, therefore, reformulated as a relation of pre-temporal origin to existence, obviating the need to explain divine acts pre-Creation.

Doctrines: Sin and Salvation

Christian theological notions of the inherent imperfection of human nature after the fall of humankind and God's concerted attempts to bring God's human creatures to restoration rise to prominence in this chapter. Because of their noteworthiness, entrenched ideas of divine freedom and human unfreedom, as eminently formulated by St Augustine of Hippo, Martin Luther and Reformed and Puritan theologians after him on the basis, *inter alia*, of what may well be the self-discoveries of St Paul, are dealt with at some length.

Such observations enable the articulation of a theology which asserts the fundamental non-validity of biological aetiologies of sin. In moving away from such theories, an alternative is offered which incorporates the findings of psychological therapeutic science in its proposals regarding the ramifications, for the internal mental life and wellbeing of an individual person, of what has become known as adverse childhood experiences (ACEs) and the usefulness, consequently, of accessing professional therapeutic support where available and possible.

Original sin is reconceived in psycho-dynamic terms where the roots of sinful disposition are situated in the presence of a compulsive evil, ushered into the life of an individual through that individual's failure to challenge and reject thought and emotional patterns suggested by parental neglect, abuse by various actors during childhood, or negative influence.

It is necessary to affirm the real benefits of a spiritual, intellectual and emotional act of renunciation of feelings, thoughts, desires and attitudes wrongfully adopted in the course of situations of neglect and abuse, particularly during one's formative years. Reflections on human sinfulness in the biblical testimony suggest a constant need to attend to introspection to mitigate the likely subtle and invisible influence of socio-economic and political factors on the spiritual and psychological wellness of the individual.

Chapter 1

Foundations I: Experience, Culture and World Religions

Given that the chief aim of this work is to adumbrate a systematic theological method for the twenty-first century, it is proper first to ask the question, in what does Christian theology consist?

In broad terms, theology designates in its Greek verbal form a presentation or exposition of God's nature.[1] Christian theology designates the study of the Christian God, its substance being the biblical teaching on God's purposes for humanity and the world. There are different dimensions to the study of Christian theology, organised as it may be around an ecclesiastical heritage, its format or the nature of its approach, its didactic conceptualisation of the Bible, core emphasis or target readership.

Systematic theology refers to the establishment of the internal and external coherence of the study of what the Bible affirms about God's nature and purposes for humanity and the world. There are a number of elements in the systematic study of theology, which can be differentiated according to whether they have to do with the presupposition or coherence of Christian theology.

In relation to the presupposition of Christian theology which precedes all other norms and sources of theology, this refers to the principle of human experience. Centred on the universal law of human nature revolving around sensitive empathy, the norm of human experience channels theological discussion in a manner that resonates with what the human

---

1. Augustine, *Civ.*, VIII.1.

conscience judges to be good, true, fair and just, and is intensely interested in issues of proper human concern. It comprehends elements as disparate as the relationship between Christian theology and culture – concerned that the meaning of Scripture is interpreted in a mode proper to a culture – and the intersection between Christian theology and non-Christian world religions, keen to relativise and chasten absolutist modes of theology.

Concerning the coherence of theology, there is: Christian Scripture, the Bible, as the substantive source of theology; the Christian tradition, that is, authoritative interpretation by theologians and councils of the theological meaning of Scripture, serving as a guide to the work of theology; and the use of human reason, which has at least two different meanings.

First, reason in the context of theology refers to the human ability to analyse and theorise using the content of Scripture in a logically consistent manner. Second, reason designates the ability to arrive at sensible and moderate conclusions, rather than extremist or fanatical ones, with the aid of advancements in the understanding of the sciences and humanities as a locus for the refinement, reconfiguration and validation of theology vis-à-vis these disciplines.[2]

The subject of theology is God's acts in the world to create, restore and perfect humanity and, through humanity, the rest of creation, comprehending various dimensions of these interrelationships and aspects of the parties involved.[3]

Experience

An essential medium through which human existence is lived, the experience of the individual person and communities encompasses emotions, desires or natural inclinations, the will or volition, goals or objectives to which commitment is attached, the means, processes, methods or instruments used to reach those goals or objectives, and the actual actions taken as a result of rational calculation or visceral instinct. A thoughtful consideration of this pattern of feeling, desiring, willing, using and acting – in short, human disposing – is central to the activity of the theological enterprise.

It may be surprising to some and felt questionable that a Christian theological project should begin on an experiential footing, particularly

---

2. Cf. Augustine's allusion to temperance as a Christian virtue to be emulated, *Civ.*, XI.22.
3. *NDT*, s.v. 'Theology' (D.F. Wright, pp. 680-81).

among those who believe that any Christian theology deserving of its name can only resort as a first and final court of appeal to the Christian Scriptures. Yet, to begin from human experience is simply to acknowledge the debt each theologian already owes, notably, to the cultural matrix from which they hail. Ignoring this setting or acting as though it does not really exist, as if, for instance, the Bible and the Bible alone determines the shape of the Christian theology in which a specific group engages, is to be, at worst, mendacious with oneself or, at best, unselfconscious. Even the very theologians who assert some form of fundamental independence of their biblical interpretation from sources external to the Scriptures operate out of some set of culturally conditioned presuppositions.[4]

Experience as a source, norm, measure or standard of Christian theology is conscious of the factual principle that each individual human person is a unique repository of experiences accumulated through their life-history. It is predicated on the observation and inference that the feelings, desires, decisions, methods and actions of a person are generally stable over a sustained period and can to a significant extent be understood in a coherent and self-consistent fashion.

This is not to suggest that people are automata or complete products of their circumstances of life, since such a theory allows for breaches in consistency and regularity, because a person may be assessed to have acted out of his own character, in the case of a shaping towards virtue, and to have overcome his personal inhibitions, in that of a shaping towards a defect of personality, character, or morality.

In spite of their often predictive or ostensibly determinative life-histories, humans remain very much in control of their actions and personal destinies. Self-transcendence is part and parcel of being human, a capacity to struggle against the negative instincts one may have inherited or come to develop through unfortunate instances of trauma or abuse, to emerge victorious in some way over one's proclivities and propensities.

Such self-transcendence is par for the course in relation to any moral question, and any purported moulding of an individual towards some form of immorality can never be brooked as an excuse for acting against the conscience. Because humanity has been created in the undestroyed divine image which, in an Irenaean framework, incorporates a free will which has been given to pursue moral good, this logic of self-transcendence does not hold for the opposite case of a shaping away from virtue. Moral self-transcendence is normative, and the question could

---

4. For more on this, see *infra*.

well be asked why a person does not act in accordance with conscience for all the positive and formative psychological-emotional impartation they might have received as a child.[5]

With respect, however, to amoral matters, such as core aspects of human identity including culture and religious profession, a settled pattern of human disposition may be regarded as normative. There is no cause for a church or theological school to attempt to alter such settled cultural or religious patterns. As a matter of fact, to do so would amount to nothing less than a deliberate effort to bring about an erasure of cultural or religious identity.

No Christian theology should permit itself, secretly as much as openly, to espouse an ideal of eradicating these personal and communal identity markers. By all means, the Church should not forbid enquiries into the substance of the Christian faith and the ways of the Christian community on the part of non-Christians keen to learn more about the faith out of their own free will. It is rather a different matter to mount a systematic campaign to reach a certain goal of a number of converts to the Christian faith, or for individual adherents to be aggressive in their approach to sharing an evangelistic message.

An important principle which the norm of experience establishes and validates is that of the fairness and integrity of an approach to human interactions. In all circumstances, the Christian believer ought always to ask himself, first, in what the unique repository of experiences accumulated through the life-history of the other person in question consists, second, how his actions towards this person might be perceived by the latter in the context of this unique repository of experiences accumulated through his life-history, and, third, whether this psychological-emotional effect on the person, if conceived and experienced as unpleasant or even offensive, is that which the Christian wishes to be visited on himself.[6]

Having established, to the greatest possible extent, the nature of the counterpart's unique repository of experiences and the likely emotional effect of an action on the counterpart on the basis of the understanding of his life experiences, if the Christian should conclude that that same

---

5. St Irenaeus also includes human reason, speech and authority over the animal realm within the conception of the image of God. A.B. Collver III, "Who Is Man?: Image and Likeness in Irenaeus," *CSJ* 22, no. 1 (Epiphany 1999), p. 32.

6. This, of course, as one would quickly appreciate, is an application of the golden rule.

effect of his action is not something he would wish to experience through a person with whom he may deal or interact, he should forbear that action. This experiential paradigm is eminently applicable in the case of an interaction with a member of a marginalised group or other cases of proper human concern, including the need to preserve a sustainable state of the earth for posterity.

Yet another principle that experience as a norm of Christian theology validates and establishes concerns the theological conception of the divine-human relationship. It should be clear that, to the measure that we wish to espouse the belief in God as love, God should not be excepted from an expectation of others that arises from an experiential paradigm. In other words, any theological conception of God's character should not neglect the possibility and theological necessity that God considers the emotional effect on human persons of God's actions, and behaves with due sensitivity towards human persons and proper regard for their dignity.

This is not tantamount to a humanisation of God, which *eo ipso* is an inappropriate theological procedure, given that, especially in a Western theological tradition, as well as an Eastern one, the line between the divine and the human has to be maintained at all times. On the contrary, such an experiential-oriented theological procedure is enjoined by the moral correspondence between God and humankind, made as the latter is in the divine image, not just in terms of human rationality and intellect, as Augustine of Hippo thinks, but in emotionality as well.[7] To require of God to be sensitive and empathetic towards human persons in their distinct stations and situations is not an unauthorised predication of God. In and of itself, emotional vulnerability, the capacity for a person to be impacted psychologically by the actions of another person, whether it be via speech, conduct or a confession of inner thought, is no defect.

A person is not called to erect a psychological barrier, shield or armour by which to protect himself against possible emotional hurt. Granted there will be situations where it may be necessary to be on one's guard against a deceptive, manipulative and callous person, yet, by and large, the human person is not consigned to a lifetime of relational self-isolation. Similarly, God is sensitively empathetic, within the divine community that is the Trinity, towards human beings both individually and collectively, and summons each human individual and community to practise the same attitude towards God and other individuals and communities respectively.

---

7. Augustine, *Civ.*, XII.23, XIII.24.

As against the viewpoint that God exploits human beings as a means by which to magnify God's own glory predominantly through their personal humiliation, extreme and unrelenting anguish, and even destruction, an experiential doctrine of the conception of God in relation to human persons and communities, hand in glove with a moral definition of the divine image in humankind, entails a conception of God as sensitively empathetic.

An engagement with the emotional repercussions of an action arises from reflection upon the meaning of the golden rule for the present time, this rule being, as Jesus elaborated it, for a person to do to others that which he or she would like for others to do to him or her. An approach which takes account of individual affectivity constitutes for Kant a universal law of human nature, in a maxim which may be expressed as follows, 'I will to demonstrate sensitive empathy toward others in a situation of a personal struggle so as to be dignified, valued, appreciated, understood, and treated as a human being myself in my own struggles'; this can, first of all, be expressed as a universal law in which every person pursues the same course.[8]

How conceivable is this as a universal law? It is a viable rule of thumb. To what extent will the individual in question and all other individuals be able to commit themselves to this line of action? Is it possible that some individuals might simply not be interested in exploring this avenue of activity? The idea of a personal struggle is sufficiently broad that people in general would be able to resonate with the concern expressed in the maxim. However, just because most people have personal struggles, does it follow then that they are to show sensitive empathy towards others who might be facing struggles of a similar nature if they expect to be treated in the same empathetic way? Yes, for the principle of reciprocity is operative in human relationships. Why should a person set themselves apart from other people as worthy of a treatment which they are not willing to extend to others? Sensitive empathy is clearly a legitimate concern for any person in any community who is keen on promoting his own happiness, given that it is a fundamental human expectation to be accorded understanding and treated with sensitivity *in extremis*.

As a matter of fact, personal abuse, with its long-standing psychological effects, is precipitated by a negligence in some way of the universal principle of sensitive empathy. In childhood abuse, typically an older person acts riskily towards the individual in question without sufficient

---

8. R. Johnson and A. Cureton, 'Kant's Moral Philosophy', *SEP* (Spring 2022), https://plato.stanford.edu/archives/spr2022/entries/kant-moral/.

and fair consideration of the impact of that action on the child's wellbeing. Having thus had its own personal space and dignity violated, the child experiences a warping and perversion of its very humanity and a corruption of its human disposition.

In a bid to cope with such a harrowing experience and prevent future occurrences of the same, the now tortured affectivity bends around the soul of the individual, in one instance forming an aggressive-protective mechanism by which the person mounts a continual protest against the injustice already suffered by reacting excessively or aggressively against provocative or reminiscent events or persons. This is no more than an attempt to find emotional release and achieve a sort of twisted reciprocity in a new world order in which gross injustice is subconsciously judged to be the norm.

In this context, anger legitimately felt towards a victimiser is projected upon any other thing, person, or feeling linked in some way with the experience. Incessant reprisal is directly or indirectly perpetrated against others.[9] Consequently, an individual might be especially heightened to the experience of injustice, personally undergone or second-hand, because of a remembered feeling of having been unfairly treated or abused as a child, or having witnessed such maltreatment.

In addition, the individual may feel that he as well as those he hurts both deserve the abusive treatment they experience. In this regard, studies have borne out a pattern through which adults, particularly women, exposed to childhood abuse or neglect, whether as direct objects of aggression or domestic onlookers, are postulated as being more likely to experience violent behaviour than their well-treated counterparts due quite possibly to the uncritically accepted belief that violence is an acceptable solution to conflict.[10] Furthermore, adverse childhood experiences have been demonstrated to be 'robustly' correlated with aggressive conduct in subsequent years.[11] Another possible outcome of

---

9. A. Cuncic, 'What Does It Mean to Be "Triggered": Types of Triggering Events and Coping Strategies', *Verywell Mind*, Dotdash Meredith, updated 10 March 2022, https://www.verywellmind.com/what-does-it-mean-to-be-triggered-4175432.

10. Child Family Community Australia, 'Effects of Child Abuse and Neglect for Adult Survivors', The Australian Institute of Family Studies, January 2014, https://aifs.gov.au/resources/policy-and-practice-papers/effects-child-abuse-and-neglect-adult-survivors.

11. J.W. Madole, S.L. Johnson and C.S. Carver, 'A Model of Aggressive Behavior: Early Adversity, Impulsivity, and Response Inhibition', *Journal*

trauma involves a person being lastingly petrified with fear and incapable of trust.

While the wounded emotionality eventually becomes twisted in its understanding of what is appropriate and inappropriate behaviour, it begins with an outrage, which though gradually repressed is never really fully absent, and returns in full force when recovery transpires. The emotionality is an extremely delicate and sensitive faculty, reeling greatly from any perceived or experienced injustice, especially that transpiring during the formative years of human existence. It is imperative for the individual to undergo a process of psychological healing and restoration in which, first, on an intellectual and, finally, emotional level, the person begins to appreciate the immoral nature of the traumatising and abusive treatment he has experienced at the hands of others, so as eventually to take a stand against such treatment of himself and others.

Before this affective clarity arrives, the person depends for his continued peaceful existence on a voice of conscience and reason ceaselessly and restlessly attempting to sound through the thick cacophony of a dark and disturbed affectivity. Such people are never to yield to their sinister impulses, however compulsively they may seem to demand an immediate or imminent release and actualisation. This is because in any world or world order, the harm of another person is never acceptable. Understanding and empathy may by all means be shown towards the suffering a person has experienced, but under no circumstances should a person's misery mitigate the gravity of any action which harms another individual.

With this doctrine of sensitive empathy as a defining characteristic of God's nature, we find ourselves in a position to closely examine, successively, the relationship between Christian theology and culture, and that between Christian theology and non-Christian world religions, including atheism-humanism.

Culture

What is the relationship between Christian theology and culture?[12] Some Christians are of the view that the Christian faith is completely determined by the content of the Christian Scriptures, which have their

---

12. For the purposes of this work, culture is defined as the beliefs, mores and social conduct associated with a distinct grouping of individuals

origin in God, and Christian religious texts alone, and that human culture has little if any contribution towards the substance of the content of the Christian faith. Such a transcultural conception of the nature of the biblical canon pervades systems of thought, including Helmut Richard Niebuhr's analysis of the different approaches of the Christian faith to a culture at large.

Niebuhr speaks of a Christian message that is set against a cultural framework of ideas, beliefs and practices, that affirms this cultural framework, draws from this cultural framework, exists in a state of uneasiness in relation to this cultural framework, or is capable of renovating this cultural framework.[13] The impression hereby given is that Christian theology is formally distinct from culture, with which it may form some kind of a more or less salutary relationship.

A transcultural understanding of the Christian message has engendered an imperialist approach to missional engagement, in which Christianity, as it has been apprehended in the Western and Middle Eastern world, is simply propagated to and imposed upon a foreign cultural group, in intact form, all in the widespread belief that Western theologies represent a restrictively correct conception of the Christian faith, being worked out rigorously from Scripture alone or Scripture and the Christian tradition – or so it is thought.[14]

The truth of the matter, however, is that there is no escaping the effects of culture in the theological enterprise. Culture operates already at the most primary and primal level, that of scriptural interpretation. Even before we become aware of it, our most deeply held convictions about the nature of reality shape the theological conclusions we reach about what the Bible teaches about God's purposes for humanity and the world.

Not even the great thinkers of the Christian faith, who attempted to articulate a correct theology free from non-biblical influences, were spared the impact of pre-existing presuppositions of a human community. Therefore, theologians such as Martin Luther, John Calvin and Karl Barth were at pains to distinguish their brand of theological teaching and argumentation from that of other theologians, whom they

---

brought together on the basis of shared social, moral or philosophical values and ethnic self- and group-identity and belonging. Cf. Hedges, *Controversies in Interreligious Dialogue*, p. 77.

13. T. Wax, '"Christ and Culture": An Overview of a Christian Classic', *TGC*, 25 February 2015, https://www.thegospelcoalition.org/blogs/trevin-wax/christ-and-culture-an-overview-of-a-christian-classic.

14. W.A. Dyrness and V.-M. Kärkkäinen, Introduction to *GDT*, pp. vii-x.

felt had overly accommodated the findings of a Christian tradition or the sentiments of a human rationality, and emphasised the importance of paying more careful attention to what the Bible actually says.

Luther believed that Scripture stood above the traditions of the Church[15] and even the human faculty of reason,[16] Calvin that Scripture was superior to the decisions of church councils, by which he simply means that his particular interpretation of the Scripture trumps any church council and that only those councils which agree with his understanding of the Bible may stand,[17] and Barth that divine revelation as it comes through Scripture must illuminate an understanding of faith quite apart from any insight nature might give.[18]

These theologians are not wrong in seeking to affirm the divine initiative behind the work of salvation through Christ. They are also not incorrect in highlighting what they perceive to be errors of biblical interpretation concerning certain doctrines of the Church or perpetrated on the part of certain thinkers. Yet, one has to realise that a mistake committed in an area does not invalidate the legitimacy of the area of inquiry itself. Just because a church went too far in articulating certain doctrines or instituting specific practices does not signify that a church should not articulate doctrines it may find to be implicit in Scripture or institute practices for the benefit of the community; and just because a thinker is thought to have crossed a critical theological line does not suggest that all doctrinal development is to be interdicted.

Foundational theologians may not have been sufficiently alive to the fundamental role of particular cultural perspectives on their thinking and systems of thought. While theologians such as St Augustine of Hippo may have expressly named philosophical systems from which their theologising may have benefited, and recognised their positive role in their own thinking, they may not have attained a sufficiently deep and fair appreciation of the relativity of their theological modes of thinking, a relativity which arises from the fact that these modes of thought themselves are culturally conditioned.

We can observe that important theologians such as Luther, Calvin and Barth did not transcend the rational categories in which their intellectual communities thought. As a case in point, they continued to

---

15. E.g. the practice of indulgences.
16. E.g. Luther, *De servo arbitrio.*
17. Calvin, *Inst.*, IV.ix.1-2.
18. See R. Holder, 'Karl Barth and the Legitimacy of Natural Theology', *Themelios* 26, no. 3 (Summer 2001), pp. 22-37.

see God as an absolute subject, that is, an all-powerful ruler who secretly holds the reins over events that are allowed to happen in the world.

Luther distinguished between a *Deus absconditus*, a 'hidden God', and a *Deus revelatus*, a 'revealed God'; Calvin and his followers developed a theology of double predestination including a divine predetermination of the human rejection of God in Christ on the part of many individuals.[19] As a modern successor of the reformers, Barth self-consciously attempted to soften the theological repercussions of such views because they appear to drive a wedge between God and Christ.[20] Even so, he persisted in his numerous references to God as a Lord who has the whole of existence at his disposal and eternally pre-decides in sovereign freedom every event that is to occur in the history of time.[21]

The idea of God as an absolute subject is premised on a legitimate philosophical insight, of René Descartes, that the doubting self provides a means to obtain a certainty of self and therefore constitutes a foundation of knowledge. This conception of the human mind and rationality as holding the key to knowledge has a precedent in the Neoplatonic notion of St Augustine of Hippo regarding an inward turn to reason and concept as affording an apprehension of God and Truth.[22]

It is also in line with an appropriation of Platonic thought by the Cappadocian Fathers in the fourth century in the idea of a human soul's journey towards the fullness of God in terms of a cultivation of mind and heart, in which the increasing knowledge of God involves a purification of one's values and priorities (carnal or spiritual) through a growth in one's relationship to and understanding of God.[23] Such an approach conceptualises God as a theoretical and ethical ideal rather than empathetic fellow sufferer.

---

19. P. Helm, 'Classical Calvinist Doctrine of God', in B.A. Ware (ed.), *Perspectives on the Doctrine of God: Four Views* (Nashville, TN: Broadman & Holman, 2008), pp. 5-28.
20. Barth, *KD* II.2, §35.1 (*CD* II.2, §35.1, p. 333).
21. Barth, *KD* II.1, §31.1 (*CD* II.1, §31.3, p. 622); idem, *KD* III.4, §54.3 (*CD* III.4, §54.3, p. 301).
22. Augustine, *Conf.*, III.11; S. MacDonald, 'The Divine Nature: Being and Goodness', in D.V. Meconi and E. Stump (eds), *The Cambridge Companion to Augustine*, 2nd edn (Cambridge: Cambridge University Press, 2014), pp. 22-26; Augustine appeals to Romans 1:20, quoted, e.g. ibid., VII.16.
23. D. Bradshaw, 'Plato in the Cappadocian Fathers', in R.C. Fowler (ed.), *Plato in the Third Sophistic*, Millennium Studies 50 (Berlin: De Gruyter, 2014), pp. 195, 197, 200.

The human subject is clearly finite; but Descartes imagined that his supposition of the existence of an infinite, perfect and absolute divine subject was universal to human consciousness. Through the efforts of Immanuel Kant and Friedrich Schleiermacher, ethical theology and a theology of experience developed in which religion was affirmed as a moral authority and the human experience of the self a potential avenue by which to know God. Johann Gottlieb Fichte and Georg Wilhelm Friedrich Hegel added to the discourse by suggesting God as the subject of God's own self-revelation and the human knowledge of God, the latter mediated through human self-knowledge.[24]

With the benefit of that history, Karl Barth worked out a conception of God as an absolute subject of God's revelation and human knowledge, and worldly phenomena. In Barth's theory of divine self-communication, this divine subject knows the truth it wishes to communicate about itself in a crystallised manner, and is able to convey this truth about itself to a human person in an unmistakable and inerrant fashion through the divine encounter, Scripture and preaching.[25] God conceived of as absolute and omnipotent subject in and of itself does not engender a theological exclusivism, and yet, mixed with a religious self-preference, it becomes possible to think of God as capable of nothing other than an absolute and exhaustive communication of doctrine, leaving no room for authentic experiences of the divine in other religions.[26]

One does well to discern that the idea of God as an infinite, perfect and absolute subject may perhaps simply be cultural, a function of self-preference, and arise from a desire for control. There is nothing wrong with seeking a clear or certain knowledge of God. However, the

24. J. Moltmann, *The Trinity and the Kingdom: The Doctrine of God*, trans. M. Kohl (Minneapolis, MN: Fortress, 1993), pp. 13-16.

25. Barth, *KD* I.1, §8 (*CD* I.1, §8, pp. 295-347); see ibid., p. 321: 'The fact that God takes form means that God Himself controls not only man but also the form in which He encounters man. God's presence is always God's decision to be present. The divine Word is the divine speaking. The divine gift is the divine giving. God's self-unveiling remains an act of sovereign divine freedom.'

26. If it is asked why God did not leave any clear and explicit witness in the Bible as to the fact that God reveals Godself in other religious traditions, just as effectively as God has done in the Christian tradition, this is because the Bible is not a descriptive textbook of a theology of world religions but a paraenesis first to the Israelite or Jewish and then the Christian people or those who would become Christians to believe in or obey their vision of God.

minute I deploy my religious knowledge as an instrument to validate an inherent sense of superiority, I cross the border from a genuine search for knowledge to dogmatism. We may call this type of theology, a sovereignty theology.

Christianity outside Israel was primarily mediated through Greek philosophy and culture. In a similar way, Christianity within Israel was mediated through the Jewish system of belief and way of life. The origins of Gentile Christianity date to the Council of Jerusalem (50) at which it was decided that non-Jewish Christians did not have to conform to Jewish rules and customs.

Since that time, the conditions were in place for the development of a classical theology in dependence upon Greek philosophical thought-forms. Patristic theologians of the Church such as Origen, Eusebius of Caesarea, the Cappadocian Fathers and Augustine of Hippo were well read in the influential philosophies of their day and attempted and executed syntheses of classical philosophy and biblical interpretation.

Augustine grappled with Neoplatonic philosophy in his exposition of divine eternity while the Cappadocian Fathers expressed the doctrine of God as Trinity in the categories of Aristotelian thought. The impact of Greek philosophy on Christian theology involved God being conceived of not just as simple, indissoluble, unmoving and unchanging, but impassible, that is, incapable of affectivity.[27] St Thomas Aquinas, an influential Western Christian theologian from the Middle Ages, completed a theological synthesis of Aristotelian philosophy and Christian biblical interpretation in his *Summa Theologiae*.

Similarly, in the twentieth century, the Korean-American theologian Jung Young Lee pioneered a new approach to Christian theology by fusing philosophical categories from his native Korean culture with his interpretation of the Scriptures. Although he was trained in classical and Western theology, he decided at some point, as early as his doctoral studies, to return to his cultural roots. Thus, he set aside for a time the Bible and the theology he had been taught and familiarised himself with classical texts of his East Asian culture.

---

27. In the patristic age, to be God is to be incapable of being 'involved in human suffering and change'. *NDT*, s.v. 'Nestorius' (H.D. McDonald, p. 457). Cf. Moltmann, *Trinity and the Kingdom*, p. 21; C. Tornau, 'Saint Augustine', *SEP* (Winter 2019), https://plato.stanford.edu/archives/win2019 /entries/augustine; Augustine, *Conf.*, XIII.ix.10, XIII.xvi.19; Barth, *KD* III.4, §53.3 (*CD* III.4, §53.3, pp. 108-109).

Lee took up the *Book of Changes* and immersed himself in its intellectual and spiritual picture of the world. He learned about the yin-yang philosophy which became a part of Taoism and Confucianism. Then he went back to the Bible and read it with fresh eyes. From then on, he developed an authentically East Asian theological interpretation of the Christian Scriptures which he called, 'God as [or theology of] Change'. This East Asian system is immanentist, this-worldly, concrete, specific and reified rather than transcendent, other-worldly, metaphysical, abstract and rarefied, traits which characterise classical and much Western theology, particularly certain strands of German idealist theology.

World Religions

While there were moments in the history of Israel and the Church when society was organised theocratically or influenced by Christianity as a state religion, today, we speak about the wish and need to promote an interreligious *modus vivendi*, a carefully, conscientiously and vigilantly forged state of coexistence, harmony and peace between the many different world religions within a single national community in a modern secular state.[28]

Since the Christianisation of the Roman Empire during the reign of Constantine the Great (r. 306-37), Christendom, the mutually beneficial alliance between the Christian Church and the state, has persisted

---

28. For the purposes of this book, religion is defined as a distinct, yet bewilderingly multifarious, socio-cultural phenomenon comprising various combinations of people, teachers, texts, beliefs, traditions, practices and histories, existing within or between cultures, arising from and preserving elements of earlier cultures, yet having the ability to transform itself through successive historical eras and cultural successions, in which some vision of human meaning or fulfilment is held out that transcends the realm of the empirically observable. This may involve belief in a positive relationship between this non-empirically observable realm and four or more of the following characteristics of a mainstream religious tradition: belief in one or more divine or spiritual beings or powers; an afterlife; a socio-ethical system of some kind; some capacity for self-transcendence; guidance in relation to prayer or meditation; and an aetiology for the state in which humanity or the world is found. Cf. Hedges, *Controversies in Interreligious Dialogue*, pp. 77-81.

through different historical eras and social systems until the fallout from the First World War.[29]

During this period, Western Europe underwent a shift from what Johnson and Koyama designate, 'conditional tolerance equilibrium', in which non-Christian groups such as the Jews were accorded limited social rights based on a symbiotic contract in which rulers lent political support to the efforts of the mainstream Christian Church to ensure conformity to its beliefs and practices and conferred further benefits in return for a legitimisation and sacralisation of the political hierarchy.[30]

This religious-political equilibrium would be shaken in the sixteenth century as a result of religious, political and economic changes. The Protestant Reformation, in which a critique of a dominant religious modality was normalised through the channel of the printing press, contributed directly to the waning of the political influence of the Catholic Church. States grew in power, size and independence with the help of military advances and the development of a general rule of law and a method of collecting taxes. As a system of governance based on cultural and religious identity failed to regain its dominance, such as in France during the reign of Louis XIV, and concessions were made in the direction of religious toleration, the vision of a secular state inspired policymakers and the path was charted towards a modern concept of religious freedom.

Even so, the paradigm of Christianity as a political vehicle has persisted up to the present time in which religious belief continues to be used as an instrument of social control. This is evident in any number of theologies which encourage or promote a restrictive interpretation of the teachings of the Christian faith in which, rather than attempting to find a harmonious place in a religious world order characterised by significant plurality, the uniqueness and superiority of the Christian faith and Church is emphasised over all other religious groups.

A modern theology gives pride of place to the awareness that people are not all Christians, and it is unreasonable for the Christian theologian to insist that the Christian faith alone has the right to decide that in which religious truth consists, and seek to enthrone only the Christian God and faith in the realm of human religious profession and leave out of consideration all other gods and faiths.

---

29. W.A. Stahl, 'Christendom: One Thing the Reformation Did Not Change', *Impetus* (Winter/Spring 2017), Luther College, University of Regina, SK.
30. N.D. Johnson and M. Koyama, 'The State, Toleration, and Religious Freedom', GMU Working Paper in Economics No. 18-18 (30 May 2018).

An inclusive Christian theology arises out of a desire to observe the golden rule of Jesus: 'So whatever you wish that others would do to you, do also to them, for this is the Law and the Prophets.'[31]

It would be understandable for a staunch adherent of a particular religious system to pronounce on religious matters with finality. Christians are not exempt from this tendency. Yet there is something profoundly flawed about the thinking of a person who insists that his or her religious views are correct and deserve to be taken with the utmost gravity and yet at the same time refuses to accord the same inalienable need and right to a member of another religion. An exclusivist orientation to Christian theology, or any religious belief system for that matter, is by nature self-imploding and self-defeating, for the exclusivist will never be able to accord to the religious other a genuine space for being who he is without in some way already pre-judging the latter to be somehow less than he is and in need of conversion.

The passionate evangelism of the Early Church in Acts arises for two primary reasons. First, the historical event of the inauguration of the institution of the Church required that a critical mass be gathered to form the foundations of this new religious community.[32] Second, the moral bankruptcy of some Jewish leaders and the Roman state and popular religious cult (as per the New Testament the former practised hypocrisy; Augustine points out the vices, indecencies and indiscretions of the Roman and Greek gods, celebrated in public theatre, evident in the latter, with moral philosophy limited only to the elite few who were believed to be worthy of receiving it[33]), entailed that the Christian gospel be preached far and wide to provide a viable and helpful alternative to the existing cult. In the same way the Old Testament prophets delivered judgements or oracles against the enormities of ancient Near Eastern religion, including the incestuous relationships, child sacrifice and bestiality practised by the Egyptian and Canaanite peoples, for which Yahweh expelled them through the Israelites.[34] A problem arises when

---

31. Matthew 7:12, ESV.
32. The religiously exclusivist injunctions in Exodus 22:18 and 22:20 can similarly be interpreted in keeping with the need of a new religious community to protect its cultic boundaries.
33. Augustine, *Civ.*, I-X.
34. Leviticus chapter eighteen. Some Jews were evangelised because Christianity came on the scene as a development of the Jewish religion, but this ought to be separated from any claim that Christianity is superior to or supercedes Judaism.

theologians attempt to draw a straight line of extrapolation from these anti-cultic denunciations to modern religion, many of which promote similar moral values and have proven themselves capable of internal reforms.[35]

Religious exclusivism is not quite identical to religious extremism.[36] Yet, an exclusive orientation towards religious faith is an impediment to authentic interreligious dialogue, understanding, appreciation, solicitude, cooperation and camaraderie.[37]

In a multi-religious world, an aspectual and relative theological approach, in contrast to an absolutist theological approach which claims to be complete or exhaustive, will pave the way for dialogue, cooperation and solidarity at a profound level between Christians and those of other faiths.

In this regard, two ways can be canvassed for approaching the issue of world religions from a Christian theological standpoint, one focussed on the moral and practical benefits of world religions and another on forging a theological affinity between Christianity and other world religions.

In the context of a discussion of Christian theology vis-à-vis the other world religions, a particular person may espouse a specific religion rather than any other religious option. For the sake of discussion, let's suppose this person is Christian. Given his religious background, he will have received some instruction about who God is and what God is like. However, take another individual, who is not Christian but perhaps Muslim. He will similarly have received some form of instruction about God's being and

---

35. A case in point being the abolition of the practice of *Sati* or widow-burning in the Hindu religion, against which Raja Rammohan Roy, a nineteenth-century reformist from Bengal, fought. K. Raina, 'How Did Sati Get Abolished In India?', *Feminism in India*, FII Media, 29 October 2018.

36. See D. Pratt, 'Exclusivism and Exclusivity: A Contemporary Theological Challenge', *Pacifica* 20, no. 3 (October 2007), pp. 291-306; idem, 'Religious Identity and the Denial of Alterity: Plurality and the Problem of Exclusivism', in P.D. Bubbio and P.A. Quadrio (eds), *The Relation of Philosophy to Religion Today* (Newcastle-upon-Tyne: Cambridge Scholars Publishing, 2011), pp. 201-15; and idem, 'Fundamentalism, Exclusivism and Religious Extremism', in D. Cheetham, D. Pratt and D. Thomas (eds), *Understanding Interreligious Relations* (Oxford: Oxford University Press, 2013), pp. 241-61.

37. J. Patton, 'Including the Exclusivists in Interfaith', *RFIA* 16, no. 3 (2018), pp. 23-33.

character, and the differences, even conflict and contradiction, between Christian and Islamic ideas of God will be noted.

These, and all other world religions, present equally valid ways of approaching and knowing about God. Let us suppose there were just one divine reality that created humanity and seeks to reach out to them; and this divine reality, this divine force reaches out to human beings in many different, and equally valid, ways, forming different religious communities for a common moral purpose.[38]

One religious group places an emphasis on the loving, forbearing and forgiving nature of God; another focusses on the holiness or transcendent otherness of God; yet another religion conceives of God not as one being but a group of beings working mostly in harmony to provide for the spiritual needs of humankind; a different religion might place a premium on the all-pervasive nature of divinity; still another group may not even teach the existence of any God, but simply uphold the need to pursue a common good or human morality and be guided by the human conscience.

Christians can hold the view that there is just one divine force working among different religions which serves the spiritual needs of differing religious communities and builds up our common humanity. One way of reconciling different religious ideas about God, the gods or the ultimate principle is to picture a three-dimensional diagram consisting of three lines meeting at a common point at the bottom and reaching outward in three different dimensions.

A first dimension is whatever promotes appreciation or gratitude for the divine, a second, whatever promotes love, empathy and compassion for fellow human beings and, a third, whatever promotes our care for the living and natural environment. On this diagram it is possible to organise much that is taught in world religion.

Certain parts of religious doctrine may not fit readily onto this structure. As a case in point, divine violence may be a historically conditioned factor which is difficult for modern people to accept and a highly nuanced treatment of this specific topic may be required.

---

38. That religions constitute a positive spiritual and moral source is recognised by world leaders including Singapore's prime minister. H.-L. Lee, 'National Day Rally 2009', 16 August 2009, Prime Minister's Office Singapore. God may disclose Godself in other religious traditions via the Father, Son or Holy Spirit in Christianity but whom other religious groups will patently call by a different name. Heim, *Depth of the Riches*, pp. 135-36.

Because of the competing needs of various religious groupings, interreligious conflict has transpired in history; sometimes it is even explicitly endorsed in religious texts. An attempt to make sense of the conflict recorded in the scriptures between different religious groups can recognise its relative inevitability during the formative years of community-building.[39] However, in the modern era it is an approach that need not any longer be espoused. Interreligious conflict was carried on to protect religious and communal boundaries during an age of martial aggression; it does not negate the validity of competing religious understandings.

Granted there were manifest instances of aggression against other religions in the Old Testament, yet these were exceptional circumstances in which the political entities whom Israel faced on leaving Egypt, where they had been held as slaves, were particularly expansionist both politically and religiously.

Sihon, king of the Amorites, was unwilling even to provide safe passage for Israel but attacked it,[40] while Balak, king of Moab, hired a prophet to curse it.[41] The peoples who occupied Canaan were assessed to be certain to corrupt the faith of Israel if they were allowed to coexist with them. Hence, the difficult decision to utterly destroy them was taken, whatever may be the interpretation of the literality of the invasions.[42]

Moreover, the communities God judged directly or through Israel were culpable of moral wrongdoing, including the promotion of adultery through temple sex, bestiality and even child sacrifice.[43]

In populating the chart of the spiritual, moral and ethical benefits of world religious traditions, one realises that what is crucial is the premise that one's religion, whatever it may be, is not fundamentally inimical to or incompatible with another religion at least as to its spiritual-moral-ethical aims; that, by learning about other religions, one stands to bolster, strengthen and clarify one's own religious beliefs because one gains a clearer view of aspects which are understated in one's own religion, such

---

39. Given a limited view of God's power, such that he is not seen as capable of changing a person's mind, the destruction of the firstborn of Egypt may be viewed as a necessary act to compel the leader of a militaristic nation such as Pharaoh to allow the Israelites to leave the land.

40. Numbers 21:21-23.

41. Numbers 22-25.

42. Judges 2:1-3.

43. P. Copan, *Is God a Moral Monster? Making Sense of the Old Testament God* (Grand Rapids, MI: Baker, 2011), p. 159.

as an aspect of a common divinity which is often also an aspect of a common humanity, and obtains a multi-perspectival view of the same divine reality, and comes to the recognition that one can with good conscience protect one's religious others and seek their greatest wellbeing.

The theory of a perichoretic constitution of the Trinity may be helpful in throwing light on the relationship between the world religions.[44] Perichoretic constitution considers how the Father is whom the Father is through the Son and the Spirit, because the Son and the Spirit contribute to constitute the full being that the Father is, while the Son is whom the Son is through the Father and the Spirit, because the Father and the Spirit contribute to constitute the full being that the Son is, and the Spirit is whom the Spirit is through the Father and the Son, because the Father and the Son contribute to constitute the full being that the Spirit is.

The divine persons may be compared to the different sides of a transparent triangle. One may look at a different side of the triangle but, ultimately, one sees the same object, the only difference being the side at which one is looking. Suppose there are pictures on each side but one cannot see the picture from the back, only the outline. Therefore, when one looks at one side, one sees the picture on that side but cannot really make out the picture on the other three sides.

In a similar manner to the triune nature of God, featuring as it does a single divine being in three distinctive personal presentations, a trinitarian theology of world religions here commended identifies the source of religious knowledge as the same one divine being, the Trinity in Christian terms, disclosing itself in differing ways, this time not as different persons but the same being in different modes, as fitted, adapted to and accommodating the spiritual needs of various communities existing in different time periods. In the case of the world religions, there are not many gods or even different persons but, perhaps, just one divine principle.

With these remarks, I turn to my second way of attempting a reconciliation of the world religions; namely, through a search for a theological affinity between these religions.

Using a perichoretic model of the divinities of world religions, it may not be imperative to discard the Christian notion of a single godhead in a bid to embrace the right of other religious groups to a peaceful existence and flourishing.

---

44. E. Z.-K. Chua, *'God-ness', 'God-ity', and God: A Historical Study and Synthesis of the Christian Doctrine of the Divine Being*, 2nd edn (New Orleans, LA: University Press of the South, 2022), pp. 80-102.

The Christian God can be conceived as the single divine reality as manifested and revealed to Christians, with the Islamic God seen as the same divine reality but as manifested and revealed to Muslims, yet there is ultimately only one divine reality.

Within each religious group, there are norms of governance and identity which obviously do not apply in other groups. It is not incorrect for a Christian or a Muslim to say that his God is the only true God, but this particular monotheistic vision has to be tied immediately to the needs of the specific religious community in question.

In this way, as soon as a Christian might say, 'The God of the Bible is the only true God', he could hasten to add, 'But the doctrine of God in the Bible is not the only way to approach or understand the only true God, who is free to manifest Godself almost as another God, a group of gods, or even an impersonal moral principle according to the needs of specific religious communities.'

Therefore, Christians do have a true knowledge of God but it is not an exhaustive one, and this very crucial space is opened up by the Christian doctrine of divine transcendence and sovereign freedom, where God is acknowledged as an immeasurable reality that eludes complete human comprehension and expectation and defies being confined to any one particular religious understanding.[45] Therefore, there is no need to force a choice between the idea that my God is either the only true God to the exclusion of other religious understandings or this God is not God at all.

A transgender person can serve as an analogy to understand God from a multifaith perspective. Whether pre- or post-transition, there is just one individual in question. Some people will know only the pre-transition person, while others only the post-transition. Even so, there is no more authentic self behind these two modes – both are just as real and authentic. The difference between God in the world religions and the transgender person, of course, consists in how God is simultaneously present in multiple, different modes of presentation in each religion rather than sequentially or chronologically.

On these terms, monotheism is fundamentally inclusive rather than exclusive in its orientation. In any monotheistic religion, there is only one God and this God makes its presence felt among all of humanity in different ways for a common, moral purpose. For this reason, a seventh-century Chinese imperial edict recognised a shared threefold structure

---

45. Cf. 1 Timothy 6:16; R. Bernhardt, 'Trinity as a Framework for a Theology of Religions', *STK* 90 (2014), p. 60; Heim, *Depth of the Riches*, p. 40.

by which the three traditional Chinese religious systems, namely, Confucianism, Buddhism and Taoism, along with Nestorianism may be classified, one comprising the Tao, symbolising the transcendent mystery to which all religions testify in multifarious ways; *sheng*, sagacious human persons hailing from different historical and cultural milieux with some grasp of the Tao; and *jiao*, specific religious systems of philosophy, instruction and practice which vary according to their locales of origin and influence, and the historical conditions associated with them.[46] It is impossible for an omnipresent God to be active and operative only in certain communities and not others. Hence, it is compelling to posit that this God is present even in those spaces as the Holy Spirit, but taking on a different name and conceptualisation.[47]

Along similar lines, the Bahá'í Faith teaches that the founders of the great world religions, such as Moses, Zoroaster, Buddha, Jesus and Mohammad, were all representatives of the same God who brought a fundamentally unified,[48] historically appropriate and sociologically relevant message[49] to their respective communities.[50]

Yet, do not different religions contradict one another? Even if so, they do not have to be perceived as making affirmations in an exhaustive manner, only those which are valid for their specific communities. Now, when it comes to issues of religious belief, one is dealing with the unfalsifiable and extremely subjective. In this regard, absolute statements about the metaphysics of God or the salvation of humankind are unrealistic and otiose. To consider Christianity and any other world religion on an equal footing as coexistent and equally valid systems, it will be necessary to venture to distil the key point of each system.

There are at least three ways for a Christian theology to engage a world religion. A first option might attempt to identify areas or secondary streams in a world religion from which it may be possible to develop

---

46. J. Gentz, *Understanding Chinese Religions*, Understanding Faith (Edinburgh: Dunedin Academic, 2013), p. 5.
47. Cf. *GDT*, s.v. 'Hinduism' (M.T. Cherian, pp. 391-92).
48. 'Essential principles' and 'divine truths' such as the idea of God as loving.
49. One which accounts for differing statutes governing human conduct in community.
50. J.E. Esslemont, *Bahá'u'lláh and the New Era: An Introduction to the Bahá'í Faith* (Wilmette, IL: Bahá'í Publishing, 2006), pp. 29-57, 129-146; The Bahá'í Faith, 'What Bahá'ís Believe: Revelation', *The Official Website of the Worldwide Bahá'í Community*, accessed 18 May 2022, https://www.bahai.org/beliefs/god-his-creation/revelation.

an interpretation of an aspect of that religious system which is considerably congruent with a Christian theology. Second, one might venture to develop a new interpretation of a doctrine of a world religion which comports with a Christian understanding. Third, one might engage with the mainstream of a world religion with a view to some form of reconciliation between Christian theology and that religion. This book opts for the third possibility because it elects primarily to engage mainstream and classical conceptions of world religions from a Christian theological angle.

With this in mind, I shall proceed to consider each of a number of the various major religions with the object of seeing how they can all be understood as differing revelations of the same God vouchsafed to different communities at different points in history.

Buddhism

Buddhists speak of *dukkha*, suffering brought about by the various stresses of life through different life phases and, generally, an attachment to people and objects which turns into anguish when those things are eventually lost, and an existential dissatisfaction with life; a karmic cycle of reincarnation, *samsāra*; and the release from these cycles through *nirvāna* or enlightenment.[51]

In Buddhist teaching, the law of Buddha is enshrined in what is known as the *Four Noble Truths*. The first principle pertains to how life is replete with suffering in the form of stresses, significant losses and existential dissatisfaction. The second principle concerns the causes of these different forms of suffering. These are, first of all, aversion, as a response to life's stresses, leading to being fixated with and consumed by distressing situations in life, due to a failure to appreciate how it is in the nature of life to be replete with *dukkha* or suffering. Second, there is an attachment to people or objects which leads to agony when they are lost, due to a failure to understand *aniccā*, or the fugitive nature of people and things in the world. Third, there is an endless craving for happiness and fulfilment which generates existential dissatisfaction, due to a failure to embrace *anattā*, or the notion that the self is not an absolute essence or factor that needs to be mollycoddled or exalted but one very much in need of enlightenment. The third principle in the *Four Noble Truths* avers that these kinds of suffering can be successfully and effectively overcome, and the fourth principle lays out the method, the

---

51. Bowker, *MaB*, pp. 231-35.

Eightfold Path, by which they can be resolved, leading the person to a blissful mental state known as *nirvāna*.[52]

The *Eightfold Path* involves embracing: right vision or perception about how human existence as it tends to be lived, in aversion, attachment and dissatisfaction, is unviable; right aims, or goals, pertaining to love of others rather than of material things or the pursuit of self-advancement through trampling on others; right speech, in which one strives to be discreet and honest; right action, whereby a person commits always to help others and never to take a life, engage in theft or promiscuity; right livelihood, where a person commits to a profession which is open and above board and does not bring harm on others or the wider community; right mindfulness, whereby an individual renounces all malicious thoughts and embraces benevolent ones; right awareness, where a person weans themselves of a fixation on bodily pleasures and other desires; and right meditation, a resolution to undertake the meditative practices developed by Buddha.[53]

Buddhism does not espouse a doctrine that there is one God. In fact, there is no Creator in Buddhism, though there may be minor deities, such as Amita Buddha, whose altruism in assisting bodhisattvas, pious followers set on attaining *nirvāna*, has been noted as similar to the Christian concept of grace.[54] All beings are interconnected through *samsāra* in the Buddhist worldview; all sentient entities were a person's mother in a previous lifetime.[55]

Buddhism makes a forceful point about how life's stresses, attachments and unbridled greed cause suffering, and this is a doctrine that Christianity is able to incorporate, given that Christianity, too, teaches the importance of facing one's challenges and taking life in its stride, the need to cherish our relationships and enjoy our possessions but without holding onto them obsessively, and the vanity of seeking earthly riches as well as the value of contentment.

Regarding karmic reincarnation, with the concept of *karma* (actions) as determining the location, form, bliss and misery of each individual

---

52. J.D. Oliver, *Buddhism: An Introduction to the Buddha's Life, Teachings, and Practices*, The Essential Wisdom Library (New York, NY: St. Martin's Essentials, 2019), pp. 62-65, 89-90; BBC, 'Life and teachings of the Buddha: Dukkha, anicca and anatta', accessed 17 May 2022, https://www.bbc.co.uk/bitesize/guides/zd8bcj6/revision/5.

53. Stark, *DG*, p. 240.

54. *GDT*, s.v. 'Buddhism' (T.C. Muck, p. 122).

55. Oliver, *Buddhism*, pp. 88-89.

soul across many lifetimes, this is centred on the importance of living wisely with a good conscience. Instructively, *karma* is not a mode of divine reward or punishment, but a natural principle of the universe governing and regulating human morality, much like the laws of nature.[56] Although Christians may not agree that human existence is structured in multiple and potentially unending cycles of reincarnation whose quality is contingent on the morality of one's present existence, they can nevertheless affirm the need to lead good and moral lives.

Christians can also recognise that they do not have a monopoly on religious truth or possess exact or exhaustive insight into matters of the spiritual realm. In charitability, they may allow that life may very well be cyclical or karmic in nature and choose not to be overly dogmatic about their own religious views.[57] They can appreciate how such a system of reward and punishment may well be beneficial for stemming evil and promoting goodwill, and grasp that belief in the existence of self-sacrificial and more approachable minor deities may have much in common with the notion of the approachability, relatability and empathy of God in their own faith.

The trinitarian divine persons do function more than a little like these minor deities, each playing a distinct role, with the others supporting, of helping people towards faith and good morality. Indeed, the celestial bodhisattvas of Mahāyāna Buddhism, who aid human supplications and

---

56. S. Fohr, *Jainism: A Guide for the Perplexed* (London: Bloomsbury, 2015), p. 7.

57. If this is the case, then it would be necessary for Christians to concede that the scenes of divine judgement such as proffered in the Book of Revelation would have to be conceived metaphorically as symbols of God's fellowship with the obedient or pious (in the case of the scene of the righteous being separated from unbelievers in Revelation 22:14-15, with the latter to be understood in the book's socio-historical context as designating people who conspired with the Roman powers in order to avoid economic consequences and political oppression for their faith in Christ) and God's timely and fitting punishment of evildoers in myriad ways (in the case of the depiction of people being thrown into the lake of fire whose names were not written in the book of life in Revelation 20:11-15, possibly referring to the perpetrators of persecution against Christians during Roman times, and Christ's remarks about those who cause the believers to lose faith in God being possibly judged by fire in Mark 9:42-48). See G.K. Beale, *The Book of Revelation* (Grand Rapids, MI: Eerdmans, 1999), pp. 28-33, and C.A. Evans, *Mark 8:27-16:20*, WBC 34B (Nashville, TN: Thomas Nelson, 2001), pp. 71-72.

needs relating to achieving *nirvāna* and worldly affairs, serve as a kind of god.[58] The difference, however, is that, unlike these deities, God in Christianity is a single and unified being. This ontological distinction need not prevent a Christian from accepting the experiential similarities between the Buddhist and Christian faiths. It is up to the Buddhist to decide whether he wishes to delve further into whether God should be conceived as a single being or as separate, minor divine beings.

Furthermore, there is a Buddhist emphasis, in the form of what is known as the Brahma vihārās, the Four Immeasurables, wondrous postures of perspective. These are *metta*, an altruistic love, sincere sociality, kindness and positive desire for the wellbeing of others; *karuna*, a softness of heart which incandescently desires that all entities might be liberated from their suffering; *mudita*, a genuine camaraderie and solidarity which exults because of the attainments and favourable circumstances of others; and *upekkha*, a sangfroid in the face of suffering.[59] It will be noted that the Christian faith promotes these very attributes as those which define God and which believers are to emulate from God.

In this regard, Christians may accept that the same God may well have been powerfully at work in the establishment of Buddhism, underscoring certain essential aspects of divinity and ultimate purpose while leaving others to human speculation and deduction.

Hinduism

Space is given in Hinduism to reflection on the need for the human soul, *ātman*, to be freed from its state of ignorance, *jiva*. This is achieved through a philosophical and experiential reunion with Brāhman, the unitary and incomparable creative, sustaining and monarchical ground of all being, the Ultimate Reality, on the presupposition that each human soul is ontologically, though not necessarily existentially, united with Brāhman.[60] Although people are rewarded for their moral actions or punished for their immoral acts in their current and previous lives through their lot in succeeding lifetimes, and people progress or retrogress morally through good or bad deeds, respectively, the most ideal state of existence consists in the *ātman* being reunited with Brāhman through the extirpation of the state of being attracted to something other than the true self.

---

58. Fohr, *Jainism*, p. 11.
59. Oliver, *Buddhism*, pp. 96-102.
60. Bowker, *MaB*, pp. 171-74, 179-82; Fohr, *Jainism*, p. 7.

This liberating reunion, *moksa*, results in an overcoming of a karmic cycle of rebirth (*samsāra*), cast in naturalistic categories of becoming different aspects of the physical world, including fire-day-time-sun-moon-thunder[61] and smoke-night-time-world of the fathers-space-moon-god's food-space-wind-smoke-mist-cloud-rain-edible plants-rebirth as creature that consumes it,[62] and *nirvāna*, an unconscious state of eternal happiness, a form of 'order', a 'dreamless sleep', 'an awakening', an ultimate liberation from earthly existence.[63]

The karmic theory in Hinduism, in which people experience different lots based on their moral conduct in a previous existence and in which such desert can be transferred from one person to another because there is a sort of ontological unity among humankind, has been reinterpreted as a testament to the fact that parents, ancestors and other actors exercise an influence through their genetic makeup or actions in a manner reminiscent to how past lives are said to affect present lives, and to the fact that people, through their personal, watched or heard experiences, are able to provide a medium, live or remembered, through which other people can have vicarious experiences.[64] The genetic affinity between Buddhism and Hinduism is clear even from this compendious summary.

Although Hinduism is popularly thought of as a polytheistic religion, in truth it is a monotheistic faith in Brāhman, the ultimate reality and being, invisible, not fully comprehensible, beyond time and even eternity, ever-existent, everywhere-present, boundless, simple, conscious and spiritual essence of the limited and dynamic universe.[65] Brāhman has various presentations, including the three main gods: Brahmā, the creator of the universe; Vishnu, the preserver of the universe; and Shiva, the destroyer of the universe.[66] This *trimurti*, 'three forms', with the intimate involvement of God in the creation, preservation, salvation and redemption of humankind, resembles the Christian Trinity in numerous

61. This is in the case of forest ascetics.
62. This is in the case of all other people.
63. Stark, *DG*, pp. 227-29; *GDT*, s.v. 'Hinduism' (Cherian, pp. 388-90); W. Doniger, *On Hinduism* (Oxford: Oxford University Press, 2014), pp. 89-98.
64. Doniger, *On Hinduism*, pp. 102-6.
65. *GDT*, s.v. 'Hinduism' (Cherian, p. 391).
66. The Editors of Encyclopaedia Britannica, 'brahman', *Britannica*, Encyclopaedia Britannica, last modified 31 October 2019, https://www .britannica.com/topic/brahman-Hindu-concept; BBC, 'Brahman', last modified 31 July 2003, https://www.bbc.co.uk/religion/religions/hinduism /beliefs/intro_1.shtml.

ways, in that, similarly, a single divinity is expressed in multiple presentations with essential functions in establishing, maintaining and perfecting the created order.[67] The distinction, of course, lies in how Hinduism conceives of God as being ultimately one rather than being both three and one at the same time.[68]

The Hindu conception of God is at once monistic,[69] sometimes pantheistic,[70] sometimes panentheistic,[71] kathenotheistic,[72] and there is typically a non-duality of the human soul and Brāhman, in which the two are not distinguished one from the other; consider how, in a Hindu tradition, all men and women are regarded as manifestations of the god-couple Shiva and Parvati.[73] Aside from being concurrently polytheistic and monistic, the Hindu understanding of God also espouses the equal value of all religions as different and especially relevant ways of approaching the same one divine reality, something which a modern Christian doctrine can learn from.[74]

There is much room for agreement between Christians and Hindus in terms of God as creative, preservative and ruling and the need for a moral lifestyle. Moreover, the idea of *karma* and *samsāra* in Hinduism, insofar as it asserts the possibility of moral change through the primacy of moral action, promotes noble and right conduct among human persons conceived of as morally self-determining agents. Given Christianity's emphasis on responsible moral behaviour, there is broad correspondence in this regard between Christianity and Hinduism. As for Hinduism's conception of God as omnipresent, boundless, simple and inexpressible, this finds correspondence in our conception of the Divine Nature.[75]

---

67. Stark, *DG*, pp. 230-34; *GDT*, s.v. 'Hinduism' (Cherian, p. 389).
68. Bernhardt, 'Trinity as a Framework', p. 52.
69. The belief that there is one impersonal ultimate reality.
70. The belief that the world is God and God is the world.
71. The belief that the world is intertwined with God but God is not dependent on the world for God's existence; consider how the existence and non-existence of the universe are tied, respectively, to the waking hours and sleep of the god, Vishnu, respectively.
72. Each Hindu god is worshipped with exclusive devotion at separate times, with the gods sometimes sharing credit for certain deeds, such as dividing heaven and earth, and also having unique traits and accomplishments.
73. Doniger, *On Hinduism*, pp. 99, 114.
74. Ibid., pp. 10-20.
75. See Chapter Seven on theodicy.

For these reasons, Christians should not have any issues with affirming that the same God revealed Godself in Hinduism, just in a different manner.

Islam

Islam teaches the necessity of submission to a powerful and monadic Creator, ruler and moral judge.[76] Allāh is incorporeal and inscrutable, subject to no limiting category, including the attributes of love, virtue and rationality, with the liberty and means even to determine the meaning of right and wrong, the course of life of the human individual, and events that transpire in the world.[77] Even so, Allāh is classically linked to such qualities as truth, radiance, omniscience, forgiveness, love, favourable disposition, mercy, wisdom, justice.[78] The specifics of the exact rules that need to be adhered to and the key prophetic authority will differ from those of Christianity, but Christians can recognise that these rules and customs have held together Muslim societies in piety and sociality.

Christians can also resonate with the pivotal importance of humility, gratitude and obedience before God, attributes highly valued in Christianity, and the common belief in God as a Creator, loving, forgiving, merciful, powerful, wise and summoning people to love God and one another. Furthermore, Christians can recognise that, although Muslims may well object to the doctrine of the Trinity as an inaccurate and misleading depiction of God who is one, these objections are based on fundamental misconceptions, such as the belief that the Christian Trinity constitutes not the Father, Son and Holy Spirit, but the Father, Jesus and Mary, and the overarching conviction that God as a single being cannot be conceived as a threefold being without splitting the divinity three ways.[79]

Christians can see that the Trinity, in effect, shores up the doctrine of God as love in essence. This is because, as an internal community of full persons, God is able to love the other in Godself and not just Godself. In this way, God's love for God transcends simple self-love and becomes a matter of genuine affection and authentic communion between divine

---

76. Bowker, *MaB*, pp. 127-28.
77. Stark, *DG*, pp. 365-67.
78. *GDT*, s.v. 'Islam' (J.D. Woodberry, pp. 425-26).
79. M. Volf, *Allah: A Christian Response* (New York, NY: HarperOne, 2011); J. Hoover, 'Islamic Monotheism and the Trinity', *CGR* 27, no. 1 (Winter 2009): 57-82, corrected version, pp.1-2.

persons in the Godhead. On these terms, Christians cannot finally subscribe to the Islamic notion of God as a single and unitary being, as one person rather than three.

Irrespective of this, they can consider how a non-trinitarian view of God testifies powerfully against any attempt to split the Godhead into separate pieces. There have been efforts, as in Marcionism, to pit the God of the Old Testament, conceived of as the Father, against the God of the New Testament, embodied and concretised in the Son, on the assumption that one reveals the holiness and justice of God, while the other, the love, forgiveness and compassion of God. The Islamic vision of God starkly reminds Christians of their own faith in God as one. It also highlights the fact that, to all intents and purposes, the Godhead does function like a single being.

Furthermore, Christianity is sufficiently theologically capacious to accommodate such a view as an Islamic conception of God as utterly transcendent even over formal and moral categories of personal attribute, and in possession of untrammelled power as subject over all reality.

The Qur'an does not take a stand on whether God predetermines all events and things in the world, or whether human beings have a role to play in carrying out or violating God's will. The teachings of the Prophet Muhammad, however, have a predisposition towards predestination.[80] As for the most commonly held view of the subject among Muslim believers, this is the notion that God foreordains all things with possibly some human contribution as opposed to human beings possessing the free will to obey or disobey God's will purely on their own initiative.[81]

Even predestinarian formulations attest, in a manner which a moderate Christian theology can accept, to the way in which God is not sub-servient in any sense to human categories of thought, and that the universe did not arise by accident but originates ultimately through or in God. Similarly, the idea of God as omniscient, found as it is in the Christian tradition, can be taken as attesting to the truth that God is either intrinsically aware, or keeps Godself aware, of the affairs of the world and is already aware of much,[82] not least the hearts of believers in whom God dwells.

---

80. F.M. Denny, *An Introduction to Islam*, 4th edn (Boston: Prentice Hall, 2011), pp. 103-4.

81. Ibid., p. 169.

82. 2 Chronicles 16:9.

In light of this, a Christian can see how it might well be that the same God chose to reveal Godself to these communities in the ways recorded and enshrined in the Islamic faith.

The Bahá'í Faith, Zoroastrianism, Taoism and Sikhism

In the Bahá'í Faith, God is not fully comprehensible, is an all-powerful, all-wise, all-knowing, all-loving, all-merciful, exalted and gracious Creator of the world and great physician of the world's soul, attributes Christians can resonate with in their own beliefs about God.[83] The world-positive outlook of Bahá'ís, in which every part of the world reveals an aspect of the Creator, bears an inherent affinity with the Christian conception of God, in which, to varying degrees, the different elements of the non-divine entitative order express certain features of God.[84] Christians, at least sectarians or fundamentalists, can also be inspired by the Bahá'í Faith's embracing attitude towards science.[85]

The Zoroastrian religion has God, by the name of Ahura Mazda,[86] as an eternal, supreme, creative, paternal, pastoral being possessed of a holy spirit, a just, merciful, righteous and holy judge, enthroned in the heavens and served by angels, a source of all that is good, of omni-potent, omniscient, and omnipresent prowess, traits which Christianity associates with God in some way.[87] Zoroastrianism underscores the centrality of human decision in the moral act. It focusses on the need to be constantly mindful of the value of expressing good thoughts,

---

83. Esslemont, *Bahá'u'lláh and the New Era*, pp. 29-57, 129-146.

84. The Bahá'í Faith, 'What Bahá'ís Believe: An Unknowable God', *The Official Website of the Worldwide Bahá'í Community*, accessed 18 May 2022, https://www.bahai.org/beliefs/god-his-creation/revelation/unkn owable-god.

85. Idem, 'What Bahá'ís Believe: The Coming of Age of Humanity', *The Official Website of the Worldwide Bahá'í Community*, accessed 18 May 2022, https://www.bahai.org/beliefs/god-his-creation/revelation /coming-age-humanity.

86. 'The Wise Lord', Ormazd.

87. J. Rose, *Zoroastrianism: An Introduction*, I.B. Tauris Introductions to Religion (London: Bloomsbury, 2012), pp. 14-26; BBC, 'Zoroastrianism: God, Zoroaster and immortals', last modified 2 October 2009, https:// www.bbc.co.uk/religion/religions/zoroastrian/beliefs/god.shtml; A.V.W. Jackson, 'Zoroastrianism and the Resemblances between It and Christianity', *BW* 27, no. 5 (May 1906), pp. 338-39.

good words, good deeds,[88] with an accent upon 'humble devotion', 'right mindfulness', *armaiti*; 'readiness to listen', *sraosha*; 'friendship', *airyaman*; and 'religious insight', *daena*. Truthful speech, faithfulness, generosity towards the destitute, diligence and frugality are important qualities pursued by the Zoroastrian.

Aspects of Zoroastrian theology include the agency of archangels,[89] angels,[90] archfiends and evil spirits,[91] including an omnipresent prime adversary, Angra Mainyu,[92] conceived as an independent force, whose evil is by choice and from the very beginning, the source of all that is evil, who is of the nature of deceit and falsehood, *druj*, malicious, craven, a tempter, traitor, perverter of good and the essence of death. Although powerful, Angra Mainyu is not omniscient.

Zoroastrian doctrine postulates a constant and ongoing battle between Ahura Mazda and Angra Mainyu. However, victory ultimately belongs to Ahura Mazda and the forces of good given that Angra Mainyu's power has a limit, but this not separate from the moral agency of human beings, by whose good thoughts, words and deeds, one gains access to heaven, and by whose evil thoughts, words and deeds one falls into hell. When this victory is secured with the assistance of a saviour, *saoshyant*, there will be a consummation of a wished-for or good kingdom, a global restoration, resurrection of the dead and the rule of righteousness.

The Zoroastrian religion gives pride of place to the family and highlights the need to care for the pristine and good creation of God through agriculture and restoration of barren lands as a mark of holiness, cleansing of the elements of fire, earth and water from contamination by dead matter or personal ritual uncleanliness, gentleness towards domesticated animals such as cows and dogs while ridding the land of reptiles and pests to atone for sin and gain merit.[93] It can readily be seen

---

88. *Humata, hukhta, hvareshta.*
89. *Amesha Spentas*, 'Beneficent Immortals', associated with various aspects of reality.
90. *Yazatas*, 'Worshipful Ones'.
91. *Daēvas*, 'demons'; *drujes*, 'fiends'.
92. 'The Destructive Spirit', Ahriman.
93. Rose, *Zoroastrianism*, pp. 14-26; BBC, 'Dualism in Zoroastrianism', last modified 2 October 2009, https://www.bbc.co.uk/religion/religions /zoroastrian/beliefs/dualism.shtml; BBC, 'Humanity in Zoroastrianism', last modified 2 October 2009, https://www.bbc.co.uk/religion/religions /zoroastrian/beliefs/humanity.shtml; Jackson, 'Zoroastrianism and Christianity', pp. 336-42; The Editors of Encyclopaedia Britannica, 'amesha

that, broadly speaking at least, Zoroastrian theology shares much in common with vital principles in Christianity.

As a matter of fact, it is believed that the henotheistic phase of the development of Jewish monotheism, in which God, like Ahura Mazda, becomes the only true God as head of a pantheon of other subordinate gods, much like the way the Persian king was seen as the king of kings and therefore the only true king, the idea of Satan as a chief adversary of God, and Jewish angelology and demonology, are indebted to the influence of Zoroastrianism.[94] It cannot, therefore, be said that the world religions are not capable of a salutary intercourse among one another.

In Taoism, the originating and ineffable principle that is the Tao is at the centre of a spontaneous, impersonal and unintentional process by which all things came into being. There are four main stages in the formation of the universe, beginning with an 'unrepresentable before', progressing to a 'primordial undifferentiation', leading on to the emergence of the yin-yang principles, then their interplay, which, in turn, brings about the five phases and all entities.[95] Qi is the fundamental essence of being and life in the universe.[96]

According to the cosmogonic account found in the Book of the Huainan Masters, *Huainanzi*, a Chinese classic from the second century BC, this is how all things came into being: in the outset, during a time called the Great Inception, there was no boundary between the heavens and earth in the dynamic and spontaneous upward and downward movement of things. Then the Tao brought about an ill-defined emptiness, which engendered the ordered state of the universe, out of which arose *qi*. The lighter and clearer accumulations of *qi* rose to form the heavens, while the heavy and cloudier sank to form earth. The former came together more quickly than the latter, and so the heavens were formed earlier. The essences in the heavens and on the earth gathered to form yin and yang, then spread out to give rise to the four seasons. Finally, the essences of the four seasons separated to form the myriad entities.[97]

---

spenta', *Britannica*, Encyclopaedia Britannica, 20 July 1998, https://www .britannica.com/topic/amesha-spenta.

94. T. Römer, *The Invention of God*, trans. R. Geuss (Cambridge, MA: Harvard University Press, 2015), pp. 227-30; Jackson, 'Zoroastrianism and Christianity', p. 338.

95. L. Komjathy, *The Daoist Tradition: An Introduction* (London: Bloomsbury, 2013), p. 104.

96. Ibid., p. 103.

97. Ibid., p. 102.

The processes of becoming in the universe are not guided by a divine person, intentionality or agency, but result purely and spontaneously from an in-built, natural process of evolution within the incomprehensible Tao, which is beyond all representation and which manifests itself in various forms of becoming and being in the humanly observable and non-observable universe.[98] This 'ecological' cosmogonic theology of Taoism sees the universe with all its inhabitants returning someday to an undifferentiated unity and a state beyond all representation.[99]

The cosmogonic element of Taoism, defined as it is by its monism or belief in a single, impersonal ultimate reality, its panenhenism, whereby nature is viewed as a sacred totality, and its panentheism, in which sacred reality is both identical to and yet also transcends the universe, constitutes a primary dimension of its theology. A secondary dimension is provided by an animistic and polytheistic worldview, incorporating local deities and cosmic divine beings, which may be primeval divinities, primitive manifestations of the Tao, or divinised human beings, ghosts and ancestors.[100]

Although the pantheonic nature of divinity in Taoism in which different gods are assigned various roles may give some pause to Christians, such functional polytheism is useful in drawing attention to the effective and responsible work of God in the world order.[101] Moreover, the principle of Tao as an underlying structure by which being, existence, nature and morality are given form and the possibility of actualisation is useful in illuminating the same structural role of God in the Christian theology which I am proposing as one by whose nature all things which exist directly receive the power of existence as posited or receive it indirectly through agents directly posited,[102] who holds all things together, materially, in Christ, through an ancient decree effectuated by the might of angels.[103] Nevertheless, there remain significant points of contrast between Christian and Taoist theology, and it will be for Taoists alone to decide if they wish to engage more deeply the issue of the nature of divinity.

---

98. Ibid., pp. 102-5.
99. Ibid., p. 127.
100. Ibid., pp. 113-15.
101. BBC, 'Taoism: Gods and spirits', last modified 12 November 2009, https://www.bbc.co.uk/religion/religions/taoism/beliefs/gods.shtml.
102. That is, the Trinity and the angels.
103. BBC, 'Taoism: What is the Tao?', last modified 12 November 2009, https://www.bbc.co.uk/religion/religions/taoism/beliefs/tao.shtml.

Important in Taoism is the need to pursue harmony between the various elements of human existence, whether it be relationship with the gods, deceased ancestors, or nature spirits. Christians can relate to the need to find peace with a divine entity, which may appear in distinct individual forms in the Taoist religion, the need to remember and honour deceased loved ones without necessarily worrying about their safety or fearing their vengeance, and the need to protect the world with its guardian spirits sent from God.[104]

Sikhism is a religion with a strongly this-worldly and experiential focus in which non-dualism is essential to viewing all of life, characterising even the divine. Human existence is to be lived in the clear understanding that all things are impermanent and not worth clutching onto too tightly. Instead, people should learn to undergo a process of 'ego-loss' in which they cease to regard themselves as the centre of the universe and the rightful owner and judge of the world around them. In this process, the individual is to remonstrate lovingly with the egocentric self within himself and correct both thought and language from the standpoint of pre-conscious, ego-relativised self-awareness of having direct access to the divine source, and being one with all other things through the universal law of birth, death and rebirth which constitutes the ethical warrant. The egocentric person is an insecure and especially vulnerable person in that he depends on circumstances being in a very specific way and the stars being aligned in order that he can experience some measure of stability and peace of mind.

As transcendent and immanent at one and the same time, the divine source is to be experienced in its transcendence through immanent, worldly modes of speech, thought, feeling, desire, will, intention and action. All actions are imprinted in the consciousness, leading to patterns of habit which can fortunately be erased through meditation on *nam*, the name of the divine source which transcends categorisation as a being, and a progressive and intrinsically desperate self-rehabilitation through transformation of one's partial self-concept. Time is both objective – as a system of measurement of the passage of our lives based on the regular revolutions of the earth about its own axis and about the sun – and subjective – as an individual perception of how life is progressing or stagnating.[105]

---

104. Corduan, *PGWR*, pp. 58-67.
105. A.-P.S. Mandair, *Sikhism: A Guide for the Perplexed* (London: Bloomsbury, 2013), pp. 131-55; cf. Augustine, *Civ.*, XI.6, in which the saint explains that, since eternity is devoid of alteration, and the idea of duration

Sikhism thus focusses on how the one God, who is ineffable and yet capable of being finitely expressed through worldly analogues, guides the faithful towards freedom, *mukti*, from the cycles of *karma* through knowing and becoming one with God. While God is not fully comprehensible, it is possible to gain some understanding of God through acts of affection, adoration and reflection upon the human soul and the world at large.[106]

Christians can appreciate how these ideas and experiences throw light on the nature and majesty of God, and find correspondences between the Sikh conception of God and a doctrine of the Divine Nature as postulated by our theological system. In particular, there is an affinity between the Sikh idea of the need for a loving self-remonstration and the call on our part to self-renunciation, in which inappropriate and wrongful thoughts, feelings, desires, intentions, resolves and actions are disavowed in one's own heart. Christians should also be able to find agreement with the Sikh notion of the interconnectedness of all things, whether or not one assumes the validity of a reincarnational view, in the tendency for actions to repeat themselves and harden into habits.

The Sikh notion that all people are able to approach God may be foreign to Christian theology. However, in Christianity the mediatorship of Christ is not so much an achievement, by which through some act of Christ, God was somehow persuaded to remove the barriers to human access to God (even though some strands of the Christian tradition continue to espouse a view of the atonement as having instrumental value as a propitiatory sacrifice), but rather a revelation, an epiphany on the part of humankind, through Christ's self-sacrificial act on the Cross, that God has never been at enmity with them but so deeply loves them that God was willing to give up God's own Son to testify to God's unconditional love and affection and remove all barriers people might erect for themselves or others in relation to access to God.

---

presupposes the existence of some object that is capable of alteration or movement so that, through the identification of some regular motion, it is possible to conceptualise an interval or unit of time, there is no recourse except to postulate time as having come into being with the rest of the universe and not rather that time already existed when the universe came into being at some point in time.

106. BBC, 'Sikh Beliefs', last modified 24 September 2009, https://www.bbc.co.uk/religion/religions/sikhism/beliefs/beliefs.shtml; Corduan, *PGWR*, p. 132.

In their own ways, these religions may be seen as valid revelations of God.

Shintoism and Other Traditional and Tribal Religions

While there may seem to be little in common between Christianity and Shintoism and other traditional and tribal religions, as a matter of fact, the affinity between them lies in the manner in which in all of them the appeasement of the divine or spiritual is a centrepiece. Although in traditional and tribal religions the spirits to be placated are not equivalent to a monotheistic conception of God, at the very least they succeed in drawing attention to the reality of the spiritual world, and how there is need to be properly reconciled to this entire domain of existence. Furthermore, as in Shintoism and other traditional and tribal religions, in which nature is given prominence as a realm inhabited by spiritual entities, Christians can assent to the need to respect and protect the natural environment which may be presided over by special nature angels or spirits sent by God to take care of the physical world.[107]

Non-Theisms

There is much in common even between Christianity and non-theistic systems. As a case in point, the ethical correspondence between Christianity and Confucianism has been observed.[108] Analogues can be found in the Christian faith to basic Confucian values and attributes such as humanity/benevolence, *ren*, righteousness, *yi*, ritual, *li*, knowledge, *zhi*, trustworthiness, *xin*, filial piety, *xiao*, loyalty, *zhong*, and yielding, *rang*, and a neo-Confucian ideal of universal affection and responsibility.[109]

Although neo-Confucianism is based on a conception of human nature as fundamentally virtuous, this need not be pitted against a Christian conception of human sinfulness, which may be construed and articulated in terms of a foreign incursion of compulsive evil through adverse childhood and other traumatic experiences.[110] Instead, this Chinese religio-philosophical tradition attests to the undeniable fact of a trans-cultural human morality and conscience which is finally primed

---

107. Corduan, *PGWR*, pp. 123-24, 138-41.
108. Gentz, *Understanding Chinese Religions*, p. 66.
109. Ibid., pp. 55, 62.
110. Ibid., pp. 57, 61.

towards self-transcendence. It points to how something mysterious and spiritual underlies the ethical quality of being human.[111]

While non-theists[112] do not accept a belief in a God, non-theism actually underscores the importance of the realm of human responsibility – people are not to rely primarily on God to do what they ought to do by means of their freedom and out of a sense of moral obligation in the first place. Nobody should use God as a shield or excuse to justify not engaging more effectively and readily in issues of human concern, much less blame their irresponsible, culpable or harmful actions on spiritual elements.

Christians can find agreement with Jains in the latter's emphasis on renouncing such passions, *kasāya* – enmity, cupidity, deceit, fury – as part of the process of salvation from the endless cycles of *karma* into a state of *nirvāna* or *moksa* through harsh ascetic practices involving the pursuit of non-violence and meditation.[113]

Christianity can learn from the humanist cause by accepting its critique of the excesses of authority based on tradition and dogma, its valid points about religious hypocrisy and an unwillingness on the part of certain religious groups to accept the insights of science.[114] Moreover, Christians can agree with secular humanistic core pursuits of the advancement and optimisation of personal enjoyment and fulfilment which, given the collective and reciprocal nature of human society, capable of functioning as an indicator towards the higher purpose of the human person, entails, on occasion, seeking the same for others, sometimes even at one's personal expense.[115] It will be for non-theists themselves to decide whether they would like to reflect further on the nature of the ultimate principle for themselves.

Christians can recognise how the insights of non-theism originate in the same God, though non-theists themselves do not believe in the existence of a God.

---

111. Ibid., pp. 62-64.
112. E.g. Jains, Confucians.
113. Fohr, *Jainism*, pp. 9-10.
114. Humanism is used here synonymously with atheism, which can be distinguished in terms of whether it is agnostic, uncertain in a reasoned way, confrontationally explicit, non-confrontationally explicit, or philosophical or practical. K. Walters, *Atheism: A Guide for the Perplexed* (London: Bloomsbury, 2010), pp. 11-12.
115. Ibid., pp. 131-34.

A Christian Engagement with World Religions

As for Christianity itself, much has been made about the exclusive nature of salvation through Jesus Christ. Yet, Jesus never taught that Christianity is the only possible or helpful religion, or that all other religions are without merit and right to exist.

Jesus did say that he is the way, the truth and the life and that the only way to the Father was through him,[116] that in order to advance into the kingdom of God, it is necessary for a person to be reborn through water – that is, baptism – and spirit – that is, faith in Christ;[117] his disciples did assert that his was the only name by which people could be saved.[118] However, all this is to be interpreted in the light of Jesus' declaration that salvation in the knowledge of the Father is mediated exclusively through him.[119]

Eternal life, or salvation, is the knowledge of God the Father, that is, the Christian God rather than any other god or gods or some other ultimate principle, through Jesus the Son. The Christian religion very much serves the group of people who are willing to commit to its idea of ultimate reality and purpose. It may seek to gain converts but, more often than not, it is centred on a specific community of faith with its particular needs.

As such, Christian theology can be framed in terms of a communally situated system of doctrine with standards, norms and criteria which are valid but only for members of the religious community in question. This entails a recognition of the existence of different religious or philosophical kingdoms and communities, each ruled by its own deity or set of deities, or ultimate principle.[120]

Jesus never denounced other religions or impugned their benefits. While he did criticise the hypocrisy of the Jewish religious leaders of his day, and even (via St Paul and St John) the church, he never spoke against other religious communities.

Christianity holds that the spirit of Jesus is vital to regenerate a sinful human heart so as to free a person from the clutches of sin. Nonetheless, it is also clear from Scripture that this refers principally to the power of the gospel message to transform a life from being characterised by

---

116. John 14:6; see also 1 John 2:23.
117. John 3:3, 5.
118. Acts 4:12.
119. John 17:3.
120. Cf. Bernhardt, 'Trinity as a Framework', p. 60.

self-obsession to self-giving love. It does not exclude the possibility of lives being equally transformed and redeemed through the medium of other religious systems. All are truly under the power of sin, as Romans chapter three intimates, but there is no suggestion here that only Christians can escape the power of sin; only that the Christian faith, notably, offers a promise of divine forgiveness of sins through the Cross of Jesus.

It is true that the Bible speaks about how God chooses people to believe in Christ and appoints them to eternal life through such faith. However, this need not be taken as implying that God secretly controls the processes of the mind and heart that determine one's religious affiliation, or that Christianity is the only way to be saved.[121]

What it does mean is that God in Christianity gives every person an opportunity to believe in Christ and receive the benefits of such faith; it is God's wish for anyone to become a Christian if they wish. And the moment they make a decision in favour of Christ, they are conferred the advantages of fellowship with the Father through the Son, Jesus.

There is indeed a warning in the Christian Scriptures against acting in such a way as to be worthy of hell and destruction, but this is limited to those who choose to live against their consciences, such as the rich man who simply ignored a poor and starving beggar, Lazarus, who was placed at his gate,[122] and members of a powerful regime who were bent on persecuting Christian believers.[123]

In the former case of a man called Dives in a Christian tradition, the harshness of the divine sentence is due to the insouciant callousness of his attitude towards the desperately and life-threateningly destitute, an attitude that is sure to lead to further and graver instances of immorality even if such ignoring of the poor might not be considered clearly immoral by certain people. One needs to bear in mind that this story occurs in the context of a hortatory dominical parable addressing a social ill, rather than constituting a literal picture of what will happen, is happening or has already happened to a specific individual.

In this light, the narrative should not be taken as a realistic portrayal of the consequences of a specifically identified instance of sinfulness. Instead it ought to be glossed as an *exemplum* warning against the dangers of continuing in such an attitude of unthinking and heedless, arrogant indifference, all because such a mentality is likely to lead to

---

121. Cf. Chia, 'Question 11'.
122. Luke 16:19-31.
123. Revelation 20:7-15.

consequences and actions that one will come to regret deeply. The same thing might be said about those who persecute Christian believers. However, it seems scripturally unwarranted to contend that God will punish with hellfire on the basis of religious affiliation. To maintain that God does this is to conceive of God in an overly punitive way.

Indeed, the exclusive orientation especially of a restrictive strand of Western Christianity is a consequence of a dogma of an absolute certainty of knowledge about God. This, in turn, is a result of the idea of God as an absolute subject, reigning in all domains of God's activity, including epistemology and phenomenality. It is a short step from the notion of an omnipotent divine potentate to a rigid dogmatism of Christian doctrine.

Recall Barth's view that the absolute divine subject has full and infallible clarity about the truth about itself and its purposes for humanity and the world, and has full and infallible ability to communicate this perfectly, and in an appropriate manner, to a human recipient.[124] When God's self-revelation was understood as human self-knowledge, the doctrines of the Church found divine legitimacy as God's perfect self-understanding, leaving no room for differing or culturally appropriate interpretation because God as the absolute subject will not cascade a relative message but only an absolute one.

The Christian faith as such does not sponsor a doctrine which condemns all non-Christian people to hell. Christianity as a faith can be interpreted as being fundamentally open to dialogue and internal reformation in accordance with interreligious and global harmony.

The Old Testament records the story of Naaman in the Second Book of Kings chapter five. In this story, the prophet Elisha heals Naaman, a commander of the king of Aram, of his leprosy. In deep gratitude, Naaman decides to become a God-fearer, a non-Jew who turns to faith in Yahweh. He asks Elisha whether God would be able to accommodate him whenever he has to accompany his master into the temple of Rimmon. The king would bow down, and he would have to bow as well because the king would be leaning on his arm. Elisha's response is for Naaman to go in peace.

Under an exclusivist interpretation, Elisha could conceivably have demanded that Naaman share his faith or testimony with the king, or quit his job altogether. God's readiness to accommodate Naaman shows that the faith of the Old Testament, on which Christianity is based, does not regard other religions as being so repugnant to itself that no concession whatsoever is possible.

---

124. Barth, *KD* I.1, §8 (*CD* I.1, §8, pp. 295-347).

In another story, Jesus heard that one of his disciples, John, tried to prevent a man from conducting an exorcism in his name; but Jesus urged his disciple not to stop the man, if only because this would serve to build goodwill with another religious community.[125]

I propose that Christians stay true to our doctrine of divine transcendence and allow that the teachings of other religions or philosophies about God, the gods, or the ultimate may well be valid, given that God is an immeasurable reality beyond the full and exhaustive comprehension of any one particular religious community.

On this basis, I contend that there is a need to reform the theology of our respective religions, by recognising the legitimacy of other faiths and studying their doctrine to see how our own might be enhanced, deepened or made more comprehensive in its scope. Such a global systematic theology, as I call it, has a number of values.

On the premise of the principle that the transcendent God is capable of expressing Godself in more ways than registered in just the Christian faith, that, indeed, it is possible that this same God has expressed Godself in other religious faiths in just as authentic and genuine a manner as in the Christian religion: one, a global systematic theology is respectful of core differences in other religious faiths *qua* aspects from which Christianity can learn; two, it recognises similarities between Christianity and other faiths; three, it is committed to pursuing goodwill towards other religious communities, and dialogue and solidarity in coming together to address issues of communal and global concern as may be pertinent to religious faith or humanity as a whole, such as religious terrorism, medical-ethical issues, humanitarian concerns, and ecological problems; and, four, it commends its respectful, appreciative, charitable and beneficent religious vision to other faiths.

A Theological Exercise in Metaphorical Compatibility: Differing Accounts of Creation

As a theological exercise, if we grant that the same divine reality is merely differently perceived by different religious groups, how do we make sense of contrasting accounts of creation? A method of metaphorical compatibility may be proposed in this regard.

In one account in Shintoism, the *Kojiki*, the universe begins with the differentiation of heaven and earth, the formation of a first group of three invisible deities in heaven, followed by the emergence of reed shoots in a

---

125. Mark 9:38-41.

pool of floating oil where land would later appear, and the coming to be of a second group of invisible deities, including the male divine being, Izanagi no kami, and his female counterpart, Izanami no kami.[126]

The *Nihon shoki*[127] offers a slightly different take, in which, in a manner reminiscent of Taoist cosmogony, the story begins from the time before the differentiation of heaven and earth and the emergence of the principles of yin and yang. Heaven and earth constituted a unitary substance akin to an egg. Within this substance, the untainted and transparent elements became heaven; this was followed by the cloudy and heavy elements becoming earth.

Heaven and earth came together in intercourse, bringing forth a reed-shoot that turned into the early divine entity, Kami Kunitokotachi no Mikoto. The heavenly divinities commission Izanagi and Izanami to create dry land.[128] The duo create Japan by dipping a jewel-encrusted spear in the ocean, stirring the waters, then retracting the spear, so that water dropped from the spear back into the ocean to form an island, Onogoro-Shima, whose location is presently unknown. The divine couple erect a castle on the island with a heavenly pillar, go around the top of that pillar in a connubial ceremony, and create eight other islands.[129]

In Buddhism, a cosmogony is provided by the *Aggañña sutta*, the 'Discourse on the Origins', which tells of how the universe began as an immense and spiritual space inhabited by beings created by the intellect which subsisted on delight and exuded light. This universe underwent a contraction and became a lightless and flooded world with no sun and moon, replete with genderless entities. Arising from an undefined source, a sweet substance begins lining the surface of the water, delighting the entities dwelling in the world and engendering desire. The succession of day and night and of seasons begins as the denizens find their bodies becoming rougher and individuated, marked by a pleasing appearance as much as a displeasing appearance, leading to conceit. Beings evolve until the present state of ignorance, greed and hatred, standing in need of enlightenment.[130]

---

126. *The Record of Ancient Matters*, AD 712.

127. *Chronicles of Japan*, AD 720.

128. H. Hardacre, *Shinto: A History* (Oxford: Oxford University Press, 2016), pp. 47-49.

129. M. Smith, 'Japanese Mythology: Cosmogony', Canadian Studies Center, Michigan State University, 29 August 2019.

130. J. Whitaker, '"The Story of God": A Buddhist Perspective on Creation', *Patheos Library of World Faiths & Religions*, 20 April 2016, https://www.

In Hindu cosmology, there are many worlds, each with its own creative process, and time flows in a circular motion, with a world undergoing multiple creative processes. These creative processes involve a divine being either fully becoming a world or permeating it. In a well-known creation story, the world came into being as a result of a Primeval One feeling unstimulated and deciding to add some excitement to its life by dividing itself into a number of shapes and presentations, constituting the physical world and its entities, through which it sought love and entertainment.[131]

In another popular creation account, the *Vishnu Purana*, Vishnu was reclining on an ocean of milk above the serpent Sesha when a lotus arose from Vishnu's naval bearing the god, Brahma. Through Brahma, all living things, including other gods and demigods, as well as the heavenly bodies, sprang into existence. When the work of Brahma was complete, Vishnu caused himself to distend, becoming Ksirodakasayi Vishnu, Paramatma, and suffused all corporeal and incorporeal reality.[132]

In *The Laws of Manu*, God appeared out of nowhere and brought internal distinction and vitality to a universe without differentiation by bringing about water, into which he spilled his semen, causing the semen to become a golden egg. Then he split the egg in two, and created the sky, earth and the atmosphere between them, as well as the eight cardinal or compass directions, time and its units, constellations and planets, rivers, oceans, mountains, the uneven and even ground, creative and purifying heat, speech, sexual pleasure, desire and anger.

In the *Shatapatha Brahmana*, the Creator is said to live for a millennium. Aware of this, he desired offspring and gave himself the power to reproduce, making the gods from his mouth, which went into the sky. He breathed downward and made the demons, and they went into the earth, forming darkness around them. Conscious that they were evil, he afflicted them with evil, presumably, pain or suffering, and they were defeated. Out of the light that appeared when he created the gods,

patheos.com/blogs/americanbuddhist/2016/04/the-story-of-god-a-buddhist-perspective-on-creation.html.

131. *Brihadaranyaka Upanishad* 1.4.
132. Patheos, 'What is the creation story in Hinduism?', *Patheos Library of World Faiths & Religions*, accessed 25 May 2022, https://www.patheos.com/library/answers-to-frequently-asked-religion-questions/what-is-the-creation-story-in-hinduism.

he made the day and, out of the darkness that appeared when he made the demons, he crafted the night.[133]

According to the Vedas, people came into existence through the sacrifice by the gods of the divine Primeval Male, out of which the heavenly and immortal beings came into existence through his rising up three quarters, and humankind through the remaining quarter, by which the Brahmin class, priests, emerged from his mouth, the Rajas and Kshatriyas, warriors, policemen and kings, his arms, the Vaishyas, commoners, who work the fields, his thighs, and the Shudras, servants, his feet. The moon developed out of the Primeval Man's mind, the sun, his eye, the middle domain of space, his navel, the sky, his head, the earth, his feet, and the skies, his ear. Another creation account has a feminine principle, Aditi, giving birth to a masculine principle, Daksha, and the latter, in turn, begetting the former, perhaps through a sequence of one being reborn in another as in a circular creation story of the origins of Brahma and Vishnu. After this rebirth of Aditi came the generation of the immortal deities. In the midst of this, Aditi also produces the earth, and the skies out of the earth.[134]

In the Taoist creation myth, there existed chaos in the form of an egg, from which emerged the first man, Pan Gu, who had a pair of horns, tusks and a hairy physique. In certain versions, Pan Gu is believed to have knowledge of the yin-yang dual principle of all reality and to be responsible for dividing heaven and earth, arranging the heavenly bodies, splitting up the four seas, forming the earth by carving out valleys and pilling up mountains. An alternative account has Pan Gu contributing to the formation of the universe through his death, in which the various parts of his body became elements of the world, his eyes turning into the sun and moon, his blood and sweat creating rivers, his hair becoming the flora, his body turning into soil, the parasitic organisms on his body developing into human beings.[135]

In Jainism, the universe is eternal, and Jains worship the transcendent, collective body of those adherents who reached enlightenment as a kind of non-creative and non-active[136] deity.[137] In Islam, Allāh created the

---

133. Doniger, *On Hinduism*, pp. 166-69.
134. Ibid., pp. 157-66.
135. The Editors of Encyclopaedia Britannica, 'Pan Gu', *Britannica*, Encyclopaedia Britannica, 20 July 1998, https://www.britannica.com /topic/Pan-Gu.
136. Enlightened Jains are freed from desires which bear the fruit of action.
137. Fohr, *Jainism*, p. 12.

world, including angels, other living things, planets, rain, for human flourishing by a fiat declaration. Allāh had angels collect seven handfuls of soil of different colours from earth and formed Adam, the first man, out of that soil, infusing him with living breath and power, and then created Eve, the first woman, from Adam's side.[138] The biblical God also commanded the universe into existence. In atheism we have no God whatsoever. Furthermore, there is also the big bang theory.

Is there any way to reconcile all these varying pictures?

It is necessary in the light of conflicting pictures to attempt to produce a metaphorical compatibility out of literally incompatible statements. One could venture a solution by asserting that there is a sense in which God is both personal and non-personal. Like a human person, God has an intention and purpose for the world but, unlike a human person and more akin to a process, God pervades the entire universe as a principle of origin. In different ways, God is both solitary and communal. Like a single person, God works with a single-minded purpose but, unlike a single person, God relates with other persons in the Godhead or empyreal community. In different ways, God is both spiritual and material. God works intimately through physical matter and principles but at the same time God is a spiritual being.

In different ways, God is both gendered and genderless. God does not have any biological parts and yet God has relational characteristics associated with men and women. In different ways, God both exists and made the world and does not exist and did not make the world. God cannot be very clearly distinguished from the processes by which God works in the world, including the evolutionary process, and may seem on empirical terms to be non-existent, yet this does not mean God is not present.

In different ways, God made the world out of nothing and out of Godself. God is the ultimate origin of the material dimension of the universe but, at the same time, the material universe is patterned after Godself. In different ways, God took no time and no great effort in creating the world and took a long time and great effort in so doing. God has always had a concrete and detailed plan for the world but in the same breath God took time to fashion the universe through evolutionary processes.

In a sense, it is unsurprising that there are many different descriptions of the divine and the origin of the world, because the divine often confounds

---

138. *GDT*, s.v. 'Islam' (J.D. Woodberry, p. 426); BBC, 'What accounts of the origins of the universe are found in Islam?', accessed 25 May 2022, https://www.bbc.co.uk/bitesize/guides/zv2fgwx/revision/8.

human understanding and stretches the limits of human imagination. The divine reality cannot be tied down to any one presentation in a literal and rigid way, and the different portrayals succeed in expressing some one aspect of the divine nature and its creative, providential and governing activity.

On the basis of our understanding of Christian monotheism, the biblical references to all people submitting to Jesus[139] may be conceived of in terms of how, since it is the same God who works equally in all religious traditions, all worship offered to a god or gods, or even merely a commitment to an ultimate principle may be considered worship of God or at least, and at minimum, an awareness of ultimacy or ultimate moral value.[140] Hence, the vision of Philippians chapter two can be fulfilled without people of non-Christian religious and philosophical traditions having to convert to Christianity *en masse*, and the verses in question are merely an affirmation that Jesus discloses his nature as that of the one God who works in all religions and philosophies.[141] The assertion in 1 John 5:11-12 to the effect that the authority to confer the divine gift of life is vested in the Son of God alone may be construed in similar terms.

---

139. E.g., Philippians 2:9-11.
140. Walters, *Atheism*, pp. 131-34.
141. By the same token, the multiple differences between religious depictions of God, the gods or the universal principle are not finally important for salvation or human actualisation, since the greatest value for human beings is ethics, that is, being a selfless and beneficent human person in the main, and the demand or call for this is secured even on the minimal, elegant and streamlined view of atheism. Cf. Romans 2:6-11.

Chapter 2

Method: Towards a Christian Global Systematic Theology

It may ring strange, particularly to Christian ears, to suggest that the same God revealed Godself through the various world religions, considering the gulf of theological differences. Be that as it may, the Judaeo-Christian message has undergone various transitions that would have been less than clearly recognisable to the people of God in former ages. As a case in point, when Jesus came on the scene, he brought teachings which effectively laid the foundations for an interpretation of God's law delivered through Moses which constituted a return to the original essence of that law and yet were perceived to be obscure by the people of Jesus' day.

It is necessary to observe that the instruction of Jesus directly to the disciples and indirectly through the Holy Spirit concerning elements of the Mosaic law, such as the food laws, is not diametrically opposed to the exhortations of God through the authority of Moses.[1] Jesus was not opposed to the food laws as such; he may have felt that these regulations were critical in providing a visual and metaphorical picture of the fact that certain actions render a person impure before God. These actions include wicked thoughts, the desire to kill another person, sexual relations with a married person, illegal dispossession, lying with the intent of harming the reputation of another person, and defamation.[2] What Jesus may have been really against was the perversion of these kosher

---

1. Mark 7:14-19.
2. Cf. Matthew 15:19-20.

rules to confer a sense of religious favour and aegis purely on the basis of an external observance of a ritual.

The same thing could be said of the Sabbatical law, which was not laid down to be so religiously observed as to be the indirect cause of harm to a person in dire need but only to enshrine remembrance of God as the origin of all existence.[3] Also, the requirement for all Jewish male infants to undergo circumcision, the purport of which was solely to image the morality expected of the Jewish community, which proscribed certain behaviour, such as theft, sexual relations with a married person, embezzlement and the unfettered worship of wealth, and all other forms of moral lawbreaking.[4] Consequently, far from encouraging the violation and jettisoning of God's law, Jesus attempted to redirect the attention of those he came into conflict with, back to the heart of that law.[5]

Likewise, in relation to the core belief of monotheism in the Judaeo-Christian faith, it should be noted that the form of the conviction pursuant to the oneness of God endorsed by the Bible has little to do with the exclusive and aggressive type usually promoted as biblical teaching, whether on the part of critics or theologians themselves. As we have already seen, if the Old Testament religion appeared to promote exclusion or the exercise of aggression towards other faiths, this was only on the grounds of gross moral violations and possible and potentially fatal incursions. Even during the formative years of Israel, monotheism was more a matter of loyalty and commitment than a universal broadside against and delegitimisation of all other religions.[6]

In a world order in which the rights of the various religious groups are protected in international and national legal and ethical systems, it is no longer tenable to insist on an exclusive fealty to a particular religion. Jesus through direct and indirect guidance led the community of believers to see the true essence of vital Old Testament laws, by which it dawned on their leaders that they were not to exclude the Gentiles on the basis of their differing cultural backgrounds and practices.

---

3. Cf. Mark 3:4.

4. Cf. Romans 2:17-29.

5. Brownson cites the kosher food laws, circumcision and the law of the Sabbath as examples of regulations which were revisited. J.V. Brownson, *Bible, Gender, Sexuality: Reframing the Church's Debate on Same-Sex Relations* (Grand Rapids, MI: Eerdmans, 2013), p. 65.

6. T.P. van Baaren, 'Monotheism in world religions', *Britannica*, Encyclopaedia Britannica, accessed 25 May 2022, https://www.britannica.com/topic/monotheism/Monotheism-in-world-religions.

This was no new insight. As a matter of fact, the Old Testament books of prophecy testify to a day in which the Gentiles would be included with the community of the people of God but without really specifying the nature of this inclusion. It was left to the apostles of Jesus to determine, with the help of the Holy Spirit, what embracing the Gentiles would entail concretely.

Jesus did not bring new teaching which served to overturn Old Testament law; and neither do I now presume to venture to overhaul the teachings of the New Testament in propounding my theory about an inclusive and irenic monotheism. However, in both cases, the intent, and, I hope, the effect as well, is simply to be faithful to the timeless truth of God in a radically changed context.[7]

Reflection on the purport of the Scriptures led Christians to throw their weight behind movements to abolish slavery and eradicate racial discrimination against black people because these were rightly seen to offend against the intrinsic equality in which all human beings originate from God. The next watershed and *status confessionis* will be the renunciation of religious exclusivism, which constitutes, in effect, if not in express intent, a marginalisation of religious others.[8] Religious communities in modern societies have learned in a practical sense to live with one another; the next challenge is for them to reform their central theological principles in keeping with this practical need.

We do well to remember that God is capable of working dissimilarly among the various religious groups and emphasising certain attributes in a religion which may not be prioritised in another, and that it is easy for a human mind to exaggerate these specific attributes at the expense of others. God is even capable of dealing differently with people according to their religious profession if need be.

The only qualities we cannot ever ascribe to God in all settings are omnipotence and omniscience. To argue that God who is good is all-powerful and all-knowing at the same time, and yet to observe the prevalence of evil, injustice and needless suffering is to commit a logical error and subscribe to a travesty of God's incorruptible goodwill. To contend that God can intervene in these situations but chooses not to for whatever reason is to demolish the idea that God is truly good.

---

7. W.S.-C. Goh, 'Doctrines: An Interplay Between Experience and Scripture', *Roman Catholic Archdiocese of Singapore*, 19 May 2022, https://www .catholic.sg/19-may-2022-thursday-5th-week-of-easter.

8. Hedges, *Controversies in Interreligious Dialogue*, p. 252.

It is not enough to suggest that God is merely non-omnipotent while possibly being simply omniscient, because of biblical testimony not only to God's non-omnipotence[9] but God's non-omniscience[10] as well. The conception of God in a Christian-based global systematic theology, as opposed to another which may be based on another religion as a primary premise, has to take account of this.

As far as a Christian-based global systematic theology is concerned, it is preferable to aver that religions which promote the ideas of divine omnipotence and omniscience may have gone too far in highlighting the power and awareness of God. Goodness, non-omnipotence and non-omniscience are essential attributes of God in any religious system from a Christian point of view. Whatever exalts the purposive goodness of God is essential to a theological conception which is inclined towards the message of Christianity.[11] Therefore, *inter alia*, the ultimate principle is a personal being rather than impersonal force, this God is Trinity rather than monad, and a single being rather than a pantheon of multiple deities.

Logically, however, it is conceivable that God is a being of irresistible power and only apparently incorruptible goodness, rather than incorruptible goodness and only apparently or purportedly irresistible power. Nonetheless, the decision has to be made as to which among these two attributes is primary, for they cannot coexist. In this system, oriented as it is towards the Christian faith, the latter is judged to be preferable because assessed to be more fitting and helpful, as an exemplum, to human conscience and moral aspiration. It is also possible to construct a global theology or philosophy on the basis of the central divine or ultimate attributes and their ordering of any other religious or atheistic system. There will be disagreement between theologians and

---

9. Mark 6:5.

10. Genesis 18:20-21.

11. That is to say, God is to be conceived as an independent moral agent whose personal vision is to bring about the highest wellbeing of all entities and whose moral and communal character undergirds these movements. It was Richard of Saint-Victor who asserted that the communal nature of God is rooted in God's divine fullness, requiring as it does perfect, reciprocal (so as to be 'orderly') and inclusive (so as to be unselfish) love which can only be consistently offered by and among perfect divine persons. Richard of Saint-Victor, *De Trin.*, III.2, 7, 11. R. Angelici, Introduction and Commentary to Richard of Saint-Victor, *On the Trinity: English Translation and Commentary* (Eugene, OR: Cascade, 2011), pp. 44-45.

philosophers of such systems over various aspects, and there will be major areas of agreement, however, this in no way translates to a sense of superiority of one group to another.

A religion or philosophy may emphasise an aspect of divinity or ultimacy which is understated in another religion or do just the reverse. The idea is for members of different religious and philosophical groups to learn from each other in order to bolster their own picture of the divine or ultimate in a more holistic fashion, being willing to prune certain, less effective facets of their theology or include other specific, more profitable dimensions not as adequately found in their belief systems to achieve this.

The question arises whether it is even fruitful for an established world religion to enter into such a constructive dialogue of mutual theological formation with another. The assumption undergirding such pessimism could be the mere assumption that a world religion has little if anything to learn from another, especially if that other world religion is already and directly condemned in the sacred text of a world religion.

An example can be adduced from Islam and concerns the Christian doctrine of the Trinity, which, as already noted, is misunderstood in the former religion as a community comprising the Father, Mary and Jesus.[12] Such an observation makes one wonder about the validity of Islamic condemnation of the Trinity and whether a Muslim theologian might have anything positive to learn about God from a proper and accurate understanding of the Christian Trinity. For that matter, it may be asked whether the God which the atheist denounces is the type of God worshipped by Christians.[13] The very same thing could be said to a Christian theologian about the central beliefs of any other world religion.

Each religion will have many positive things to say about itself and perhaps some negative things to say about other religions.[14] The key is to get beyond the self-enclosed space of a religious faith, to begin a productive conversation with other faith groups and to clarify one's opinions about

---

12. Hoover, 'Islamic Monotheism and the Trinity'.
13. G. D'Costa, *Theology and Religious Pluralism: The Challenge of Other Religions*, Signposts in Theology (Oxford: Basil Blackwell, 1986), p. 93.
14. As examples, consider the Islamic teaching that the Christian Scriptures have been corrupted (Hoover, 'Islamic Monotheism and the Trinity', corrected version, p. 2); the Jain and Buddhist shared idea that Hindu gods are stuck in *saṃsāra* and so are inferior to Mahāvīra and Buddha (Fohr, *Jainism*, p. 11); and the Zoroastrian belief that some of these earlier gods are in the party of a destructive, hostile and malicious spirit or inspiration, Angra Mainyu (Rose, *Zoroastrianism*, pp. 17, 22).

other religious faiths so as to change one's perspective from negative to positive, with a view, finally, to bolstering the constructive holism of one's own faith. Ideally, each religion should be able to arrive at an accurate conception of the faith of its counterparts and attempt as far as possible to integrate what has been learned into their own systems of belief.[15] Be that as it may, each religion should be properly and duly understood on its own terms and not on those of the religion whose adherents seek to understand in order to appreciate and learn from the former.[16]

A unified system of religion that reconciles all religious traditions cannot be achieved, given that each faith or philosophy will espouse its own commitments to a specific ordering of particular principles of the divine, ultimate or meaningful.[17] The open-minded theologian or philosopher of any religious or philosophical persuasion will attempt a systematic theology or philosophy which weans itself off unhelpful or anti-communal perspectives,[18] upholds values, premises, categories, paradigms assessed to be quintessential to the system,[19] redresses

------

15. The Archbishop of Canterbury, writing on the issue of fostering peace in an often violently torn world on the occasion of the publication of a book on reconciliation, recommends – as one of three 'transformational habits' to bring relational healing, form relationships with people who are different, and mitigate the impact of factors that keep people apart – the virtue of curiosity in people who may be different from us, in order to develop an accurate understanding of what these people stand for, and ways in which they may be able to contribute to other communities, and the value of humility in seeking to benefit from what other people may have to say. J. Welby, 'The Big Idea: Is a World without Violent Conflict Really Possible?', *The Guardian*, 6 June 2022.

16. We note the Dutch theologian Hendrik Kraemer's (1888-1965) concern about violating the 'totalitarian' integrity of a religion in attempting to assimilate or come to terms with it. D'Costa, *Theology and Religious Pluralism*, p. 55.

17. Such an understanding is necessary to avoid the type of criticism levelled against a thinker such as John Hick, who has attempted to construct a theology of world religions based on the idea of an Eternal One, Divine Reality or the Real at the centre of a universe of faiths which, in D'Costa's estimation, ultimately impresses as being Christian in substance, concealed as pluralist. D'Costa, *Theology and Religious Pluralism*, pp. 43-45.

18. E.g. the idea that one religion is better than another's or even the only true way to salvation.

19. E.g. the personal nature of God, the immanence of God, the transcendence of God, God's struggle with evil, humanity's resemblance to

imbalances[20] and charts a path of metaphorical compatibility of literally incompatible beliefs across religions.[21]

Can any one such religious or philosophy-based system be deemed to be superior to another? To the extent that a system does its level best to overcome anti-communal tendencies, promotes a broad suite of universally binding pro-social values, redresses imbalances and manoeuvres between the competing claims of the various religions and philosophies, it can be considered to be a fair, good and meritorious attempt which need not be pitted against another similarly fair attempt. Each religious or philosophy-based systematic theology is valid because it encapsulates and is premised upon some vital aspect or aspects of the divine being.

The Method of a Global Christian Systematic Theology

If the Bible already makes clear statements of truth, what might be the possible contribution of a culture and non-Christian religion? Augustine of Hippo availed of the classical philosophy of his day, accepting ideas which he felt agreed with and bolstered Scripture and rejecting those which he felt contradicted it.[22]

Built into the biblical writings already are facets of a distinctive Hebrew and Graeco-Roman culture which make different assertions about reality.[23] This includes the absolute sovereignty of God in an ancient Near Eastern worldview.[24] Consider the statements regarding God's

---

God, God as the redeemer and hope of humanity, the goodness, love, justice, compassion, gentleness, patience, trust, empathy, purity, wisdom, power of God.

20. E.g. focussing more on God as personal than non-personal.
21. E.g. what a theistic system can learn from a non-theistic system and how the former may incorporate an interpretive and significatory essence of the idea that God does not exist, a possibility being the following: a theistic religion can learn from a non-theistic system that God bears not just a personal dimension but an impersonal one, in which God is conceived in terms of being the origin of all things and a principle, or at least an ultimate source, of material evolution.
22. Augustine, *Conf.*, VII.ix.14-15; XIII.xi.12.
23. Newman, *DCD*, p. 352.
24. Rulers in the ancient Near East were regarded as taking responsibility for everything their subjects did, whether or not these went to plan, and the incorporation of this element into a monotheistic faith guaranteed

providential control over good fortune and disaster in Isaiah 45:7 and Ecclesiastes 7:14. Indeed, the Hebrew Bible owes much to a Persian religious influence, via Zoroastrianism, in terms of its development of a henotheistic idea of God as the only true God, head of a pantheon of other, subaltern gods (much like the Persian king was thought of as the only true king because he ruled over other kings and Ahura Mazda was believed to be the head of the Zoroastrian pantheon), of the notion of a powerful chief adversary in the person of Satan, inspired by the figure of Angra Mainyu, Ahriman,[25] and its ideas of angelology and demonology, in general. Furthermore, the biblical writings, especially the primeval history, were shaped by Mesopotamian texts such as the epic of Gilgamesh and accounts of creation and a flood.[26]

Christian Scripture also includes thought-forms from Greek philosophy. John Henry Newman (1801-90) detects Gnostic and Platonic language in the Johannine writings, noting that unitarians have suggested that the doctrine of Christ's divine nature proceeds from Platonism, while Gibbon observes that the notion of an incarnation was pioneered by Gnostics. To Newman, regardless of their source, these ideas are successfully and efficaciously synthesised in a self-confident Christian theological tradition. We may add that the Ephesian reference to Satan as the 'prince of the power of the air'[27] and the general New Testament cosmological framework may have profited from a Platonist classification of the demons as inhabiting the air as their proper abode, human beings as inhabiting the earth, and the gods[28] as dwelling in heaven.[29]

As a matter of fact, we cannot fail to discern traces of Aristotelian and Platonic philosophy in the New Testament writings.

---

the attribution of responsibility for all events to the one God. G. Boyd, *Is God to Blame? Beyond Pat Answers to the Problem of Suffering* (Downers Grove, IL: InterVarsity Press, 2003), pp. 90, 188.

25. On the characteristics of Angra Mainyu, similar as they are to Satan's, the reader is directed to the account of the substantial likeness between Judaeo-Christianity and Zoroastrianism on p. 40.

26. Römer, *The Invention of God*, pp. 227-30, 232; Jackson, 'Zoroastrianism and the Resemblances between It and Christianity'.

27. Ephesians 2:2.

28. The equivalent in Christianity of good angelic beings such as thrones, dominations, principalities, powers.

29. Augustine, *Civ.*, VIII.14, 24.

In Aristotelian thought, there are such skeins as God's perfection, immutability,[30] immovability,[31] impassibility,[32] eternality,[33] immateriality,[34] non-potentiality,[35] self-contemplative[36] nature and ability to move all things forever, not through direct action upon those things which are moved,[37] but by being possessed of such pulchritude and wholeness that it draws the love, *eros*, of all things as an 'unmoved mover'. God cannot be related to anything for, if God were so, God would by definition become dependent on that thing, for, as a case in point, God's status as a Lord, but God is independent and perfect in a self-sufficient sense.[38]

Many of these threads are detectible in New Testament depictions of God as an independent, eternal, incorporeal, morally perfect, powerful, wise divine ruler, origin and guarantor of an economy of salvation in the cosmos, and deserving recipient of praise and glory.

This includes the idea of God: as independent rather than being dependent on how circumstances turn out as in the case of Noah,[39] Saul,[40]

---

30. This is because, if God is perfect, any change in such a perfect being will necessarily involve a move away from perfection and toward imperfection.
31. This is because the movement of all things must ultimately end in some unmoving cause or origin.
32. This is because the ability to be affected by another being implies change but God is unchangeable because perfect.
33. This is because the movement it causes continues indefinitely.
34. This is because it has no beginning and is incapable of becoming something else.
35. This is because, in order to keep the world moving without end, it cannot have anything less than the nature of pure actuality, and potentiality suggests the ability to change but God is immutable because perfect.
36. This is because there is nothing more sublime than philosophical contemplation, such contemplation about the supreme entity, and such contemplation about such contemplation, a 'thinking of thinking'.
37. This is because action involves change.
38. Aristotle, *Metaphysics*, Book XI, cited in A.J.P. Kenny, 'Aristotle: The unmoved mover', *Britannica*, accessed 13 July 2022, https://www.britannica.com/biography/Aristotle/The-unmoved-mover; J. Sanders, 'Historical Considerations', in C. Pinnock, R. Rice, J. Sanders, W. Hasker and D. Basinger, *The Openness of God: A Biblical Challenge to the Traditional Understanding of God* (Downers Grove, IL: InterVarsity, 1994), pp. 65-66.
39. God regretting that God created the world, seeing how evil it turned out to be.
40. God having second thoughts about the election of Saul in view of his disobedience.

Job[41] and Jonah;[42] non-bodily, rather than having parts which can be compared to components of a human body; blamelessly perfect, rather than being subject to accusations of an unjust handling of human affairs as in the case of Job; irresistibly powerful, rather than having God's will repeatedly foiled throughout the history of Israel; wise, reliable, and steadfast, rather than being liable to a change of mind as in the cases of Noah, Saul and Jonah; and having complete providence over the order of salvation, rather than occasionally lacking the ability to keep God's own people under control, as in the time of Saul, David, Solomon and many kings of the northern kingdom of Israel and certain rulers of the southern kingdom of Judah.

This development of a theology of God with a strengthening of its view of God's power is possible only because between the Old and New Testaments, there is a decisive and radical shift in the conception of God's role from that of a military ruler, predicated as it is on the ability of a deity to bring well-nigh completely unpredictable and uncontrollable political affairs to a successful outcome, to a spiritual saviour and liberator from the power of sin, predicated as this is upon the ability of a deity, well within its realm of disposal, to assure forgiveness of transgressions against that same deity through the symbolism of an utterly sacrificial act on the part of Jesus. In this manner, while there is indeed an evolution of theology in regard to the doctrine of God, in light of their distinct purviews, both an Old and New Testament understanding of God are mutually compatible.

Platonic philosophy grapples with God, the Beautiful or the Good, as a source, norm and goal of goodness and beauty.[43] Socrates believed that the will of a true and supreme God accounted for the existence and ordering of all things, a God whose being constituted an immaterial splendour and the approach to the truth of whom could be had only by means of a moral purification.[44] Likewise, in the New Testament, such as the First Epistle of John, God is portrayed as the paragon of goodness and love for believers to emulate, in 1 Timothy 6:16, as dwelling in unapproachable light, and, in John 1:6-9, even as the true light, as Platonists also believe.[45]

---

41. God resolving to subject Job to trials on the advice of an accusing angel.
42. God deciding against overthrowing Nineveh because of its collective repentance.
43. Bradshaw, 'Plato in the Cappadocian Fathers', pp. 195, 197, 200.
44. Augustine, *Civ.*, VIII.3.
45. Augustine, *Civ.*, X.2.

In a cultural-philosophical principle's role as a source of inspiration in guiding the theological interpretation of Scripture towards ever increasing specificity, it is understood that there is no wholesale adoption of the systems whose individual elements are being assimilated and translated into a new intellectual context. Purely those components or aspects of the cultural-philosophical thought-form are co-opted which are perceived to be capable of extending the apprehension of general scriptural affirmations about God's nature and purposes for humanity and the world. As such, Aristotle's notion of the eternity of the universe and the idea that all human beings share a single rational soul, this according to Averroes, as two cases in point, are not carried over into a patristic Christian theology which otherwise benefits from his insights.[46] In contrast to Aristotle, Plato, though not the Alexandrian Neoplatonists, held that the universe had a beginning.[47]

While culturally conditioned metaphysical frameworks such as Aristotelianism and Platonism colour the concepts and even the language of the Scriptures, they do not exhaustively and exclusively dictate the complete and full meaning of the truths Scripture seeks to convey.

This may be because, in the case of the Old Testament, of the Hebrew culture's disinclination towards metaphysical developments of its doctrine of God and, in that of the New, of a Hellenistic Jewish group's similar unwillingness (although rooted in a culture in which certain key thinkers are given to exercises in intellectual speculation, such as about the nature of the true, good and beautiful) to go into any great depth concerning God's ontological nature. (Nonetheless, the New Testament writers did bequeath to posterity such technical philosophical conceptions as that of the *Logos*, understood as the effectuating influence of God to bring about the world and coordinate its intellectual and ethical capacities.[48]) Such a reticence on their part should give pause to scholars, inclined towards patristic and classical thought-forms, thinking that the widespread Greek philosophical milieu in which the nascent Church found itself unequivocally sanctions a direct, rigorous and exclusive application of Greek philosophical ideas to the exposition of a theology of God in Scripture.

While Plato's notion of divine transcendence is one possible way of developing the idea in Scripture of a God who dwells in unapproachable light, it is not the sole approach. God can be transcendent in either a

---

46. *NDT*, s.v. 'Aristotelianism' (A. Vos, pp. 43-45).

47. Augustine, *Civ.*, XII.12.

48. A. Harnack, *WIC*, p. 202.

dimensional or qualitative sense, or a little of both. As a matter of fact, the literary context of that particular depiction of God's other-worldliness, to wit, 1 Timothy 6:13-16, does not explicate that description.

Indeed, Scripture may be attempting a merely doxological proclamation of the qualities of God as having full personhood in portraying God with the ability to adjust God's response to changing human conduct,[49] as emotive, having regret,[50] emotional stirring,[51] affliction and grief,[52] and as having the ability to bleed in atonement[53] as well as being transcendent[54] and unchanging.[55] None of these verbal effusions of passion and incandescent feeling are to be isolated from variant expressive descriptions and appropriated as, in themselves, a sufficient and exhaustive basis for constructing a philosophical theory of God's nature.[56]

There are numerous possible scriptural adductions for the doctrine of God's sovereignty.[57] During the Old Testament era, God presented and allowed Godself to be presented as a sovereign heavenly monarch. This constituted an instance of divine adaptation to the political circumstances in which Israel found itself, that is, as a fledgling and often threatened national community with an exigent need to defend itself from stronger neighbours. Such a religious vision of an all-powerful and all-determining divine reality informed personal piety in a reassuring way, coupled as it was with the appropriate and frequent angelic interventions.

Nonetheless, though capable of executing many mighty acts at different points in human history, as seen in the events of the exodus from Egypt, the military campaign against Canaan, the sacking of the northern kingdom of Israel and southern kingdom of Judah, and the Jewish return from exile, God is ultimately only able to bring about God's will in inconceivable ways only some of the time, and for a critical purpose of shoring up the stability of Israel at that. No other aim justifies such blatant use of physical or military force on the part of God, which, unlike suasion in the direction of psychological awareness and moral renunciation, is no solution to the problem of sin and evil.

---

49. The Pauline letters, Hebrews and Johannine letters.
50. Genesis 6:6.
51. Judges 10:16.
52. Isaiah 63:9-10.
53. Acts 20:28.
54. 1 Timothy 6:16.
55. Malachi 3:6, James 1:17.
56. Mozley, *Impass.*, pp. 1-6.
57. E.g. Exodus 4:11, 21:12-13; Proverbs 16:33, 21:1; Ecclesiastes 7:14; Isaiah 40:15, 17, 45:5-7; Daniel 4:34-35.

While having scriptural pedigree, the doctrine of a divine sovereignty is called into question as a component of a cultural worldview by a cardinal doctrine of the loving Father preached by Jesus, a Father who, if all-powerful, cannot possibly be completely good and, if thoroughly good, cannot conceivably be omnipotent.[58] This is because of the presence of gross injustice, in the face of which only a God less than perfectly benevolent, who could bring Godself to assign instrumental value to gratuitous and unprovoked innocent suffering, could withhold from sufferers God's supremacy of capacity, and only a God less than irresistibly and insurmountably powerful, who could not have prevented evil and injustice, could stand the test of moral goodness.

There will always be a tension between cultural worldviews and biblical truth, which can hopefully be retrenched through an intercultural and even interreligious critique and contribution, along with a fuller integration with non-theological academic disciplines.[59] In this process, different, text-based, cultural or world religious frameworks, modalities or worldviews 'fill out' the meaning of Scripture in a culturally relevant way, posing to Scripture questions which Christian theology may not have or may have only little considered. Cultural or religious modality in this context designates the most deeply held philosophical sensibilities of a culture or religious or philosophical tradition.

A case in point is the primacy of an already and always perfect, simple, unchanging and timeless being over temporal succession as defining the conception of God in Western traditions mediated by classical and neoclassical Greek philosophy, as compared to the primacy of temporal succession over being as a means of approaching the knowledge of the divine in many Asian traditions.[60] The classical Christian conception of

---

58. John Mozley designates the doctrine of divine love in Scripture as 'the very core of true Christian thought about God'. Mozley, *Impass.*, p. 176.

59. Cf. The discussion regarding the way in which the translators of the Septuagint misrendered Genesis 6:6 in order to fit a precommitment concerning the way in which God should be conceived as being beyond sorrow and grief. D. Castelo, 'Qualified Impassibility', in R. J. Matz and A. C. Thornhill (eds), *Divine Impassibility: Four Views of God's Emotions and Suffering*, Spectrum Multiview (Downers Grove, IL: IVP Academic, 2019), p. 60; Sanders, 'Historical Considerations', p. 72.

60. Sanders, 'Historical Considerations', pp. 68, 99. According to Sanders, the Church Fathers found themselves situated in an intellectual milieu where Middle Platonism was predominant. Sanders, 'Historical Considerations', p. 59.

God as simple is more than a matter of historical interest; it continues to exert a measure of influence as a distinct view on offer to theologians and Christians alike. More importantly, perhaps, it provides a model for engaging in a culturally sensitive and integrated approach to Christian theology.

Cultural and religious modalities are to accord due respect to the Christian Scriptures, allowing them to set the boundaries and delimitations for further discourse. The first step to a culturally guided development of the theological interpretation of Scripture, then, is to erect a theological scaffold around some doctrine, built out of only the clearest and unequivocal indications from the Scriptures, in which whatever these Scriptures explicitly assert is accepted and whatever they categorically deny is renounced.

As an example, a doctrine of God articulated purely on the basis of express scriptural affirmation would outline the monotheistic nature of God, which Newman singled out as a 'cardinal distinction' between Christianity and the religious and philosophical systems with which it coexisted in the patristic age, including paganism, non-revelatory philosophies, dualistic Gnosticism which incorporated some form of angel worship and the belief that the Testaments were produced by two different sources.[61] This theological principle being core to scriptural attestation is not subject to alteration by means of the assimilation of cultural material, but appropriates that material in a manner that serves to refine Christian doctrine as based on the affirmations of the Bible.[62]

A theology of God based on explicit scriptural affirmation would also highlight the transcendence of God,[63] God's unchanging moral nature,[64] God's being as love,[65] the threefold nature of the community that claims the name of or some form of equality with divinity,[66] the possibility of divine action in an economic or worldly sphere of things,[67] God's full personhood and ability to adjust God's response to changing human

---

61. Newman, *DCD*, p. 338.
62. B. Murphy, 'The Development of Doctrine', *Simply Catholic*, Our Sunday Visitor, accessed 22 July 2022, https://www.simplycatholic.com /the-development-of-doctrine.
63. 1 Timothy 6:16.
64. Malachi 3:6, James 1:17.
65. 1 John 4:8, 16.
66. E.g. Matthew 28:19-20.
67. E.g. Exodus 3:14.

behaviour,[68] and the possibility of God being affected by events in the worldly domain with regret,[69] stirring emotion,[70] affliction and grief,[71] undying love,[72] and through suffering for the atonement of the Church.[73]

Next, these cultural modalities and frameworks are permitted to provide greater specification from their most deeply felt instincts and intuitions to the vague conception based only on explicit scriptural indication, insofar as these developmental directions are not contrary to the express affirmations of Scripture.[74] This entails a highly creative intercultural synthesis, in which the Bible as the primary source of theology encounters the texts and traditions of other cultures. In this engagement, the biblical material is closely examined in such a way as to produce doctrinal statements predicated only on what the Bible expressly affirms to be doctrinally correct, while the non-biblical cultural material is just as closely examined in such a way as to provide the creative inspiration to address any questions, issues or cruces left over from the biblical engagement which aims to provide answers to those questions from the express doctrinal affirmations of the Bible alone.

The manner in which this non-biblical cultural material is brought into the discussion will of necessity be dynamic, eclectic and selective. By its very nature, such a cultural supplemental approach to the theological interpretation of the Christian Scriptures will not be capable of doing full justice to the non-biblical cultural material used in this form of engagement. The aim of such use of non-biblical cultural material will be more modest, involving only a carrying over into theological formulation of ideas from non-biblical cultural material, to develop what the Bible expressly affirms doctrinally in response to various questions about doctrine, in such a way as not to directly contradict what the Bible expressly affirms doctrinally. In this regard, the role of non-biblical cultural material may entail a lending of a particular emphasis on a

---

68. E.g. Pauline, Johannine writings and Hebrews.
69. E.g. Genesis 6:6.
70. E.g. Judges 10:16.
71. E.g. Isaiah 63:9-10.
72. E.g. Hosea chapter eleven.
73. E.g. Acts 20:28.
74. David Brown implies that the Bible itself does not adjudge with satisfactory specificity on possible questions of the Christological doctrine of the Incarnation and that at Chalcedon and on other occasions, some prior philosophical commitment was necessary to take theology where the Church wished to go. D. Brown, *The Divine Trinity* (Eugene, OR: Wipf & Stock, 2011), p. 226.

specific dimension of reality to the theological formulation of a biblical doctrine.

As a case in point, in Jung Young Lee's innovative cultural appropriation in his theological interpretation of the Scriptures, he borrowed from a Chinese classic, the *Book of Changes*, a yin-yang metaphysical paradigm of change, which intimately addresses divine participation in the changes of the world in their interrelationships, to supply the Christian doctrine of God with a greater emphasis on how God is immanently related to each entity in the spatio-temporal tellurian realm.[75] As Lee does so, patently he finds himself in a position where he has to reject aspects of the doctrine derived from the hexagrammic patterns of the *Book of Changes*, such as the idea of God not as a living and active Trinity capable of relating with other entities, but as an entelechy, an organising and animating principle at the heart of all being and becoming.

A caveat is in order at this juncture. In whatever comments are made in the succeeding sections about an Asian or Western theological tradition, one does well to bear in mind that an attempt is being made here only to identify and discern dominant or still influential paradigms which may to varying degrees be effectively contested in more balanced versions of these respective traditions. There is no intention to stereotype an entire Asian or Western theological tradition.

Having said that, it is quite impossible for a proponent, whether of an Asian or Western theological system, to baldly disavow the influence of the theological themes that have achieved prominence in the history of Christian theology, that is, unless one wishes to gainsay altogether this intellectual heritage. At the very least, an innovative and more balanced modern articulation of Western theology, insofar as it is and sees the value of being conscious of its theological lineage, and engaged with it, would seek to grapple with, relativise and contextualise these themes as a type of baseline or starting point for theological discussion. Western theology is not without a past, however one might be inclined positively or negatively to view it.

Far, then, from tarring all Western theology with the same brush and assuming that the theology of St Augustine of Hippo, for instance, is completely and exhaustively representative of the Western tradition,[76] the maximal suggestion that is made in these pages is that a Western theology

---

75. Z.-K. Chua, 'Jung Young Lee's Biblical-Cultural Trinity: A Systematic Theology from East Asia', PhD diss., University of Otago, 2021.
76. It is patently not such an archetype in the sense of exhausting all the creative possibilities of Western theology.

will have themes and questions which it will, if it does not already more or less conscientiously subscribe to, at the very least have to come to grips with, simply because they saliently characterise a historically dominant stream of thought and patrimony of the Western theological tradition, and it is only in this sense that we dare to speak of a foundational theological theme or paradigm in Western history.

As to the rationale for employing a historical Western theological tradition, such as found in St Augustine, as an object of comparison with Asian and other theologies, this is only because, in Augustine's theology, we find both the explicit influence of a cultural paradigm[77] on a Christian theology, as well as a theological system which became a consequent point of reference for subsequent theologies.[78]

Due to the import of Augustine's theological system in the Western theological tradition, his thought functions either as a plumbline, norm, standard and point of identification, or a starting point, point of departure, of discussion, or of differentiation for subsequent theologies in the Western mould. Even in the latter instance, Augustine's thought remains prominent in that it furnishes a basic structure on the premise of which modifications are made. A debt, whether it be adjudged a good or bad one, remains a debt.

Consider Jürgen Moltmann's reinterpretation of the classical theological doctrine of immutability and impassibility, in which he does not actually reject what the doctrine affirms about God's eternity, but only what it fails to affirm about God's ability to interact with and be affected by God's creation through 'active suffering' experienced as a result of a conscious, sovereign, personal choice of coming into an interpersonal relationship with God's human creatures in which God allows Godself to be emotionally vulnerable to human beings because God allows Godself to care, as a relational *primus inter pares* rather than absolute despot, for those very beings.[79]

---

77. In this case, Platonism and Neoplatonism.
78. St Augustine is credited as a major influence on medieval and modern Christian theology, whether of a Roman Catholic or Protestant persuasion. The Editors of Encyclopaedia Britannica, 'Top Questions', *Britannica*, 23 May 2019, https://www.britannica.com/biography/Saint-Augustine; idem., "St. Augustine," *Britannica*, February 16, 2000, https://www.britannica.com/biography/Saint-Augustine.
79. Moltmann, *Trinity and the Kingdom*, pp. 21-23.

Moltmann does not completely repudiate his ties with classical Western tradition as he continues, as a case in point, to speak of an eternal generation and procession in the Trinity, recalling classical theology's construction of a transcendent, unchanging divine being outside time and space,[80] or, at the very least, some idea of God as having always existed in some form of time prior to the creation of the universe;[81] he conscientiously stands within the classical Western tradition and only endeavours to refine it so as to formulate an articulation which is more holistic and balanced.[82]

Even in the cases of Western theologians who attempt to adjust the doctrine of impassibility in a direction more congenial to their desire to assert the idea of God's true solidarity with humankind, references to a divine eternity remain, however this is conceived, whether purely in terms of duration or also categorically transcendent and otherworldly quality or dimensionality. Very few, if any, working within the mould of classical theology, influenced as it has been by Greek metaphysics, would think to depart from the notion of God as eternal, although the ideas of omnipotence, immutability and even impassibility may be called into question, as a non-Western theological system might be willing to do.[83] This only suggests that the classical theological paradigm of God as simple, immutable and impassible, as we have identified it as rooted primarily or essentially in Augustine of Hippo, functions as a model with which Western theologians have reckoned and will continue to reckon.

In Taoist cosmology, the universe develops by means of an evolutionary process by which an ill-defined, nebulous and abstract whole increasingly gains definition, specificity and detail through parts being separated one from another, boundaries coming into place and divisions coming into existence. Mere tendencies coagulate and form themselves into matter, which amasses in ever denser quantities until first objects, then

---

80. Classical or atemporal eternity.

81. Temporal eternity or sempiternity.

82. Moltmann, *Trinity and the Kingdom*, pp. 182-85.

83. Mozley, *Impass.*, pp. 140-66; *NDT*, s.v. 'Time and Eternity' (J.E. Colwell, pp. 688-89). This section of Mozley's monograph surveys the landscape of theological response from 1866 to 1926; consider the four views of God's relationship to the temporal dimension articulated in G.E. Ganssle (ed.), *God and Time: Four Views* (Downers Grove, IL: InterVarsity Press, 2001).

plants, animals and, finally, human beings come about, in which a later evolved entity is possessed of more dimensions and therefore greater uniqueness, specificity and concreteness than an earlier one. Universal, uniform unity becomes particular, heterogenous diversity.

This is similar to how in classical Augustinian theology there is a movement from the simplicity of God, to which everything in the world in its fullness can only dimly approximate, to the diversity of things in the universe which in their concrete qualities and dimensions express what God is in God's elegance by illuminating ever new dimensions represented in God's being.[84] The primary distinction is that in a Taoist cosmological system, the ultimate force, Tao, being always already in existence spontaneously brings forth or posits the one, the two and the three, which, in turn, bring about all other things, whereas in Christian cosmology, a personal God exists already in the beginning and consciously creates all other things.

In an Asian system, a theological construction will imagine a Divine Nature as a positer which posits all other things including the primary elements,[85] which, in turn, authorise[86] the creation of, actually create[87] or indwell[88] some of the material principles of the universe.

The angels roughly correspond to the Platonic Demiurge, a subaltern artificer deity which shapes and orders formless or chaotic material in accordance with their affiliated eternal and rational archetypes, except that these angels also create matter from nothing and they do so in accordance with the divine will and design.[89] The existence and power of angels do indeed arise from the Divine Nature through a process of position, yet this determination as well as all others does not emerge from the volitional choice of the Divine Nature, but from its being fundamentally structured the way it has been, to give power to angels but not to its own entitative form in the Trinity. Being only a

---

84. E.g. the spatiality in God's being through material objects, the sentiency in it through animals and the personhood of God through human beings.
85. In this case, the Trinity, the one, animal souls, the two, and angelic and human souls, the three, in a logical rather than chronological progression.
86. The Trinity being subjects.
87. The angels being subjects.
88. The angels and spirits being subjects.
89. The Editors of Encyclopaedia Britannica, 'Demiurge', *Britannica*, 20 July 1998, https://www.britannica.com/topic/Demiurge; Augustine, *Civ.*, XII.26.

structural framework, the Divine Nature cannot exercise its power in any personal sense.

To the objection that this is to restrict God's power, it may be noted that, even in a classical theological formulation of the conception of God, God's power is limited, by the very fact that God cannot be any other than supreme or perfect in the way supremacy and perfection are construed, that God has no choice in the matter and, even if God wishes to have an option, can have no possible choice in it. Classical theologians would underscore that God would not desire anything other than what God already is, and that therein lies God's perfection and fullness, to which response we might offer that God in our theory also desires nothing other than what God already is, and that the definition of supremacy and perfection in classical theology falls short of the kind of supremacy and perfection we imagine as befitting God, in light of the theodictic dilemma thrown up by these classical notions.

In this manner, the biblical attestation to a creation by God of all things is not undermined, seeing as God remains the ontological premise, as the Divine Nature which sets the universe in motion and empowers its activities, of all things in their variety and evolution. God, therefore, exists in the same realm and time as other things.

In contrast, a classical theological system would posit a purposeful God as a conscious and all-engendering origin of all things. God does not exist in the same realm or time with other things but in a different realm or in a time before the time of other entities. Moreover, in either system, there is always a distinction to be drawn between God or the Divine Nature and the Trinity, which functions as a source and paradigm for all other things, and those other things, which by their nature, ontological structure and spiritual, intellectual, emotional or physical form approximate to God in some way as God's symbols or analogies.

There is a point, therefore, in historical time beyond which even the Trinity does not exist, simply because this is a horizon of all possibility, beyond which there is no possibility of existence or subsistence, and therefore not even the Trinity. The Divine Nature is precluded from consideration of whether it belongs anywhere in this chronological progression because it is not a being *per se*, but a ground or substratum of being, not an entity, but an ontological framework, structure, condition, law or principle. For this reason, the Divine Nature does not exist so much within a universe as conditions it. Although the divine Trinity is an entity within the universe, it is also naturally attached to the all-conditioning, though not all-determining, Divine Nature.

As such, it is worthwhile juxtaposing Augustine's system and those which build upon it to those which arise from other cultural-philosophical modalities. As we shall see, a historical Western theology might try to explain away the texts that deal with God's emotions as anthropopathism, while an Asian theology perhaps needs to guard against a tendency to reduce God to a mortal and overly limited being.[90]

---

90. Cf. Mozley, *Impass.*, pp. 1-6.

Chapter 3

Case Study: A Classical Theology of God and Its Philosophical Debt

Greek philosophical notions, particularly Platonic ideas of God as simple, transcendent, immaterial, immutable, inexpressible yet capable of being grasped to an inadequate degree through desultory visitation of the sagacious akin to a flash of lightning; supra-human, and supra-angelic ultimate mover, greatest of goods, for whom being, living, understanding, and beatitude are equally intrinsic; the definition or essence of all things, the first or ultimate form, rather than the things which it creates, comprising as they all do both a form or nature and the matter which is shaped by that nature;[1] a definition or essence which is perceived by the mind and enables it to make physical and musical aesthetic distinctions and attain to an understanding of the divine through created analogies in the world, the essence of life itself rather than an instance of life, intellectually perceived rather than sensibly;[2] the uncreated source of existence, truth, and happiness, the power of knowledge and understanding; and the one the love of whom through knowledge and emulation is blessed (whether this be in angels or human beings), the

---

1. Augustine, *Civ.*, XII.25.
2. Accordingly, Augustine opines that the image of God in human beings consists in nothing other than their rationality and intellect, and this in order to express their superiority over all other creatures which lack those faculties to the degree in which human beings possess them. Augustine, *Civ.*, XII.23.

inspirer of love – all this made their way into Christian theology through Augustine of Hippo.[3]

Plato's God being perfect, that is, lacking nothing, needing nothing, dependent on nothing, this God is incapable of change since change for such a perfect being would imply a movement away from perfection and towards imperfection. God as the best and most beautiful being imaginable is the epitome of reason, goodness and beauty, incapable of malice or deceit, omnipotent, omniscient, timeless.[4]

An Augustinian emphasis on impassibility may have entered Christian thought through Plato's formulation of the idea of God as beyond the capacity to be affected with delight, sadness or pleasant feeling, sealed off from active providential intervention in the world and even love for the world because love must be directed at an object of need, but God is in no way deficient, an aspect which is challenged in Christian theology.[5]

The motif of impassibility in Augustine's theology may also owe something to a Platonist conception of a threefold hierarchy of rational souls. This is a taxonomy which classifies gods, demons and human beings. Gods[6] belong to heaven,[7] possessed of invulnerability to passions or emotional impact, goodness, blessedness, honour and immortality, some of whom attained that status through a process of deification.[8] These gods possess bodies of flame, are composite in nature, being

---

3. Augustine, *Civ.*, VIII.5-8, 25, IX.16, XI.25; idem, *Conf.*, XIII.iii.4, fn. 4; T. Ainsworth, 'Form vs. Matter', *SEP* (Summer 2020), https://plato.stanford. edu/archives/sum2020/entries/form-matter; Augustine, in *Civ.*, VIII.17, 25, expresses that he thinks it the greatest obligation in religious matters for a believer to emulate the God who is worshipped, through which perfect wisdom and healing can be attained; from the Platonic point of view, things which are composed of matter and capable of being perceived by the physical senses are beneath those which, while not composed of matter, are able to permeate, organise and vitalise it and are capable only of being perceived by the rational mind. Augustine, *Civ.*, IX.17.

4. Sanders, 'Historical Considerations', pp. 62-64.

5. Ibid.

6. These are akin in Christianity to good angelic beings like thrones, dominations, principalities, powers.

7. These are affiliated with the elements of fire and ether.

8. E.g. Mercury, the grandfather of Hermes Trismegistus, Aesculapius, Atlas, Hercules, and, in Augustine's view, even Saturn and Jupiter, who may well have been a human father and son whose relationship was marked by the strife of the son against the parent because of their own or another's impiety, *Civ.*, VII.18, VIII.26, XVIII.8.

constituted of a physical body such as a heavenly body, the world or a body of water, and a mind made up of ether, and therefore dissoluble, yet kept from ontological cessation through the sustenance of the supreme God. Although the Demiurge is credited with the creation of the world, the lesser deities function to construct human beings and other earthly entities.

The province of demons is the air and they function by virtue of physical nearness as mediators between the gods and human beings, with both the gods and demons capable of being invoked through cultic arts into images and mysteries. Demons are possessed of vulnerability to passions, emotions which are not guided by any moral code,[9] vanity, misery and immortality. Some demons are said to be good. Human beings belong to the earth and are possessed of vulnerability to passions, susceptibility to immorality, capacity for a moral life, through which they may access immortality.[10]

Another view of God which Plato held, of God as the true existent and truly real as that which is uncreated and does not change, may have originated, so Augustine thinks, from Plato's possible exposure to the record of the divine appearance to Moses in the event of the burning bush, whereby God revealed Godself as, 'I am who am.'[11]

Hellenistic theology contributed its predilection for a vision of God as unchanging, not subject to time and dependable, rather than changing and subject to the vicissitudes of time, as a mark of power and freedom from death and defect as opposed to enervation and decay, as united rather than existing in separate parts, incorruptible rather than subject to deterioration and destruction, and fulfilled rather than always only seeking fulfilment. Christian theology adopted the Greek philosophical differentiation between a realm of the existent as opposed to that in pursuit of existence, one of true being as opposed to that which merely seems to be true, the former occupied by a God characterised by the mind and freedom from time and change as a non-relational, non-temporal and

---

9. One which prescribes avoidance, for instance, of anger, venality, self-inflation, partiality, intellectual and emotional unrest, malice, unrighteousness, pride, envy, deceit, vindictiveness.

10. Augustine, *Civ.*, VII.23, VIII.11, 14-18, 21, 23-24, 26, IX.2, XIII.16-18; T.K. Johansen, 'Review of S. Broadie, *Nature and Divinity in Plato's Timaeus* (Cambridge: Cambridge University Press, 2012)', *NDPR*, University of Notre Dame, August 2012, https://ndpr.nd.edu/reviews/nature-and-divinity-in-plato-s-timaeus.

11. Augustine, *Civ.*, VIII.11.

unchanging basis for a world marked by temporal passage and shifts, and the latter by that dynamic world itself.[12]

It can be readily observed that the classical, still influential, patristic doctrine of God as simple, immutable,[13] impassible, immoveable, blessed, perfect, incorruptible, self-sufficient, spiritual, intellectual, and incomprehensible because incapable of being directly perceived or experienced, draws directly from a Platonic and Neoplatonic Greek cultural paradigm.[14] The classical theological paradigm of a God defined by the canon of simplicity has been traced to the confluence of the political notion of a monarch and Aristotle's idea of an Eternal Thinker.[15]

The comprehensive scope of influence of such a biblical-classical synthesis in the form of the notion of God as simple and immutable can be seen in the way Augustine's soteriological concept of divine predestination, involving the corruption of the human nature and the necessity for divine election in salvation, was calculated to safeguard God's independence and omnipotence from being eroded by the suggestion that salvation is mediated through human free will and simple foreknowledge and therefore ultimately contingent only on human decision rather than the divine will.[16] In addition, divine love is to be understood only in terms of the divine engendering in the world of being and delight.[17]

John Mozley, an early twentieth-century minister and theologian, believes that a strong Hebrew view of divine sovereignty prepared theologians in the first Christian centuries to take up the Greek

---

12. Sanders, 'Historical Considerations', p. 68.
13. Therefore, in Augustine's theology, time is separated from eternity so as to keep the latter unaltered, seeing that time by definition involves change and succession, which necessitates the existence of creatures capable of movement by which time may be measured, whether in terms of the rotation of the earth or some other movement prior to the creation of the world. Augustine, *Civ.*, XII.15.
14. Such a doctrine may be referred to at times as a classical one because it owes its essence to influential patristic theologians and continues to exercise an influence, whether a positive one leading to emulation or a negative one leading to reaction, in theology from its origins up to the present time. John Mozley in *The Impassibility of God* refers to the doctrine of divine impassibility as an 'ancient and medieval tradition' (p. 173) and as 'traditional' (p. 176).
15. Mozley, *Impass.*, pp. 136, 163.
16. Sanders, 'Historical Considerations', p. 81; Augustine, *Civ.*, V.8-11.
17. Sanders, 'Historical Considerations', p. 96.

philosophical idea of a divine One in contrast to the non-divine, remaining Many, where the divine unity stands apart from the world, completely insulated in its proper domain from questions of the orientation of the world and its emotionally stirring images.[18]

If it is asked, as it may rightly be done, why God has to be conceived of in these ways, which might come across as odd to members of certain non-Western ethnic groups, no answer of objective justification, based on ways of assaying the quality of one type of response against another, may be proffered. This is due primarily to the fact that what one culture prizes is to a significant extent connected with its influential thinkers, and these thinkers with their unique personal histories come to focus on specific aspects of reality according to how their intuitions guide them; in the same way, the pathbreaking and paradigmatic intellectuals of other cultural groups will, being the specific individuals they are, emphasise the things that draw them most strongly.

As people even within the same precinct may be diverse, so it is unsurprising that the guiding lights of diverse cultures should place more attention now on abstract logic, now on concrete phenomena of nature, now on the individual person or familial or communal unit. By their remarkable charisma, the historical circumstances that enabled them to come to public prominence, the public actions taken by these individuals themselves, in short, by numerous accidents of history coming together at suitable times and in favourable ways, one intellectual comes to exercise an imprint of knowledge, brilliant insight or discovery that subsequently defines or redefines the course of thinking for a people group or society; and that figure comes to be exalted above the rest for their intellectual influence. For the majority of individuals in a given community, it will be sufficient to follow these well-trodden paths.

Once a critical mass of a following is secured by dint of favourable historical accident in tandem with the brilliance and clarity of the idea to promote adherence to it, a school of thought is established and holds promise of thriving and flourishing in the ages to come. In just this way, members of a particular cultural group will veer towards a specific conception of God which is not immune to questions of logical necessity, biblical justification, theological coherence and practical relevance.

Therefore, having recourse to a historical Western emphasis on the primacy of substance over process, we may have a development of the

---

18. Mozley, *Impass.*, p. 173. See also pp. 164-65.

doctrine of God in which divine transcendence is expressed in the form of a morally perfect[19] and unchanging being.

According to a classical conception of divine simplicity, which takes from Platonism and Neoplatonism, and which thinkers at least since the time of Augustine developed, God is simple, not a synthesis of disparate elements such as universal/particular because *actus purissimus*, fully actualised being (Aquinas), form/matter or measurable parts because incorporeal spirit, subject/accidents because without distinctions, essence/existence because necessarily existent, nature/personality/ subjectivity because God's nature and existence are 'absolute pure act', potential/actual because pure and simple act, essence/attributes, essence/ knowledge (thought/wisdom), essence/will (decision/decree), essence/ action, knowledge (thought/wisdom)/will, because God is pure act and without potentiality (Quenstedt),[20] quiescent/active because God as living is completely active, passive/active and self-willing/world-willing because both are identified as a result of the absolute decree, essence/ morality, essence/ability, will/ability (Schleiermacher).[21] In short, God as simple is objectively devoid of distinction.[22]

Divine Simplicity in Thomas Aquinas' Doctrine of God

Thomas Aquinas develops the conception of divine simplicity and incorporeality on the basis of Aristotelian hylomorphism and its act-potency distinction. The hylomorphic paradigm, which constitutes a

---

19. That is, good, transparent or trustworthy.
20. Johannes Andreas Quenstedt (1617-88), a German Lutheran of the Lutheran scholastic tradition, professor of theology at the University of Wittenberg (1660-88). See Dorner, *DI*, art. 2, pp. 95, 104-5, 115; the idea of a unity and identity of divine understanding and will was present already in Aquinas. Dorner critiques determinism on p. 106, p. 107, fn. 44, pp. 108-10, highlighting that it makes too little of human freedom and is in danger of positing phantoms, the fact that, in order for God to be free, God has to be more than a being driven by bare and pure necessity, and how a conception of an absolutely simple eternal divine decree, as opposed to a mediated one, leads to dualism in view of the presence of evil, and is also unable to permit real divine action and interaction in the world. Dorner also provides an outline and critical examination of the doctrine of divine immutability, taking his primary material from various sources including Quenstedt.
21. Dorner, *DI*, art. 2, pp. 122-25.
22. Ibid., p. 136.

key doctrine in Aristotle's natural philosophy, postulates the existence of two fundamental and metaphysical principles, namely, primary matter (potential) and substantial form (actual), as defining all of worldly reality.[23]

God does not possess a body because with matter, change and division are possible but God is unchangeable and indissoluble; matter entails the possibility of the actualisation of what the form of the matter dictates it should become, yet God is fully actualised; matter receives its perfection and goodness from being shaped by the primary (God) and intermediate agents to assume its proper, specific form, but God is already perfect[24] and good; and matter is the passive-receptive principle of a thing but, God being the self-actuating principle of all activity, God can only be form and not or also matter. God appoints intermediate causes to promote structure and pulchritude in creation, such as human persons, in order to share the honour of being a cause.

Unlike material things, which receive their individuality from the individual matter of which they are composed and which their forms shape, God as form itself has individuality in being form without the possibility of assuming matter because God cannot be other than fully realised. Even though the angels may be form without matter as well, God differs from them in that God is, and alone is, unlimited.

Because God is not composed of matter taking form, in God the abstract[25] and the concrete[26] are completely unified in one perfect form, God being God's own nature. Furthermore, because of the fact that in God there is no accident or anything that is not part of God's substance, every aspect of God's existence defines God's substance, so that God is identical to God's wisdom and power.

It is in this manner that God is simple, that is, God's identity and self are exactly identical with God's nature, existence, goodness, wisdom, power, relationships, actions and all other attributes of perfect and active existence, without division and divisibility. Active power or action designates the ability to act upon a second thing as opposed to passive potentiality or passion which refers to the ability to be acted upon by a second thing. God can only be spoken of as having active power without any passive potentiality.

---

23. The Editors of Encyclopaedia Britannica, 'hylomorphism', *Britannica*, 20 July 1998, https://www.britannica.com/topic/hylomorphism.
24. That is, completely actualised, realised according to one's ideal form.
25. This is typically associated with form.
26. This is typically associated with matter.

God being simple, God is a being fully engaged in one continuous act of existing, understanding, willing, loving, planning and acting; as such, in God, the faculty of understanding is equivalent to the content and expression of understanding, and the faculty of the will is equivalent to the content and expression of the will, there being no potentiality in God, only full actuality.

God's nature is identical to God's wisdom, being self-determined. God is most perfectly living because God moves Godself, in a fully actualised sense, rather than being moved by another. God's will is presupposed by God's understanding, because God's understanding presupposes the knowledge of and attraction to that which is good, that is, God.

God's goodness leads God to communicate God's good to others, that is, God's creatures, out of the same love God has for Godself, making them as they are so as to find their fulfilment in God alone, though not in order to attain some state of perfection, since apart from God's creation, God is already perfect; therefore, God is not compelled to create anything.[27]

Divine goodness is the foremost agent and ultimate goal of all things. God can be said to love, though not in the mode of passion[28] but an act of the will, because love is at the heart of the will, which, in typical human beings literally and in God figuratively, is always inclined to some good. The will experiences delight when this good is had, and displeasure when it is absent or obstructed. God wills and brings about the good that is in all God's creatures, treating human beings as rational creatures as God's friends, and the greater the love, the greater the good. God tends the creation with prudence, planning in eternity what God executes in temporality in terms of God's providential care for creation.

God does not possess emotionality and is not unsettled by sorrow for pitiful creatures, and so self-control, bravery, mastery of anger are attributed to God in a solely figurative manner. Even so, God maintains the natural and moral state of the world via a distributive justice in which God is just and generous with those in need, in an unchanging and principled way as though bound by some law but not actually bound to any, since God is completely free and acts only according to God's pure will, and so as to actualise God's wisdom and will and disclose God's goodness in the world, and grant God's creatures according to

---

27. In Augustine, God does not create the world out of some internal mechanism in the divine being which necessitates such creation nor in order to satisfy some desire of God's own. *Civ.*, XI.24.

28. Another word would be carnal desire.

their natural needs. God is also merciful in distributing good things according to the need of the creature and lavish in so doing, simply out of goodness.

God's power, being based on a limitless substance, is itself unlimited. Divine omnipotence is not tantamount to the capacity to engage in contradictions, such as existing and not existing in one and the same sense simultaneously, sinning,[29] or changing the past, though it is indeed possible for God to resurrect the dead. God's power is most perfectly demonstrated in God's sharing of goodness with creation, as well as God's forgiveness and mercy.

God is happiness actualised, which involves a mental act on the part of a rational being. Some human beings are invited into a participation in divine happiness, which constitutes the archetype of all human happiness; contemplative persons find their delight perfected in God's own enduring and self-confident mental dwelling on Godself and all other things; active persons find theirs perfected in God's administration of the cosmos; and earthly pursuits of sensuality, wealth, dominance, position, and popularity are surpassed by God's delight in Godself and others, God's self-confident ownership of the effects of wealth, God's omnipotence, rule over all creation, and the worship offered to God by creatures.

God wills all things, including those things which have a possibility of not turning out according to their initial intended purpose, either through flaws in natural processes or the use of free will, such as certain individuals who do not respond to the offer of salvation, but even these are willed by God to happen the way they finally do.

God cannot do evil, does not directly will evil, nor is God unable to prevent evil, whether natural evil or moral evil, including reprobation and rejection, but God simply permits it for a larger purpose of natural order and justice in which evil for one thing serves the good of another, with the death and deprivation of one thing constituting the birth and gain of another, so much so that were God to preclude such evils, the universe would be less than perfect. God eternally determines all things, even the free acts of human agents. As such, God chooses whom God predestines, some for eternal life in the future direct knowledge of God through granting them what is necessary for salvation, and some whom God rejects, reprobates, and punishes through refusing them these necessary things.

---

29. This entails being unable to successfully execute an action and is thereby beyond God conceived of as omnipotent.

Only one entity is God, without any possibility of a second like that God, since the two would be indistinguishable, and, if God, as the ultimate and primary cause of the world,[30] were not one, the world, too, would lack fundamental unity and the diverse things of the world would lack their limited, accidental ability to form a unified whole. God is God's own essence because there is no composition in God, no accidents,[31] no instantiations,[32] no potency.[33]

God cannot fail to exist because existence is part of the nature of God and God is existence in itself. God's existence has to define who God is in order to preclude the possibility of God receiving God's existence from an external source, as well as God plausibly possessing being in a state of potential existence, impossible scenarios because God is fully actualised being. Indeed, God is most perfectly defined by God's existence, being "He who is". Because God is absolutely simple, God is not patient of classification under some genus, regarded as an instantiation of some genus, or as having properties in the sense of traits that can be realised – again, because God is fully realised being. God is not the form or matter of the world itself, because God is the ultimate cause.[34]

The reason God cannot be composite is that, if God were made up of different parts, whether separable or not, each of which do not constitute the whole but contribute towards it, then God's being would be dependent on something more basic than it, that is, its parts, as well as to the agent of composition which unites the parts.[35]

For Aquinas, God is above alteration because God lacks the requisite qualities for mutability, including the ability to be in a potential state so

---

30. By this, we understand God as not just shaping the world but also creating the very material from which the world is shaped.
31. This is because nothing in God is outside God's essence.
32. This is because God's essence by its own power exists individually and independently of any matter.
33. This is because God is fully realised being.
34. Thomas Aquinas, *Summa*, Ia, q. 3, generally, and arts 1-8, q. 4, arts 1-2, q. 5, arts 1-6, q. 6, arts 1-4, q. 7, arts 1-4, q. 11, arts 1-3, q. 13, art. 7, qs 18-23, qs 25-26, q. 28, qs 40-41, art. 4; idem, *SCG*, I, ch. 21, arts 1-6, ch. 22, art. 10.
35. This, as well as other aspects of divine nature in an impassibilist understanding of God's being, is explained in J.E. Dolezal, 'Strong Impassibility', in R.J. Matz and A.C. Thornhill (eds), *Divine Impassibility: Four Views of God's Emotions and Suffering*, Spectrum Multiview (Downers Grove, IL: IVP Academic, 2019), pp. 13-37.

that one can progress from potential to actual,[36] the property of having components so that one's state is alterable through the modification of certain parts,[37] and the quality of being imperfect so that there it is possible to move towards perfection.[38] Even though God alone is impervious to change, all other things are subject to change, to begin with, through being brought by God, as existence itself, into existence, and having been so engendered, possess each their own potentiality to evolve and develop according to the divine plan and design.[39]

The doctrine of divine simplicity is extended from the Christian doctrine of God's nature, which Aquinas believes it is possible for natural reason to access, to the doctrine of the Trinity, into which God's revelation guides but not in as probative a manner as the Christian doctrine of the divine nature.

In Aquinas, the Augustinian preference for interior over exterior analogies for the Trinity is maintained by means of the application of the example of a mental word, in which a person conceives of an idea which expresses the individual's understanding of some concept, reproduces (begets) to the mind what it actually knows, and thereby unites mind and thought, to the begotten God the Son, and that of an impulse of love, whereby a lover experiences a strong and spontaneous feeling of affinity and attraction towards the object of love like a breath which animates the soul and which thereby unites idea and will, to God the Holy Spirit. Given that in God, existence and understanding, mind and will are completely identical, the three persons of the Trinity are certainly internally differentiated but also completely united in a numerically identical substance.

Aquinas anchors his exposition of divine personhood on Boethius' definition of the person as *naturae rationabilis individua substantia*[40] and Aristotle's distinction between substance as the definition of a thing[41] and substance as subject. This latter is anything that subsists independently and not within another thing (subsistent), constitutes a concrete example of a nature (natural thing) and is attached to properties

---

36. God, however, is fully actual.
37. God, however, is uncompounded.
38. God, however, is endlessly perfect.
39. Thomas Aquinas, *Summa*, Ia, q. 8, arts 1-3, q. 9, arts 1-2, q. 13, arts 10-11.
40. An individual substance of a rational nature.
41. That is, substance as Greek, *ousia*, Latin, *essentia*, and English, is-ness.

(substance). The person is a species of the subject, being the subject of a class of subsistent beings with a rational nature.

Given that the person constitutes the highest form of existence, in the view of Aquinas, God whose nature is perfect in every way is necessarily a person, though in a manner far superior to any creature. God is the supreme expression of independent and intelligent being. God's rationality is to be conceived of not as open to the mode of the acquisition of knowledge and understanding through argumentation or reasoning, but as being essentially defined by an intellectual capacity fully actualised. God's individuality is to be construed chiefly in terms of God's natural and ontological distinction from all other things, and God's substance is to be interpreted as the fact that God has existence of Godself.

Although in humanity, personhood declares a distinct instantiation of a human nature, in the Godhead, personhood refers to distinct relations of origin. These relations of origin exist in being identical to God's nature. An example of a relationship within the Godhead is paternity, or the Father, a divine person. The divine person is an independently existing or subsistent subject, a *hypostasis*, which exists in the divine nature and is to be completely identified with it. The idea of divine personhood unifies the dimensions of nature and relationship in the Godhead. As relationship that subsists in the form of a subject or *hypostasis*, the divine person is first of all a relationship and then an expression of a nature, whereas as the divine nature conceived of as a subsistent or independently existing subject or *hypostasis*, the divine person is primarily expression of nature and only secondarily a relationship, capable of being distinguished from all other things in virtue of its nature.

Aquinas believes that in the trinitarian Godhead, the category, person, is applied to designate the fact that these rational subjects and subsistents not so much constitute an instantiation of a nature which they share in common[42] but signify that the Father, Son and Holy Spirit exist in a differentiated and determinate way in the single divine nature, in which the Father, presumably cited as a case in point, possesses the fullness of the divine nature.

To eschew the Arian stance which imagines Father, Son and Holy Spirit to be three substances, it is necessary to assert that the divine persons are distinguishable, yet not dissimilar or varied in their nature or existence, and standing apart or segregated as are sections of a larger fullness, or

---

42. A case being a word such as 'a man'.

differing in dignity, lacking affinity or alien. In order not to subscribe to Sabellianism, which postulates that God is just one person, Aquinas is persuaded that it is imprudent to discourse about any divine person as the peculiar or utterly distinctive God, or as severally composed or isolated.

The knowledge of the Trinity is intimately related to the understanding of salvation, which is procured by the incarnate Son through the bestowal of the Spirit. Aquinas distinguishes five notions in the Trinity, concepts which spell out the particular relationship between the divine persons as well as distinguish the persons one from another. Therefore, the Father is distinguished by the Father's unbegottenness, having no origin in any source, the Father's paternity, being the source of the Son, and the Father's common relationship, with the Son, to the Holy Spirit, as the source of the Spirit. The Son is distinguished by the Son's filiation, originating as the Son does from the Father, as well as the Son's common relationship, with the Father, to the Holy Spirit, as the source of the Spirit. The Holy Spirit is distinguished by the Spirit's procession, originating from the Father and the Son. Among the five notions, only unbegottenness, paternity, filiation and procession, and not also the common relationship of the Father or Son as source of the Holy Spirit, are exclusive identifying markers for the divine persons, while only paternity, filiation, common origination of the Holy Spirit and procession, and not also unbegottenness, pertain to the relationship between the persons. The reason the divine persons can be conceived as identical to their relationships is that, in God, there is no division between the abstract and the concrete as in the case of matter taking form.

Aquinas defines a divine person[43] as a relationship existing in the divine nature, only rationally distinct from this nature but not actually dissimilar to it, and truly differentiated from and standing over as an equal counterpart against the other relationships to which it stands in a give-and-take and mutual bond. This may be difficult for us to grasp as we have only directly encountered creatures differentiated as subjects only by their various natures, and not the relationships in them because these relationships do not possess an independent existence.

Since there is no movement in God, who is simple, that is, fully actualised, having only active power without passive potentiality, whatever is said about action in God arising from the relationships of begetting (paternity), being begotten (filiation), shared origination or procession are to be regarded as the relationships between persons said

---

43. *Elohim* in Hebrew, *hypostasis* in Greek and *persona* in Latin.

to bear different roles based on action[44] and passion[45] always already actualised and hence without any connotation of passion or movement.

Even though God's existence and the Father's begetting imply the presence of a will, such will does not refer to an external action foisted upon God by an extrinsic agent or goal, but represents an internal, necessary movement of the divine will in which God approves of being God and source of the Spirit as expression of God's love and as love itself, the Father of being source of the Son. The begetting by the Father of the Son transpires not as God creates the world and the very materials by which God forms the world, but in a manner akin to the generation by a father of a son, yet without the implication that the Father's substance is shared with the Son, since God's substance cannot be apportioned, but that the Father conferred the Father's entire substance on the Son without losing any of it, and in such a way that the only difference between the Father and Son is constituted by the identity of the Father as originator of the Son, and the Son as originating from the Father.

In the natural world, the source of a product may require time whether for physical maturity or the progress of an action, as in the case of the begetting by a father of a child. While human beings choose to have children, the Father begets the Son not by will but by the Father's eternal and sublime divine nature, not through a succession of stages because the generation of the Son is not a corporeal event. In this way, the Son has been in existence coeval with the Father in and from eternity, as has the Holy Spirit.

The Father and Son being the same in their essence and splendour are respectively the perfection of paternity and filiation. The Son is the peak of filiation in a manner that believers can by predestination attain through divine grace. The Son as the Word[46] constitutes a kind of mental concept brought about by the Father from what the Father knows of the Son, and to name the Son Word is not to indicate the divine substance in itself but rather only the person distinguished by means of its source. The mind is to the process of awareness and understanding as existence is to the existent. Although in humans the act of knowing something does not produce the object of knowledge, in God the subject and object of knowledge are completely identified. Since in God existence and

---

44. This involves the moving of an external object.
45. This involves a being moved by an external subject.
46. This is possibly known as begotten understanding and conceived awareness.

knowledge are completely identical, God's Word is a dimension of God's nature and exists independently in God.

The names of the divine persons refer exclusively to God's personal relationships within the Godhead and not also those with creatures. These names indirectly refer to the person's nature as divine as well as their analogical relationship to creatures; therefore, the Son as begotten God is also the unbegotten Creator. The Son is further named Image as something which originates from something else and bears a likeness to it in virtue of being of the same species because the Son as Word is of a similar kind as the Father, akin to how a prince is of the same nature and species as his biological father, the king.

Though the Holy Spirit is also like God in being God's love, it is not called image or begotten because to be an image is to be of the same kind as the source but the Spirit is primarily God's love and love does not entail being of a similar kind to another. The Holy Spirit as love is a movement of the will towards the object of affection. The divine persons are not differentiated by having different natures since they subsist in the same nature but only by mutually opposed relationships such as paternity and filiation, each of these being a divine person. These mutually opposed relationships in God are all relationships of origin, of originator to originated and vice versa. The Son originates the Holy Spirit rather than the other way round because affection for something presupposes some mental concept of it, a word.

Just as the act of knowing creates a mental concept by which the subject of knowledge unites itself with an intellectual concept of the object of knowledge, the act of loving produces an emotional stamp, a persistent feeling of affection by which the subject of love unites itself with a desire for the object of love, as does the object of love for the subject of love in a reciprocal manner. Love as applied to God can designate God's affection for God's object of affection, in which case it refers to an aspect of God's nature, no different than God's awareness or understanding; it can designate that which issues from a loving nature as an expression of affection, in which case it refers to the Holy Spirit; or it can designate the act of such an affective impact being established, like the process of breathing, in which case it refers to the mode by which this person originates and comes to fullness in the lover and the beloved, similar to how the Son is mentally spoken or begotten. Just as to speak is to produce a word and to blossom is to produce a flower, so to love is to breathe out an expression of love.

The Father speaks the Son and Word as well as creatures into their respective forms of existence, the Father and Son express affection towards themselves, each other, and human beings in the Holy Spirit understood as the love which arises in them. The Spirit originates as the expression of God's affection, based on God's intrinsic goodness, for Godself and God's creatures.[47] By virtue of their origin, the Son belongs to the Father and the Spirit to both the Father and the Son. The divine persons can be offered as gifts to human beings as rational creatures by their receiving God's Word and the affection arising from God in order to be able to know and love God correctly. Such a gift is presented not in order to receive something in return but purely out of the goodwill of love. Although the Son as well is the gift of God to the world out of God's love, the name of Gift is properly attached only to the Holy Spirit, given that the Spirit originates from the Father as the Father's affection, because the idea of a gift is closer to the notion of an expression of love than that of a word or image.

Aquinas discourses of the Son and Holy Spirit as sent in time even as they issue or proceed in eternity, the Son and the Spirit as God. To speak of an issuance or procession of the divine persons is to emphasise their source, to speak about their begetting or breathing out is to describe the eternal act in which those persons come to exist in a new mode of being, while to speak of their sending is to describe a temporal objective and the way in which the Son, for instance, may be sent into the world to exist in a new way in the flesh or both the Son and Holy Spirit are given to believers, in an invisible fashion. Although God subsists in general terms in all creation through God's substance,[48] presence,[49] and power,[50] God is also able to live in the hearts of believers, as rational creatures, as in a temple, as object of knowledge and affection, and therefore as the possession of believers.

It is through divine grace that the Son and Spirit are sent forth and bestowed in time, and that believers are able to exercise their created faculty of divine grace to delight in these persons and receive God as a gift that the eye cannot perceive. Furthermore, God's grace sets the stage for the believer to have ownership of the divine person, the Holy Spirit, who is given and who gives itself. Among the divine persons, only the

---

47. Augustine of Hippo understands the Holy Spirit as quite possibly the divine goodness which Father and Son share together, given that the Spirit is in both, much as the Spirit seems to be an essence of holiness that unites the other two divine persons. *Civ.*, XI.24.
48. Here God is understood as cause of all.
49. Here God is understood as being aware of all.
50. Here God is understood as having authority over all.

Son and Spirit can be said to have been sent into the world, for sending presupposes an origin and the Father is without an origin. Nevertheless, all three divine persons can be said to share in the common task of bringing about divine grace and indwelling believers by means of grace. God's gift of grace seeks and achieves the conformity of human souls to God, in which, as the divine persons are sent into the human person, they are made to resemble the particular divine person. Therefore, the Holy Spirit being an affection, when it is sent into the human soul, this soul becomes loving as the Holy Spirit, the gift of affection. Concerning the Son as the Word which breathes out an affection, the sign that this gift of a divine person is conferred on a believer is that they become not just wise but full of the wisdom that engenders affection.

The Holy Spirit, arising as affection, constitutes a sanctifying gift of God, while the Son, being origin of the Spirit, is the source of this sanctification. Consequently, that people might learn of the invisible sending of the divine persons through visible symbols, the Son as source of sanctification was made a human being, uniting with a visible creature, with rational mind and perfect self-mastery, backed by the Holy Spirit as the sign of his authority. Aquinas opines that it is not imperative for the Holy Spirit to be incarnated simply because any creature can be a sign of sanctification. There is no need for every sending of a divine person, physically undetectable, to be manifested in visible forms. Even so, the Spirit was powerfully delivered upon Christ, his apostles, and some saints of the Early Church at the baptism of Jesus, through the sign of a dove, a fertility symbol connoting Christ's role as a bestower of the grace of a spiritual rebirth, at the Transfiguration, through the sign of a radiant cloud as a representation of plentiful guidance, at the original Pentecost through the signs of a powerful gust, indicating authority to serve the sacraments, and flaming tongues, highlighting the call to teach. As the Son reveals the Father, the Spirit reveals the Son. The following distinction has to be struck between eternal issuance and processions[51] and temporal sending: in eternity, the Father alone is source of the Son, and the Father and Son alone are source of the Spirit, whereas in time, the whole Trinity is involved in delivering the divine persons as the effect of divine grace.[52]

For Aquinas, to exist is to be capable of being mentally grasped. Relating to divine knowledge of creation, in Aquinas' theology, in correspondence to Augustine's appropriation of Platonism, this is possible because God

---

51. This might be conceived of as a form of sending.
52. Thomas Aquinas, *Summa*, Ia, q. 27, qs 29-43.

is fully realised awareness and God's knowledge is not unrealised or deficient in any way. Consequently, God knows everything about the world through direct knowledge. God is identical to God's single and endless act of infinite awareness, always fully realised, concerning God's being and activity and that of the world and merely possible things.

God's knowledge through God's will brings about all things, both their material and assumed forms. God knows the future through a foreknowledge of future events without directly or certainly determining their occurrence because some creatures have freedom of choice. God brings about the universe in its array through the reality conceptualised by Plato, that is, Ideas, substantive forms of things and designs for each thing, according to which they are made and by which they can be comprehended.

In relation to human knowledge of the divine, God brings God's intelligible self before a mind, which God aids with a supernatural light of apprehension. This supernatural light occasionally furnishes stimulating inner images[53] or external presentations[54] and presents facets of faith not accessible to natural reason such as the Trinity. A greater measure of this supernatural light is conferred on those who love more and thereby desire this light more.

God cannot be physically perceived or mentally depicted, only understood, but not in such a way that the limitless God is fully known by a finite mind, only through the successiveness of time and dividedness of human attributes such as wisdom which are applicable to God in a simple sense.[55] Other things by their mental existence allow the well-fitted created mind to understand. The processes of the mind enable it to extrapolate from material things to attain to a comprehension of things which do not exist materially and even in themselves, that is, God.

Like Augustine, Aquinas believes that God is the source of all being and understanding, and the source of understanding in that God sustains truth by eternally holding all truths in God's mind, such as mathematical truths or shapes, or the truth of events that would transpire. The Greek term, *theos*, referring to God, directly signifies God's engagement in all-encompassing planning and governance, and because God is not directly perceived but only perceived through God's effects or ordained acts in the world, 'God' ultimately stands in only for the idea of an indefinable being whose nature it is to bring all things and events about,

---

53. This happened with the prophets.
54. This happened at the baptism of Christ.
55. In the case of wisdom, this defines God's essence, ability and life.

is distinct from and transcends all creatures, and excels them all. God's other names relate to different dimensions of God's being or existence: YHWH relates to God's individuality and Goodness relates to God as the source of all that is.[56]

In the theology of Augustine, Martin Luther and John Calvin, in line with God as the ultimate mover in both Aristotelian and Platonic philosophy, God's knowledge of all things is due to the fact that God predetermines everything from the beginning, whether this be the creation of spirits or bodies, their natures, their powers, though not rational wills *per se*, their degree or extent, or the way they are put together or fit together, at least not in a unilateral way, for such creatures can either choose good or ill, though ultimately even these decisions are determined by God.[57]

Divine Simplicity, Immutability and Impassibility

God is an ontologically, instrumentally and ethically absolute[58] being, which brought about all contingent and changing being, itself dwelling in unperturbed and imperturbable beatitude comprising joy, delight, care, love, grace *par excellence* (according to Thomas Aquinas).[59]

Love, as unconditional desire for the highest wellbeing of the other, exists in God, according to Aquinas, because God has will, and therefore desire, and because all desire is ultimately rooted in love of something deemed to be good or aversion of something viewed as being the opposite to what is regarded as good. Divine love does not involve sensory organs, only the intellectual faculty, and is impassible, that is, not exposed to being affected by anything that happens in the realm of the world, while God's joyful delight is unitary and simple in nature. Sadness, anger and regret are far from God's nature because

---

56. Thomas Aquinas, *Summa*, Ia, q. 12, arts 2-13, qs 13-17; Aquinas did not consider the activity of understanding to be a faculty of the human body but, presumably, the immaterial soul alone.

57. Sanders, 'Historical Considerations', pp. 87-90; Augustine, *Civ.*, V.8-11, XI.10, 15, 21, XVII.6-7.

58. That is, ontologically necessary, omnipotent, omniscient, omnipresent, eternal, conscious, loving, just, beautiful, harmonious.

59. Dorner, *DI*, art. 2, pp. 88-95, 100, art. 3, p. 176, fn. 31; Moltmann, *Trinity and the Kingdom*, pp. 21-22; A.W. Oei, 'The Impassible God Who "Cried"', *Themelios* 41, no. 2 (2016), p. 243; in Augustine, God, whose mind has no limits and is capable of fathoming all numbers, has existed in perfect bliss even prior to creation. *Civ.*, XII.17-18.

these emotions imply imperfection, deficiency and passion, understood as the ability to be genuinely affected by events in the world.[60] In Anselm of Canterbury, God expresses divine compassion for humanity through bringing about effects in the world in which sinful people receive help in a time of desperate need but not by actually experiencing a feeling of sympathising kindness.[61]

God cannot change or suffer. This is because God is absolute, self-sufficient and therefore 'timeful' – that is, God experiences all of earthly history already and simultaneously and thus regards the elect with loving pleasure at having already attained their ultimate state (Quenstedt).[62]

God is incapable of change – that is, God has no possibility of transitioning from less morally perfect to more, and from potential to actual in terms of beginning, prosecuting and completing an activity (Isaak Dorner).[63] There is no hint of succession in God because God is already ultimate perfection and always in a state of having already achieved what in human terms progresses through the various levels of learning and growth, and thought, feeling, desire, intent, resolve and action.[64] In this regard, God is not static or dead, but fully actualised and stably flourishing in infinite dynamism and life (Schleiermacher).[65]

In the view of Augustine, God is beyond the capacity for suffering in the sense of being affected in a negative manner. Since God is not a physical being, the only suffering God could undergo is psychological. Yet, God is not even exposed to this kind of suffering. For this reason, God is not liable to negative emotions such as regret, pity, anger, jealousy or patience,[66] though God brings it about through God's agents acting in the world that the sources of what seems to be divine regret, pity, anger or jealousy are dealt with through what appears to be a making

---

60. Mozley, *Impass.*, pp. 114-16.
61. T.J. Oord, 'Strong Passibility', in R.J. Matz and A.C. Thornhill (eds), *Divine Impassibility: Four Views of God's Emotions and Suffering*, Spectrum Multiview (Downers Grove, IL: IVP Academic, 2019), pp. 134-35.
62. Dorner, *DI*, art. 2, pp. 100-3; P. Helm, 'Responses to Bruce A. Ware: Response by Paul Helm', in B.A. Ware (ed.), *Perspectives on the Doctrine of God: Four Views* (Nashville, TN: Broadman & Holman, 2008), pp. 124-25.
63. Dorner, *DI*, art. 2, p. 88.
64. Dorner, *DI*, art. 2, pp. 105, 124-25; Augustine, *Civ.*, XI.21, XII.17.
65. Dorner, *DI*, art. 2, p. 122.
66. This is not a negative emotion but one which is predicated on a tolerance which involves some form of restraint and therefore suffering.

good, liberation, punishment or revenge.[67] In short, in Augustine's theology, divine feelings as attested in Scripture are to be regarded as anthropopathisms standing in for God's variegated and appropriate action among humankind in effectuation of a moral good or purpose.[68]

In a similar way to how God's ascribed and perceived feelings are to be divorced from God's impassible eternal reality, Augustine believes God's knowledge of God's creatures and ascribed and perceived dealings with them as they exist in time, such as in hearing and answering their prayers, is set at a distance from the dynamic interactions in which the latter are involved, in which God in eternity already knows all things which will inexorably happen, knows how God's mediators make God known to God's creatures in time, knows God's creatures' attempts to interact with God, and God's respective responses to each of these specific

---

67. Augustine, *Civ.*, XV.25, XVII.23; Augustine extends this logic to scriptural descriptions of God as moving from one locality to another (by recourse to a theory that God simply causes God's creatures to become especially aware of God's presence in a supernatural way) and exercising God's faculty of sight (by recourse to a theory that God simply causes God's creatures to become aware of the spiritual reality of the phenomenon God is said to perceive). *Civ.*, XVI.5. The example taken is of God's confrontation of the builders of the Tower of Babel. In the event of the nearly executed sacrifice of Isaac, because it is impossible in Augustine's theology that God should not know or perceive any one thing, God is said to come to know Abraham's obedient faith or see God's provision of a sacrifice in place of that of his son, because God brought about the knowledge of Abraham's obedience both to Abraham himself and to the world, and because God brought about the vision of God in the event of the provision of the ram (*Civ.*, XVI.32). Though God might appear to people in a supernatural way, God never does so directly or immediately but ever indirectly or mediately, through some agent (*Civ.*, XVI.29). See also *Civ.*, XXII.2, in which Augustine also discusses how God's differential response to a formerly righteous person who has fallen into sin in moving from kindness to wrath is analogous to the manner in which the same sun could formerly appear gentle and pleasing and seem to damaged eyes to be overly glaring and a cause of discomfort, inferring that, while God does not actually change in any way, yet the unchanging deity brings it about that sources of immorality or wickedness are remediated in time and space and at scale.

68. Mozley, *Impass.*, pp. 119, 174; Augustine, *Civ.*, IX.5, XII.1-9; Augustine believes that the angels of God are similarly impassible and immune to emotions such as anger, merely carrying out actions which seem to people like acts of vengeance.

interactions in one still, unmoving eternity, completely unaffected by the progression of time. God in eternity does not engage in utterance, which has temporal boundaries marking an onset and a termination, but, whatever God does in eternity, God does wholly and continuously.[69]

John Scotus adds that God's love is manifested not in a direct action but the movement of all things in an active and passive movement of love towards God and towards a unity of all being, while John Calvin asserts that God is represented as loving in order to facilitate these movements.[70]

Furthermore, in the view of Augustine of Hippo, if God is to be spared any form of emotional distress, God has to be incapable of being caught by surprise or moved to act in a manner that breaks God's perfect composure and causes God to act irrationally and against principles.[71] There is only a placid benevolence in God in the knowledge that God brings effective aid to those who may need assistance.[72]

As we can see, Augustine effectively subordinates divine emotionality under divine rationality. Not only is God a different kind of being from humankind but one who dwells in a completely different dimension. Human persons are not to emulate God's serene outlook presumably because the circumstances of divine and human life are antithetical to one another.[73]

In Gregory Thaumaturgus, we have a clear exposition of divine impassibility.[74] God's perfect state is not degraded by God's sufferings for the redemption of the world – conversely, God's blessedness is not added to by any earthly joy. In any divine participation in earthly conditions of abuse and violence, there is no weakening of God's complete self-sufficiency in that God Godself elects to suffer those sufferings for the world.

God is in no way perturbed – subject to passions, that is, emotions that overcome composure and override a person's rational ways of dealing with a matter – by the events of the world even in God's direct experience, in the Son, of such a grievous episode as death. On the contrary, by God's actions in the world whether directly in the Son or indirectly through

---

69. Augustine, *Civ.*, X.12-13. Because the God perceived in time in various forms is not the eternal divine reality, Moses asked to see God in God's true character (Exodus 33:13). *Civ.*, X.15.
70. Mozley, *Impass.*, pp. 109-11, 120-21.
71. Augustine, *Civ.*, XV.25.
72. Mozley, *Impass.*, pp. 104-9.
73. Ibid., p. 108.
74. Ibid., pp. 63-72.

God's ministers, God brings about punishment or moral progress in people.

Since the notion of suffering typically implies some notion of being unwillingly subject to some form of pressure, distress or unpleasant physical sensation, it is not appurtenant to the dignity of God's nature to ascribe to God any manner of suffering in a human sense.

In the estimation of Duns Scotus, God is immoveable and impassible, that is, incapable of being acted upon, simply because it requires a material form to be acted upon, and God is immaterial.[75] To John Gerhard, God is impassible because God is immutable, immortal, infinite, simple and independent.[76]

Divine immateriality is a baffling doctrine which would make little sense except under certain specific conditions. It postulates that God not only has no physical or spiritual form or body but that God's being does not actually have a location anywhere in the universe, that God in a very real sense does not properly or actually exist in the world but rather in a different domain altogether where time does not flow, but everything, all God's reality and experience, is always present in the same way forever.[77] God's proper form is undetectable and imperceptible, because it is the substratum of all being. This structural positing factor of all being we assign to the Divine Nature, in distinction from the entitative Trinity, to which the Divine Nature properly belongs.

In Augustinian theology, God is capable, through an extension of God's reality, of being fully present or absent at any point in space and time.[78] Thomas Aquinas develops this idea by postulating that God's presence does not entail God's substance being attached to the creaturely domain, but rather has reference to God's all-encompassing efficacious and purposeful activity among creatures in the world. As comprehensive as the scope of this determining and influencing divine activity is, necessary because God is existence itself, so God may be said to be omnipresent in 'power', as well as in 'presence', through God's awareness of all that happens everywhere, and 'substance', insofar as this designates only God's causal activity in the world, to bring it about that things exist, that providence is maintained and that the desired knowledge of God is brought as a gift of grace before the human mind desiring to know the one it loves. As much as God is present in all places

75. Ibid., pp. 117-18.
76. Ibid., p. 124.
77. Augustine, *Conf.*, XI.xi.13.
78. Augustine, *Civ.*, I.29.

and in all things, God as the unchanging being is eternity itself, eternity defined (according to Boethius and building on Aristotle's insight into eternity's non-successiveness) in terms of the state of having in one perfectly rich and eternally unchanging moment the fullness of one's whole existence (rather than lastingness) and indivisibility.[79]

This doctrine of a bipartite God bears much in common with a Platonic doctrine of the divine as subsisting as both a Demiurge, the active component of God through which all things come into being, and Living Creature, the archetypal component of God according to which all things are shaped and directed.[80]

Yet, it can hardly be denied that God suffered in Christ. Consequently, the theological doctrine of divine impassibility has to be expounded and defined in terms of God's complete incapacity for being deprived of God's blessed, immutable and incorruptible perfections, in terms of God's inability to undergo any kind of psychological suffering, whether intended or not, and to be thereby extracted from God's eternally blessed state of a more or less peaceful perfection of love and joy. This imperviousness to being subjected to a loss of an eternal happiness is rooted in the idea that God is independent, self-sufficient, transcendent and categorically different in nature from humankind.[81]

Accordingly, while physical deficiency and attendant physical desire, such as hunger leading to the search for food, fatigue resulting in the pursuit of rest, or suffering entailing a physical instinct to avoid it,[82] may be possible in the incarnate Son owing to the Son's physicality, there is no psychological turmoil (Gregory Thaumaturgus) or at least none leading to sin (Gregory of Nyssa) even in all circumstances including these.[83]

In the view of Marshall Randles, a nineteenth-century Methodist theologian, God's perfect and eternal love is not so peaceful as patristic

---

79. Thomas Aquinas, *Summa*, Ia, qs 8-10.

80. Bradshaw, 'Plato in the Cappadocian Fathers', p. 197.

81. Mozley, *Impass.*, pp. 173-74. In contradistinction, those of a dissentient school of thought in regard to the subject of God's impassibility major on scriptural descriptions of God's loving nature, immanence with the processes of nature and human experiences and the Cross as a reflection of God's eternal feelings. Ibid., pp. 175-77.

82. Might we say that this includes sexual tension or desire?

83. This may be juxtaposed to Gregory of Nyssa's theology which, all other things appearing to be equal, seems to admit of psychological distress in Christ, so long as this does not lead towards sin, achieved through a redefinition of passibility as any sense of need or desire to fulfil it which does not urge toward sinful conduct. Mozley, *Impass.*, p. 81.

theologians such as Gregory Thaumaturgus and Augustine of Hippo might maintain.[84] Indeed, in writers such as Horace Bushnell, a nineteenth-century American Congregational theologian, God has suffered as much as Christ did on earth from all eternity.

On the other end of the theological spectrum is Robert Mackintosh, an early twentieth-century writer, who avers that God's simple and unfailing foreknowledge of all future events assures God of hope and happiness even in the interim.

Between Bushnell and Mackintosh would be writers like Maldwyn Hughes in the early twentieth century, for whom God chooses to allow suffering into God's mind from a creation endowed with free will but has a sure grasp of how events in history will unfold with an ultimately optimistic outcome.[85]

St John of Damascus defines passions in terms of wounds and diseases, in the case of the physical body, and desire and anger, in that of the mind, whereby, in the latter respect, a mind is caused to become attracted to some good thing while, on another occasion, it is caused to be repelled by some bad thing both in such a way as to depart from a person's rational ways of dealing with matters.

Given this broader definition, and to the extent that impassibility is identified with the inability to experience passions, technically defined, and not simply equated with an incapacity for suffering, to speak of God as impassible is to attest to God's fundamental inability to be affected whether by good or ill events, to either undergo psychological uplifting or distress, and thereby God's self-sufficiency; in the incarnate Son, there is an allowance for amoral passions including physical[86] and certain types of emotional[87] suffering.[88]

In summary, there are five ways of apprehending the notion of passions and passibility.

The word, 'passion', itself comes from the late Latin word, *passio*,[89] a word which indicates the action of being made to go through pain or distress, being subservient to, being put through some process, being

---

84. Ibid., pp. 167-70.
85. Ibid., pp. 170-72.
86. E.g. hunger, thirst, death.
87. E.g. fear.
88. Mozley, *Impass.*, pp. 99-102; at the beginning of his monograph, on p. 1, Mozley equates the notion of impassibility with the inability to undergo suffering.
89. This, in turn, has its origin in another Latin word, *patī*.

immersed in a situation or set of situations, or patiently coming to terms with or being resigned to difficulties being experienced. Therefore, it designates an act or circumstance in which a person is subject to the action of another, whether externally or internally.[90]

First, there is an Augustinian and Thomistic definition of impassibility in terms of the structure of God's nature as impervious to being affected in any way by the affairs of the universe or even being self-affected; that is, God is ontologically impassible.[91] 'Passionless' emotions fit within this category, insofar as these, whether love, delight, relenting or envy, do not involve God being subjected to the influence of the actions of an agent.[92]

This conception of passion arises from a Platonic notion of fourfold basic human emotionality, namely, desire, fear, joy and sorrow, as 'diseases', 'passions' (Greek, *pathē*), and 'perturbations' (Cicero, who distinguishes from these *perturbationes* three *constantiae*, Greek, *eupatheiai*, namely, will, contentment and caution)[93] originating from the human body, naturally accursed with mortality as it is, being constituted of earth, and infecting the soul, from which arise all human callousness.[94]

These regular affections are, of course, merely movements of the human will either towards or away from the object in which desire,[95] fear,[96] joy[97] or sorrow[98] is concentrated, and are good or evil as the will involved is good or evil, with exemplifications of the former being longing, fear, rejoicing or sorrow related to obtaining and keeping themselves in the hope of the deliverance of God through observing God's laws or avoiding perdition and a life of sinful obsession whether for oneself or others.[99] The Lord himself, according to Augustine, was as a man in possession both of an authentic physical human body as well as an authentic human soul with all its authentic emotionality, and he experienced desire, for the fellowship of his disciples at the last supper, joy, that he was not present at the deathbed of Lazarus in order that he might have opportunity to perform the miracle of delivering his

---

90. Dolezal, 'Strong Impassibility', p. 15.
91. Augustine, *Civ.*, V.8-11.
92. Dolezal, 'Strong Impassibility', p. 17.
93. Augustine, *Civ.* (Dods, trans.), XIV.5, p. 447; Augustine, *Civ.*, XIV.8.
94. Augustine, *Civ.*, XIV.3, 5-7.
95. A seeking to have something it loves.
96. A seeking to depart from something which causes it agony.
97. An enjoying of what it already has and loves.
98. An enduring of what causes it agony.
99. Augustine, *Civ.*, XIV.7, 9.

friend from the state of death, and sorrow, because some people present were self-righteously insouciant regarding the misery of a man with a withered hand in the synagogue amongst them, because Lazarus had died, and because of his own impending death.[100]

For this reason, Augustine was incisive concerning how in a world of sinfulness and attendant agony, *apatheia*, the inability to experience emotions of longing, fear, joy or sorrow, is no virtue at all; indeed, love and joy but not fear or sorrow exist in eternal life. At the same time, he averred that Jesus had entered such a world by choice from a position of power and thereby burdened himself with these dire straits which he could have elected to avoid, seeming therefore to imply that God is exempt from the standards of Crantor, an Academic thinker quoted by Cicero, regarding non-emotionality being not fitting in a world of agony and as a matter of fact a reason for human conceit or a sign of inhumanity, because God being perfect is of philosophical necessity exempt from the ability to undergo change of any sort, including that related to empathy in suffering.[101]

God is truly at peace, having a love and joy mixed with a perfect foresight so that God is not drawn to things which possess some beauty apart from God but only that which has been given by God, nor does God rejoice over things for virtues they inherently possess apart from God but only that with which they have been endued by God. Since God ordains all things, nothing in the world can make God afraid or sorrowful. All the developments and trajectories of the emotions of human beings throughout the history of the world – from the past through the present into the as yet undefined (for us) future – are likewise predestined so that it is impossible that God should be truly sorrowful or even empathetic (in place of which God may hold out the hope that the sufferer more fully understands and embraces the good reason and purpose for their present misery) that anybody is caught in the midst of suffering since, if the omnipotent God so wished, God could very well have ordained that that person does not, or does not continue to, experience that particular episode of sadness in question,[102] but that he does under God's providence

---

100. Ibid., XIV.9.
101. Ibid., fn. 78.
102. E.g. by preventing the fall of humankind, by preventing that of the angels through granting all of these the sufficient gift of perseverance through temptations whether at the point of creation or that of temptation. Cf. ibid., XII.9.

suggests that God has a reason and purport even for that time of sorrow, as well as other negative events.

These accomplish at least four things: present a suitable occasion for God to reveal God's intransigent opposition to evil as well as work for God's liberation and healing of God's creatures, chasten and warn the proud, prove and console the righteous.[103] In addition, God is unafraid about the prospect of some people not finally receiving divine salvation since it was God who elected the chosen and rejected the reprobate in the first place, and this in order only to reveal both God's mercy and righteousness without concealing either by acting only in a manner suggestive of the opposite.[104] If God appears in human history or experience to display a desire or joy that is dependent on human response, or to exhibit any form of fear or sorrow, or change of mind, this is only by appearance, resulting from the provision arranged by divine providence for the comfort of the human soul.[105]

Second, there is a definition, adopted by John of Damascus and John Mozley, which understands passion in terms of emotional disturbance or elation.[106]

Third, there is an Augustinian definition of passion as an irrational, mental perturbation of an immoral quality, a sinful, disordered emotional disorder[107] which gives pride of place to how, with passions, there is a disruption of psychological and rational composure in an immoral way.[108] Augustine was of the view, following Plato (*Republic*, IV), that anger and lust being inclined towards violent excess are in need of regulation by the reason, adding that, antecedent to the fall of Adam, anger and sexual desire were moderate and self-regulated, oriented towards the promotion

---

103. Cf. ibid., XIV.11, 26-27, XV.21.

104. Ibid., XXI.12.

105. Ibid., XIV.11.

106. The capacity for such being termed 'emotional passibility'.

107. The capacity for such being termed 'sinful disordered emotional passibility'.

108. Augustine, *Civ.*, VIII.17; in contrast to human emotional passibility, understood as irrational and immoral deviations of feelings and behaviour, God is master of God's anger, incorruptibly righteous, beyond petty revenge, boundlessly loving and merciful, and friend of redemptive affliction. J.C. Peckham, 'Qualified Passibility', in R. J. Matz and A. C. Thornhill (eds), *Divine Impassibility: Four Views of God's Emotions and Suffering*, Spectrum Multiview (Downers Grove, IL: IVP Academic, 2019), p. 97.

of justice and the reproduction of the human race, the latter activity being carried out without shame.[109]

Fourth, there is a notion, in the thought of theologians such as Gregory Thaumaturgus, of passibility in terms of the ability to alter one's own emotions.[110] Fifth, John of Damascus defines physical passibility in terms of being wounded or diseased.[111]

On the basis of these notions, it seems that the patristic architects of the doctrine of divine impassibility distinguished between experiences proper to the Father and the Son in their eternity[112] and those that may have been proper to the incarnate Son,[113] as well as between physical and emotional passibility or suffering, with some attributing to Christ the ability to suffer only physically[114] or both physically and psychologically but without sin.[115]

While none were inclined to attribute passibility to God *per se*, and many disinclined to ascribe any form of suffering to the Father in any form, theologians could find some place for speaking of the suffering of Christ, in the process of which they drew a distinction between physical suffering, which Christ did indeed suffer, and emotional suffering, which Christ may (e.g. Gregory of Nyssa) or may not (e.g. Gregory Thaumaturgus) have suffered; to the extent that Christ has capacity to suffer emotionally, it may be said that Christ's soul was passible (e.g. Aquinas).[116] Given Damascus' definition of physical passion as wounding, it is necessary to say of Christ's physical body that it was also passible.

Theologians such as Gregory Thaumaturgus, Augustine of Hippo and John of Damascus were also concerned to underscore the purposive control God or Christ had even over physical or emotional suffering as an instrument by which humankind would be cleansed or redeemed through the symbolism (in the case of the Father) or presence (in that of the incarnate Son) of God in suffering.

---

109. Augustine, *Civ.*, XIV.19, 26.
110. The capacity for such being termed 'internal passibility'.
111. Peckham, 'Qualified Passibility', pp. 87, 103.
112. This is where they are conceived as ontologically impassible.
113. This is where he is conceived as not ontologically impassible in the human nature, with the divine still impassible.
114. Physical passibility without emotional passibility in the human nature, with the divine still impassible.
115. Physical passibility with emotional passibility but without sinful disordered emotional passibility in the human nature, with the divine still impassible.
116. Mozley, *Impass.*, pp. 116-17.

As Calvin put it, commenting on Genesis 6:6, the eternal God is certainly 'not sorrowful or sad, but remains for ever like Himself in His celestial and happy repose',[117] while William Temple, of the classical theology school, in his *Christus Veritas* describes God as 'incapable of suffering'.[118]

It is not incorrect to attribute to God a lack of passions insofar as it is presupposed that God is indeed the sovereign and all-determining Lord and ruler of the universe. A problem arises only if and when the idea of God as sovereign is contested, such as by a theological system based on an Asian cultural paradigm. Consequently, a Greek Platonic and Neoplatonic theological system is self-consistent as an unfalsifiable edifice.

In the latter view, God is not susceptible of affect – including time-shaped love, jealousy and hate. God is immune to suffering, learning, willing, regret, form, movement.[119] Nonetheless, God has the disposition, an inclination, if you will, in the presence of particular situations, for change, affect – including time-shaped rather than eternal love, jealousy and hate – suffering, learning, willing, regretting, taking form, moving. God's nature is such that, if God were spatio-temporal, God would love, envy, hate, suffer, learn, will, regret, have form and move.[120]

As such, God is able to experience change, affect, including time-bound love, jealousy and hatred, suffering, and learn, will, regret, and take form in a mediate, proximate, extra-dimensional modality, akin to the Incarnation whereby God assumes an additional mode of existence without relinquishing God's original mode of existence (Bruce Ware and John Frame), where, presumably, God is real to human beings but human beings are not real to God in the sense that God's mediated presence affects the human experience but human existence does not in any way affect God, who is beyond change; this is the case, problematically, also for the Incarnation (Gerhard).[121] This mediated presence is only for the

---

117. This is cited in ibid., p. 120.

118. This is cited in ibid., p. 163.

119. Compare this doctrine with J.I. Packer's revised understanding of divine immutability, in terms of a 'moral consistency', and divine impassibility, construed as the ability to avoid all 'involuntary' suffering, in *NDT*, s.v. 'God' (J.I. Packer, pp. 274-77); 'time-shaped' is a neologism deployed to distinguish between God's divine emotionality in eternity and human feelings, signifying the latter, which, in contrast to the former, is directly situated in a space-time nexus of interactions and relationships.

120. Oei, 'The Impassible God Who "Cried"', pp. 244-47.

121. Dorner, *DI*, art. 2, pp. 100-1.

sake of bringing human beings into a covenant relationship with Godself with a view to leading people towards the vision and embrace of God's eternal bliss, according to Calvin's doctrine of divine accommodation and condescension.[122]

It has been supposed that in traditional doctrine the God who is experienced in time and space is not the God who truly exists in God's eternal nature but merely a projection from atemporal/aspatial infinitude into a temporal/spatial finitude.[123] Consequently, God is not really or actually in a certain location or in all locations, or thinks, feels, learns, decides, acts, responds. On the contrary, the absolute God is simply represented or symbolised in relative terms without ever taking from or affecting God's actual essence. Within its temporal-spatial field of activity, the divine projection is competent at all points in time and space to express and reveal the fullness of this relative expression of divine being (Schleiermacher).[124]

The nineteenth-century German Protestant theologian, Isaak Dorner has observed that this conception of divine immutability, as formulated by Schleiermacher, has implications for the reality of sin and salvation, and the necessity for a redeemer in Christ. To what extent can a person sin against God if God is not affected by the world? Also, to what extent can God save a sinner if God does not really exist in the changing world but only via what may be merely a projection?[125]

---

122. B.A. Ware, 'A Modified Calvinist Doctrine of God', in B.A. Ware (ed.), *Perspectives on the Doctrine of God: Four Views* (Nashville, TN: Broadman & Holman, 2008), p. 89, main text and fn. 22; cf. P. Helm, 'Responses to Bruce A. Ware: Response by Paul Helm', pp. 121-23.

123. To what extent can it be said that God is infinite in God's eternal and transcendent essence? Is such infinity to be taken in a potential or actual sense? If divine infinity is taken in the former sense, it designates God as having power and wisdom capable of being revealed beyond limit; while, if it is understood in the latter sense, it implies some quantitative conception of God's power and wisdom as being of infinite intensity, appearing in the form of glory or brightness of power, so that God's power can very well be said to be actually and not simply potentially infinite, and God's wisdom is infinite in the sense of God knowing that infinite intensity of God's power and thereby being also infinite in quantity. In some way, this is a moot point seeing that infinity cannot exist in practice, but only conceptually, and even then, only negatively, in that one can only say what infinity is not rather than what it actually is.

124. Dorner, *DI*, art. 2, p. 124.

125. Ibid., pp. 128-29.

Perhaps, even if God is not directly affected by sin, sin represents the intent to rebel against God and is therefore wrong even if it does not offend or affect God. As for the necessity for a saviour, even if God is not personally and directly present in the world, the power of salvation emanates from God. All this represents a distinction within a creational idea, an experience of God of all times and places of world history in one eternally continuous present moment, which is real yet nevertheless not indicative of any distinction within God's eternal being, but, rather, a God-conceived storyline and drama involving God and human beings in which God's being is analogically expressed.

The truth of the matter, however, is that the earthly projection of God, while not directly or properly God, is nevertheless truly God, given that the eternal being of God imagines and thus creates and fashions the whole divine-human drama, putting itself emotionally into each act of the narrative. Though existing only as a single simultaneous point gathering all events in history, this drama constitutes a multifaceted emotional-active structure which expresses the detailed content, substance, and spirit of God's eternal blessedness in eternal cognitive-experiential accompaniment by other entities. In time, we see only the separated threads now of God's joy, then of God's disappointment, then of God's disillusionment, then of God's frustration, then of God's anger, then of God's resignation, then of God's sorrow and, finally, of God's hope. We forget the joy, disappointment, disillusionment, frustration, anger, resignation, sorrow, then the hope, or we might have some recollection of them, and yet the present experience once it has faded is forever gone. In eternity, God experiences the joy, disappointment, disillusionment, frustration, anger, resignation, sorrow and hope all at once and in a continuous manner.

The joy, disappointment, disillusionment, frustration, anger, resignation, sorrow and hope are facets of God's blessed love, who is glad not because there are no troubles or anguish, but solely because God truly cherishes the human other and selflessly desires only its highest good, delighting thereby in each person as God's own child, though he may disappoint, resist, or even oppose and hate. The conventionally negative emotions of disappointment, disillusionment, frustration, anger, resignation and sorrow are always tempered and bracketed by the sustaining positive emotions of the joy of creation and the hope of repentance. God has time and grants God's creatures the gift of time.

Consequently, God, because of God's relation to creation, is not merely monolithically or flatly joyful or blissful even in eternity, but feels always the strong pull, passion and sentiment of love in constantly experiencing the complete flow of world history with its full range of emotions. In eternity God relates authentically in an emotional way to all moments in time at once and therefore also to each individual moment and person. As such, God is not actually without emotions or unable to really interact with human beings in time and space. God does relate authentically but is not limited to a specific point in time but referred to every event all at once. We may experience God as relating to a specific moment and person but, in fact, God relates to every moment. This body of constant and sublime experience also includes God's experiences and interactions with Godself within the Trinity both in the world and before and after it. All events and emotions are from God and ultimately determined by God.

God is therefore disposed to feeling emotions in time but not thereby indisposed to feeling any of them in eternity, only that the domain of eternity collects all that is in the temporal realm and for that reason disposes for the latter. God in time is no mere mediator or projection of an actual reality, but a slice of the immense eternal divine experience which gathers up the googolplex events, moments and emotions in world history in one continuous, unchanging, indivisible and endless moment. God's decreed experience of all of time in a simultaneous way is the effective cause of any event, emotion or experience in time. This is how I understand Barth's reinterpretation of the classical doctrine of divine immutability with respect to eternity and time, in which the concept of timelessness is jettisoned in favour of a still unchanging divine experience, yet one filled with all manner of engagement and interaction in worldly settings.[126]

Although creation as subject to and characterised by 'plurality, process, change, contingency' is fundamentally different from God, creation need not be simply grounded in God's nature (Aquinas), which leads to acosmism, a pantheism in which the world is simply God's illusory projection of Godself in terms of worldly attributes, or God's will (Duns Scotus), which means that there is no more epistemological connection leading from the world to the knowledge of God.[127]

Instead, creation, which is not eternal,[128] is brought about by and reflective of the free goodness of God,[129] through an eternal will or

---

126. Barth, *CD* II.1, §31.3, pp. 612-13.
127. Dorner, *DI*, art. 2, pp. 95-99.
128. Augustine, *Civ.*, XII.16.
129. Ibid., XII.17.

decree (Schleiermacher)[130] in a concrete expression in time and space of an eternal idea (Gerhard and Quenstedt),[131] which incorporates the ability to develop or evolve in a chronologically sequential manner, as determined by eternal divine decree (Schleiermacher).[132]

In the theology of Thomas Aquinas, creation can be conceived as an analogical image of God's nature, in which God's interpenetrating and infinite attributes and perfect or pure act are separated, made finite and reduced to a temporal process. This involves the realisation of the form of matter through primary[133] and intermediate agencies, and yet the attributes and act contain within their separate, finite and temporal natures conceptual-logical-peripheral intimations rather than a direct sensible experience of an overcoming of such separation and finitude, expressed in the reality and knowledge of God.[134] For Aquinas, the creature is to God as an effect is to a cause, a partial realisation to what is completely actual, without potentiality as yet unactualised. Every creature bears a likeness to God and is a sign and symbol of the divine, because every feature that makes a creature complete can be traced to a unity of the all-comprehending consummation of these qualities in God.[135] As a matter of fact, God cannot properly be said to be related to creatures, only creatures to God, since God subsists in a dimension completely distinct from that in which creatures subsist.[136]

---

130. Dorner, *DI*, art. 2, p. 124; Augustine, *Civ.*, XII.14.
131. Dorner, *DI*, art. 2, p. 102.
132. Ibid., pp. 124-25.
133. I.e. God as the origin, archetype and end of all goodness, or the inherent worth, attractiveness or usefulness of all things, granting each thing its existence, properties and the ability to attain its specific goal.
134. Thomas Aquinas, *Summa*, Ia, q. 3, art. 7, q. 4, arts 1-2, q. 5, art. 2, q. 6, arts 1-4. Cf. Dorner's criticism of the ostensible lack of reality in creational distinctions posited in Schleiermacher's articulation of the classical doctrine of divine immutability, *DI*, art. 2, pp. 125-27.
135. We can imagine, therefore, a two-way cycle affording the knowledge of God, in which the divine is accessed through the perfection of creaturely morality and, once that is in place, the divine is contemplated so as to emulate it. While the second step may not be precisely possible in an atheistic worldview, in that there is no personal deity which reflects the perfections of creaturely moral attributes, human morality is nevertheless still gathered up in an ultimate principle governing human existence in the form of a rule to which the enlightened human person adheres strictly.
136. Thomas Aquinas, *Summa*, Ia, q. 12, art. 1, q. 13.

Divine omniscience as an attribute is not capable of division between eternal and temporal realms. For while it may be possible to insulate God's eternal immutability from the dynamic realm of creatures, and posit a dynamic, mediated form of God's existence in the creaturely domain without compromising either aspect, this cannot be done with the extent of God's knowledge of the affairs of the world. God either knows everything, whether it be within the Godhead or within the creaturely domain, or God does not know everything, because God does not know all that goes on in the creaturely sphere.

It is not possible for God to be omniscient in the eternal realm and, at the same time, possess limited knowledge in the creaturely realm – as certain scriptures seem to suggest (i.e. Genesis 18:17-21) – unless one postulates that the mediate form of God's existence either pretends not to have full knowledge of all the goings-on in the world, the eternal form of divine existence, although in possession of all knowledge, is unable to communicate this knowledge to the mediate form (giving rise to a mediate existence that does not know everything, resulting in a split within the divine nature), or this form of divine existence does not really arise from the eternal mode, considering that there is no correspondence or consistency between the nature and extent of God's knowledge in the eternal realm and in the creaturely domain.

For God to remain omnipotent, and for the theory about divine inclinations expressing themselves in space-time to work, God needs not only to be all-knowing in the eternal realm, but also needs to have the spatio-temporal equivalent of eternal omniscience, which is knowledge of all affairs in the world.

In other words, the divine essence remains what it always is in its simplicity and imperturbable nature, yet the outflow of this essence in the created realm vibrantly manifests the dynamics of the divine nature in time and space towards human beings in covenant with God. Divine impassibility is an important quality because this being's will is completely grounded in this being's internal choice and decision and not affected in its substance or resolve by any external circumstance. This being is properly the Father, represented by the Son, Jesus, and works through the Spirit in the world, with different versions of the Trinity, ranging from constructs where Jesus is ontologically divine to ones where Jesus is merely a functionary of God.

As a specific example of a Western theological deepening of scriptural attestation, we turn to Bruce Ware's glossing of passages such as Psalm 102:25-27, Malachi 3:6, and James 1:17, which deal, respectively, with God's everlasting nature, God's permanent covenantal commitment to God's people and the incorruptibility of God's love and goodness, in terms not just of an ethical immutability but also an ontological immutability.[137] While scriptures such as 1 Timothy 1:17 do indeed describe God as a being dwelling in an inaccessible quality of glorious brightness, this comes short of a full-fledged and express affirmation regarding God's atemporal or timeless eternal nature, and simply depicts God as Son as surrounded in a heaven of heavens by blinding light in the presence of splendid angels. Another instance of allowing prior philosophical commitments to guide one's theologisation from the Scriptures can be found in the work of W. Bingham Hunter, who adduces Numbers 23:19 and 1 Samuel 15:29 in support of his contention that God is incapable of having a change of heart.

These passages, as John Sanders has correctly noted, only go as far as to intimate, in a manner reminiscent of a vow, that God has determined in the specific scenarios indicated in those places, namely, that God has resolved to bless rather than curse Israel[138] and that God has rejected King Saul in favour of another king.[139]

Not all Western theology has taken an Augustinian approach to God's nature, with modern thinkers such as Wolfhart Pannenberg and Jürgen Moltmann having sought to revise the understanding of God as immutable[140] and impassible.[141]

In contradistinction to historically important emphases in a Western theological conception, with an Asian evolution of the doctrine of God, there will be a focus on the primacy of relationality and process, whereby a development of the facet of the doctrine of God which underscores God's nature as love, as community, and God as active in and capable of being affected by the worldly sphere brings it about that God becomes a being that is intensely relational, relatable and accommodating, as opposed to occupying a categorically different dimension often thought to render God fundamentally inaccessible, aloof and transcendent.

It will be observed that in each of these traditional developments of the one scriptural doctrine of God, an aspect of the doctrine will be more

---

137. Ware, 'A Modified Calvinist Doctrine of God', pp. 90-91.
138. The case being Numbers 23:19.
139. The case being 1 Samuel 15:29; Sanders, 'Historical Considerations', p. 95.
140. According to Pannenberg, God's deity, which depends on the effective governance of humankind, is in principle subject to risk of being undermined in the event that the worship of God is not comprehensively adopted among people.
141. According to Moltmann, God suffers with the crucified Christ.

developed than others. In the case of a historical Western articulation, divine transcendence will be prioritised above the areas of God as love, community, active and affected, while, in an Asian formulation, the neglected dimensions will take precedence over those emphasised in a historical Western construction. It is the burden of each cultural theological construction to explicate the way in which their articulation does not run counter to facets less attended to. Consequently, a Western theology of God might adjust its transcendent doctrine by adding a second dimension of God's consciousness which allows for God's activity and emotions, while an Asian theology might modify its immanent doctrine of God by re-expressing transcendence in terms of a boundlessness of God's love, mercy, compassion, empathy, justice and goodness.

Cultural modalities are also allowed to pursue different directions according to their distinctive concerns and interests not adequately, if at all, covered by the essence of the doctrine formed on the premise of explicit scriptural indications, illuminating those areas from their native frameworks in ways that are not contrary to the explicit affirmations of Scripture. Therefore, in the Asian theology of Jung Young Lee, God is conceived as a cosmological pattern and complementary logic as much as a living entity, whereby God is present in every relationship, to God, self, human others, fauna and flora and the rest of the world, assuming the relational position of each party invisibly behind that party and relating with other parties invisibly behind them.[142] Such a conception is not expressly forbidden by Scripture and thus it is permissible.

The recognition of the cultural relativity of the Scriptures should not preclude a straightforward interpretation of objective events recorded in the text. For instance, the Old Testament depicts God as actively working in the world, sometimes quite dramatically, as in the liberation of Israel from Egypt, while the New Testament has reference to God as dwelling in inaccessible light and the Son as sustaining the universe by mighty speech.

A Christian theology that recognises cultural relativity should not prevent a theologian from accepting the account of the exodus as an objective report, albeit possibly with some embellishment, of what actually transpired supernaturally, or espousing the view that God is mysterious beyond full human comprehension and Christ is an eternal Son and God who authoritatively decreed the coming to being and development of the material universe through the immense power of angels.

---

142. Chua, 'Jung Young Lee's Biblical-Cultural Trinity: A Systematic Theology from East Asia'.

It may, however, be necessary to limit the scope of the application of such ideas by clarifying that God, while occasionally and in specific instances sovereign through the power of angels, is not always sovereign, that God, while forever incapable of being fully apprehended, is in many ways intelligible and comprehensible, and that the Son, though able to announce a decree of creation, is nevertheless not almighty but works through angels imperfectly in the world.

Expressions of Cultural Influence on Specific Skeins of Christian Theology

Seeking an affinity between the Bible and culture and religion generates relevance in theology for particular people groups. Additionally, a culture or religion may possess a certain outlook which subserves the theological interpretation of the Bible, lending further specificity, in a culturally meaningful way, to what the Scriptures are comfortable asserting about God.

This has happened in the case of Jung Young Lee, who studied the Asian concerns embodied in the ancient Chinese text, the *Book of Changes*, and took these questions and metaphysical governing assumptions to his reading of the Bible, allowing the philosophy of the *Book of Changes* to specify biblical teaching in areas of cultural relevance and interest.[143]

An Asian cultural text such as the *Book of Changes* may underscore the importance of attending to the dynamic nature of all things in the universe. Such an outlook would suggest a possible conception of the God mentioned in the Bible in terms of change, movement and interaction as opposed to a divine being dwelling in a dimensionally different eternity. The philosophical system based on the *Book of Changes* could also suggest a way of conceiving of the Christian God, not so much in terms of being infinite, transcendent and inaccessible, but finite, immanent and accessible.

The *Book of Changes* is able to promote a Christian theology which prioritises affinity between God and the rest of the existent order. The metaphysics of yin and yang and of change that came to be associated with the classical Asian text conceptualises the ultimate principle in terms of dynamism in interplay and complementarity. Pegged to a Christian doctrine of God, as in Lee's system, God is redefined as the cosmological pattern at the heart of the universe, dynamic in itself and its relationality with each entity both directly and through each other

---

143. Cf. ibid.

entity, revealing itself as the relational model and paradigm for every entity.[144] Accordingly, an Asian theological approach centred on the insights of the *Book of Changes* is capable of paving the way towards an interfaith approach to Christian theology.

The complementary system which evolved out of the *Book of Changes*, with its exposition of the principles of yin and yang as paradigms for the roles played not only by natural elements such as the day/sun and night/moon but men and women in society and the wider world, serves also to emphasise the need for different actors to fulfil their particular functions, duties and responsibilities relative to each other to promote the common good. This conception of the parts of a greater whole working together for a common purpose is able to throw light on the distinct responsibilities of human beings and God in the biblical story without overstating the divine role in the economy of salvation.

As an example from a non-Christian religious tradition, a Hindu understanding of the Christian God and faith might emphasise an intellectual and spiritual movement away from temporal and carnal interests towards true selfhood in God, shedding light on the dimension of self-identity in the individual's progress from sin to salvation, in contradistinction to a conception which prioritises character and behavioural modification and transformation.

In all these cases, we are dealing with matters which the Bible does not define exhaustively.

With regard to the nature of God, Scripture does not exactly articulate whether God is to be thought of primarily as a changing or unchanging being or both in equal degree. The Bible does not fail to depict God as faithful and unchanging with respect to God's purposes. At the same time, Scripture is clear that God is able to interact with people. However, it does not elaborate on whether this is a direct interaction, in which case God would be a changing entity, or an indirect interaction, in which case God would be an unchanging being.

Furthermore, the Bible represents God as occasionally changing God's mind on how best to deal with a community,[145] but leaves unaddressed the question of whether this represents a genuine change in God's attitude towards human beings, in which case God is capable of change, or merely portrays a phlegmatic and cold working out of one

---

144. Ibid.
145. Examples cited of this include the world in the time of Noah; Israel in the time of Moses at the incident of the golden calf; Assyria in the time of Jonah.

of multiple possible decisions taken because of the specific presenting circumstances, perhaps with complete certainty from the beginning that events would pan out in the way they have.

A historical Western theological framework would be inclined to the notion of God as dwelling primarily and properly in an inaccessible realm transcendent to our own and, within that sphere, completely incapable of any form of shift or change and therefore direct and genuine interaction, relying for God's dealings with human beings on any number of mediators, including, quite possibly, an accommodated mode of divine existence and presence in the ever-changing spatio-temporal domain, such as the incarnate Son and perhaps an accommodated Father and Holy Spirit, or angels. This is a theology of an unmoved mover as opposed to one of a moved mover.

A theology based on the *Book of Changes* might rule in favour of God as directly interacting with humanity in an authentic manner whereby human beings possess true freedom to make their own decisions which God is able to some extent to anticipate but unable always to prevent and as compelled to adjust God's response to human beings in accordance with their response to God. Here we find a moved mover theology, in which God though Creator is able to be affected by God's creatures, as opposed to an unmoved mover theology.

Relating to the issue of whether God is essentially infinite and transcendent or finite and immanent, the Scriptures do not rule definitively or authoritatively on this matter. On one hand, the biblical God is presented as dwelling in inaccessible light and, on the other, God is also portrayed as having come to human beings in their own fleshly mode. Because of this, a historical Western approach would propose that God be understood as transcendent, infinite and inaccessible in God's true nature; while an approach guided by the *Book of Changes* would have a predilection for a conception of God as immanent, finite and accessible.[146] There is, therefore, a transcendent God theology in a historical Western theology as opposed to an immanent God theology inspired by the philosophy of the *Book of Changes*.

Concerning the affinity and difference between God and the rest of the order of entities, once more, Scripture does not rule definitively on the question. Although the Bible is clear that God is set apart from the rest of the universe by the fact that God alone is the Creator, it is quick to add that humankind, out of all entities in the world, was created in the divine image.

---

146. Augustine, *Conf.*, XIII.xi.12, in which Augustine speaks of the divine persons as boundless.

In a Greek philosophical conception and a historical Western theological framework influenced and shaped by it, God is the transcendent subject of God's revelation through the dogmatic teachings of the Church, and the dogmatic teachings of the Church are fully constitutive of God's special revelation to humankind through the Church.

Although the Bible does say that God bestows wisdom on God's people to see and know the truth about God's faithfulness and the ends of those who are righteous and who do evil,[147] and God the Father is the source of all knowledge about God the Son,[148] there is no implication that such knowledge is only obtained through a participation in divine wisdom and non-transferable to a human mind.[149] If such direct participation and non-transferability were the case, there would be no possibility of such knowledge being inexhaustive, incomplete, uncomprehensive or in any other way imperfect or inadequate. Yet, God does not privilege any human being with such definitive knowledge about Godself.

It remains to be explicated how theological exclusivism could lead to the idea that divine revelation is exhaustive and impatient of being complemented by religious teachings found in other cultures. Theological exclusivism supposes that God specially favours one religious community above all others and grants God's full and exhaustive revelation to that one community rather than the others.

This arises from a possibly unconscious emulation of God who in a historical Greek-Western conception assumes the form of a supreme being with complete mastery of the reality around itself. The dominant key here is difference and superiority, a difference of superiority, what has been called 'transcendent otherness'.[150] Similarly, the Church fancies itself a master – better, mistress – of the religious world through a special dispensation of the supreme ruler of the universe. This leads to the interpretation of seemingly exclusivist passages in simplistic terms, engendering a theory of God's selection of a limited number of people and consequent rejection of the rest.

In an Asian worldview, God as the cosmological source and model of the dynamic and ever-changing universe is fully integrated in the worldly domain. Rather than a supreme being who stands above the rest of reality, God is defined by God's relationality and sociality as a fellow sojourner, crusader and sufferer along with the rest of the universe.[151]

---

147. Psalm 36:9.
148. Matthew 11:25-30.
149. Compare with Augustine, *Conf.*, XIII.iv.5, fn. 6.
150. Ware, 'A Modified Calvinist Doctrine of God', pp. 76-78.
151. *Pace* Oei, 'The Impassible God Who "Cried"'.

Indeed, God can be found in any and every place, person, culture and teaching. The operating principle is affinity and equality, an affinity of equality. In this regard, the seemingly exclusive passages of the Bible, especially in the New Testament, are to be regarded as designating the message and vocation specially adapted to the Christian community with its particular inclinations, aspirations and needs, without the strong implication that similar, yet also different, messages and vocations might not be specially adapted in other times and places to the peculiar inclinations, aspirations and needs of other religious communities.

It is granted and it cannot be gainsaid that the New Testament comes down hard on religious idolatry. Nonetheless, it is unnecessary to assume that these criticisms apply to any but a maximal distortion of non-Christian religious faiths of the apostolic age from an authentic connection with spiritual deities, through the use of figures/figurines as symbols of unseen qualities and indications of presence rather than as equivalents of the deity in question, into a magical manipulation of and fixation upon material figures and figurines for selfish reasons and without any real intent of seeking to know what these religious figures might represent.[152]

As Wolfhart Pannenberg has incisively observed, biblical religion does not repudiate the existence of other gods. In point of fact, the conception of Yahweh itself owes something to pre-existing notions of the gods of the surrounding communities and peoples and the attributes of these deities. For instance, Yahweh is understood in intimate relation with El, a Canaanite god responsible for creation, Ahura Mazda of the Persians, the supreme god and creator,[153] and Baal, a Canaanite god of fertility.[154] This is a salient angle to bear in mind and capitalise on in an interfaith theological evolution, development and construction, strongly implying as it does that the revelation of God to all cultures is one, though differently perceived, and the gaping need for each religious community to come to terms with the fact that no one religious tradition is sufficient for a complete understanding of God and that all need to learn of one another, in as appreciative and respectful a manner as possible.

With respect to the human and divine role in the economy of salvation, Christian Scripture is reticent about whether the faith of the believer – that is, the believer's openness to dependence on or reception of that which God freely and graciously does for and through the believer in

---

152. See Pannenberg, *ST* 1, 3.4, pp. 178-87.
153. Ezra 5:11; 6:9-10; 7:12ff.
154. Pannenberg, *ST* 1, 3.4, p. 179.

saving and liberating them from the sinful principles which hold them captive[155] – or the volition, will, determination and resolve of the believer is more basic to a successful moral life[156] or whether both aspects are just as important.

Treating the possible implications for scriptural interpretation of a historical Western theological paradigm in relation to this subject, it may be that Western theologians in a historical orthodox school of thought prefer to conceptualise God as an absolute sovereign, exclusively responsible for the fact that any Christian believer is brought from a state of sin and non-salvation into one of holiness and salvation, and that the believer is only ostensibly or at most secondarily active in pursuing their own salvation. This is a sovereign God as opposed to an invitational God theology.[157]

As for a theology erected on the premises of the *Book of Changes*, this might cast its lot in with an exposition which privileges the joint responsibility of God and humanity in the actualisation of salvation, in which humans are fully capable of making, and called upon to make, a decision to embrace all that God has provided for their salvation in the way of appropriating the blessing of the atonement of Christ. This is an invitational God as opposed to a sovereign God theology.

Hence, a cultural theology is free to develop the conception of God in any one of these directions in its attempt to form a self-consistent and externally harmonious system.

With respect to the nature of the movement from sin to salvation, Scripture again does not take a firm stand on whether spiritual and moral progress should be predominantly understood as epistemological (knowledge-based) or pragmatic (action-based) in nature or both to an equal extent. Scripture does highlight the need for Christian believers to act upon their faith convictions regarding the people God has called them to be, as well as draw attention to the way in which believers are to understand themselves as having their identities fused with Christ in his death and resurrection.

Accordingly, a historical Western theological interpretation of the theological signification of Scripture might develop a formulation of the doctrine of sin and salvation which primarily explores and accentuates the positive, practical impact of a Christian faith on moral behaviour, both in the inward thought life and outward conduct. This is a works-primary as opposed to a faith-primary theology.

---

155. A major theme in the Pauline writings.
156. A major theme in James and First John.
157. Helm, 'Classical Calvinist Doctrine of God', pp. 49-50.

As for a theological interpretation of Scripture based on insights from Hindu religion, there might be a focus on how the behaviour of the believer is driven, shaped and transformed by an increase in his awareness and knowledge of who he already and actually is in Christ.

A case in point is the distinctive theology of Singapore megachurch pastor, Joseph Prince, formerly Xenonamandar Jegahusiee Singh, a Chinese-Indian, whose father was a Sikh priest. Prince's theology is emphatic about the spiritual identity of the Christian believer as a child of God deemed forever and unconditionally righteous before God from the point of conversion and the power of Christian self-identity to counter addiction to pornography, alcohol, nicotine and drugs, as well as a negative self-concept.[158]

To be sure, Prince does not explicitly assert an Indian religious root undergirding his theology, and there is no attempt on my part to suggest that he is mixing religions, only that perhaps his personal background may have contributed to his peculiar emphasis on Christian self-knowledge and self-identity as a means of overcoming the psychological roots, in a low self-esteem and sense of personal unworthiness, of unhelpful thoughts, feelings and behaviour. Such teaching has borne fruit, predominantly because it squarely addresses and attempts to resolve a contributing factor in physical and mental health issues such as depression, anxiety, smoking tobacco, alcohol abuse and drug use.[159] Because of his central concern, theological emphasis and ethical methodology, Prince tends to say less about the direct actions a believer should take.

We can christen this type of theological modality a faith-primary as opposed to a works-primary theology.

These are just some of the ways in which a Christian theology might be developed on the basis of differing philosophical and religious frameworks.

In light of the foregoing, it might be useful and accurate to designate a systematic theology based on a culture or religious system as a

158. Koorong, 'Joseph Prince', Koorong Books, accessed 30 May 2022, https://www.koorong.com/meet-the-author/joseph-prince; J. Prince, 'Receive Two Gifts to Reign Over Addictions', three parts, accessed 8 June 2022, beginning at: https://blog.josephprince.com/two-gifts-to-reign-over-addictions; cf. idem, *Destined to Reign: The Secret to Effortless Success, Wholeness and Victorious Living* (Tulsa, OK: Harrison, 2007).
159. WebMD Editorial Contributors, 'Signs of Low Self-Esteem', *WebMD*, last reviewed 16 December 2022, https://www.webmd.com/mental-health/signs-low-self-esteem.

cultural-guided or religious-guided Christian systematic theology, to give, for instance, an Asian cultural-guided Christian systematic theology or a Hindu-guided Christian systematic theology, because culture or religion serves as a guide to a more specific conception of biblical teaching on the various aspects of a polyvalent Christian theology. All such variations of a Christian systematic theology may be unified in a coherent system known as a global Christian systematic theology, which encourages and offers an olive branch to other versions of a global systematic theology, such as a global Islamic systematic theology, a global Hindu systematic theology, a global Buddhist systematic philosophy or a global humanist systematic philosophy.

Members of different cultural and religious groups should not be afraid to theologise from their cultural predilections, emphases, inclinations and preferences as enshrined in their classical cultural texts. As we do so, however, we shall need to be aware of how our thinking, foci and priorities, as wired by our integration within our respective communities, may influence the way we interpret Scripture and what it says about God's purposes for humanity and the world. This is so that we may act to ensure that whatever doctrine we may formulate will be balanced rather than lopsided in its emphases.

While each cultural and religious tradition will have its blind spots, with a countercultural critique whereby a cultural and religious systematic theology subjects itself to scrutiny by other cultural and religious systematic theologies, it is possible to attain to a fairly high level of accuracy of a holistic, conceptual articulation of the biblical witness.

It will be observed that, in many instances, each cultural and religious tradition contributes an essential angle to the debate, and the key is to be able in some way to hold together complementary perspectives in creative tension. Let us consider what this could mean in each of the examples earlier cited.

In the case of whether the biblical God is to be thought of as an unchanging or changing being, an attempt at a synthesis from the direction of a historical Western theological framework could venture to re-conceive an unchanging God as translating God's existence from a non-temporal into a temporal state, while one from the direction of a paradigm guided by the *Book of Changes* could articulate a changing God as in possession of unchanging and perfect attributes.

As another example of an intercultural theological critique, the theories of divine infinity in historical Western theology[160] and apophaticism

---

160. WCF 2.1.

in Eastern theology emphasise the vastness of God and how God ontologically grounds all of reality. The insights of these theologies are not to be treated lightly. On the other hand, Asian theology will underscore God's this-worldliness. A synthesis attempted on the side of a historical Western rationalism might formulate a view of God as being infinite in nature but having in some authentic way accommodated Godself to human understanding. As for a synthesis ventured from the direction of the *Book of Changes*, this might be one in which God is hypothesised not so much as an infinite or unknowable being[161] but as a being whose good nature can never be fully manifested.

Apropos the question of the extent to which the Christian God is to be apprehended as fully responsible for the salvation of humankind, as opposed to being only partly responsible for the same, a bid to reconcile these contrasting perspectives on the part of a historical Western theological paradigm might fathom God as the ultimate authority behind the economy of salvation but not without a human contribution in the form of an authentication of what has been decided in advance by God. In contrast, a *Book of Changes*-inspired synthesis could begin from the standpoint that God and humans cooperate in the work of salvation and yet also grant that it is God from whom the design of human nature and morality comes, as well as moral scruples which endlessly lead towards the splendid vision of humanity.

Regarding the issue of the degree to which the salvation to which God brings humankind is to be grasped as being moral rather than epistemological in nature, a historical Western theological system could attempt a reconciliation of different viewpoints by means of a theory concerning how salvation consists primarily in moral change and action, and yet that this moral transformation comes about through a prominent emphasis on a growing consciousness of God's own moral nature and the fact that this divine moral nature constitutes the vision for human morality. As to the contribution a Hindu-guided construal of biblical theology might make to this topic in the form of a synthesis, this might well take the shape of a proposition regarding the centrality of a human self-identity anchored in God in Christ, yet which is maintained, strengthened, endorsed and confirmed by each good, proper and right moral act.

Some may worry that a Christian theology which is accepting of other religious traditions could be in danger of syncretism. The idea of a syncretism or a mixing of beliefs from different religious traditions

---

161. This may be so for the Divine Nature alone but not also the Trinity.

typically carries a negative connotation for mainstream Christians such as evangelicals. The approach we are propounding is not innocent of any attempt to bring insights from other religious faiths into theological discussion and even construction; it is, therefore, more akin to an assimilation, to use Newman's chosen term for the development of Christian doctrine via taking on board material from the surrounding philosophical milieux.[162]

Be that as it may, this is not so as to erode the biblical foundation, seeing that other religious and cultural traditions function merely as inspirations to further guide theological interpretation of the Bible rather than supplant the primary and decisive role of the latter. One should not be blind to the fact that Christian theology throughout its history has consistently accommodated insights from other religions and philosophies.[163]

---

162. Newman, *DCD*, pp. 73-77.
163. Cf. a test for syncretism by determining whether a religious reconstruction changes the tradition at large to a considerable degree or causes it to become something its adherents can no longer identify as the particular religious tradition in question. H. Gustafson, 'Is Transreligious Theology Unavoidable in Interreligious Theology and Dialogue?' *OT* 2, no. 1 (2016), p. 258.

Chapter 4

Foundations II: Faith, Scripture, Tradition and Reason

What is it that unites the Christian Church as a diverse set of communities?

The Christian faith is more than a moral code, philosophy and cult. According to Thomas Merton (1915-68), a Trappist monk, introducing and interpreting the theology of Augustine of Hippo as expressed in *De civitate Dei*, Christianity is the experience and expression of the life of Christ in its self-denying and selflessly loving nature. It is a reconstitution of humanity in its original design as a community of persons whose constant knowledge and unchanging treasure is God, and whose goal for action is divine love for God and one another for God's sake, God serving as the source of and reason for a communal unity of selfless affection. Such a life pursues God as the highest good and employs other things to that end. Its vision is set over against the pursuit of selfish interests as the highest good, in which God is seen as dispensable and only embraced insofar as God is able to fit a self-centred agenda. Such a vision necessarily forces people apart as mutual competitors and mutually suspicious players in an endless game of success.[1]

With this overview in mind, I should like to suggest that the grand themes of the fall of humankind and the atonement of Jesus both express the main emphases of Augustine's exposition of the Christian faith and unite Christianity as a global religion.

---

1. T. Merton, Introduction to Augustine, *The City of God*, trans. Marcus Dods (New York, NY: Random House, 1993), pp. xi-xvii.

The Fall and the Atonement

The Father through the Holy Spirit created the universe as a gift to the Son in that the Father, Son and Spirit created and sustain the world through angels for the sake of the Son. In practice, this means that God the Father, Son and Holy Spirit jointly formed the universe as it currently exists by approving of the Son's authorising of the angels to generate, maintain and develop the material principles of the universe.[2] In this way, the universe attained its present form, with all its components, the sun, moon and stars, the sky, the seas, the land and vegetation, birds and fishes, land animals and reptiles, and human beings, as well as every other creature that is not named. God blessed or commanded the plants, animals and humankind to reproduce and fill their respective domains. To human beings, God gave the mandate to rule over the world.

God breathed God's Spirit into the first human being, Adam, planted a garden, Eden, and left Adam to till the crops. God made many beautiful fruit-bearing trees, including the tree of life and the tree of the knowledge of good and evil. God caused a river to flow out of Eden and split into four different rivers. God saw that Adam could not find a companion among the animals and so God created a woman, Eve, out of a rib from Adam's side, and they became a couple. Before creating Eve, God gave Adam the permission to eat the fruit of any tree in the garden, except that of the tree of knowledge of good and evil, because, if he did, he would die.

Then, one day, while Eve was walking around the lush and green garden which was named paradise, a devious serpent, whom Augustine believed to be the devil in masquerade, seeking out of envy to cause humanity to be deposed from the good graces of God just as the devil had been[3] – whose own fall took place as a result of its not having been endued by God with a sufficient gift of perseverance in the face of temptation, whether at the point of creation or temptation[4] – emerged

---

2. Cf. Augustine, *Civ.*, XI.9, fn. 21, in which Dods cites Vives' observation to the effect that Plato, the Greek theologians and Jerome all espoused the view that God made spiritual beings first and then had them bring into existence the material world, in contradistinction to the perspective of the Latin theologians and St Basil of Caesarea that God alone created all things directly in simultaneous fashion. John 1:3, Hebrews 1:3.

3. Augustine, *Civ.*, XIV.11.

4. Augustine, *Civ.*, XII.9.

and questioned her regarding God's prohibition against consuming the fruit of the trees in the garden.

The serpent asked Eve whether God had indeed forbidden them from eating the fruit of any tree in the garden. She retorted that God allowed them to eat the fruit of any tree in the garden, with the exception of the tree of the knowledge of good and evil, because if they did so, they would be in danger of death.

Then the serpent went on to suggest that it was not a foregone conclusion that they would die from eating the fruit, rather that God denied them the fruit from that particular tree simply because it was actually good for them, in that their eyes would be opened and they would become like God, knowing good and evil.

Eve believed the serpent's lies, coveted the fruit of the tree for its supposed benefits, thinking it would make her wise, and ate it. She also handed some to Adam and he ate it. The primal couple's coveting of the fruit was guided by the seduction of the serpent, beginning as a purely intellectual exercise, a toying with possibilities.[5] When, however, neither husband nor wife restrained themselves and permitted the prohibited thought to remain and bear fruit, the rapacity was confirmed and started distorting their emotions, engendering the fall of humanity. So Adam and Eve ate the fruit, and their eyes were indeed opened, they realised they were naked, and they made loincloths for themselves out of fig leaves.[6]

---

5. Cf. N.T. Wright describes these possibilities as pretexts, *Evil and the Justice of God* (Downers Grove, IL: IVP, 2006), p. 51.

6. Augustine poignantly discussed the nature of the shame with which humankind was cloaked in just punishment of their Edenic transgression, where: in seeking independence of God, humankind was instead enslaved to sinful and sexual passions (*Civ.*, XIV.15); in seeking to satiate themselves, humankind was instead condemned to discontentment (*Civ.*, XIV.15); in refusing allegiance to God, human beings found themselves in a state in which allegiance was refused to their soul by their unruly emotions and sensual desires (*Civ.*, XIV.15); in seeking to become more than human through turning to themselves, human beings which were destined for participation in divine glory instead received humiliation (*Civ.*, XIV.13), the soul being more noble than the physical body yet being controlled by the physical body (*Civ.*, XIV.23).

In this way, their moral condition degenerated by means of the following sequence of thoughts: temptation by the serpent;[7] cognitive consideration on the part of the couple;[8] surfacing of doubt about the temptation;[9] extended contemplation;[10] further assault on the part of the serpent;[11] further consideration;[12] final attack;[13] final decision.[14]

While it was a grievous sin for the first couple to distrust God, covet what God has forbidden and seek to become like God in God's wisdom, and foolish, considering that, as opposed to what the serpent promised, human beings did not quite become like God in God's wisdom but only became starkly aware of their own nakedness, the principle of proportionality in punishment does not permit God to do any more than penalise these human beings perhaps by withdrawing some of God's aid. Contrary to the theory of original sin, God did not punish humanity for Adam's sin by corrupting their nature or permitting their nature to be naturally corrupted by the act of sin or supernaturally corrupted by

---

7. 'God is keeping the fruit away from you because God knows that in the day you eat of it you will become as wise as God.'
8. 'Could all this be true?'
9. 'Could the serpent be lying to us?'
10. 'Either God or the serpent is lying to us. If the serpent is lying and we eat the fruit, we will be punished by God. If God is the liar, and we eat the fruit, we will become as wise as God. Between attempting to become as wise as God and risking being punished by God and forgoing the potential advantage of wisdom to avoid punishment, which is preferable? This is a difficult choice, so let us think further. What motivation could the serpent have for lying to us? It could be desiring our downfall. And what motivation could God have for lying to us? It may well be that God does not desire our highest good. Well then, does the serpent have any incentive for telling us the truth? Perhaps, considering that the serpent is one of God's wise creatures. And does God have any incentive for being truthful to us? Yes, as well.'
11. 'But, you see, God is, in fact, not interested in any of us attaining our highest good. See, God demoted me just because I wanted to share God's glory.'
12. 'You may be right, but it is not befitting for us as God's creatures to desire what God has.'
13. 'True, but what could you lose by testing God's integrity? If it turns out you are wrong, you will be punished but I'm sure God will forgive and restore you. But if I happen to be right, and you give up this opportunity, you wouldn't know what you missed. Are you sure you wish to do that?'
14. 'The serpent has a point. Let's go for it.'

some avenging angelic forces[15] such that they can only be bound for everlasting damnation.

One interpretation of the Edenic story is that Adam and Eve distrusted God, not believing that God had their best interests in mind. They were forewarned about the consequences of eating the fruit of the tree of the knowledge of good and evil. Even though they did not literally die upon tasting and digesting the fruit, something had changed.

In coveting what was not good for them, they gave in to sinful passions and rejected the friendship of God, considering God a competitor and thinking that God saw them as competitors for wisdom, thus reducing the image of divinity to dust, choosing to trust in the seductions of a serpent, a creature made by God, rather than the Creator.

Augustine of Hippo, tapping on St Paul's perspective, was of the opinion that Adam was not actually deceived through the serpent, the devil working through the great snake, but only Eve (cf. 1 Timothy 2:14, Genesis 3:13),[16] and that the husband was simply going along with the wife in being complicit in her transgression, not really intending

---

15. It is as if an act of sin, however grievous or heinous, could remove the possibility of free will; Augustine, *Civ.*, XIV.15.

16. The idea of deceit (*nsh'* [hiphil], to trick, deceive [*CHALOT*]; *apataō*, to deceive, cheat, mislead [*SLGNT*]) here may not involve Eve's conveniently forgetting that God had said that it is wrong and harmful to consume the fruit from a particular tree but her doubt that such consumption would be harmful for her (as God advised Adam) and her indulgence of the idea that it might contrarily be good (as the serpent advised her over against divine counsel). The stratagem worked by playing on the woman's fancies for wisdom, as great as that of God, selfish desire and vanity overcoming her scruples over breaking God's command, her lack of trust in God, and, quite possibly also, her desire to be wiser than her husband by having received new teaching he did not have and being vindicated in adhering to that new counsel, therefore becoming his teacher rather than only he being hers. Therefore, Eve's heart was deluded by vanity in seeking to be equal to God in wisdom and, before even eating the fruit, already considering her viewpoint more viable than that of God, distrust of God in making of God a mere rival, and competition with her husband, into thinking that what God had clearly declared to be harmful was, in fact, salutary. In a very real sense, the woman was deceived by her own ambition, greed, cunning, wit and personal envy; she was misled by the serpent, not because there was no other option for her, but simply because she had accepted a way of thinking and a way of life which promoted self-aggrandisement, scepticism and conflict. The serpent may have been at

disobedience as much as the woman, albeit performing actions which suggest disobedience, and thinking it a lighter sin for him to commit the act out of a sense of marital loyalty and solidarity.[17]

The sin in which both were involved was the greater because of the facility with which they could have kept the sole commandment to refrain from eating the fruit from a single tree when they had been offered that of every other tree in the vast garden.[18] Furthermore, Adam has no defence in the fact that he deferred to his wife in the matter of the consumption of the fruit, nor Eve in the fact that she heeded the serpent's suggestion, because both by the very act of eating the fruit revealed that they placed some person or thing before God, and they were therefore fully culpable for their insubordination.[19]

Although the human soul was crafted by God out of nothing at all, the human body was created out of created earth, and God fused both together to form a living, human being.[20] Because the nature which God crafted for human beings was created by God, it is good, but because this very thing was created by God out of nothing, it is capable of a descent into sinfulness through being misguided by an evil will. The sinful will is nothing other than a movement of the soul into itself, seeking its own glory rather than that of God, who alone is able to lift up a creature into divine glory, apart from which all creatures perish in humiliation, even if they desire and work all their lives to be greater than they are and to be self-subsistent.[21]

As for Satan, the fall of this angel took place in a slightly different manner. Therefore, Lucifer coveted what Lucifer's eyes glimpsed of God's glory. The thought occurred to Lucifer how good it would be to be as splendid and sublime as God. When Lucifer did not restrain Lucifer's mind, but allowed the forbidden thought to linger, it blossomed into a disordering of the emotions and resulted in Lucifer's thoroughgoing de-purification.

Satan being filled with all manner of enmity, discord, jealousy, resentment and, most of all, conceit, which sits at the head of these sins

---

fault in suggesting such a way of thinking and way of life, but the woman was at fault for accepting them.
17. Augustine, *Civ.*, XIV.11, 13.
18. Ibid., XIV.12, 15.
19. Ibid., XIV.14.
20. Ibid., XIV.11.
21. Ibid., XIV.13.

and others, this is how the angel's thought process was prosecuted:[22] sight;[23] thought;[24] reflection;[25] self-doubt;[26] revisitation;[27] decision.[28]

According to Augustine of Hippo, the fall of the angels came about not through a defective creation, but a good creation of an angelic being with the love of God and love for God imbued in it, which in its pride substituted an inferior good[29] for a supreme good,[30] and this either because God did not, in the case of angels which defected, grant them sufficient assurance and embodiment of divine love, or assist them adequately against temptations to turn against God. It is not necessary in my opinion to charge God in any way for failing to keep errant angels from their evil acts but only to assert that these, out of the boredom and contempt of complacency, elected to tease their fancies by envisaging an alternative theocracy of the universe in which they would be head rather than the one in and for whom they ought to find their greatest and deepest joy and delight, and through whom alone they can find them. Augustine defines the people who live in alignment to God as those for whom God is fount of true bliss and who seek to live out God's purpose for their lives as God's creatures, against the people who live in

---

22. Ibid., XIV.3.
23. 'What a glorious sight!'
24. 'How good it would be to enjoy that splendour!'
25. 'But how could I, a creature, dare to imagine that? Besides, God had informed all of us angels to keep our proper places. Perhaps I should just be content with my position in heaven. But why would God tell us to be content with our respective positions? God says God is God and we are God's creatures, and there is no way for God to make us like God. It is a limitation of God's power. Even if such a thing might be impossible for God, perhaps it is not impossible for me. Could it be possible so long as I replace God?' Augustine of Hippo explains that the root of the arrogance of the demons is constituted by the fact that they are cognisant of so much more than human beings, yet without love, humility and service to underpin it. *Civ.*, IX.19-20.
26. 'How could I think of doing something so ungrateful?'
27. 'Then again, could it be that God has been fooling us all along? That would justify my attempt to supplant God. But what if I am wrong about this? Then God would punish me. And what if I am right? I would have done right by myself.'
28. 'Well then, I will go ahead and attempt a rebellion, just to test God's integrity. No pain, no gain. I don't want to ever regret not having been bold enough to seize my own future.'
29. The power of God in the angel.
30. The power of God respected in God.

alignment to themselves as those for whom they themselves are fount of bliss and who seek to live out their own purpose for their lives.[31]

The first couple alienated themselves from God by their own free choice and fulfilled the meaning of the words, 'of the knowledge of good and evil', by making themselves moral arbiters, moral judges, of what is good and what is evil. They became godless and set themselves up as gods.[32]

Because they wilfully alienated themselves from God, they experienced pangs of shame as they discovered their moral disorientation and spiritual bankruptcy. They hid from God with whom they previously had close fellowship. Moreover, when God looked for them and tried to find out what had happened, Adam made excuses, blaming Eve for passing him the fruit to eat and even blaming God for giving someone like Eve to him; Eve, in turn, accused the serpent of deceiving her.

This led God to curse the serpent to an existence of crawling on the belly, and being crushed by a descendant of Eve, a prediction of how Christ, who as a human being is a descendant of Adam and Eve, will defeat the serpent, which symbolises the devil. God consigned Eve to painful childbirth and a difficult relationship with Adam, and Adam to the arduous toil of tilling the ground and anxiety over his mortality.

---

31. Augustine, *Civ.*, XII.1-9, XIV.4. In the latter reference, Augustine finds his doctrine of the earthly and heavenly cities in the scriptural oppositions of carnality and humanity against spirituality and of God's truth against the dissimulation of the devil and people who follow the devil's example, interpreted as categories of people in terms of their response to God's command, whether it be obedience or disobedience, and promise that they will find their happiness in God alone, whether it be to take refuge in God or to disdain and abjure God.

32. Augustine was of the view that the tree was so named because of the knowledge it afforded of two states: a first being the ease and blessedness of a life lived under and in dependence on the grace of God and in submission to God's commands; and a second being the accursed nature of a human existence eked out in separation from God's provision and rule. *Civ.*, XIV.17. Although Augustine clearly intended his remarks in the context of a Christian theological framework, just as well might these profound thoughts be applied to a non-Christian or even non-theistic setting, in which case, divine grace may be substituted with 'an admission of the existence of a worthy other in the form of a divine being or universal principle (whether this be personal or impersonal in nature) for which one is grateful or delighted', while divine rule may be substituted with 'a desire to be in an intellectual or moral alignment with such a divine being or universal principle'.

God made clothes of skin for the couple. So that they would not eat the fruit of the tree of life and live forever in misery, God had the couple evicted from the garden, and placed angels and a turning, flaming sword to guard the route to the tree of life.

Not long after this, we read that Eve gave birth to two sons, Cain, the elder, and Abel. The brothers each brought an offering to God, Cain from his crops and Abel from his flock. However, when Cain saw that God preferred Abel's offering, he was enraged with jealousy.

Through this incident, God intended to teach Cain the importance of humility and gratitude, the recognition that God did not owe Cain anything at all and that, if God decided to favour Abel, whose name means breath, vapour or vacuity,[33] it was not because of Abel's own merits, but God's own graciousness.

God conferred with Cain and urged him to learn this vital lesson. However, Cain decided against humbling himself, allowed a lurking power of sin to pounce on him and proceeded to arrange a meeting with Abel during which he killed his own brother.

God looked for Cain and asked him where Abel had gone. Cain gave a cold reply to the effect that he was not responsible for his younger brother. Then God heard the voice of Abel's blood crying to God from the ground and condemned Cain to a life of difficult toil working the ground, of constant migration in search of fertile fields and of being constantly on the run from people seeking his blood. Cain lamented to God about this and God had pity on him and set a seal of protection on Cain, so that anybody who dared to murder Cain would be paid back sevenfold.

From that time on, human existence was riddled with myriad sins comprehending anti-social, solipsistic, impious, inhumane, unethical, immoral tendencies of the psyche, speech and conduct.[34]

Although God could have decided to abandon humanity in its sinfulness, rebellion and disobedience, the response on God's part was to send God's own Son, Jesus Christ, to be born as a human being but not in such a way as to compromise the Son's divinity, to save humankind from sin.

This salvation was achieved through Jesus arriving as the face of God, the face of the Father.[35] By revealing the fatherly and loving disposition

---

33. A. Park, *The Genesis Genealogies*, God's Administration in the History of Redemption 1 (Singapore: Periplus, 2009), p. 97.

34. Romans 1:28-32.

35. John 1:18.

of God towards humankind, Jesus sought to invite people to enter into a relationship with God the Father as the Father's children. All who believed in Jesus, that is, who took the image of the Jesus who preached, taught and healed throughout Israel, as revealing the compassion and empathy of the Father for the people the Father created, had the opportunity to become, recognise and identify themselves as the children of God the Father. This is what it means to be a follower of Jesus, a Christian.

Throughout the history of humankind, from the earliest days, God has always sought out humanity, whether it be during the time of Adam and Eve, Noah, or Abraham, Isaac and Jacob, or their descendants. One can discern traces of God's graciousness, mercy and loving empathy in the Old Testament but, in the person of Jesus, one is exposed to the fullness of who God is and how God relates to us.[36]

This is a God who provides everything that we need. It is a God who forgives our sin and always gives us a second chance. It is a God who has always wanted a relationship with each and every one of us, in spite of the things we may have done. So great is the love of God for humanity that God offered even God's Son, Jesus Christ, as an atoning sacrifice on the Cross, so that we may never be alienated from God in doubt or distrust ever again.

Jesus died an innocent death, executed by reason of a conspiracy between religious leaders and the occupying force of the day. There were a number of reasons Jesus gained enemies in Israel where he was born and where he preached, taught and ministered. In general, Jesus met opposition from Jewish religious leaders across three main groups.

There were the scribes and Pharisees, experts in the revered scribal or oral law which comprehensively lays out how the religious life is to be lived down to the smallest detail. There were the Sadducees, Jewish aristocrats who worked with the Roman government; and there were the priests, members of elite families who performed sacerdotal functions and benefited greatly from the sacrificial system.

Some of these religious leaders conspired to put Jesus to death and succeeded in so doing, manipulating Jesus' own followers and even the Roman governor to their own ends. The reason they did so was that they felt threatened by Jesus' teaching, ministry and actions.

Jesus' ministry of compassion for the lost and hurting directly challenged the authority of the scribes and Pharisees. His immense popularity raised the spectre of a revolution and a violent Roman reaction which would in all probability see the Sadducees ousted from their

---

36. Hebrews 1:1-3.

positions of privilege and influence. His claim to represent the interests of God and attempts to reform the sacrificial system struck directly at the benefits of the priestly class.[37]

Yet, what really hammered the nail into the coffin of Jesus' earthly existence, at least until he rose again on the third day after his crucifixion, was his own claim to be the Son of God. In designating God as his Father, Jesus was effectively claiming equality with God. The Jerusalem leaders as described in the Gospels perceived this act with lucid clarity and denounced Jesus for what they felt was an act of blasphemy against God, since they did not believe Jesus to be the Son of God, merely a human being. The reason that these Jewish religious leaders could not tolerate Jesus' claims to be the Son of God was that they saw them as undermining Judaism's nature as a monotheistic religion.[38]

In this way, Jesus became for them as 'a stone of stumbling, and a rock of offense'.[39] This is a stunning statement. It suggests that what God intended as a good thing, a cornerstone by which some Jews, alongside converts from other communities, would go on to be forged into a spiritual temple, had lamentably become a curse, a frustrating obstruction that trips a person.

How did this come about? Jesus came as God's appointed representative to save the world through the power of God's forgiveness released to the world on and from the Cross. Yet, many Jews simply could not accept Jesus' claims. In rejecting Jesus' messianic claims, they, in effect, repudiated God's offer of grace and revelation through Jesus.

In the face of the human conspiracy to lead Jesus to his death, God gave God's Son to those who sought to take his life as an atoning sacrifice for deliverance from the power of sin. This was not a decision God made on the spur of the moment, as though God were caught by surprise; God had decided in advance that this would be the way God would act if the specific circumstance of a rejection of Christ obtained.

John Watts, in his *Isaiah 34-66*, makes an instructive observation about the identity of the sufferer mentioned in Isaiah 53:3 – who is not to be equated with the 'servant of Yahweh' in other passages in Isaiah – which gives credence to an interpretation of the Crucifixion and atonement as an event certainly preordained of God and employed by God but, at the

37. W. Barclay, *The Mind of Jesus* (New York: HarperCollins, 1976), pp. 150-66.
38. Deuteronomy 6:4.
39. 1 Peter 2:8, ESV.

same time, a result of a divine appropriation of a prior sinful human decision to execute the Messiah.

Watts argues that the original referent of the Isaianic sufferer was Zerubbabel, a sixth-century BC Jewish governor, and that he was put to death by the territorial governor because he led a rebuilding of the Jewish temple and the territorial governor did not believe that the work had been officially approved and mistook it as an attempt at rebellion during an unstable period of political contestation for the throne of the Achaemenid Empire.

Later on, when the governor and his leaders realised that the project had been given the green light by Cyrus and endorsed by Darius as well, they were put in a difficult position. Nevertheless, they acknowledged their error and the Achaemenid emperor absolved them of guilt in order to strengthen the unity of his empire. Scripture is thereby saying that God had taken the unjust death for a guilt offering, as a satisfaction paid to God for the sins of others to bring about unity and restoration.[40]

To the extent that this, too, is illustrative of the destiny and mission of Jesus, it can be inferred that there, too, we see God coming to terms with the sinful acts of human beings in executing his Son unjustly, by taking it for a guilt offering and propitiation on behalf not just of the people actually and immediately or more indirectly responsible for the crucifixion, but of all humankind.

God may have long predicted the possibility of something like the Cross being the result, and God's prediction may have been confirmed by the strong opposition of certain Jews towards Christ's ministry among them. Christ, too, saw a fateful end coming. Moreover, at some point during the earthly ministry of Jesus, both the Father and the Son realised that the only effective response to the opposition and rejection of their people would be an atoning death and vicarious propitiatory sacrifice. In this manner we may understand also the possible, even anticipated, rejection by the Assyrians of God's warning to them, through the prophet Jonah; the way in which God knows how God would respond to each option taken, whether that of rejection or of acceptance, and therefore repentance, as an instance of how what is concretely written or prophesied in the pages of Scripture, whether Assyrian judgement or Christ's rejection, need not necessarily be the only possible outcome in a situation, and that, although Jesus was sent to die in atonement of sins, as it were, this would merely constitute a sorrowful expectation on God's

---

40. J.D.W. Watts, *Isaiah 34-66*, rev. edn, WBC 25 (Grand Rapids, MI: Zondervan, 2005), pp. 201-3, 227-33.

part out of which God in God's supernal ingenuity would nevertheless bring good from evil.[41]

It is proper to refer to Christ's atoning work as a propitiatory offering (Romans 3:25). As a revelation of that which was spoken of in the Old Testament (Leviticus 17:11), Christ was sacrificed (indeed, Christ sacrificed himself) that we might know God as favourable to us, always forbearing, ready to forgive and desiring reconciliation rather than seeking revenge or retaliation. Contrary to popular supposition, such propitiation is neither instrumental nor transactional: Christ did not by his death alter the disposition of God the Father from wrathful to kindly towards all who present Christ's atoning sacrifice towards the Father, seeing that he paid the price for human sinfulness (that would be to make it impossible for God to express anger in the form of loving correction towards sin). On the contrary, Christ reveals the very and unchanging attitude of the Father as beyond vengeance and retaliation by showing in himself, as the revelation of the Father, just how the Father would respond to utterly unjust treatment leading to the Father's hypothesised unjustified execution, were the Father to have become human instead of the Son – in just the same way that the Son responded to it. On this count, classical theology has constantly found it trying to reconcile Christ as divine with Christ as human. The fact is that the Father and Son, even as incarnate, are one and the same in their character and disposition – both humble and meek, ready to do the will of the other.

In light of the repudiation of his ministry, Jesus surrendered to the will of God and went the way of the Cross. Christ died on the Cross in order to provide a clear and definite means by which any person could be assured of God's forgiveness for past wrongs, when we ask for it, for God is the end of all vengeance.[42] The logic is that, whatever might cause a person to believe that God may hold a grudge against him, he is able to recognise that any punishment God might wish to mete out, or any score God might wish to settle, has already been fully settled at the Cross, on which the unblemished and innocent Son of God died for sinners.[43]

---

41. Cf. Matthew 21:33-44.
42. While forgiveness designates the desire on the part of a wrongdoer to remit a perpetrator's guilt, which in itself does not suggest that boundaries should not be erected for safety, forbearance is the mental and emotional decision of the will not to pursue retaliation or vengeance of any sort, active or even passive, and to any degree.
43. Acts 10:43.

It should be borne in mind that the Cross as an instrument by which to obtain forgiveness for sins is a mechanism established by God for the resolution of guilt through turning to God in Christ in sincere repentance; it is not that, when Jesus died on the Cross for the sins of the world, all the world's past, present actual and future, potential, wicked inner or outer acts have been atoned for and thus there is no longer warrant for God to be wrathful at unrepentant evildoers and so moral condemnation of evil and corruption should be proscribed. The Cross is not a means of altering God's appropriate attitude towards moral evil, even if a purported new posture is construed only as something which God assumes by virtue of what Christ has achieved on the Cross in favour of humanity, for God's attitude towards sin is incapable of being changed; what God regarded in the past as evil God still regards as evil.

Instead, the Cross constitutes a concessionary and merciful act on God's part, in which God helps the penitent sinner deal with the psychological guilt and remorse due to their wrongful actions through a symbolism of sacrificial atonement which bespeaks forgiveness, compassion, kindness, mercy and friendship, so that the repentant sinner can truly leave behind their lives of sin and begin a new chapter for themselves. Therefore, the Cross is not an obligation for God to act in a certain way – even towards an unrepentant evildoer – in which God is mistakenly thought of as being unjustified in any condemnation or punishment of sin, but, rather, merely a concession.[44] In other words, the Cross removes the feeling that God stands in judgement over the sinner but not the sin, which must be repented of in order to be removed, or the effects of sin, which are only eliminated along with the sin itself, and substitutes in its place a warm and affectionate feeling that accompanies a confidence in God's unremitting love and goodness.[45]

Scripture

Nourished by the human interpretation of the words of Scripture, Christian theology is patently not Scripture itself, but an earnest and rigorous attempt to access the meaning of the Scriptures for an understanding of what these Scriptures might say about God, humanity and the world.

Christian theologians have historically regarded their Scriptures as a revelation, a disclosure coming ultimately from a God who dwells in

---

44. Cf. Ware, 'A Modified Calvinist Doctrine of God', p. 91.
45. Barclay, *Mind of Jesus*, pp. 284-85.

heaven. Many theologians today as well as a great many adherents of the Christian faith worldwide continue to regard the Bible as a divine revelation.

God can be thought of as having in some way directed the process of scriptural production using many different authors, methods of author engagement, editorial procedures and genres. This God does without eradicating the idiosyncrasies of personality and writing style of each author, warranting a great differentiation in authorial styles.

Sometimes, indeed, God does exercise the biblical writer and causes him to speak or write whatever God dictates. We see this happening most clearly in the prophets. On other occasions, however, there is more leeway for a biblical writer to produce a text by accessing his own rich, individual store of spiritual and pastoral insight, as St Paul did. The latter was an apostle, an authorised messenger and follower of Christ who bequeathed letters such as First Corinthians, where he offers guidance for believers on marriage, singleness and widowhood.[46]

In still other instances, there may be a divine stirring of human hearts to take of what is already available and compile a religious history which would be spiritually encouraging and socially meaningful to people of the time.

Consider the case of the first five books of the Bible, the Pentateuch. Many scholars today believe that the Pentateuch in the current form emanated from at least four different pre-existing sources, J, E, D and P, each representing a rather different set of theological and socio-logical concerns. These were oral traditions which existed for a long time and were progressively interwoven within the communities of Israel, reaching canonical form in the Pentateuch. This four-source theory of the Pentateuch, known as the 'documentary hypothesis', was developed by a nineteenth-century German scholar, Julius H. Wellhausen.[47]

If there is a tension of literary form in the Bible, there is also theological tension between different biblical books. As a case in point, New Testament scholars have repeatedly analysed, compared and attempted to synthesise the distinctive theologies of James the Just, the half-brother of Jesus, eponymous author of a New Testament epistle, and of St Paul, author of many letters in the New Testament. St James generally majored on the role of works in the salvific process while Paul focussed on that of faith.

---

46. First Corinthians chapter seven.
47. T. Longman and R.B. Dillard, *An Introduction to the Old Testament*, 2nd edn (Grand Rapids, MI: Zondervan, 2007), pp. 42-45.

There is also the famous theological tension between the Old Testament and the New Testament depiction of God's nature, which led the second-century theologian Marcion to reject all the books of the Old Testament, much of the New Testament, and parts of New Testament books he accepted, as being not of divine origin.

Naturally, theology is occasionally able to drive literary considerations as well. A good example is the prophetic book of Isaiah in the Old Testament, which is said to have been written by up to three different authors. Key to this argument is incredulity that the prophet Isaiah could have correctly predicted an event such as the rise of the Achaemenid king, Cyrus the Great, whom the book mentions by name, and even the coming and sacrificial death of Jesus Christ, believed by some to be prophesied in a passage about a suffering servant of Yahweh in Isaiah chapter 53; some writers hold that the actual author of Isaiah is a man named Meshullam, oldest son of Zerubbabel, on the basis of Isaiah 42:19 which is said to contain his name.[48]

In order to avoid the conclusion that Isaiah was written by a prophetic author possessed of the ability to precisely predict events in the distant future, scholars have conceptualised an 'after the fact', *ex post facto* composition of such predictive passages. While these scholars are well entitled to their own point of view, I believe that we do not have to rule out the possibility of authentic prophecy as a matter of principle.

The divine origin of the Christian Scriptures was recognised through a long and gradual process of canonisation, a protracted process based on a lengthy background of communal use of the books in question and, therefore, a process not so much of deifying the scriptural books as confirming their divine provenance.

The reason it is crucial to examine these specific examples is in order to recognise that the Bible as we have it today did not drop down from heaven as a timeless book comprised exclusively of universal truths patient of straightforward, literal interpretation. As any reader of the Bible will be able to tell, the sacred anthology is filled with references to concrete events involving particular people, groups, cultures and nations in specific places and at specific points in human history.[49]

---

48. J.D.W. Watts, *Isaiah 1-33*, WBC 24 (Nashville, TN: Thomas Nelson, 2005), pp. xliii-xliv.
49. That this is the case is evident in the fact that the canonical biblical narrative is oriented around the establishment of divine covenants cut with various specific individuals in particular socio-historical contexts.

Obviously, a doctrine of scriptural inspiration must not preclude a proper consideration of any of the multiple human factors possibly entailed. At the same time, our ideas of humanity and the world need not hold us back from treating accounts in the Bible as veracious and attesting to true occurrences of divine speech and action towards, through, about and for human beings, and the Bible itself as divinely inspired, that is, capably superintended by God at every stage of the process of its production.

Tradition

It is necessary also to consider the historical development of Christian theology in terms of its authoritative expressions of doctrine, otherwise known as Christian tradition.[50]

With a survey of church history before us, it does not take one very long to observe that certain factors, such as culture and politics, were more prominent in shaping the growth and evolution of historical theology.

Some early Christian thinkers embraced their surrounding culture. As cases in point, St Justin Martyr and St Clement of Alexandria in the second century and St Augustine of Hippo in the fourth and fifth centuries took the view that, even though some of what non-Christian culture contained had to be rejected, such as polytheism, materialism, world eternity and transmigration of souls, classical philosophy was by and large an ally and not an enemy of Christian theology, possessing useful moral truth.[51]

Such Early Church Fathers saw how philosophy could be deployed to counter polytheistic conceptions and sought in accommodating philosophy to demonstrate the universality of the biblical God and this God's ability to crown the most elevated teachings of the day, while taking care to critique that philosophy *ad libitum*.[52]

---

50. For an authoritative survey of the historical development of Christian doctrine, one may profitably consult J. Pelikan's *The Christian Tradition: A History of the Development of Doctrine*, 5 vols (Chicago: University of Chicago Press, 1971-89).

51. The Editors of Encyclopaedia Britannica, 'Christianity: Christianity and Classical Culture', *Britannica*, 28 July 1999, https://www.britannica.com /topic/Christianity/Relations-between-Christianity-and-the-Roman-gove rnment-and-the-Hellenistic-culture#ref67428.

52. Sanders, 'Historical Considerations', p. 72.

Augustine, for instance, personally believed that Greek philosophy contained valid philosophical truth which a theologian like himself could exploit so far as it was shorn of polytheistic notions.[53] Furthermore, he espoused ideas which must have originated in Neoplatonism. These include: the idea of God as being beyond the world and non-material; the fact that things which cannot change are superior to things which are capable of change;[54] and the idea that there is a ranking in which God is superior to the soul and the soul, in turn, is superior to the body.[55] He borrowed: the idea that the soul is non-material and cannot be subject to death; the idea of a division, opposition and contrast between a world that is perceived by reason alone and another world that is perceived by sense alone;[56] and the idea that rational concepts are discernible in the world of sense.[57]

In addition, Augustine subscribes to the idea of God as the cause of creation,[58] the presence of conceptual or Platonic forms in the mind of God and their function as archetypes for sense phenomena,[59] and the idea that rational concepts are situated in the inner being and that God and Truth can be discovered by looking into the soul.[60] Moreover, he proffers the idea that evil is not a metaphysical reality but a negation of being, of goodness,[61] and the idea that human affection for God is to be seen as a semi-sensual attraction towards true beauty.[62]

Augustine accedes to the Platonic concept of an intellectual or spiritual ascent, persuaded that progress towards the supreme being that is God and Truth is achieved by an upward and inward movement from the body to the soul, that is, from the knowledge of objects to the knowledge of oneself, and from the world of sense to the world of reason.[63]

Augustine also holds that Christianity and Platonism both affirm that God is the ultimate cause, the supreme good, and the basis and

---

53. Augustine, *Conf.*, VII.ix.14-15.
54. Cf. Plato, *Tim.*, 28a-b.
55. Augustine, *Letter* XVIII.2.
56. Augustine, *Civ.*, VIII.5-6.
57. Augustine, *Civ.*, VIII.6; idem, *Ver.*, XXXIX.73.
58. Augustine, *Civ.*, VIII.5-6.
59. Augustine, *Div.*, XLVI.
60. Augustine, *Ver.*, XXXIX.72-73.
61. Augustine, *Conf.*, VII.xii-xiii.18-19.
62. Augustine, *Conf.*, X.xxvii.38.
63. Augustine, *Conf.*, VII.x.16, where he appeals to Plotinus' teaching on an inward discovery of truth; idem, *Div.*, XLVI; MacDonald, 'The Divine Nature: Being and Goodness', pp. 22-26.

archetype of knowledge.[64] However, he considers that Platonism lacks redemptive capacity, because it is not capable or ready to accept Christ as intermediary, and so is flawed.[65]

Similarly, the Cappadocian Fathers looked to Platonic philosophy for language and a conceptual structure in constructing their own systematics, tapping on the Platonic idea of God as the source of all that is beautiful or good, the Good and the Beautiful, which exists as a Mind or Reason, an 'active' Demiurge, which expresses the creative power and mediates the creative activity of God, and an 'archetypal' 'Absolute Living Creature', 'the Form of the Good and Beauty Itself', according to which the Demiurge creates all things, and which concretises the substance of the divine Mind or Reason, and exists directly or indirectly (through other, mediate principles) in lower beings as the source of their goodness and beauty, and of humanity as created with an all-encompassing desire to seek the good that is in God, an aim which is achieved through cultivation and mentoring of the mind and heart (Gregory of Nyssa).[66] Eusebius of Caesarea and Origen of Alexandria also synthesised Platonic philosophy and biblical interpretation.[67]

Aside from culture, we have the influence of politics in the formation of Christian theology. An instance of a political influence on theology was the interference of the fourth-century Roman emperor Constantine the Great, who became a Christian after he won a battle in 312 at the Milvian Bridge in the environs of Rome against a rival emperor, Maxentius, in the belief that the victory was given by the Christian God. In the year 313 he and his co-emperor Licinius, through the Edict of Milan, brought an end to the sporadic persecution of the Christian community by declaring Christianity legal and thereby started the process of the Christianisation of the Roman Empire. Constantine founded Constantinople as a Christian city and the new Rome.

He presided over the Council of Nicaea (325) at which the Christian Church defined its commitment to the belief in Jesus as equal to God, rather than just an exalted creature, against the teachings of the priest, Arius.

64. Augustine, *Civ.*, VIII.5-8.
65. Augustine, *Civ.*, X.32; Tornau, 'Saint Augustine'.
66. Bradshaw, 'Plato in the Cappadocian Fathers', pp. 195, 197, 200.
67. G. Karamanolis, 'The Platonism of Eusebius of Caesarea', in R.C. Fowler (ed.,) *Plato in the Third Sophistic*, Millennium Studies 50 (Berlin: De Gruyter, 2014), pp. 171-92.

However, this was not the end of the theological conflict on this matter as, subsequently, Constantine himself became sympathetic to the Arian view, and his successor Constantius II was an avowed Arian. Indeed, Arianism continued as the orthodoxy of the empire for four decades after the death of Constantine.[68] Exacerbating the instability of the Church during this period was the short reign of the emperor Julian the Apostate, who was strongly opposed to Christianity.

The Nicene party returned to dominance when the emperor Theodosius I came to power, declared the Creed of Nicaea the official interpretation of Christian orthodoxy and sought to strengthen this interpretation by convening the second general council at Constantinople (381). In this way Christianity became the main faith of the Roman Empire.

Reason

The Bible is not a collection of books whose primary purpose is to detail theological principles and concepts. This much is evident to any person who has had opportunity to inspect the pages of the Christian canon. Because Scripture is no theological text, theologians have to set their minds to the task of inferring the theology of the Bible and the doctrines which crystallise it.[69]

Therefore, the Church has to define concepts which express biblical teaching on God's purposes for humanity and the world. In this manner, theologians have articulated, *inter alia*, doctrines such as the divine inspiration of the Scriptures, the providential care of God, the atonement of Christ, conversion and new life in Christ through the Spirit. Oftentimes, theologians arrive at differing interpretations of doctrinal teaching, such as in the case of the doctrine of the Trinity, in which the early and later divines developed more or less contrasting proposals.

---

68. J.F. Kelly, *The Ecumenical Councils of the Catholic Church: A History* (Collegeville, MN: Liturgical, 2009), pp. 16-18, 25-29; J.F. Matthews and D.M. Nicol, 'Constantine I', *Britannica*, 26 July 1999, https://www.britannica.com/biography/Constantine-I-Roman-emperor; M. Hudson, 'Battle of Milvian Bridge', *Britannica*, 12 February 2021, https://www.britannica.com/topic/Battle-of-the-Milvian-Bridge.

69. This dovetails with the paradigm of rationalism identified in Barth's *Die Kirchliche Dogmatik* and later theological work. G. Hunsinger, *How to Read Karl Barth: The Shape of His Theology* (Oxford: Oxford University Press, 1991), p. 5.

More importantly, however, reason as a source of theology serves a moderating role. To aver of reason that it is a norming factor in the theological enterprise is to ensure that the latter is grounded in the domain of the rational and sensible. In so doing, reason draws on the insights of the modern sciences and the study of the humanities.

The credibility of Christian theology is contingent, in the first instance, upon the degree to which its doctrines are internally consistent.[70] This might necessitate an inter-doctrinal critique bringing about a recalibration. Without such a safeguard, it is easy to be carried away in the articulation of any one particular doctrine. As a case in point, consider how in Christian theology, the doctrines of human free will in connection with those of depravity and grace tend to override clear biblical statements to the effect that the people of God have the moral capacity whether to obey or disobey the commandments of God and, by implication, vitiate the system of teaching on ethics and deontology.

Augustine of Hippo allowed a doctrine of sin and grace as predeterminant of human moral action to blunt the direct force of the laws of God, particularly in the Old Testament era, as reasonable and viable prescriptions for moral conduct so as to focus all attention on the psychological implications of a failure to uphold those laws. Consequently, God in dispensing God's requirements never intended for God's laws to be properly kept, only continually violated so as to bring God's people into a state of complete desperation and dependence through their anticipated moral failures.[71]

In this way, an implication of the disobedience of the moral laws of God is elevated to a be-all-and-end-all undergirding their promulgation, and the incisive object of the divine laws is fully concealed behind this indirect purpose. On this basis, theologians worked backwards from what appears to be a human experience of total depravity and crippling moral powerlessness first to a watershed during which the moral state of humanity deteriorated beyond repair, and then either to a divine foreknowledge that human beings would fulfil the conditions for their moral state so to deteriorate, or even further to a point prior to creation at which God decreed that humanity would be destined to walk the road of moral ruination, some for good.

The moral state of humanity is, however, far from being a *fait accompli*. When St Augustine formulated his doctrine of original sin, he did so from

---

70. Cf. A.C. Outler, 'The Wesleyan Quadrilateral in Wesley', *WTJ* 20, no. 1 (Spring 1985), p. 9.

71. This is a major thesis undergirding Martin Luther's *De servo arbitrio*.

the standpoint of a person riddled with what mental health experts today would have little hesitation in recognising as psychological disorders of various kinds.[72] Suffering as he did from such mental health challenges as binge-eating disorder and compulsive sexual behaviour arising from a difficult and painful childhood, in an age when these conditions were not well understood, Augustine is no longer in an ideal position to theologise in a general and universal manner about the moral and spiritual condition of humankind from the vantage point of his personal experience of doing his level best to submit to the commandments of God.

For one thing, Augustine was by no means representative of the general population and the average person. Accordingly, he joined issue with the British monk Pelagius on the question of the human ability to observe the moral laws of God. Evidently, Pelagius had a different experience of keeping God's commandments from Augustine which could go some way towards explaining his sanguine viewpoint.

My construal of the Christian doctrine of human free will avoids the charges of Pelagianism and semi-Pelagianism. Contrary to Pelagianism, which asserts the possibility of human morality and even salvation apart from divine grace, I aver that morality is lodged in the human person through an omnipresent Divine Nature, which not only provides an overarching moral vision and inspiration but regularly prods a person to do what is morally right, so that no human person can by his morality oblige God to do anything – because people, in disposing themselves morally, are only following the design of their nature and doing what they ought to in the first place (Luke 17:7-10) – and that salvation, that is divine pardon for sinfulness, is completely and exhaustively provided through the Cross of Jesus.

Contrary to semi-Pelagianism, which argues for the possibility of a good human intent and desire, produced by the person in question without any divine contribution, which attracts the gift of salvation, again, I do not propose that a person is capable of mustering up any good moral thought, feeling, desire, intent, resolve or action apart from the possibilities provided by the substratum that is the Divine Nature

---

72. While it may seem, at least in a popular perception, as though Augustine experienced a carefree childhood and hedonistic adolescence, in reality his strenuous and dogged pursuit of personal fulfilment masked a profound and abiding anguish. The necessarily indirect and inferential evidence and my findings based on these will be taken up substantively in Chapter Eight.

and, further, that nobody can act in such a way as to oblige God to be favourably disposed to them.[73]

Second, Augustine patently did not possess the means to penetrate beyond the thick, emotional cloud of depressive thoughts and guilt typical of those who struggle with disorders of sexual behaviour and compulsive eating. He perceived himself entrapped in his addictions, which afforded him no relief even in his sleep, in that he experienced undesirable and unsettling dreams involving himself engaging in compulsive sex acts. Augustine therefore philosophised regarding his instincts and deepest attractions and came away with the conclusion that he was intrinsically flawed, and that this sinfulness could be traced, biologically, right back to the days of Adam and Eve.

On their own, because these feelings and thoughts are beyond the control of the individual, the inclinations of a food or sexual compulsion in the case of Augustine, the thoughts and feelings which Luther in his excessive religious scrupulosity judged to be indicative of a sinful nature, and those with which Paul struggled in his post-traumatic stress disorder, do not constitute acts of a conscious moral choice.[74] It is incumbent on the individual simply to choose against acting on these thoughts and feelings, consistently to renounce these thoughts and feelings and, if such help is available, seek psychological treatment addressing possible underlying and root causes. Although not sinful volitional behaviour as such, these kinds of negative behaviour-inducing thoughts and emotions represent a compulsive evil that is to be put down as soon as possible through repudiation and probing analysis of the dysfunctional consciousness (e.g. Matthew 5:21-30, Genesis 4:2-7).[75]

Therapeutic solutions for each of these mental health conditions do not involve a simplistic decision not to think, feel or desire in unwanted ways but entail learning salutary ways of thinking and behaving through cognitive behavioural therapy (compulsive sexual behaviour, binge-eating

---

73. For a succinct summary of Pelagianism and semi-Pelagianism, see R.E. Olson, 'The Classical Free Will Theist Model of God', in B.A. Ware (ed.), *Perspectives on the Doctrine of God: Four Views* (Nashville, TN: Broadman & Holman, 2008), p. 166, fn. 10.

74. These inferential diagnoses will be discussed in Chapter Eight.

75. This harks back to the teaching of the influential fifteenth- and sixteenth-century Neo-Confucian scholar, Wang Yang-ming, on how wicked thoughts have to be arrested as soon as they are detected in view of their virulence and compulsive nature. Cf. Gentz, *Understanding Chinese Religions*, p. 64.

disorder, post-traumatic stress disorder), picking up interpersonal skills (binge-eating disorder), facing one's greatest fears and learning how best to respond to them (religious obsessive-compulsive disorder).[76] These treatment pathways strongly intimate that these thoughts, feelings and desires are not conscious moral choices.

The danger arises, however, when a person, in their earnest desire to be pure and holy before God – not just in outward conduct but even the internal life of thoughts, feelings or desires – begins to internalise, identify with and even define themselves by these thoughts, feelings or desires, over which – apart from psychological introspection and abjuration – they have no control, in terms of the ability to stop them from arising in the first place, coming away with the incandescent conviction that they are terribly sinful, flawed and broken.

In this regard, it is always necessary to strike a distinction on a number of levels. First, one should distinguish between non-volitional elements, such as inappropriate, impure or vindictive thoughts, feelings or desires, and volitional acts, such as the acceptance of these kinds of thoughts, feelings or desires, any form of intention, planning, resolution or action based on them. Second, it is necessary to differentiate between thoughts, feelings, desires, intentions, plans, resolutions or actions, which are truly morally defective, corrupt and wicked – such as anything that promotes enmity, disloyalty, injustice or destruction – and those which are less than immoral, though nevertheless defective, such as thoughts or feelings associated with inordinate depression or guilt, a sense of personal unworthiness or a desire to engage in self-harm.

Non-wicked non-volitional thoughts, feelings or desires need not occasion any guilt; non-wicked volitional thoughts, feelings, desires, intentions, plans, resolutions, or actions may be defective, but do not

76. A. Felman, 'What to Know about Compulsive Sexual Behaviour," *MNT*, Healthline Media UK, 8 October 2019, https://www.medicalnewstoday.com/articles/182473#treatment; Mayo Clinic Staff, 'Binge-eating Disorder: Diagnosis and Treatment', Mayo Clinic, Mayo Foundation for Medical Education and Research, 5 May 2018, https://www.mayoclinic.org/diseases -conditions/binge-eating-disorder/diagnosis-treatment/drc-20353633; Z. Villines, 'Religious OCD: Separating Shame from Spirituality', *GoodTherapy*, 2 November 2018, https://www.goodtherapy.org/blog /religious-ocd-separating-shame-from-spirituality-1102184; NHS, 'Treatment – Post-traumatic Stress Disorder', last reviewed 20 May 2022, https:// www.nhs.uk/mental-health/conditions/post-traumatic-stress-disorder -ptsd/treatment.

deserve moral condemnation. Wicked non-volitional thoughts, feelings or desires may be a cause of personal concern requiring efficacious attention so that they do not degenerate into a manifestation of compulsive evil through uncontrollable, seamless and spontaneous wicked volitional action,[77] but they should not be conflated with a person's own acts.[78] Wicked volitional thoughts, feelings, desires, intentions, plans, resolutions or actions should be regretted and avoided at all costs. The last group of actions may be met with criminal punishment to preserve the stability of society and world, as well as moral condemnation.

Is a person who is predisposed to commit some act of harm towards another person responsible for succumbing to their weakness, given that herculean effort is required on their part to refrain from evil? This is ostensibly an all-or-nothing situation, where, if the person succeeds in the moral struggle, they are rightly commended for their perseverance and moral strength – but really only by way of an encouragement, seeing that it is only their duty to win the moral fight – whereas, if they fail to overcome their temptations, they will be reproached for not having done enough to avoid wrongdoing, which it is the duty of every person to eschew, whether so predisposed or not. Unfortunately, violence towards another person can never be justified, not even to a partial degree by the fact that the attempt to do right by another person is riddled with all manner of difficulty. It is the responsibility of a person always to maintain a clear mind regarding the rightness or wrongness of an action even if the entire world appears to be pressing hard on him.

The question of morality tends to be obfuscated by the intensity of the inner moral struggle against latent and potent propensities. One is likely to be so caught up in personal anguish that we imagine that giving in to our baser instincts might be pardonable. However, there are two different kinds of anguish, one justifiable, which it is right to attempt to relieve by any ethical means, another unjustifiable, which does not seek relief except through unethical methods. Unacceptable anguish, which provides a strong inner justification to the individual in question for committing evil, is to be tamed at all costs – in the way that God suggested Cain domesticate his primal instinct to kill his brother – by

---

77. Cf. Genesis 4:7; Romans 6:6-23, 7:7-25.
78. As a matter of fact, Augustine was of the view that the sensual bodily responses of a woman during an act of rape are akin to the involuntary movements a body may make during sleep and not to be charged to her as wrongdoing, provided she does not go on to willingly entertain excitement and pleasure. Augustine, *Civ.*, I.25.

exerting self-restraint over one's emotions and refusing to allow these to overwhelm us, and by being clear that such instincts, which are beyond one's control and not to be permitted to give rise to guilt, and the actions they recommend, are evil, and to be subjugated and extirpated at all costs.

Concrete examples will be instructive here.[79] In a first, a person might have a parent who does not believe in taking personal responsibility for his/her actions, whether towards other persons or towards the first person in question, the child. This means that the child experiences great difficulty in being accountable for its own actions, because it has never really learned at whatever stage of its life the importance of being accountable for one's actions.

A second example may involve someone who has been mistreated and sexually abused and comes to develop a proclivity towards sexual fantasies involving assuming the role of a woman being abused and an addiction to pornography. Having been maltreated as a child, the person develops a warped view of the source of his own sexual pleasure, believing himself to be deserving of sexually abusive behaviour as well as, perhaps, being drawn to videos or pictures of other people undergoing sexual abuse as a means of attaining a vicarious sense of erotic fulfilment.

Finally, an individual who experiences gender dysphoria,[80] seeks feminine beauty and envies attractive women might decide that it is justifiable to downplay the importance of feminine beauty as a method of coping with a lack of a good quality in another gender perceived to be the only source of sexual pleasure, self-esteem and self-confidence, perhaps because of having been, as in the second example, sexually mistreated at some point in their lives.

If a thought, feeling or desire involves wickedness, it presupposes a compulsive evil having previously entered the person's soul. As to how this may have happened, it was either invited through overstepping one's boundaries, as in the case of the devil, or allowed uncritically to enter and remain in the person's soul following an abusive action perpetrated against that person, as in the case of a victim of childhood or adolescent abuse, who, in the absence of proper teaching on the ethics of human psychology and conduct, may have come more easily to accept that the sinful way he or she has been treated is the right way to be treated and to treat others, or embraced such ways as a means to survive in a harsh

---

79. These examples are anecdotes from the lives of actual people.
80. There is no inference here that all persons who experience gender dysphoria feel, think, or behave this way, only certain individuals, one of whom is known by the author.

world or to get ahead. Evil, however, has become a compulsive force through the agency of the devil, who in the devil's desire to surpass God has set for the devil the life goal of opposing all that God wills and does among people and otherwise in the world. Those who do not renounce evil in the form of wicked thoughts, feelings or desires at every turn have to be content to allow the devil to begin or continue to wreak havoc in their lives; those who do disavow it are kept from his assaults.

In all circumstances, a person should pursue: *clarity* through therapy and self-introspection as to the emotional reasons for their thoughts, feelings or desires and the rightness, wrongness or defectiveness of these; *concession*, the acceptance of these reasons and where they stand on the moral spectrum; *commitment* not to continue in volitional acts spurred by these inappropriate, defective or immoral but non-volitional thoughts, feelings or desires; a *covenant* to lovingly and patiently guide oneself away from these thoughts, feelings or desires by gently counselling oneself that one does not have to think, feel or desire in the defective way in which one does; and *consult* necessary help through therapy or spirituality.[81]

The real object of the fourfold schema earlier presented is to underscore the fact that non-volitional thoughts, feelings or desires should under no circumstances be conflated with their volitional equivalents. They are not at the disposal of the individual and should not be regarded as moral actions or factors. Similar to how menstrual discharge or leprosy were regarded in the Mosaic law as forms of uncleanness to be shunned and dealt with strictly, so there are forms of non-moral imperfections in all people in the shape of non-volitional thoughts, feelings or desires.

In contradistinction to menstruation and leprosy, however, these non-volitional wicked thoughts, feelings or desires have a potential, if left

---

81. The Christian Church has experienced paradigmatic shifts in human knowledge of the physical universe, as well as a tectonic change in our understanding of the world of the human psyche. If God is indeed comprised of a structural framework that – as developed in the chapter on theodicy – acts as an ontological substratum for all entities, a Divine Nature, and, if the active and entitative dimension of God, the Trinity, is itself posited by the Divine Nature, which properly belongs to the Trinity, then the Trinity does not come into the world with perfect understanding of sociological, scientific, medical, psychological, moral and even religious matters, and, to a very large degree, seeks understanding in these matters from the Divine Nature, progressing and growing towards this understanding, but at a quicker rate than humanity, thereby inspiring them towards advances.

unaddressed or unresolved, to blossom into volitional wicked thoughts, feelings, desires, intentions, plans, resolutions or actions. While non-wicked thoughts, feelings and desires, such as feelings of unworthiness or suicidal ideations, may not be morally wicked, they should not be left untended, for these, too, have the tendency to lead to something greater – in this case, unwholesome intentions, plans, resolutions or actions. As with the unwholesome, so with the wholesome. Good non-volitional thoughts, feelings or desires, coming as they do from the Divine Nature which permeates every human person, also have the capacity to turn into volitional thoughts, feelings, desires, intentions, plans, resolutions or actions.

Church figures like Augustine, Martin Luther and St Paul did not strike a clear distinction between volitional and non-volitional thoughts, feelings or desires, nor did they comprehend that not every defective thought, feeling or desire had to be deemed wicked and corrupted. Although Augustine was not mistaken in asserting a lineage of sin, he went too far in contending a biological or natural source of human immorality.[82] His theory engendered a culture of self-flagellation and feigned humility within the Christian community in which it became fashionable and befitting of a pious person to be obsessed with his purported profound personal wickedness in order that the grace of God might be fully and perfectly magnified.

While an Augustinian theology of sin does indeed succeed in directing pious minds to the Cross of Calvary as the only solution to human misery, it does so only at the very great cost of maligning a natural affinity between religion and medicine and psychology, and obscuring the steps psychologically burdened individuals like Augustine himself need to take in order to attain a greater freedom of mind.

---

82. This is a view, a conception of Adam as having a natural or realistic headship, through a traducianist process by which an infant receives its soul from the pneumatological substance of its parents, as opposed to a federal one, spelled out in Augustine's *A Treatise on the Merits and Forgiveness of Sins, and the Baptism of Infants*, 1.8-11. See Erickson, *CT*, p. 578. Augustine, *Civ.*, XIII.14: the seeds of the essence of individual persons who would come to be were in Adam weakened and denounced by his voluntary transgression, held captive by the power of mortality and righteously denounced by God, and all people after Adam's fall would be born in such a state of deterioration and rejection. This happened before these unborn individuals could be given their specific individuality.

By referring the matter of sinful action directly to the divine court, such a theology renders moot any appeal for clarity or assistance with respect to penultimate authorities in the form of mental health professionals. The emotional roots that shape and influence a person's bedside manner are bypassed and ignored in favour of a dysfunctional belief that a disturbed mental state characterised by shame and self-blame is an ideal spiritual state, at least for the ultra-pious. Such theology ultimately encourages moralism, the simplistic conviction that it is possible and desirable for a person to conform to all religious and moral rules, and that to the extent that a person fails to do so, he or she is to be chastened and brought soon back into the fold.

If the irresistible sin-grace doctrine of Augustine fails to comport with the rest of Christian theology and thus incites extreme and unbalanced ways of thinking, feeling and behaving, it also fails the test of proportionality. In the hands of the followers of the sixteenth-century reformer, John Calvin, who himself tried to stay true to an Augustinian conception of human sinfulness, everything, ranging from the most commendable to the most egregious, including the fall of the first man, became a theatre to display the fullness of divine glory.[83]

Therefore, even if God had the means to prevent Adam from collapsing into a lamentable condition of utter depravity that would infect and affect all his progeny, if only God was pleased to endow the first man with a greater measure of perseverance in face of temptation from the serpent, yet God desired and decreed something far different – the sin and misery of the human creation – in order to secure the total necessity for the atonement of Christ and everlasting gratitude towards and submission under God in Christ.[84] This is all well and good, until one realises the titanic cost of this theocratic vision.

The pious will have to content themselves with recognising, seeing, thinking of and identifying themselves as sinful beings and falling at the feet of a bloodied Christ hanging above them nailed to a cross in payment of their wretchedness. The impious, so to speak, will have to be satisfied to be fodder for the righteous as instruments to display the holy wrath of God. Neither the righteous nor the unrighteous will be capable of altering their destinies, nor will they be able to mount a legal challenge against the heavenly sovereign for this king's decisions pertaining to their

---

83. Calvin, *Inst.*, III.xxiii.8.
84. Calvin, *Inst.*, I.xv.8, III.xxi.5; J.N. Anderson, 'Why Did God Allow the Fall?', *TGC*, 27 June 2017, https://www.thegospelcoalition.org/article/why-did-god-allow-the-fall.

moral fates, simply because, it is thought, just as the righteous have been purified inside-out by the work of the Holy Spirit, so the unrighteous are left unholy inside-out, have less than a scintilla of a desire to be removed from their spiritual estate so as to be right with God, and more than a mountain of will to persist in their sinful obstinacy.

Human pain, at best, leading to salvation and the consummation of salvation and, at worst, leading to everlasting damnation, even if this be the agony of inveterate sinners, as Calvinists would call them, is dismissed out of hand as a direct consequence of the Adamic fall and a sinful nature which God does little, if anything, to salve, except arrange for the death of God's Son on a cross to atone for the sins of a limited number of the elect.[85] Before a wrathful God, it is ludicrous to speak of an emotional empathy for the transgressor, just as much as the victims of a crime or the officers of a judicial system could underscore emotional affinity and rapport with a wrongdoer. Calvinist theology and the ambience it creates among its adherents is matter of fact and sterile in its forensic nature.

Augustine and his successors paint a gloomy picture, a black-and-white depiction of the causes and the reality of the moral darkness that reigns among human beings. It lays not the blame but the reasons for the spiritual state and therefore the ultimate hope of the human creation at the door of an all-powerful heavenly potentate. Apart from the proclamation of the Gospel, there is little if any need to engage in a struggle against sin in the manifold realms of human activity, since there is no human way to change the sinful person, little need to be so involved in the building and development of society.[86] There is, of course, no necessity for a Christian person to be engaged in any type of dialogue with an adherent of another religious profession, because, so one thinks, there can be no compromise between the Church and other religious institutions.[87]

---

85. This is according to one of the five dimensions of seventeenth-century Reformed orthodoxy, as articulated at the Synod of Dort (1618-19) convened by the Reformed Church of the Netherlands in response to the Dutch Arminians, the Remonstrants, led by Jacob Arminius. The Editors of Encyclopaedia Britannica, 'Synod of Dort', *Britannica*, 20 July 1998, https://www.britannica.com/event/Synod-of-Dort.
86. Calvin, *Inst.*, II.i.8-9.
87. Cf. P.C. Potgieter, 'Calvin and Other Religions', *AT* 24, no. 1 (2004), pp. 148-49.

The inner logic behind an Augustinian theology is rarely so lucidly spelled out. This is not a critique of Augustine as a theologian *per se*, but merely an attempt to illustrate the excesses of a theology detached from the moorings of integration with other equally biblical doctrines.

Given the considerable influence of the Augustinian conception of sin, it will be no mean feat to attempt a viable alternative view which does justice to the biblical testimony. A fundamental critique of the classical theology of sin makes it necessary to alter also a classical understanding of the manner in which the grace of salvation originates and reaches humankind, as well as of the very nature of that salvation.

A doctrine of salvation that coheres with a biblical apprehension of deontology will continue to affirm the central place of Jesus and his redemptive act on the Cross, simply because this is what Scripture itself affirms. It will not baulk at agreeing with the biblical attestation that, when Jesus came, it was to save sinners, ruined as we all are by the primeval acts of our first ancestors who decided that it was better to covet what God had not freely given than simply to be content with the plenitude God had already graciously distributed.

This ancient sin of avarice and suspicion towards divine authority has terrorised humanity in many a form, running the gamut of transgressions and immoralities, besmirching families from childhood to adulthood, oftentimes spilling over in myriad types of corruption into wider society and community. A reasonable and rational theology would not vacillate to affirm that these things are true and that Jesus came, providentially, to rid the human conscience of the bugbear of guilt as well as the gadfly of anxiety concerning God's alacrity to receive a sinner back into God's own fellowship. The mission of the Son of God was to put an end to the perception of divine enmity against sinful humanity, to assure and reassure of an eternal path leading back to the home of humanity in the heart of God. Jesus is the Son who represents the fatherly concern of God towards errant humankind and invites one and all to come to the table of feasting and company, in the presence of an affectionate God and origin of all that is.[88]

---

88. A vivid picture of this is supplied in the parable of the lost son; the Cross demolishes the typical depiction of God as wrathful by accomplishing something which the devil in all its cunning ingenuity can never bring itself to achieve and thereby replicate – come to earth in an inferior form and die a humiliating death.

This is not a truncated Gospel but an unconditional promise of forgiveness and fellowship, so long as forgiveness is sought in contrition and fellowship in repentance, or at least the sincere willingness to change one's old ways. Even for the obstinate, there is the prodigal love of a father who waits for his lost son to return.[89] Salvation is divine pardon and absolution, and there is nothing left for God to do before it can be enacted and effected in a human heart. God has done everything necessary for people to be able to understand and receive God's promise of forgiveness. It is possible to choose to accept the gospel invitation. If there is any hindrance, this is not placed by God, but a result of human misunderstanding based on unfortunate past experiences, encounters with people who made the Christian faith look smaller than it really is, or narrow-minded and rigid, arrogant and hypocritical, or even contemptible.

God actively speaks in the human heart and attempts to draw people to God, whether through the Christian faith or another world religion. As such, God subsists in two main ways. There is a passive and substantial aspect of God, in which God is omnipresent and active in every being but only as a presupposition or substratum of that being's good thoughts, feelings and actions. Then, there is an active and entitative aspect of God, in which God exists in a concrete spiritual form. In order to preserve the lack of omniscience on the part of the entitative dimension of God, the entitative aspect of God's existence is not aware of all things despite the fact that the substantial aspect exists everywhere. This is because this substantial dimension is not an actual living entity *per se* and lacks a personal consciousness. It is rather a fertile realm for the emergence of moral entities, an ontological-moral-existential framework which facilitates thoughts of love, selflessness, purity, wisdom, sensitivity, empathy, patience, graciousness and affection. Therefore, there are not two Gods, but just one God.

Even when we speak of God as manifested in different religions, it is the same God who appears in different ways, perichoretically, so that in

---

89. God's predominant mood and disposition toward humanity is one of situational joy (because of goodness among human beings), sorrow (because of tragedy or minor human deviation from the paths of righteousness) or anger (only because of dramatic or categorical human deviation from righteousness), along with an everlasting and unchanging undercurrent of delight (because human beings, along with all other facets of the world, arise from God).

the form that God takes in any one religion, the fullness of God's being is present in that form. There is no higher or lower presentation of God, just as we do not say that the Father is superior in being to the Son or the Holy Spirit. Furthermore, the different religious presentations of God do not exist at the same time, but are the same being rotating endlessly to serve different constituencies.

God responds to the needs and prayers of humankind, commanding God's angels to attend to these human concerns.[90] God is neither high and mighty, unsympathetic, impassive, nor impassible. In the encounter with the pain and misery, anxiety and fear, joy and cheer, sorrow and grief, hope, despair, God shares in what is bad and takes pleasure in what is good. God identifies with every human person in his deepest struggle and basks in his highest delights. God strengthens the weak, comforts the sorrowful, lifts up the despairing, and commissions and empowers the ready. There is no human affair in which God is absent. Even in the depths of sin, God is present, in trembling, in mourning for that which is presently lacking and desire for what is better.

At the very moment that a human person begins to appreciate the vast extent of God's affectionate love and intimate solidarity with all creation, the way is opened into the very presence of the divine. This experience is one of such epiphanic splendour that it can scarcely be described, and the wisest of men fumble to call it, rather prosaically, a rebirth of sorts. Without being born again, it is impossible to see or enter the kingdom of God, as Jesus apprises Nicodemus, and this is completely true.[91]

Those who receive the good news of God's fatherly love are translated from their current and now past state of self-condemnation and doubt

---

90. Above all else, prayer profits the intercessor, ideally prodding him to examine his motives for entering into intercession in the first place, and making him a more loving, humble, healthy, wholesome, better person. Prayer does not affect God's response for the most part, since in many cases God already knows the needs of people given that God dwells in the hearts of the believers in the Holy Spirit, and God is already working to the best of God's ability to bring relief, peace and flourishing to their circumstances, from the very inception of the specific need in view, and the sudden awareness of the need to pray is simply an intuition of God's desire and will to serve the need in question, beginning with the intercession of the Spirit in the believer's heart, invoking God for help through the angels (Romans 8:26-27). Cf. Schleiermacher's view on prayer, Olson, *Journey of Modern Theology*, pp. 142-43.

91. John chapter three.

regarding God into a glorious place of new and hopeful expectation.[92] Their hearts are renewed, regenerated as it were, and from a dark and dank previous existence in which their souls and minds were numb and dead, they were raised to a new kind of existence; and so stark is the contrast it can only be adequately hinted at using the imagery of death and resurrection. A sanctification, a renewal of patterns of thought and ways of behaving and relating with God, other people, and the world is almost certain to follow in the wake of the divine-human encounter, as people glimpse the divine love and affection and seek to model it in their own lives towards other people.

Moved to explore in a deep way what could have shaped them to be the people they have come to be and to be ashamed of being, both through spiritual reflection and professional therapy, they are released into the freedom of the children of God, a liberated condition of existence in which the duties and obligations of the kingdom of God are not onerous but joy and life-giving.[93] More and more, they realise that God had always had each of them in mind, in God's positive affections. God has always intended for each of them to know God's mind and feel God's perfect love. This is an experience which can only be termed a form of predestination, a foreknowledge, an election and appointment to eternal life.

To be sure, this is a far cry from an ornate Reformed theology of sin and grace with its differing and distinctive grasp of foreknowledge, predestination, regeneration, saving faith, justification, sanctification, glorification through an exclusive understanding of salvation.

It is not on that account an inferior theology. There is no real loss in offering a view of the process of salvation which removes God from meticulous activity in the spiritual realm in order to situate human activity in its network of interpersonal and ethical relations within a broad system of divine affection and graciousness, in which people are free to be who they really want to be, liberated as joyfully responsible, grateful and affectional individuals within their own communities.

Nor is it harmful to suggest that the Christian faith is not the only route to spiritual wellbeing and an authentic relationship with the divine. On the contrary, such a theology requires a good dose of humility both to propagate and accept. Indeed, the capacity of God to manifest Godself in

---

92. Colossians 1:12-14.
93. Matthew 11:28-30.

different and profitably adaptive ways to various religious communities
with their specific histories, struggles and hopes is a manifesto that attests
to the endless creativity and insurmountable humility, loving affection
and self-giving nature of God.[94]

---

94. It may well be that a sense of spiritual-existential hopelessness
    underpinned by a notion of original sinfulness helps to further the desire to
    alleviate inner tension by relativising the laws of God through speaking of
    a morally non-respecting and unconditional divine love (Augustine, *Civ.*,
    XXI.18), as well as to produce restrictive, absolute and universal statements.
    These may pertain to moral aetiology, as in the case of the theory that the
    reason a loving God should permit humankind to be susceptible to moral
    weakness at creation and, through the Fall, to be punished with the state of
    original sin, is to be ascribed respectively to the divine purpose for humble
    human dependence on God and the gravity of the Adamic offence. There
    may also be absolute statements regarding eternal, final destinies, such as
    those which postulate that the reason a loving God should permit people
    to suffer forever after the final judgement is to be attributed to the severity
    both of Adamic sin and its offshoot in some actual sinfulness which even
    a loving God is within rights to punish utterly considering the putative
    seriousness of the offence. Such belief systems are typically based on
    literal and often context-disregarding interpretations, or those which tend
    to ignore the insights of modern science. See Augustine, *Civ.*, XXI.

Chapter 5

Doctrines: The Trinity

By and large, Christian doctrines attempt to summarise and conceptualise biblical teaching on specific subjects. However, the Christian doctrine of the Trinity has the distinct honour of not so much describing and naming what the Bible teaches on certain topics but, rather, reconciling different strands of Christian theology. To the extent that the Trinity straddles doctrines, two things are necessary: to highlight the various doctrines the Trinity sits between; and outline its special province.

Place in a Systematic Theology

Regarding the question, with which doctrines the Trinity ventures to cohere, clearly, the doctrine of Christology is involved. Although the Christian Church had always operated with some form of understanding about God, Jesus and the Holy Spirit, as emergent in the pages of the New Testament, there was little need to codify and substantiate the teachings of the Church on this particular issue until a challenge to the divinity of Jesus gained traction in the Roman world in the time of the Libyan presbyter, Arius (c. 260-336), and his patriarch, Alexander of Alexandria. Along with a rising trend of subordinationism, Arius taught that, the Son being subordinate to the Father and God incapable of being subordinate, the Son is therefore not divine, and indeed has a beginning in time as created of God.[1] This challenged the doctrine of the Trinity, which depends for its lifeblood on the expansion of divine

---

1. Kelly, *The Ecumenical Councils of the Catholic Church*, pp. 19-21.

status to include not just Jesus, the Son of God, but also the Holy Spirit of God.

If the Trinity possesses a horizontal aspect of the incorporation of two other entities under the category of divinity, there is also a vertical dimension. It is imperative to resolve these new divine entities back into a Christian doctrine of God, whose requirement is essentially monotheistic.[2] For this reason, the Trinity ties at least three different doctrines together: the doctrine of Christ and of the Holy Spirit into the doctrine of God.

Regarding its special purview, the Trinity probes these three doctrines variously. Concerning Christology and pneumatology, it is interested in establishing the scriptural basis for the argument of the Son and the Holy Spirit as having divine status. There is a forward motion in that sense. However, regarding theology proper – the doctrine of God – the Trinity tries to achieve a compromise of sorts with the monotheistic ideal of Christianity, which it inherited from Judaism and holds in common with Islam. A backward movement may be here observed. Obviously, one should not neglect the fact that antecedent to the doctrines of Christ and of the Holy Spirit, the doctrine of God was already present as the soil out of which the Trinity grows.

Preamble

The Divine Nature

In classical theology, the Christian God is spirit rather than corporeal matter, self-subsistent rather than contingent like the universe (because the Divine Nature is proper to the Trinity but not the rest of the universe, which is, therefore, dependent on the Divine Nature as its source and origin; the Divine Nature is the only thing that exists on its own without needing to be posited by another),[3] exists in an eternal present rather than a temporal domain, to our mind eminently authoritative, knowing (through the respectful surveillance of the angels), present (through the worldly movements of the Holy Spirit who dwells in the heart of

---

2. Ibid., p. 19.
3. St Augustine has a scintillating statement in *Conf.*, XIII.i.1, iv.5, of how God has entirely no need of the human being, whether to relieve God of God's burdens, make God feel better or stronger through the reverence that a person might give, or bring God delight, but that, as a matter of fact, it is Augustine who relies on God to find virtue.

believers), blissful and source of bliss, simple (having no distinction between its essence and specific form of existence, that is, its specific attributes or characteristics),[4] ineffable (in having a boundless nature whose concrete expressions can never exhaust it) and perfect in love.

How is it scriptural to suggest in a revised understanding that God as entity is neither omnipotent, omniscient, nor omnipresent?

Regarding why God is said to fall short of omnipotence, this is an inference from the disparity between God's desired outcome for humanity as a people who would practise love one towards another and the actual reality of their relations. Concerning the question of why God is neither omniscient nor omnipresent, this relates to the account of the crisis of Sodom and Gomorrah. In that incident, Yahweh had to make a personal visit to the land in order to ascertain the truth of the reports that had presumably been brought to Yahweh by angels (Genesis 18:20-21). If Yahweh were all-knowing or everywhere present, Yahweh would not have had to depend on reports about the cities to discover that something was awry. If Yahweh were everywhere present, Yahweh would not lack certain, personal and intimate knowledge about the goings-on in the world. Likewise, it was necessary for a report about how the Israelites were suffering in Egypt to make its way to God in heaven; the account in Exodus 2:23-25 suggests that angelic messengers observed the gross injustice that was taking place in Egypt and brought the news to God, who took an expedition to the land.

Similarly, in Daniel 9:24-10:21, when Daniel fasted and prayed over prophecies of Israel's ruination, attending angels almost immediately heard his prayer, conveyed his words to God and a mandate was given to an angel to bring divine illumination about the fate of Israel to Daniel. John 21:17 is to be interpreted in terms of Jesus' knowledge of all that was going on in the heart of St Peter at the very moment in question, rather than of an omniscience, which Jesus himself disavowed.[5] Hebrews 4:13 is not a statement concerning divine omniscience, but rather a commentary on the extent to which God is able to probe a human heart. Although God cannot see the future because it has not yet happened, God can predict events with reasonable accuracy and estimate the human capacity for wickedness and righteousness beforehand.[6]

---

4. Augustine, *Conf.*, XIII.iii.4, fn. 4, viii.9.
5. Cf. Matthew 24:36; Mark 13:32.
6. E.g. Jude 1:4-5.

The Divinity of Jesus Christ

The three major types of viewpoints regarding the divinity of Jesus revolve around: (1) the choice of Jesus as Son of God (the elective/adoptionistic view); (2) the role/identity of Jesus as Son of God (the functional/psychological view); and (3) the nature of Jesus as God (the substantial view).

According to what can be known as the elective or adoptionistic view, Jesus was born an ordinary human being, and at the point of his baptism, he was chosen by God for adoption into the Godhead as God's Son, thus conferring on him special powers by virtue of his being filled with the Holy Spirit of God.

The strength of this perspective lies in the fact that the Scriptures do indeed depict Jesus as a man who was filled to the utmost with the Holy Spirit, revealing the fullness of the Godhead in his being and person. At the same time, it downplays the passages which intimate Jesus as being in the very beginning of time with God and, as a matter of fact, being God himself – things we would not normally say about an ordinary human being.

In a functional or psychological understanding, Jesus is thought of as a powerful agent of God of some angelic or superhuman nature or as being taken up into the divine identity of the one God. Sent by God into the world to act on God's behalf, Jesus brings with him the full authority or status of God, like an ambassador, to execute God's will in the world.[7]

The advantage of this viewpoint is that it takes seriously the biblical testimony concerning the agency of angels in the execution of God's mission, including the mysterious 'angel of Yahweh' who along with other angels carries out the will of God.

A shortcoming concerns the way the Scriptures, nevertheless, distinguish between God and God's angels, and to designate Jesus an angel of God, even with full divine authority, is to confer on him a status that is less than divine.

This leaves one with the substantial view of Jesus as having the nature of God.

It is a perspective that best accounts for the scriptural testimony relating to how, first of all, Jesus alone sees the Father by virtue of his living directly

---

7. J.D.G. Dunn, *Did the First Christians Worship Jesus?: The New Testament Evidence* (Louisville, KY: Westminster John Knox, 2010), pp. 141-51; L.W. Hurtado, *One God, One Lord: Early Christian Devotion and Ancient Jewish Monotheism* (London: SCM, 1988), pp. 129-30.

in the Father's presence.[8] Second, it accounts for the Bible's teaching that Jesus has first-hand knowledge of the Father and is capable of disclosing that knowledge to the people with whom he chooses to privilege that knowledge.[9] Third, it expresses the biblical notion that Jesus alone is able to perfectly reveal the character of the Father.[10]

Although Jesus became a human being, he is not merely a man, but God. As the *Logos* or the Word, the Son expresses God's mind, and executes God's will and purpose in the world, including bringing about, sustaining and developing the material principles of creation through the Son's ancient decree to angels.[11] In his nature, Jesus is superior to the angels.[12] Even then, being God-man in no way precludes his capacity to be filled with the Holy Spirit, and also to represent the Father in his earthly ministry.

It is not surprising then that, since the earliest times of the Christian Church, adherents of the faith have offered their worship not just to God the Father but also to God the Son, the Lord Jesus Christ.

With the acceptance of the divinity of Jesus, the Christian faith effectively takes Judaism from a unitarian to a binitarian model of God's nature. The doctrine of Christ's divine nature was only the inception of the doctrine of the Trinity and created a momentum which led to the inclusion and definition of the Holy Spirit as the third person of the Trinity.

The Divinity of the Holy Spirit

Concerning the Holy Spirit, it is both less and more challenging to demonstrate the divine nature of this person than that of Jesus.

It is less challenging to show the divinity of the Holy Spirit in that there is a very natural affinity, an inseparable link, between God and the Spirit of God, so that there is no doubt at all in the first instance that the Spirit has something at least to do with God. The pneumatomachians in the fourth century denied that the Holy Spirit was either divine or a person. However, scripturally, as an integral part of the Godhead as

---

8. John 1:18.
9. Matthew 11:27.
10. Hebrews 1:3.
11. John 1:3, Hebrews 1:3.
12. Hebrews 1:5-14.

God's own Spirit, the Holy Spirit is equally divine. St Peter in the account of Ananias and Sapphira identified the Holy Spirit with God.[13]

It is more challenging in a sense because the Scripture, particularly in the Old Testament, is rife with copious references to the activity of God through God's Spirit. When Yahweh wished to empower a person to act on Yahweh's behalf, Yahweh would send the Spirit of God to come upon the person. Under these circumstances, it is easy to think of the Spirit as nothing more than a medium of God's action in the world.

Nevertheless, can the Holy Spirit be understood as a person rather than an impersonal force?

The New Testament ascribes not just actions but personal emotions and relational actions to the Holy Spirit, allowing for the possibility of the Spirit's being grieved,[14] being blasphemed,[15] betrayal of trust,[16] speech,[17] cognitive scrutiny and deep-level communication.[18]

The Spirit's ability to be grieved suggests that the Spirit has feelings which are susceptible to being adversely affected by an unwillingness to practise the lifestyle the Spirit endorses. This lifestyle is characterised by goodwill, empathy, gratitude and self-restraint[19] and, when a professed Christian believer deviates from this pattern and refuses to do anything to change themselves, the Holy Spirit who dwells in the believer is pained.

What about the Spirit's capacity to be treated in a sacrilegious way? This can happen if a believer witnesses an activity of the Holy Spirit, such as in a miraculous healing of a person, but chooses to think of it as a work of demons.

During the earthly life of Jesus, it was clear that he was performing miracles through the power of the Holy Spirit. Yet some Pharisees chose to dismiss this possibility out of their strong prejudice against Jesus and failed to correct their own misconceptions. This resulted in the offence of the Holy Spirit, who would have felt completely and unfairly misunderstood by the people the Spirit had come to succour.

The Spirit is capable of having the Spirit's trust betrayed. There is a story in Acts chapter five, to which we have already referred, about a couple by the names of Ananias and Sapphira, who were believers. They were

---

13. Acts 5:3-4.
14. Ephesians 4:30.
15. Matthew 12:31.
16. Acts 5:3.
17. Acts 13:2.
18. 1 Corinthians 2:10-16.
19. Galatians 5:22-23.

guilty of lying to the Holy Spirit when they sold a piece of land, retained some of the proceeds for themselves and brought the rest to the apostles, giving the impression that they had donated all the money they received from selling the property. From this account, we are able to observe that the Holy Spirit has a relationship of trust with the believers of Christ and this trust can be breached through acts of dishonesty.

The Holy Spirit is also capable of communicating with believers through speech, as when the Spirit asked the church at Antioch to set apart Barnabas and Saul for a missionary journey. Moreover, the Holy Spirit is capable of understanding the mind of God and making God's thoughts known to the believer in a deep way (1 Corinthians 2:10-13).[20]

On such grounds, the Church recognised the Holy Spirit as a divine person deserving of adoration as much as the Father and the Son.

If we have a sufficient basis for asserting everything in the foregoing – if our arguments are sound and rigorous, our evidence valid, and our exposition coherent and persuasive – then there are good reasons for the Church's doctrine of the Holy Trinity.

Definition

The Christian doctrine of the Trinity posits that there are three persons in the one God. The doctrine can be expressed in seven interconnected statements.

The first three statements relate to how each of the three persons are fully divine. Contrary to subordinationism, the Father is not more fully God than the Son and the Spirit. The Son is not merely a powerful and pre-eminent archangelic figure; the Spirit is not inferior in terms of the Spirit's essence and being to both the Father and the Son.

Therefore, the Father is God; the Son is God; and the Holy Spirit is God.

The next three statements touch on the differentiation between the three persons. Contrary to Sabellianism, the three persons are not merely different forms of the same person. Consequently, the Father is not merely God assuming the role or guise of a father; the Son is not merely God assuming the guise of a son; and the Holy Spirit is not merely God assuming the guise of a spirit. In other words, the Father, Son, and Holy Spirit are not simply hand puppets.

Therefore, the Father is not the Son; the Son is not the Holy Spirit, and the Father is not the Holy Spirit.

---

20. Cf. Basil, *Spir.*, 10.24 (*OHS*, 10.24, p. 55).

However, it is the final statement of affirmation that causes a centuries-old offence. This statement affirms that there is only one God. It directly counters the doctrine of tritheism, in which the Father, Son, and Spirit are conceived of as three separate and independent divinities or deities, three gods who would do very well on their own but who nevertheless choose to work together for the good of humanity and the world.

The Christian belief in the Trinity is considered blasphemous in the Islamic faith, which holds that God is one, cannot possibly produce a son and has no equals or associates. It has to be noted, though, that the Trinity to which Islam objects comprises not the Father, Son and Holy Spirit, but the Father, Son and the Virgin Mary, the human mother of Jesus, and this is a misinterpretation of the Christian doctrine.[21]

The Christian doctrine of the Trinity caused offence in the days of St Gregory of Nyssa, a fourth-century Church Father typically grouped together with his brother, St Basil of Caesarea, and their common friend, St Gregory of Nazianzus, collectively known as the Cappadocian Fathers. Among other things, St Gregory of Nyssa was falsely and mistakenly accused by his theological opponents of propagating a doctrine of tritheism.

Existing Conceptions: Strengths and Weaknesses

Let us canvass some major views regarding God as Trinity.

Tertullian: Economic Trinitarianism

An early form of trinitarianism was economic trinitarianism. Economy here refers to God's plan of salvation for the world beginning with its creation. The architect of this doctrine was a third-century theologian by the name of Tertullian.

Tertullian is believed to have given us the term, 'Trinity', in its original Latin form, *Trinitas*.[22] He sought to strike a delicate balance between God being one and there being three divine persons by positing the Trinity as the form the one God takes in acting in the world.

According to Tertullian, prior to creation, God was a single being, with God's reason, the *Logos endiathetos* or the Word immanent, within

---

21. Hoover, 'Islamic Monotheism and the Trinity', pp. 57-82, corrected version, pp. 1-2.
22. P. van Inwagen and D. Howard-Snyder, 'Trinity: The Logical Problem of the Trinity', in E. Craig (ed.), *REP Online* (London: Routledge, 1998).

God. At the point of creation, God brought the Word immanent into external existence as the Son, who is the *Logos prophorikos* or the Word expressed.

The Son, in turn, brought the Holy Spirit into existence out of the Son's own being. In this way, God is actually one, and was so in eternity, but, when God acted to create the world, God generated two persons to aid in the creation and ruling of the world.

The strength of this formulation is that it tries to hold in creative tension the conception of God as one and of the existence of three divine persons. The disadvantage from which it suffers is that which afflicts all unitary theistic systems. This is that God as a monad would not be fundamentally capable of the kind of relational and interpersonal love which is supposed to characterise the essence of God in Christianity. Furthermore, it appears to be based on speculation about the forms God might take whether in eternity or history. It also gives short shrift to the fact that, according to the prophetic section of the Bible, God did not cease being one after creation.

The Cappadocian Fathers: Same Substance, Distinct Relations of Origin

I wish to dedicate slightly more space to a discussion of the Trinitarian theology of the Cappadocian Fathers.

Although the Cappadocian Fathers were wrongly accused of tritheism, their thinking was somewhat more nuanced and intricate. They did emphasise the distinctness of the persons through a concept of relations of origin. However, they also made it clear that the Father, Son and Holy Spirit are *homoousios*, or 'of one substance'.

There are two ways of conceiving of Father, Son and Spirit as being of one substance. First of all, in what is called the generic view, they are of one substance in that they are members of a common category of divine beings. This is unlikely to have been the view of the Cappadocians because it implies the existence of three Gods, a position they were anxious to disavow.

A second, and more plausible conception, views the Father, Son and Holy Spirit as being of 'numerically' the same substance. According to this perspective, there is only one divine substance, essence or nature and this incomprehensible and ineffable nature is shared in as complete and perfect a manner as possible between the Father, Son and Spirit.

Because there is only one divine substance, St Basil refused to allow a numbering of the members of the Trinity, that is, he was hesitant to refer to them as 'three' because to do so would be to detract from the essential oneness of the Godhead.

In the Nicene Creed (381), Jesus is said not to have been made by God but begotten of God. In other words, Jesus was not created by God at some point in time, but begotten, or fathered, by God the Father. Now, when did God the Father beget God the Son? The Cappadocian Fathers were insistent that the begetting, generation or fathering of the Son by the Father is not something which took place in time, at some point in the history of the universe, or even before the universe was created.

On the contrary, the begetting, generation or fathering of the Son is no less than an eternal act. However, when we speak of an eternal act, we do not actually mean this in the sense of an action that took place in the distant past. What we mean can be expressed by the term, perfection, or, completion. When we think of an action, there are basically three states in which an act can exist. It can either exist as a potential act, or an act that has yet to be performed and consists only in an idea or plan, it can exist as an act in the process of being performed, or it can exist as a completed or actualised act, an act that has actually been performed concretely.

In Christian theology, God exists in both an eternal realm and a temporal realm. The temporal realm is the universe in which we live. The eternal realm is an inaccessible place beyond the universe and beyond time itself, where God the Father, the Son and the Holy Spirit dwell together in a realm of perfect acts, such as the act of the decision to create, or the act of loving fellowship among the persons of the Trinity. Time does not flow in the eternal realm, such that the present becomes the past, and the future becomes the present. There is no change in divine eternity. God just exists in pure and eternal, loving fellowship. The Son and the Holy Spirit, as much as the Father, are part of this eternal being.

When we say of the Father that the Father begets the Son, and the Son is, correlatively, begotten of the Father, this is meant in two different but related senses.

First of all, the Father eternally begets the Son and the Son is begotten of the Father in a non-temporal process. The Cappadocians do not really elaborate on what it means to say that the Father eternally begets the Son or the Son is eternally begotten of the Father, simply describing the eternal process as 'ineffable'.

This is understandable. It is counterintuitive and even paradoxical to speak of a birthing of a son which does not actually take place in time. Nonetheless, perhaps what the Cappadocians mean is not so much that it is impossible even to attempt to understand the process of the eternal generation of the Son, but rather that human minds will not be able to completely grasp the fullness of what it means to describe God as being Father in relationship with Son and Son in relationship with Father.

So how does it happen that the Son is eternally begotten of the Father? The causative act of begetting does not and cannot exist in the eternal realm. That is, there was never a change of state from non-begotten to begotten on the part of the Son. The Son is always already begotten. Therefore, to speak of the begetting, generation and fathering of the Son is to speak of an eternal *fait accompli*, an eternal done deal. It is to speak of a familial relationship between the Father and the Son that has always existed. It is in this way that the Nicene Creed speaks of the Son as 'begotten from the Father before all ages … begotten, not made'.

We can see something of the relationship between the Father and the Son at the baptism of Jesus.[23] God the Father said to God the Son, Jesus, 'This is my beloved Son, with whom I am well pleased.'[24] These are words of paternal affirmation and acknowledgement. It will not be the only time Jesus hears these words from heaven. They will recur during his experience of transfiguration, when Jesus is filled with divine radiance, on Mount Tabor. Clearly, there is a loving and very affectionate father-son relationship between God the Father and God the Son.

Moving on to the third person of the Trinity, the Nicene Creed designates the Holy Spirit as 'the Lord, the giver of life', titles reserved for God alone. There is a long scriptural tradition of referring to God as the Lord. As for 'giver of life', God alone is the Creator and therefore the source of all life.

The Spirit 'proceeds from the Father'. Once more, there are no potential acts in divine eternity. So this procession of the Spirit is something which is always actual, and the Spirit never went from non-proceeding to proceeding. The Spirit represents the essence of the Father. The Spirit's procession from the Father amounts to the total self-giving of the Father towards the Son. This is an eternal act that is always completed and never only began to happen.

In other words, the establishment of the loving communion between the Father and the Son in which the Father gives of the Father's entire self, and the Son reciprocates, never began to take place because it has always existed. Accordingly, the procession of the Spirit signifies the processive, outgoing and loving nature of the eternally existing relationship of loving communion between the Father and the Son.

---

23. Matthew 3:13-17.
24. Matthew 3:17, ESV.

We can glimpse something of the outgoing and loving nature of the trinitarian relationship between the Father and the Son in the way in which Jesus spoke of the Holy Spirit as a divine gift to believers from the Father through the Son.[25]

Jesus told his disciples in this passage that the Father was ready to grant the Holy Spirit of God to anyone who asks the Father for this gift. Through the gift of the Holy Spirit, Christian believers are able to experience the loving nature of the relationship between the Father and the Son, because like the Son, the believer is able to receive the Holy Spirit, who proceeds from the Father, and to relish the conscientious care of the heavenly Father.

This construal of the procession of the Holy Spirit within the Trinity is necessary because the Holy Spirit proceeds from the Father and the Son (in Latin theology) only towards the created order; and it gives new meaning to the descriptions of Jesus being filled with the Holy Spirit in the Gospels, which can function as analogies of the life of the Trinity.

St Augustine of Hippo: A Critique of Divine Personhood

Although the Cappadocian Fathers made significant advances in trinitarian theology, there was an abiding sense particularly among Western theologians that the unity of the Godhead can be still better safeguarded than has been conventionally done through a theology of divine personhood.

Augustine of Hippo saw the limitations of applying the concept of personhood to the Trinity.[26] He recognised that theologians only spoke of the Trinity as a community of persons because they needed to avoid what they regarded as the twin errors of Sabellianism and tritheism.

Sabellianism, as we have seen, posits that God is just one person who takes on the form of a father, a son and a spirit. Tritheism is the view that the Father, Son and Holy Spirit constitute three Gods.

By using the term, 'person', theologians sought to indicate that, even though there is just one God, there are three things in God, which had to be called by some term. As for indicating that there is only one God, theologians employed the term, 'being'.[27]

---

25. Luke 11:5-13.

26. Augustine is known for his psychological analogies for the Trinity: memory, understanding, will, and being, knowing, willing. Cf. idem, *Conf.*, XIII.xi.12.

27. Augustine, *Trin.*, VII.3.4.9, VII.3.6.11.

St Augustine developed the idea of a numerically identical substance among the persons of the Trinity using an analogy of gold statues and human individuals. There is more gold or human essence in two or three statues or human individuals compared with one statue or one human individual. This, however, is not the case with the Trinity, where there is the same amount of divine essence in any one person as there is in all three persons.[28]

While human personhood is an inadequate analogy for the distinct personalities in the Godhead, it remains a useful heuristic device for attaining a deeper and clearer apprehension of the nature of the Father, Son and Holy Spirit.

Each of the divine persons possesses six crucial attributes of full personhood. They reveal themselves to be persons in the sense not just of the roles they play but in the sense of being self-identifying, feeling, thinking, willing, speaking and acting subjects.

The Father, Son and Holy Spirit are conscious of their self-identities, speaking of themselves in the first person;[29] they are able to experience emotion;[30] they are able to think;[31] they are able to will;[32] they are able to speak;[33] they are able to act;[34] they are able to relate with one another.[35] With these qualities of personhood, the divine persons freely enter into relationships with each other, angels and human beings.

Augustine contemplates the possibility of seeing the Holy Spirit as the divine goodness which Father and Son share together, given that the Spirit is in both, akin to the perspective of the Spirit as an essence of holiness that unites the other two divine persons. This logical move is tied to the theologian's need to explore the extent to which the three fundamental queries posed and addressed in Genesis chapter one – to wit, who made all things, how did the Creator make all this and why the Creator made it all – hint at the existence of the Trinity, in which: God the Father creates all and enables temporal creatures to acquire

28. Ibid., VII.3.6.11; idem, *Civ.*, XI.24.
29. E.g. Exodus 3:14-16, John 11:25, Acts 13:2.
30. E.g. Hosea 11:1-9, John 11:35, Ephesians 4:30.
31. E.g. Psalm 139:17-18, Mark 3:4, 1 Corinthians 2:6-16.
32. E.g. Jeremiah 31:31-34, Acts 13:2, Hebrews 10:5-9.
33. Exodus 3:14-16, John 11:25, Acts 13:2.
34. Genesis 1:1, Matthew 4:12-25, Acts 2:4.
35. The Father and the Son: John 12:27-28; the Spirit with God, on God's mission to take God's wisdom to impart to believers: 1 Corinthians 2:6-16.

their purpose for existence by existing in the Father's unchanging and immortal existence; God the Son is the means by which the Father made all things and enables knowledge-seeking creatures to participate in God's unchanging and immortal existence by meditating on the Son's verity; and God the Holy Spirit represents the goodness for which God made all things and enables joy-inclined creatures to obtain a share in God's goodness by participating and remaining in the goodness of the Holy Spirit.[36]

The bishop of Hippo goes on to identify another *vestigia Trinitatis*: being, knowledge and love as an image of the Trinity, in that a person knows that he exists through knowing that, even were one to be deluded in this opinion, it would only serve to demonstrate that one actually does exist, since only that which exists can be deluded in its opinion, such a person being therefore at the very least a carrier or bearer of erroneous thoughts. However, the knowledge that one is a bearer of thoughts accomplishes more than proving one's actual existence; it proves also that one is capable of knowledge or thought, whether this be right or wrong. If this is so, in a typical person who seeks happiness for himself and joyfully embraces his own existence in seeking it, there is also an affection for both his existence and the knowledge of it. As such, the human person whose existence consists in the inseparability of being, knowledge and love images the Creator God whose being, knowledge and love are similarly intertwined, whose boundless being is veracious and whose veracity has boundless being, whose love has both boundless being and veracity, and who is a triune God who has boundless being, veracity and love, all without conflation or division.[37]

The question remains of how we might resolve the three persons into the unity of the Godhead.

David Brown: The Trinity as Society

British philosopher David Brown attempts a solution by viewing the divine persons as one God in that they constitute something of a society.[38]

---

36. Augustine, *Civ.*, XI.24.
37. Ibid., XI.25-28.
38. D. Brown, 'Trinitarian Personhood and Individuality', in R.J. Feenstra and C. Plantinga, Jr (eds), *Trinity, Incarnation, and Atonement: Philosophical and Theological Essays* (Notre Dame, IN: University of Notre Dame Press, 1989), pp. 64-73.

These persons form a single community and unit which takes on personal characteristics. The way in which this is possible is that there is a shared or collective consciousness among multiple distinct entities. These entities, in turn, do not think of themselves and they are not conscious of themselves primarily as separate or isolated units but rather as a single, collective whole.

Such a situation arises whenever a society reaches some form of unanimity or majority view on a common approach to an issue, or when a people agree generally on how one ought to think about a particular group. Such a society functions in a manner akin to a single person.

While this is an innovative approach to the doctrine of the Trinity, it succeeds only in underscoring a unity of consciousness and function among the members of the Godhead rather than actually addressing the question of the numerical issue in trinitarian theology on an ontological level, that is, on the level of the being of the persons.

Proposition: Advantages and Prolepses

The key idea to understand how God can be one and yet there are three divine persons is interdependence.

As human beings, we are interdependent entities. Modern psychology has disclosed the extent to which relationship is central to the development of personhood.

Philosophical analysis has unearthed the insight that it is impossible to have a personal identity without relationship because it is only in our interactions with other people that we can develop a self-identity, become aware of ourselves as individuals and live out such a self-identity.[39]

Without being taught to do so, we should be unable even to speak, dress or relieve ourselves. This is borne out in the case of the feral child, a child brought up without a human connection. Genie Wiley was abused by her parents, shut away in a small room for most of her life and frequently tied to a potty chair. At the age of thirteen, she was found by a social worker while her mother was looking for health services.

At the time, Wiley was only 59 pounds, walked like a bunny, was given to spitting and could not stretch her arms and legs. She was quiet, unable

---

39. G. Versaldi and A.V. Zani, 'Male and Female He Created Them': Towards a Path of Dialogue on the Question of Gender Theory in Education (Vatican: Congregation for Catholic Education, 2019), p. 14, para. 27, pp. 18-19, para. 33.

to control her bowels, could not chew and only knew her name and the word, 'sorry'.[40]

According to a study co-authored by psychologist Louise Hawkley, the state of being alone may lead to issues with physical and mental health, including depression, poor sleep, impaired executive function, accelerated cognitive decline, poor cardiovascular function, impaired immunity and premature death.[41]

The fact that we are interdependent can be seen also in the way our self-validation is contingent on our external recognition by the surrounding community. Should the people around us wish to be extremely manipulative, it would be possible and conceivable, though by no means ethical and right, to cause an individual to question their own sanity. If people were truly independent and non-contingent beings, requiring nothing of social validation, it would be impossible for a person to be wrecked and destroyed in this systematic fashion.

We are made for community; and this link between who we are as human persons and the relationships in which we are embedded provides a hint to a fuller understanding of God as Trinity.

Not unlike human beings, the Father, the Son and the Holy Spirit are not independent beings, at least not insofar as their interrelationships are concerned, but interdependent persons.

To each divine person, the other two persons bring an essential element to the mix without which the first person would be affected. The Father cannot be the Father without the Son and the Spirit; the Son cannot be the Son without the Father and Spirit; and the Spirit cannot be the Spirit without the Father and Son.

This is clear to anyone who analyses the very names of the divine persons.

The first person of the Trinity is the Father. A father is a father by virtue of the fact that he has a child. If a man does not have any children, it would not be correct to refer to him as a father. Similarly, a man is a son only insofar as he has a biological father and a mother. Hypothetically speaking, if a man is without biological parents, it would not be possible to call him a son.

40. K. Cherry, 'The Story of Genie Wiley', *Verywell Mind*, Dotdash Meredith, last updated 28 October 2022, https://www.verywellmind.com /genie-the-story-of-the-wild-child-2795241.

41. A. Novotney, 'The Risks of Social Isolation', *Monitor on Psychology* 50, no. 5 (March 2020), https://www.apa.org/monitor/2019/05/ce-corner-isolation.html.

The case with the Spirit is a little trickier.

Here the analogy shifts to the tripartite structure of the human person. The person is made up of a spirit, representing the essence of a person, a soul or mind and a body. In this example, the person is an integrated being, with an inner core or identity, a mind and a body.

As persons in their own right, the Father and Son, too, are interconnected with the Holy Spirit and with one another, with the same closeness that obtains between a human person and his or her spirit,[42] with the human spirit playing a unifying role in the body similar to the way in which the Holy Spirit mediates love between the Father and the Son in the triune being.[43] The analogy of the spirit also points to the fact that each divine person is co-constituted by the other two persons each conceived as an internal, backgrounding element,[44] much as the spirit of a human person invisibly undergirds all that the person is and does outwardly. The human being has just as much necessity of a spirit, which functions as an inner core or a source or seat of personal identity, as the Father and Son have of the Holy Spirit, which forms a quintessential part of their being and life.

In this manner, the Father, Son and Holy Spirit would not be the persons they are in the absence of their counterparts in the trinitarian relationship and communion.

This interdependence runs so deep that not just would the Father, Son and Spirit be less than full persons without one another, but, without any one of them, the other two would not even exist.

This is because each divine person is constituted as a person by the other two persons. The essential elements that allow a divine person even to exist as the persons they are, are possessed by the other two divine persons. Therefore, the absolute interdependence of the divine persons is posited.

---

42. This is not intended to be a literal analogy, and there is no suggestion here that the first and second persons of the Trinity are comparable to a bio-socio-physical being without its inner soul, and that the third person of the Trinity amounts to nothing more than the inner soul of the presumed 'person'.

43. It is not that apart from the Spirit, the Father and Son have not love for each other but simply that the Holy Spirit adds to the paternal-filial relationship by facilitating communion between them.

44. This is to use the nomenclature of the Korean-American theologian, Jung Young Lee.

An analogy would be helpful here. Suppose we take a dry sponge, and we place this sponge into a small amount of coloured water in a bowl, and allow it completely to absorb the water. Then we decide to discard the wet sponge. Where does the coloured water go? It goes with the sponge into the bin. Similarly, whatever befalls the Father, Son or Spirit, befalls the other two persons as well.

This is not just true on an ontological or existential level. It is also true on lower levels, such as that of emotionality and the psyche. There is an intimate connection between the divine persons, an intimate sharing of minds and hearts. The divine persons find their unique identity in communion with the other persons. They cherish each other's presence, pursue each other's highest good, and rejoice, anger, sorrow, mourn and hope together.

The German theologian Jürgen Moltmann rightly speaks of the way in which, when Jesus, the Son of God, was crucified, the Father grieved the death of the Father's Son.[45] Likewise, Jung Young Lee wrote about a horrifying experience of death on the Cross which was shared by the Father and the Holy Spirit as well.[46]

If there is an ontological, existential and emotional-psychological interdependence among the members of the Trinity, there is also a complete harmony of action.

Conscious that they depend on the other members for their being, existence and emotional-psychological wellbeing, the divine persons do everything together. In whatever the Father does, the Son and Spirit jump in and join along. In whatever the Son does, the Father and Spirit jump in and join along. In whatever the Spirit does, the Father and Son jump in and join along.

For this reason, the Scriptures record Jesus as saying that he acts in complete solidarity with the Father,[47] that, just as the Father discloses to Jesus how the Father raises the dead and gives life to people, so Jesus gives life to those he chooses.

At this juncture, I should like to introduce the doctrine and notion of *perichoresis* as applied to the Trinity. This is a concept worked out by the seventh- and eighth-century theologian, St John of Damascus, on the

45. J. Moltmann, *The Crucified God: The Cross of Christ as the Foundation and Criticism of Christian Theology*, trans. R.A. Wilson and J. Bowden (London: SCM, 2015), pp. 192, 203, 214, 216-18, 227, 229-30, 243, 245, 247-49, 252-56, 267-78.
46. Lee, *TiAP*, pp. 82, 91-94.
47. John 5:19-38.

basis of earlier insights. The notion of a *perichoresis* of the divine persons postulates that the divine persons each envelop and are enveloped by the other divine persons. This agrees with the statement of Jesus in John 14:8-11 that he is in the Father and the Father is in him.

Perichoresis has been deployed to interrelate disparate yet connected skeins such as God and matter, the divine and human natures of Christ and, more famously, the divine persons in the trinitarian communion. It combines ideas expressed in two related Latin words; namely, *circuminsessio* and *circumincessio*. The two categories are to be distinguished in proportion as they exist either in a passive (*circuminsessio*) or active (*circumincessio*) mode.

The passive dimension, taking from *sedere* and *sessio*, signifying a seat, the state of being seated, or the position where one is seated, describes how the elements of a perichoretic relationship, in this case, the divine persons, are surrounded and filled by the other elements; whereas, in the active meaning, derived from *incedere*, meaning to pervade or suffuse, the elements and divine persons surround and fill the other elements.[48]

The traditional approach conceives of the divine persons as permeating, interpenetrating and indwelling one another. As such it is preoccupied with the social, communal and cooperative dimension of the life of the persons of the Godhead.

In contrast, and without denying the validity of the social approach, the current approach utilises the notion of *perichoresis* as interpenetration and indwelling in the context of the structure of the being, essence, nature and psyche of the individual divine person.[49]

With the Trinity, we do not simply have the Father, Son and Holy Spirit as three separate beings. We have the Father containing the Son and Spirit, the Son containing the Father and Spirit, and the Spirit containing the Father and Son, in a mutually inclusive, ever-revolving triangle of persons. In other words, the whole of the Godhead is present in each divine person.

Therefore, the Father is fully divine, the Son is fully divine and the Holy Spirit is fully divine. At one and the same time, there is only one God, because the three divine persons form a completely integrated and interdependent whole.[50]

---

48. L. Boff, *Trinity and Society*, trans. P. Burns (Eugene, OR: Wipf & Stock, 2005), pp. 135-36.
49. Cf. Chua, 'God-ness', 'God-ity', and God: A Historical Study and Synthesis of the Christian Doctrine of the Divine Being, 79-102.
50. Heim, *Depth of the Riches*, p. 105.

As a matter of fact, there are three distinct and different ways of viewing the one God.

There is the angle of the one God existing as the Father, in which the Son and the Holy Spirit co-constitute the being of the Father and allow the Father to exist and function as the Father. In this manner, the Father exists and has full personhood and function through the being of the Son and the Holy Spirit and relates with these other persons as Father.

There is the angle of the one God existing as the Son, in which the Father and Spirit co-constitute the being of the Son and allow the Son to exist and function as the Son. In this manner, the Son exists and has full personhood and function through the being of the Father and the Holy Spirit and relates with these other persons as the Son.

There is, moreover, the angle of the one God existing as the Holy Spirit, in which the Father and the Son co-constitute the being of the Holy Spirit and allow the Holy Spirit to exist and function as the Holy Spirit. In this manner, the Holy Spirit exists and has full personhood and function through the being of the Father and the Son and relates with these other persons as the Holy Spirit.

Therefore, the Father is the only God because in the Father we already find the Son and the Holy Spirit. The Son is the only God because in the Son we already find the Father and the Holy Spirit. The Holy Spirit is the only God because in the Holy Spirit we already find the Father and the Son.[51]

This is just what it means to say of the Christian God, that there is just one God but three divine persons, God the Father, God the Son and God the Holy Spirit.

In the Nicene Creed, the Son is 'Light from Light, true God from true God ... of one substance[52] with the Father'. This involves the eternal communication or imparting of God's very substance from the Father to the Son. Once again, there are no potential acts in eternity. So, when we speak of the eternal communication of substance from Father to Son, we have in mind an eternal *fait accompli*, an eternal done deal. The Father never moved from a state of non-communication of the Father's substance to a state of communication of the Father's substance. The Son has always had the Father's substance and never not had that substance.

---

51. Cf. Augustine, *The Trinity*, trans. E. Hill, 2nd edn, The Works of Saint Augustine: A Translation for the 21st Century (Hyde Park, NY: New City, 1990), p. 230, fn. 36.
52. Greek, *homoousion*.

This is the doctrine of *homoousios*, the idea that the Son is of the same substance as the Father.

Between the Father, Son and Holy Spirit, there is just one divine substance, which the Father eternally communicates to the Son. We can assume that in the same manner, the Son eternally communicates this substance to the Holy Spirit, so as to complete the picture of the mutual communion among the three persons.

This pattern, sequence and order affords us a glimpse into the inner structure of the Trinity. The biblical book of Proverbs[53] contains a curious passage in which the wisdom of God personified relates events that took place before the creation of the world.

In this poetic passage, wisdom is narrating the things that happened in the beginning, before even the world was created, how God 'possessed', 'acquired', 'fathered' or 'created' wisdom 'at the beginning of [God's] work [or way], the first of [God's] acts of old'.

Now, who is this wisdom? The Proverbs passage reads a lot like the prologue to the Book of John. Consider John 1:1-3; the Word in this context refers to God the Son. In another passage in the New Testament, 1 Corinthians 1:30, Jesus is named, 'wisdom from God' (ESV). God the Son seems to be the personification of wisdom in Proverbs 8:22-31.[54] This is a fair assumption. The passage speaks of God as 'fathering' this personification of wisdom, a verb which normally applies only to the Son. It discusses wisdom as being God's 'master workman' just as God the Son was the agent through whom God made everything in John chapter one. Finally, it describes wisdom as being 'daily [God's] delight', which is what we saw God the Father expressing at the baptism of Jesus. There is no issue with this personification of wisdom being female in gender, since God the Son, apart from becoming Jesus, is a purely spiritual being and has no gender.

In this way, we are given creative space by this poetic passage to imagine what it could mean for God to have 'possessed', 'acquired', 'fathered', 'created', 'set up' and 'brought forth' the Son. This is what I believe the passage is talking about: there are three divine persons, the Father, the Son and the Holy Spirit. These three persons are inseparable and have always existed. There has never been a time when any one of them did not exist. It is impossible to separate the persons of the Trinity. However, in order more fully to understand the unity of the Godhead, it is necessary for me to paint a completely hypothetical, notional and – I

---

53. Proverbs 8:22-31.
54. Augustine of Hippo, for one, took this view, *Civ.*, XVII.20.

should say – impossible scenario in which the persons become separate one from another.

So, let us suppose that something could be done to the Trinity such that the divine persons became separate one from another. If this impossible thing were done, and they were separated, the Father, Son and Holy Spirit would not be the full persons they are. They would be pre-persons or proto-persons.

A proto-person is an incomplete person, a person who lacks an essential attribute of personhood. It is akin to a disembodied brain. So 'proto' is used here in the sense of 'primitive', an incomplete form of something which awaits development and fullness. There would be a proto-Father, a proto-Son and a proto-Holy Spirit.

Now let's assign key attributes of a personal being to each of these proto-persons. Let's assign to the proto-Father, the attribute of wisdom, since Christ is 'wisdom from God', meaning wisdom from God the Father. In this case, wisdom becomes what it is in Proverbs 8:22-31 through being possessed and acquired by the proto-Father as wisdom. The true wisdom (the Father) sets up and brings forth wisdom (the Son); and what of the proto-Son? Let us assign to this proto-person the attribute of the will, since the Gospels portray Jesus the Son as being filled with resolution and determination, even to hasten towards a place where he would be killed.[55]

So, thus far, we have the proto-Father as wisdom, the proto-Son as will and, with regard to the proto-Holy Spirit, we shall assign the attribute of agency of action, because the Spirit of God is the agent through whom God, especially in the Old Testament, works in the world. Consider the anointment of David by the prophet Samuel in 1 Samuel 16:12-13.

As the inner essence of the loving relationship between the Father and the Son, the Spirit also possesses the attribute of feeling or emotions.

So the proto-Father is wisdom, the proto-Son is will and the proto-Holy Spirit is agency of action and affect. In a first phase, the proto-Father moves towards the proto-Son and shares the proto-Father's wisdom with the proto-Son, thus setting up and bringing forth the proto-Son as a being of wisdom. In so doing, the proto-Father possesses or permeates the proto-Son. In turn, the proto-Son permeates the proto-Father. This means that the proto-Father and proto-Son are in communion with each other. Through this communion, the proto-Father who is wisdom acquires the attribute of will, while the proto-Son who is will acquires the attribute of wisdom.

---

55. Luke 9:21-22, 51.

However, these two proto-persons still do not possess full personhood, for it is not enough to have wisdom, that is, the ability to think and plan, and will, that is, the ability to decide. Moreover, the proto-Holy Spirit is still languishing with only the attributes of agency of action and affect.

Therefore, a further act of communion is needed, in which the proto-Father and proto-Son now in communion move towards the proto-Holy Spirit, and together they possess and permeate this proto-person. In this way, all three acquire all the fundamental attributes of personhood, with the Father, Son and Holy Spirit having: wisdom, the ability to think and plan; will, the ability to decide; and, finally, agency of action, the ability to act, and affect, the ability to feel.

It is in just this way that we are able to speak of the Father, Son and Holy Spirit as having one common essence or substance. They do not constitute three Gods but just one God because they are who they are individually and respectively only in inseparable communion with one another, a communion and fellowship which consummates the fullness of each person's being.

Each of the divine persons is fully God and the only God. This is because the divine persons contain one another within themselves. If this is the case, it means that the Father, for instance, who contains the Son and the Spirit within the Father's being, is already all that God is. The same state of affairs obtains with the Son, who contains the Father and the Spirit, and the Spirit, who contains the Father and the Son. Jesus himself testified that he is in the Father, and the Father is in him.[56]

Consequently, when we speak of the one God in Christianity and we ask who this one God is, there are three ways to answer the question, because there are three ways in which the one God exists. The one God exists as the Father, containing the Son and the Spirit, as the Son, containing the Father and the Spirit, and as the Spirit, containing the Father and Son. There is thus an overlapping of the being of each divine person without any person getting in the way of another, but acting harmoniously and cooperatively with one another in wielding the same divine substance.

I favour the analogy of a transparent tetrahedron as an excellent illustration of the ontological interdependence of the divine persons. Whichever side you view the three-dimensional triangle through, you will see the other three sides, and it is immediately evident that the side you are observing the triangle through exists in the way it does only because the other sides also exist.

---

56. John 14:8-11.

Similarly, the Father is all of the Godhead but with the identity, awareness and behaviour associated with being the Father, and the Son is all of the Godhead but with the identity, awareness and behaviour associated with being the Son, and the Spirit is all of the Godhead but with the identity, awareness and behaviour associated with being the Spirit.

Perichoretic constitution draws on the patristic insight as to how the Father depends on the existence of the Son to exist as Father. In the case of St Athanasius, God as origin of God's Word and wisdom, radiant light and spring of water depends on the existence of that Word, wisdom, radiance and water, while, in the case of St Augustine, God as eminent, benevolent, ever-existent, all-powerful, just and sagacious depends on the existence of that benevolence, ever-existence, power, justice and sagacity.[57]

The mutual dependence of the divine persons in the Trinity is attested in the theological doctrines of divine simplicity, unity and love and the philosophical-psychological theory of a relational element in the development of self-identity and personhood.

Divine simplicity proposes that God is not a composite being made up of parts, where one part of God differs from another part. As such, the Trinity is not a being made up of three parts, one being the Father, another being the Son and a third being the Spirit, but there is a perfect evenness, in which every part of the divine being is as much the Father as the Son and the Spirit.

The doctrine of divine simplicity posits that the multiple attributes of God, whether it be God's benevolence, wisdom, power or righteousness, do not constitute parts of the divine being such that one portion of God's being is constituted by God's righteousness while another part of God's being is constituted by God's benevolence. It is not therefore that, to the extent that God is righteous, God cannot be benevolent and, to the extent that God is benevolent, God cannot be righteous. God's righteousness and benevolence, and, for that matter, any other seemingly opposing pair of divine attributes, are not mutually exclusive attributes. God is merciful in being righteous, and righteous in being merciful; divine benevolence is tempered by divine righteousness, and divine righteousness is tempered by divine benevolence.

Accordingly, God's righteousness does not consist in pure and rigid legalism, a demand for an adherence to legal principles without respect

---

57. Athanasius, *Contr. Ar.*, I.14 (*Against the Arians*, I.V.14, pp. 314-15), Augustine, *Trin.*, VI.1-2 (WSA, VI.1-3, pp. 205-7).

to some higher, moral purpose, but solely in divine kindness and mercy. It is because of God's mercy that God bestows on humanity a code of moral law by which to organise the relationships between individuals and communities. Conversely, it would be less than merciful of God to leave humankind in chaos and anarchy. Similarly, God's benevolence does not consist in a permissiveness and laxity which condones all manner of immoral behaviour, but rather it is a goodness of God's character which is based on clear moral boundaries. Even within the Godhead, not just God's love but God's justice as well is operative, as an expression of how each divine person will never stoop to hating or harming one another based on their mutual and reciprocal love for one another; justice, therefore, functions as an important dimension of inner-trinitarian divine love that is not, however, positively expressed within the Trinity, simply because there is no possibility of its expression among authentically and completely loving persons. It is, however, a disposition within the Godhead which is able to be positively manifested towards errant entities beyond the Trinity.[58]

We do well to note that having definite moral boundaries does not entail that God has to be punitive, retributive or draconian in God's approach to human sin. What it does imply is that there is a clear notion of a moral ideal to which all should aspire, but the way towards that ideal is not through condemnation, whether of self or other, but soberness and forgiveness, soberness so that people are urged always to strive to live diligently and not to exploit God's mercy, and forgiveness so that people may always start anew. God's righteousness completely permeates God's benevolence and God's benevolence completely permeates God's righteousness, as all God's other attributes permeate one another.

Likewise, in the being of God as three persons, the Father does not constitute one part of God, the Son, a second, and the Spirit, a third, such that the Father excludes the Son, the Son excludes the Spirit, and the Father excludes the Spirit. Therefore, the Father, Son and Holy Spirit completely permeate one another.

The doctrine of divine unity also results in the doctrine of a perichoretic constitution, because divine unity entails that the divine persons be so grouped together and identified with one another that only one God emerges from the total picture and net effect of the doctrine of three fully divine persons. The persons of the Godhead cannot be separated

---

58. Cf. J. Sanders, 'Divine Providence and the Openness of God', in B.A. Ware (ed.), *Perspectives on the Doctrine of God: Four Views* (Nashville, TN: Broadman & Holman, 2008), p. 197, fn. 1.

from one another not just in a socio-communal sense, but even in an ontological-existential and emotional-psychological sense.

In the theological doctrine of divine love, it is necessary for God to be more than a single person, so that God would not be in need of humanity in order to have the nature of love, since love requires another person in order to be actualised. While God does not need us in the sense that we do not have anything to offer God that God does not already have and has had from the very start or anything to add to God's infinite perfection, we must be careful to clarify that this only means that, were we somehow to be taken away from God, God would continue to exist in God's perfection and bliss.

Nonetheless, having brought us into existence in the sense of positing us with all other things, God is committed to our welfare as a rightfully responsible parent is devoted to the wellbeing of their child, in a relationship in which God cannot simply pull away from us without harming God's own conscience, be emotionally unaffected by our agonies, miseries and tragedies, or feel no love or desire for our presence and a flourishing relationship with us. God plumbs the deepest depths of our sorrow and hopelessness without ever being permanently debilitated or crippled, rises to the highest heights of our joys, comforts, hopes and satisfactions without ever thinking to dampen our mood out of envy or dourness or taking a naïvely optimistic view of the situation.

A conception of God as aloof and emotionally detached, in a bid to keep God independent of contingent reality, should be evaded, in possible interpretation even if not actual meaning, in preference for a view concerning God as ontologically but not psychologically non-reliant upon human beings.[59] Indeed, God is unable to hold back revealing that God cannot bring Godself to abandon God's people, Israel, in Hosea chapter eleven, and that this inability to harden God's heart against the people of Israel is properly characteristic of God alone.[60]

As for the philosophical-psychological theory of a relational element in the development of self-identity and personhood, this theory suggests that it is crucial for there to be other people in order for a person to develop a self-identity and therefore personhood.

I would like to underscore here, again, that this theorised separation of the Trinity is neither an actual nor possible scenario, but completely hypothetical and notional, purely a teaching aid to assist us in our understanding of the oneness of God.

---

59. Cf. Ware, 'A Modified Calvinist Doctrine of God', pp. 78-85.
60. Cf. Hosea 11:8-9.

As a result of an interdependence of being among the proto-divine persons, each brings an essential and unique personal attribute to the greater whole. The Father, Son and Holy Spirit are individually a personal centre within an identical being, inseparable from one another. Each person has a unique and inalienable sense of who they are as distinct persons, yet the ability to exist and act as full persons, with the attributes of feeling, thinking, willing and acting, come from their being who they are in communion with the other divine persons.

Think, if you will, of the divine persons as akin to three brains each in need of being connected to a common brain-controlled robotic suit in order to exist and function as persons. This, of course, is not a physical suit, but an invisible system and framework that enables the three persons to move around freely in three different hubs or personal forms. Each person has a primary hub which they share with the other two persons as secondary occupants.

These hubs and personal forms are interchangeable between the Father, Son and Spirit; and, if at any point the Son, say, wishes, the Son may exchange the Son's hub or personal form with another divine person. This is because each of the three hubs or personal forms do not belong to a specific person *per se*, but they are part of an integrated system constituted through the communion between the Father, Son and Spirit.

Even though we speak of the divine persons in terms of brains and robotic suits as analogies, there is no way to distinguish between a divine person and the divine substance, so completely interpenetrated and interpenetrating, and mutually suffused and suffusing they are. Furthermore, even as we employ the analogy of a robotic suit and hubs, the invisible framework that is the divine substance is not an external part of the divine persons but basic and fundamental to their very being.

Nevertheless, analogies remain useful in helping us to grasp that, when, for instance, the Bible depicts God the Father as being in heaven waiting for the Son to ascend to the Father's right hand, whereupon the Holy Spirit would be sent into the world to infuse the hearts of believers, we are not to apprehend the Father, Son and Spirit as being separated from one another by the horizon between heaven and earth.

It is not as though they were simply something like three human persons, one an astronaut in outer space, another a farmer on earth and a third parachuting somewhere in the sky.

On the contrary, the divine persons are more like three groups of three people, except that we have to conceive of each group as being like a single person, with a primary occupant, and two secondary occupants living in the being of the primary occupant. Of course, the Holy Spirit being the spiritual companion of every Christian believer is in many places at one time, and if the Spirit is in many places at one time, the other persons being contained within the Spirit, are also in many places at any one time.

Therefore, when Jesus prayed to the Father, he was immediately and directly heard by the Father dwelling secondarily within his physical body, soul and spirit. However, because the Father is only a secondary dweller in the being of Jesus, if the Father wishes to act, the Father has to do so in the Father's primary personal form, which is in heaven. Alternatively, the Father may choose to act through the Son. For this reason, Jesus says in John 14:10-11 that God the Father speaks and works through Jesus and that these representative acts Jesus performs on behalf of his Father testify to the way in which Jesus is in the Father and the Father is in Jesus.

Because each divine person has a primary hub, at his baptism, Jesus himself went down into the water and emerged from it, while the Father almost separately spoke from heaven and the Holy Spirit alighted on Jesus. Furthermore, Jesus says of the Father that the Father shows him what the Father is doing, as though the Father and Jesus were in separate places rather than identical in position, and Jesus simply emulates what the Father is doing, such as in giving life to the spiritually dead.[61]

There is a complete and perfect union of spirits, hearts and minds in each of the three hubs, but each person can only execute their activity in their own primary personal form. For this reason, when Jesus hung on the Cross in great agony, the Father and Holy Spirit suffered in anguish along with him. Although the Father and Spirit being purely spiritual entities are incapable of feeling physical sensations without a physical body, they are able to experience the psychological pain, the sorrow, fear, misery, doubt and despair of Jesus going through his travail. If ever the Trinity were on the brink of separation, it was at the Cross of Calvary, where brutal torture attempted to split apart even the mutually indwelling divine persons in the body of Jesus one from another into ghettoes and huddles.

Not many may be accustomed to feeling the emotions and agony of Jesus, with our tendency to sanitise images of the Cross in our art and preaching. The pain Jesus endured was no ordinary agony. It amounted to an abject rejection and betrayal on the part of human beings who had conspired against the loving guardian and protector of all humankind. As much as it was unbearable physical pain, it was just as intolerable as an emotional assault of gross and incalculable injustice. God had never been

---

61. John 5:19-21.

in so much pain; and all that Jesus, the Father and the Spirit did and went through was for our salvation, to provide atonement for human sin.

In light of the foregoing, the Trinity is a rational doctrine of the Christian faith, not a self-confounding contradiction in terms, as it has been regarded by various critics of the doctrine. There is no shortage of opponents of trinitarian doctrine, even within Christian circles. Nonetheless, I should like to canvass that we retain this crucial piece of Christian theology – if only because it enables us, more than any other Christian doctrine, I have to say, to appreciate and recognise the value, in Christian terms, of a connectivity, mutual sensitivity, sympathy, empathy, solidarity, co-solicitude and commiseration among persons. The Trinity, therefore, goes to the heart of what it means to be human.

Chapter 6

Doctrines: Christology

Definition

Christology constitutes the academic theological study of the person and work of Jesus Christ as expressed in the biblical writings. It is difficult to overstate the importance of Christological doctrine for the Christian faith, particularly in a codification which adheres to a classical framework.

As a subset of Christological doctrine, ontological Christology refers to an approach to Christology which focusses on the person of Jesus Christ, in particular, the substance, being and nature of his personhood. Such a doctrine considers, specifically, what it means to say that Jesus is divine and human at one and the same time.

Place in a Systematic Theology

An ontological Christology defined as the study of the substance, being and nature of the personhood of Jesus Christ occupies a metaphysical-philosophical place in the systematic study of Christian theology. The benefits of such a Christology, therefore, are equivalent to those enjoyed by any metaphysical conception, including a classification of different entities one alongside another for better apprehension through inviting a comparison of similarities and differences.

Specific to systematic theology, knowledge of the metaphysical dimensions of Christ's person is a crucial skein in that certain aspects of the Christian theological edifice depend on an assessment of Christ's nature, most notably, the soteriological doctrine, but also the creational design for humankind in both formal and substantive terms reliably disclosed through Christ the human being.

In the study of ontological Christology, we are interested in probing the central question of how a dual nature on the part of Jesus Christ as God-human lines up against the idea of him as a single, unitary personality. Both aspects of Christ's being have to be held in tension, if only because the Christian Scriptures appear to suggest their importance and necessity to any exposition of his nature as God and human. Perhaps the challenge of any doctrine that seeks to articulate the connection between Christ's dual natures and his unitary personhood is the proportionality of emphasis on one side in relation to the other.

Does Christ's nature as a human person, therefore, hold slightly greater weight than his divine nature, or is the contrary conception closer to the mark? Or should equal prominence be given to each nature, as far as this is possible? Of necessity, this is not such an easy question to address as it might first appear to be. Whilst a glib and abstract statement to the effect that Christ is as fully human as he is divine may be prescribed, yet there is a need to connect that discussion with an entirely different and competing dimension of Christ understood as a single personal entity. If it was once simple to declare of Christ that he possesses both divine and human qualities in equal measure, this is no longer the case once it is realised that the abstract, metaphysical and rarefied is in need of specification, concretisation and reification in the context of the personal consciousness and experience of Christ himself.

Although the doctrine of God precedes that of Christ in certain manuals of systematic theology, this is true only ontologically, and such an ordering should not be permitted to obscure the fact that, in reality, the intimations in the Scriptures concerning the person of Christ are noetically antecedent to the edifice of God, for, indeed, it is through the Son that the Father of the Son is known by humanity.

Existing Conceptions: Strengths and Weaknesses

Patristic theologians struggled to articulate an ontological Christological doctrine concerning the relation between Christ's divine and human natures in a unitary personhood for the reason of a gaping chasm between that which belongs to humanity and that which belongs to God in terms of the attributes and qualities of each.

There were a series of metaphysical oppositions which rendered any fusion suspect if not logically impossible; namely, a distinction between God as immutable and humanity as changeable,[1] between God as impassible and humanity as passible or vulnerable to pain and

---

1. Pelikan, *Chr. Trad.* 1, pp. 52-53, 230-31.

suffering,[2] between God as self-subsistent or necessary and humanity as contingent,[3] between God as eternal or immortal and humanity as created mortal,[4] between God as spiritual and humanity as material,[5] between God as simple or indivisible and humanity as diverse or various,[6] and between God as all-moving or omnicompetent and humanity as moved, finite being.[7]

In light of this philosophical dilemma, several solutions were suggested.[8] A first set of answers attempted to resolve the contradiction by downplaying either the human or divine nature of Christ. Docetics, whose thought left its mark on Christian history as early as the days of the apostles, proposed Jesus of Nazareth as a phantom of sorts, having no real, only ostensible, bodily existence, thereby affirming Christ's divine nature yet at the expense of his humanity.

Pursuing a rather different solution, adoptionists, the Jewish-Christian Ebionites among them, tried to reduce the antinomy by exalting Christ as a fully-fledged human person in the first instance, later conferred divine attributes at his baptism.

Arius and his followers promoted the doctrine of Christ as a semi-divine figure, the most exalted of all God's creatures, superior even to humanity and angels, yet nevertheless beneath God. In this manner, they sought to elude the implication that there were two divine figures, two Gods.

Adding to the complexity of the theological discussion, a monk from Constantinople, Eutyches (378-456), suggested that Christ being both divine and human may have undergone a process of the two vastly contrasting natures intermingling to form a mixed divine-human nature, or in such a way that the divine nature won out over the human.

The Church Fathers, however, discerned traces in the Scriptures which obliged them to maintain an uneasy tension in which it had to be granted that Christ was human and divine at one and the same time,

---

2. Ibid., pp. 52-53, 229-31.
3. Ibid., p. 53.
4. Ibid., pp. 229, 231.
5. Ibid., p. 53.
6. Ibid.
7. Ibid., p. 54.
8. The following overview profits from a survey I had previously done on ontological Christology: E. Chua, 'How Is Jesus One Person with Two Natures? Heresies and the Mainstream "Chalcedonian" Position', *The Courier* (January 2019), pp. 36-38.

neither divine and only apparently human (docetism), nor human at first and only later divine (adoptionism), nor partially human and partially divine (Eutyches), nor superhuman (Arius).

However, even members of the victorious orthodoxy of the fourth century could not but teeter on the edge of subscribing to an adoptionistic doctrine. St Athanasius of Alexandria, for instance, expressly intimated of Christ that he was created of God as a human, and constituted by the fusion of the eternal Word and Son of God with that created human being, no doubt seeking to do justice to a reference in Proverbs chapter eight to Christ, with whom Wisdom is identified, as having been formed by God in the beginning.

The prevailing orthodox fathers espoused a doctrine not just of a dual nature of Christ but a dual will to accompany it, comprising a human will and set of desires as well as a divine will and set of desires. From this, the theology of the fourth-century bishop of Laodicea, Apollinaris, marked a substantive departure. He sought to unify the two natures of Christ in a single person on the level of the desire and will, arguing that Christ only had a divine will and desires (monothelitism).

The fathers of orthodoxy, such as Gregory of Nazianzus (329-90), Pope Leo I (400-61) and John of Damascus (676-749), devised a way of speaking about the two natures and wills of Christ which underscored an ability on the part of the God-man to experience life both as a divine and human being by a mutually beneficial and harmonious arrangement or synergy between his divine and human natures.

According to this scheme, whenever required by his mission on earth, Jesus could alternately choose, in an operation of his divine will to which the complex of his human nature-will-operation was ultimately subservient, to undergo experiences peculiar to human beings, as opposed to God, such as physical and emotional needs and suffering (including hunger, thirst, exhaustion, fear, sorrow and even death), or those peculiar to God, as opposed to a human being, involving omnipotence and omniscience.

Consequently, the divine subject, Jesus, could decide, on some occasions, to allow the human complex momentarily to express itself in his mind and body with the divine complex playing a dormant role. On other occasions, the same divine subject could decide that it was time for the divine complex to express itself in his mind and body with the human complex playing a dormant role.

In the Chalcedonian view, Christ is divine in a manner unmolested by the vicissitudes of the world in that his original being remains in a timeless eternity, shut away from interaction with the divine economy, while a human body which enables Christ to establish a direct and authentic presence in the world is capable of being affected by that which happens in the world. However, these two natures are indissolubly unified across the eternal and temporal realms without confusion, change, division and separation in just one subject, Christ. In any case, the attributes of the divine nature are functionally expressed even in the spatio-temporal world at the behest of a divine subject which determines when a divine or human nature is evinced.

The patriarch Nestorius of Constantinople (386-451) thought that it was critical for an ontological Christology to avoid the possibility of Christ's divine nature overtaking his human constitution and the conclusion that God, in Christ, was born of a woman. Nestorius dissented from the use of the title, *theotokos*, 'God-bearer', of Mary, suggesting instead *anthropotokos*, 'bearer of man', or *Christotokos*, 'bearer of Christ'. Hence, he tried to resolve the latent ambiguity generated by patristic philosophical categories, which sharply differentiated between Christ's divine nature as eternal and human nature as created and having a beginning, through more explicit statements regarding a juxtaposition of human and divine natures in Christ which underscored their clear distinction.[9] Unfortunately, Nestorius' political and ecclesiastical opponents viewed his theological statements as tending to bring about a dissociation within the single person of Christ, charging him with teaching Christ as a composite being made up of two different persons, a human being led by a divine person within a single body.[10]

In the twentieth century, the Canadian Jesuit priest, philosopher and theologian Bernard Lonergan (1904-84) sought to build on a Chalcedonian theology by arguing for a dual consciousness of Christ, as a single divine subject,[11] both as human and divine on the basis of his twofold nature, will and principle of action,[12] providing a psychological interpretation of a classical doctrine of the two natures of Christ.[13]

---

9. Athanasius, *Contr. Ar.*, II.47 (*Against the Arians*, II.XIX.47, p. 374).

10. *NDT*, s.v. 'Nestorius' (H.D. McDonald, p. 457).

11. This is contrary to what was condemned as Nestorian heresy.

12. This is contrary to monophysitism (Christ as having one nature, a divine one and not also a human one), monothelitism (Christ as having one will, a divine one and not also a human one) and monergism (Christ as having one principle of action, a divine one and not also a human one).

13. Lonergan, *Const. Chr.*, 6.2, §91, pp. 224-25.

Lonergan begins his Thomistic-Aristotelian Christological doctrine by laying the terms of reference for affirming a hypostatic union of Christ.[14] His pivotal emphases concern how in Christ there is but one subject, and this is the divine person and not also a human person. Essentially, in the Incarnation, the triune God elected for the Son alone to undergo a process of assuming a human nature in addition to the Son's pre-existing and eternal divine nature.[15] This addition of a human nature to the divine subject that is the Son is conceptual on the side of the divine nature – improperly speaking, since nothing can alter an already perfect divine nature – and real on the side of the human nature.[16]

The process of incarnation is characterised not by a moral or spiritual union between a human Christ and a divine Word, such as human beings experience in sanctification, but by an integration with a human essence itself, 'undivided in itself and divided from everything else', though without a separate human person with 'its proper act of existence'.[17] The combination of the divine and human natures in Christ can only be described as a supernatural process on the human side, since it is impossible for a human nature of its own capacity to associate itself with an infinite divine subject.[18] Ultimately, it is the divine subject that is the Son who 'causes' or constitutes and maintains the hypostatic union by the Son's own 'infinite act of existence', which in the Godhead, is exhaustively united with the divine understanding and willing; the hypostatic union is not maintained by the act of assumption itself.[19]

Lonergan defines human consciousness in terms of an 'experience' by a subject of itself and its own actions, rather than a 'perception' of internal facts and psychological activity as objects, whereby 'experience' refers specifically to a 'preliminary unstructured sort of awareness that is presupposed by intellectual inquiry and completed by it'.[20]

Experience concerns the unstructured awareness that the subject of awareness exists and acts when it sees, understands, judges, wills, grieves or performs any other action, and this is prior to any conceptualisation,

---

14. In Lonergan's theology, essence does not really exist, only the things constituted by essences. Lonergan, *Const. Chr.*, 4.4, §72, pp. 146-47.
15. Ibid., 4.2, §61, pp. 110-11; ibid., 4.4, §70, pp. 134-37.
16. Ibid., 4.2, §60-61, pp. 108-11.
17. Ibid., 4.4, §71, pp. 142-45; ibid., 4.3, §66, pp. 122-23.
18. Ibid., 4.4, §70, pp. 140-41.
19. Ibid., 4.4, §72, pp. 148-51; ibid., 4.4, §70, pp. 134-35.
20. Ibid., 5.1, §75, pp. 156-57.

rational assessment or moral judgement. Consciousness in Lonergan's Christological exposition designates an awareness of being alive, rooted in the present moment, and conscious of one's existence and activity.[21]

In contrast, consciousness as perception presupposes as a pre-requisite for consciousness in a being, some form of knowledge about its existence or actions, whereas consciousness as experience treats of a basic awareness of its existence and actions in the present time prior to any conceptual organisation of these facts.[22]

The 'I', which is the person in question himself, the 'ultimate subject of attribution', in the sense of being the thing which does all the acts the person does, is capable of engaging in acts of sensory perception, conceptualisation, rational assessment and moral choice by which the person is rendered 'conscious' at these various progressive stages, intelligibly, rationally and morally, in a way that builds on the initial awareness. The subject and the action are inseparable; the former engages in the latter as separate to its being, while the latter 'perfects' the former.[23] The human subject is related to its operations (i.e. sensing and understanding) as the subject of consciousness or wielder of an operation is related to the type of consciousness and the operation itself. The faculty of sense or intellect in and of itself is neither conscious nor senses or understands; it is the subject that is conscious, senses and understands through those faculties.[24] Consciousness is a quality of a being, marking a degree of its 'ontological perfection'.[25]

In sum, 'a human being attains himself or herself under the formality of the experienced through his or her human operations and in proportion to the perfection of these operations'.[26] The operations of a human person include physical reactions,[27] bodily reactions,[28] physical actions,[29] mental acts[30] and acts of the will.[31]

God is conscious of Godself in an analogical manner, and this consciousness is never preliminary or unstructured but always complete,

---

21. Ibid., 5.1, §75-76, pp. 156-67.
22. Ibid., 5.2, §79, pp. 172-73.
23. Ibid., 5.2-3, §77-82, pp. 168-89.
24. Ibid., 5.3, §82, pp. 184-85; ibid., 6.4, §99, pp. 248-49.
25. Ibid., 6.4, §99, pp. 248-49.
26. Ibid., 6.2, §87, pp. 212-13.
27. I.e. the experience of being scourged.
28. I.e. the experience of being hungry.
29. I.e. the act of seeing.
30. I.e. the act of understanding.
31. I.e. the acts of willing, desiring; Lonergan, *Const. Chr.*, 6.2, §87, pp. 212-13.

with the subject, the act and the object united, without the possibility of increasing clarity about self and without a need for an accompanying intellectual or moral process to complete that consciousness or preliminary awareness.[32]

According to Lonergan, Christ is conscious of himself as a single divine person as having a human nature and, at the same time, also conscious of himself as having a divine nature. He is separately conscious of himself whether as being of divine or human nature through a preliminary unstructured human awareness of his existence and actions as a subject with a human nature and through a perfect divine awareness, via a 'beatific vision', of his existence and actions as a subject with a divine nature. The unity of his personhood is secured on the human side through his understanding and affirmation of his existence and actions as a human, divine and divine-human person.[33]

Christ as 'psychological subject', that is, as a subject which is conscious of itself through experience, or a preliminary unstructured awareness of some sort, precedes Christ as 'ontological subject', that is, as a subject which has through empirical, intelligible, rational and moral operations come to perceive its own being.[34] Christ is ontologically one in that he constitutes only one, divine person. He is psychologically one in that as a single divine person he is conscious of himself through a divine consciousness and a human consciousness. He is ontologically two given that he exists in a divine nature as well as a human nature. Moreover, he is psychologically two because by means of his divine consciousness he is conscious of himself as having a divine nature, and by means of his human consciousness he is conscious of himself as having a human nature.[35] For the latter two reasons, there are two 'I's in Christ, 'I' as a subject conscious of its endless and complete divine nature, and 'I' as a subject conscious of its finite human nature.[36] It is necessary to take Christ seriously as having a human nature and therefore human consciousness because of scriptural and traditional proof.[37] Christ has a human nature through gaining that nature.[38]

32. Ibid., 6.1, §84, pp. 192-93.
33. Ibid., 6.2, §87, pp. 204-5; ibid., 6.2, §88, pp. 220-21.
34. Ibid., 6.2, §89, pp. 222-23.
35. Ibid., 6.2, §88, pp. 220-21.
36. Ibid., 6.2, §91, pp. 224-25.
37. Ibid., 6.2, §87, pp. 210-11.
38. Ibid., 6.2, §90, pp. 222-23.

196 Experience, Culture and Religion in Systematic Theology

Christ as divine subject, aware of his present being and actions as a subject with a human nature, undergoes the human processes of consciousness building, as earlier described, in which experiences are accumulated and self-understanding grows in time which affect the manner in which he perceives his present existence and actions. At the same time, at different points, Christ is either privy to the processes of his human consciousness or the perfection of his divine consciousness.[39] There is only an awareness of there being one person or subject in Christ rather than a concept of himself as a human in opposition to a concept of himself as a divine being.[40] The same divine person and subject that is Christ operates in both the divine and human consciousness.[41] It is not the divine and human natures of Christ that are linked or identified *per se* but the divine person and subject that Christ is.[42]

According to Lonergan, 'the one person of the Word is the ontological and psychological subject of both his divine consciousness and his human consciousness'.[43] This means that in his humanity-associated suite of sensible, conceptual, rational and moral processes driven by a divine person and single subject as rooted in a preliminary unstructured awareness of his present existence and actions or reactions on sensible, conceptual, rational and moral levels – in short, his finite and sequential human consciousness of what he himself is and is sensing, doing, thinking, assessing, deciding in the present moment – Christ is also aware, through a supernatural operation of a beatific vision, of an infinite and always complete divine consciousness of himself as the 'natural' Son of God with the Son's 'infinite act of existence'.

Seeing that it is the Church's doctrine that all the externally oriented actions of the Trinity are performed as entirely by one divine person as another, Lonergan seems to suggest a loophole in order to avoid implying that the Son as human being engages in acts which involve neither the Father nor the Holy Spirit, namely, human acts, which neither the Father nor the Spirit, being non-human, can perform. He pronounces that, when Christ performs acts of a human nature, he does so passively or reactively rather than actively. Therefore, the sensations and understanding which he achieves as a human being are acts of receiving rather than

---

39. Ibid., 6.2, §91, pp. 224-27.
40. Ibid., 6.2, §91, pp. 226-27.
41. Ibid., 6.2, §92, pp. 226-29.
42. Ibid., 6.3, §95, pp. 242-43.
43. Ibid., 6.4, §96, pp. 242-43.

direct action.[44] Consequently, the addition of Christ's human nature essentially just enables him as a divine person to receive sensations, physical and emotional, and even mental pictures, but at the same time, and more importantly, he holds a supernatural and direct vision of his divine nature and origin with complete understanding of himself and his thoughts, decisions and actions, with their conceptual, rational and moral value. Through the objective perception of the beatific vision, the human consciousness is able to receive the data to engage in its intelligible, rational and moral activity.[45]

On these terms, it would seem that Lonergan is arguing for Christ as primarily a psychological and then ontological[46] subject with regard to his human nature, but as primarily an ontological[47] and then psychological[48] subject with regard to his divine nature. As human sensations and stimuli are sensed and perceived by the human Christ, the divine subject chooses when the beatific vision of sonship shall modify the human experience through a consolation of sorrow and, we can imagine, the performance of miracles in situations of need, mostly, of other persons.[49]

As such, because the divine and human consciousnesses of Christ 'mutually communicate on the side of the object, so that Christ as God knows himself to be this human being and Christ as man knows himself to be the natural Son of God', in his human mode of consciousness, as divine person and subject with a human nature, Christ is aware both of human awareness processes and, through a beatific vision which mediates information from his divine mode of consciousness, of that divine mode of consciousness, as object, in proportion to what the human mode of consciousness can receive and accept; in his divine mode of consciousness, as divine person and subject with a divine nature, Christ is aware both of his complete divine awareness and, through the natural perfection of this divine mode of consciousness, of his human mode of consciousness, as object.[50]

On this view, Christ experiences reality from a divine vantage point as well as a human one. These two vantage points contrast widely in that a

---

44. Ibid., 6.2, §95, pp. 240-41.
45. Ibid., 6.5, §102, pp. 264-65.
46. However, this is only through the objective perception of the beatific vision.
47. This is having full understanding of one's being.
48. This is having an awareness of presently existing and acting.
49. Lonergan, *Const. Chr.*, 6.2, §91, pp. 224-25.
50. Ibid., 6.4, §96, pp. 242-43.

divine consciousness is non-temporal, simultaneous and non-potential pure and beatific act, while a human consciousness is temporal, sequential, always at some point along a potentiality-actuality spectrum, and exposed to weakness. However, this double consciousness is united in the one person that is Christ in a manner not subject to alteration on the part of either consciousness or a mixture of both.[51]

In this way, Christ both experiences reality in these two contrasting ways and he is aware in his person that he experiences reality in these two very different ways, presumably through an internal mechanism by which he is able to regulate and predetermine which consciousness, which experientially and subjectively unified nature, will and operation, he is able to experience at any one point in time.

There are three other major views concerning the nature and personhood of Christ associated with modern theology: a kenotic,[52] grace[53] and mythological[54] doctrine of ontological Christology.[55]

In a kenotic model, such as Thomasius', God the Son as second person of the Trinity is divested of the Son's divine attributes, especially the Son's instrumental qualities of being omnipotent, omniscient and omnipresent, but perhaps not of the Son's infallible moral nature, in becoming incarnate, and at the Resurrection regains these divine attributes. The difficulty of this conception is that, contrary to the Chalcedonian requirement that Christ have both a fully divine and fully human nature at the same time, Christ only possesses a divine nature before and after his earthly existence.

In a grace-oriented conception, such as found in Wolfhart Pannenberg, the accent is placed on the true and full humanity of Christ, which includes human personhood in an enhypostatic sense and not just a divine subject living in a depersonalised human nature in anhypostatic terms. Christ constitutes the long-awaited human being who actually does God's will fully, whom God in God's impeccable foreknowledge has anticipated would execute such obedience and eternally decreed that for reason of Christ's completely submissive response, at his resurrection, Christ would be exalted to divine status. Although this interpretation of ontological Christology is faithful to the need to safeguard Christ's authentic humanity, it does not succeed in integrating the divine nature,

---

51. Ibid., 6.1, §84, pp. 190-94; 6.4, §96-99, pp. 242-49.
52. God became a man.
53. A man became God.
54. A man is like God.
55. Brown, *The Divine Trinity*, pp. 231-39.

which is present only in God the Father and not also God the Son, who, in this case, is merely a human being who becomes god, another kind of god.

In a mythological view, Christ is to be regarded as an incarnate Son of God only in the sense of his ability to perfectly express God's love towards humanity and God's desired response from humanity. A problem with this viewpoint is that it reduces Christ's divine nature to a metaphor.

Yet another perspective is a 'divine preconscious model' of the Incarnation, which preserves intact and reconciles permanently the divine and human natures of Christ by suggesting that divine omnipotence and omniscience may be postulated as always existing in Christ as latent attributes which can at any moment be brought by a single consciousness to the fore, much like the way in which information stored in the human preconscious may be brought forward at any point in time at will. The weakness of this position lies in the extent to which one is able to speak of a person with such divine attributes, even if conceived of as latent attributes, as being authentically human, given that, obviously, no truly human person possesses such superhuman capabilities, dormant or active.[56]

On the one hand, it is surely important to see how far it is possible to retain both divine and human natures in Christ, 'without confusion, without change, without division, without separation; the distinction of natures being in no way annulled by the union, but rather the characteristics of each nature being preserved and coming together to form one person and subsistence, not as parted or separated into two persons, but one and the same Son and Only-begotten God the Word, Lord Jesus Christ'.[57]

On the other, it is necessary to accord with what Scripture describes concerning the nature of the consciousness and experience of Christ. When it comes to this, it is clear that nowhere in the depictions of the

56. A.T.-E. Loke, *A Kryptic Model of the Incarnation*, Ashgate New Critical Thinking in Religion, Theology and Biblical Studies (Farnham: Ashgate, 2014), 73.

57. Translated in H. Bettenson, *Documents of the Christian Church* (Oxford: Oxford University Press, 1947), p. 73, cited in Anglicans Online, 'The Chalcedon Formula', 23 May 2017, http://anglicansonline.org/basics /chalcedon.html. A more recent rendering may be found at D. Fairbairn, 'The Chalcedonian Definition: Christ's Two Natures', *Credo Magazine* 11, no. 2 (12 July 2021), https://credomag.com/article/the-chalcedonian -definition/.

life of Christ are there any indications of a categorical and unqualified divinity, of Jesus as a completely divine person operating mightily at every point in the creaturely sphere.

As a matter of fact, Christ exhibits a lack of omniscience, an attribute customarily thought to be characteristic of a deity in the Christian sense, in how he concedes that he is not aware of the time of the final judgement, of which only the Father is cognisant. Furthermore, Christ does not declare the possession of an untrammelled ability to accomplish his will but at a critical point of his life relates that he is able to have recourse to the Father's aid if he so desires, rather than saying that he is capable of changing the situation on his own authority. For the reason that he does not possess omnipotent ability, Christ finds himself exposed to hunger, thirst, sorrow, fear and even the possibility and actuality of death. On these terms, any theological statement about Christ's divinity has to be a scripturally qualified one.

If the divine nature of Christ cannot simply be equated with a voguish philosophical conception, his human nature is also repugnant to a jejune correspondence with the experience of typical human persons, if Scripture's attestations are anything to go by. Instead, the biblical writers who saw fit to record vignettes from Christ's life and his teachings, and compile a theological biography of the personage, were at one in their presentation of Christ as a man with, at times, divine powers, able to turn water into wine, calm a storm, multiply bread and fish, heal the sick, cast out demons and even raise the dead.

Although some have laid claim to performing miracles in the name of God, both the intensity and frequency of those performed at Jesus' hands far outpace these claims. Yet the objective is not to establish a firm connection between the performance of miracles and superhuman or even divine status, or on these terms to rule out the possibility that Christ had a human nature, which are impossible tasks, but rather to insist on the scriptural basis of any theological affirmation, especially apropos of such central issues as the nature-person problematic of ontological Christology.

In addition to expounding a disposition and synthesis of human and divine natures in Christ as manifesting at different times in his life, patristic theologians perceived the value of speaking about these two natures as being in 'communication' with or 'indwelling' (*perichoresis*) one another and, by virtue of the fact that they exist and coexist in the same single person, patient of an interchangeable use of defining attributes of each nature across the two natures. Consequently, as they contended, one could not be prevented from declaring of Christ that in him God was born, suffered and died, or a human being has no beginning.

From the days of a patristic ontological Christology, there evidently remains a dilemma not so much pursuant to a question of whether Christ is fully divine and fully human; of this the fathers of the prevailing orthodoxy were clear. What they did not succeed in resolving was the issue of the unitary personal experience or consciousness of Christ.

They did articulate a doctrine of a twofold, divine-human, nature-will-operation complex, the concrete expression of which was ultimately managed on the part of the Son as single divine subject, and yet there is a strong sense in which the duality in Christ in the scriptural depiction existed on the level not so much of his psychology but rather his ability. In short, Jesus did not show signs of sometimes being dominated by a divine consciousness, in which he was not and could not be subject to change and movement, even as on other occasions he was seen to behave in a rather human-typical way. Another way in which a patristic-inspired Christology is inadequate lies in how it cannot seriously grapple with the lack of omniscience on the part of Christ, who conceded that, unlike the Father, he did not have exact knowledge of the day of his return.

Proposition: Advantages and Prolepses

The typical ontological Christological doctrine is challenged by the necessity to reckon with the idea of God as simple, indissoluble, immoveable, all-moving, impassible and immortal because human beings stand in antithesis to these classical divine attributes; people are not simple but made up of different body parts, capable of dying and decomposing after that, not immoveable but, as a matter of fact, affected by all manner of circumstances and factors, do not have the power to decide all fates and outcomes, not even their own, but perhaps only their most mundane choices, affected by emotions, and certainly do not live forever, at least not in their current physical embodiment.

Consequently, classical ontological Christology had to explicate the manner in which fusing human and divine in the one Christ respects both sets of antithetical properties, indeed, embraces each fully without thus running into self-destructive self-contradiction. The earlier survey has canvassed the ways in which the Fathers of the Early Church attempted to resolve the dilemma, whether by emphasising the divine at the expense of the human, or the human at the expense of the divine, or trying to hold both in tension through some theory of mutual communication of divine and human attributes. It was clear to St Gregory of Nazianzus, Pope Leo I and St John of Damascus that there are both sets of contrasting attributes in the one Christ; however, they do not manifest at one and the same time in the single Christ, and the divine subject, the person of Christ, holds the prerogative of deciding which set of attributes is to be displayed at any one time.

In our theory, even God the Son in spiritual state is not immoveable, all-moving or impassible. Nonetheless, the persons of the Trinity remain simple, indissoluble and immortal. Concerning the complex of reasons that makes it possible to designate the incarnate Son as authentically and fully human, this entails arriving at a definition of what it means to be human rather than something else. To be considered human, an entity has to possess a human body, comprising recognisably human DNA, human organs and human body parts. The body need not be complete or fully functioning; a person lacking a body part or suffering from a physical disability is not on that account less, sub-human or non-human. The human body referred to in this definition comprises not just physically functioning parts but the brain with its cognitive, emotional and volitional capacities as well.

Does the human body account for the entirety of the human person? There is certainly what may be called a person, a spiritual essence, a unique relational identity, hub or node living within the body which recognises and identifies itself as an 'I' or 'me' as opposed to 'you' or 'them', or as nothing at all. This personal essence, however, is hardly a substantial form but a living essence which requires a form, being or substance by which it is able to perceive, understand and relate both to itself and the world around it.

Therefore, there is no really and distinctively human essence as opposed to a non-human sentient essence. The essence which inhabits the animal form is not very different from the essence, the human person, which inhabits a human body. Gender, too, as a psychological phenomenon is a matter of neurology tied to biology but not necessary for all beings. Only sentient beings with physical bodies have gender, which is normally determined by the presence of particular permutations of chromosomes which in turn determines the type of genitalia that will develop in the embryo. A sexual differentiation of the brain occurs later than a sexual differentiation of genitalia, resulting in a brain more or less typical of a biological sex type.[58] Without physical bodies, sentient entities, whether

---

58. D.F. Swaab, 'Sexual Differentiation of the Brain and Behavior', *Best Practice & Research Clinical Endocrinology & Metabolism* 21, no. 3 (September 2007), pp. 431-44.

animal or human, have no gender. Similarly, without a particular spiritual or physical bodily form associated with being angel, human or animal, a sentient being is neither angel, human nor animal but, according to our theory, is capable of either remaining as an angel (in the case of the angel and the pre-incarnate human soul) or nature spirit (in that of the pre-incarnate animal soul) or becoming either human or animal depending on the type of physical body it takes on.

Perchance a human being was originally an angel, while an animal was formerly a spirit, both of which subsequently put aside their angelic or spiritual bodies and took on those of human beings or animals.[59] The ages of spirits and then material beings comprise the 'eternal times' of which Titus speaks (1:2). The spiritual body of an angel differs from that of a spirit, the former being superior in intellectual and emotional capacity to the latter. These angelic or spiritual entities, however, were not directly created but posited by the Divine Nature in their unique identity, mental and emotional capacity and personality. Designated angels individually put aside their bodies and take on a human body at the time of their call into humanity, which differs from person to person. These angelic bodies are reserved for re-assumption at the time of the resurrection, when people shall be as the angels.[60] The function of the body, whether it be angelic or human, is to represent the unique personal identity in a visible manner, whether this be in a spiritual or physical sense, as well as to facilitate its life and relationships in a spiritual or physical world through affording principles of spiritual or physical operation, enabling angelic or human beings to act towards themselves, one another and the rest of the world, in spiritual or physical ways. The body is both shaped by and shapes the soul inhabiting it; in turn, the world around the inhabited or ensouled body is shaped by and shapes the inhabited or ensouled body.

The motif of resurrection is thus double, in that, on the one hand, the physically dead among human beings, having lost their physical bodies, will be raised up at that event – that is, given new physical bodies reminiscent of the old, possibly, that at the prime of youth, as Augustine believes[61] – while, on the other, these same persons *qua* angels who have

---

59. Augustine leaves open the possibility of a pre-existence of human souls, *Civ.*, XII.23.

60. Matthew 22:30, Mark 12:25.

61. Augustine, *Civ.*, XXII.15. Thus we see the intimate link between creation and resurrection understood as recreation of an old physical body in its glory.

lost their angelic bodies and are thus 'dead' in terms of having lost their former bodies for a time, will thereby regain their angelic forms and thus receive resurrection in a deeper and more penetrating way. The Bible makes it clear that the resurrection is the experience not of recovering our human bodies but of becoming as the angels. This experience is limned using the agricultural image of sowing and reaping applied to the transmogrification of the body of the human person in which the person puts aside corruption and mortality and puts on incorruption and immortality, mooting not so much a slight modification of the faculties of the human body as a translation into a new – and yet at the same time, familiar – mode of existence.

The resurrection consists in a blending or fusion of the original angelic spiritual form of a human being with the acquired human body. This process is attested by Scripture, which depicts humankind as having come from the pre-existent breath of God,[62] suggesting, along with the idea of God's pre-creation, an election of human persons – implying as it does the pre-existence of human beings in some form without which an election would have no concrete target and therefore be impossible in a literal or direct sense (except in thought) – and that human beings were previously angelic beings. These originally angelic sentient entities are planted like a seed through a human incarnation,[63] only to be elevated later in a resurrected form, brought back to something of their original form, where their suppressed angelic memories and powers will return in full force, in an angelic body fused with a human one to compose an angelic body made physical.[64]

The fact that human beings are spoken of as having been sown in their current physical bodies for resurrection into immortal life suggests that

---

62. Genesis 2:7.

63. 1 Corinthians 15:35-49.

64. That human beings after death will experience a reunion of body and soul, regardless of their spiritual state, rather than being left as a disembodied soul, is attested in Jesus' saying that it is more fearful to disobey God than incur the wrath of the devil, since the former is able to throw both soul and body into hell (Matthew 10:28). See Augustine, *Civ.*, XIII.12. Prior to that resurrection, the temporarily disembodied human soul, if it is one of a person who has lived in a manner displeasing to God or that violates a universal human morality, experiences the punishment of being vaguely aware of their eternal destiny, should they persist in their ways, and, if it is of a person who has pleased God or whose life has agreed with morality, experiences the pleasure attached to a similarly nebulous consciousness of a pleasant, future eternal state. *Civ.*, XIII.20.

they pre-exist their present forms, and that these pre-existent forms were taken by God's authority for sowing on the field of the earth. The language in 1 Corinthians 15:42-49 bears this out, describing human beings as having been 'sown' in their present bodies rather than created out of nothing. Such speculation arises from how the analogy presupposes two distinct concepts, each of which requires a referent: first, the object of the act of sowing, which, in this case, is the incarnated angelic soul; and, second, the act of sowing the object being sown, which, in this case, is the incarnation of the angelic soul.

Although the memories of dwelling in a heavenly form have been suppressed in a human being, the emotional sentiments guiding along a path of angelic and holy morality are retained during an earthly existence, resulting from the way in which angels in directly beholding the glory of God are certainly and permanently shaped into God's very moral image. Thus, the moral framework of the human being was etched into its soul during its life as an angel gazing upon the face of God, this radiating divine moral feeling, comprising moral direction and the pangs of conscience, being so strongly experienced that it is still remembered.[65] Such a theory accounts for the reason that religious or philosophical knowledge is universal and human knowledge is always guided, to be sure in rational terms, towards some idea of the divine, ultimate or truly significant; that we have the intrinsic ability to determine what is right or wrong, true or untrue, without denying that matters of religious or philosophical truth and ethics are never easy to agree upon, for the very fact that one is inclined to engage in such discourse already presupposes a general consensus pertaining to truth and ethics; that whatever we learn about morality and truth seems to be commonsensical the moment we grasp it, that is, something we wondered how we could ever have taken so long

---

65. See Matthew 18:10. Therefore, those angels which defect from God are those which choose to look away from the glory of God, first, to themselves and, finally, to the world apart from the divine radiance, migrating there, far from God, to make their home in it. Such a conception of human beings harks back to the Socratic theory of recollection depicted in Plato's *Meno*, which is predicated on the undying nature of the human soul and its ability to learn through a remembrance of things, facilitated by dialogue and reasoning, which it already knows inherently, even prior to its current, physical embodiment (*anamnesis*). See G. Keehn, 'Does the Theory of Recollection Preclude Learning? A New Dimension to Platonic Nativism', *Philosophy of Education* (2014), pp. 158-65.

to realise; and that there is no higher court of appeal beyond a common morality.[66]

Morality is here defined as moral probity expressed in an integrated and complementary sense of love, justice, humility, empathy, compassion, graciousness, mercy, passion, perseverance, honesty, purity, patience, hope, faith, trust, gentleness, loyalty, faithfulness, dedication, responsibility, diligence, excellence, respect, peacefulness, rationality, reasonableness, self-restraint, moderation, *inter alia*, comprehended in the notion of goodness.[67] It is an ultimate end in itself rather than an instrumental factor that requires justification of some sort.

Because human beings were originally spiritual angelic beings, they are able to put aside their natural bodies and receive again spiritual

---

66. Such a conception steers a middle course between a natural and supernatural approach to theology. For a statement of natural theology, where reason is applied to observations of the regularities of nature, see *SCG*, III, ch. 38, cited in Thomas Aquinas, *Summa Theologiae: A Concise Translation*, ed. T. McDermott (Allen, TX: Christian Classics, 1989), pp. 9-10.

67. Not all these values will be equally emphasised in each culture through historical time, yet many, if not most, of them will be regarded as a meritorious ideal to be strived for. Some values may be downplayed, but these will only be done in order to serve some practical purpose or to avoid a practical consequence, implying that the value or values thus ostensibly opposed are not flatly contradicted, but only stand in need of tempering and refinement in light of practical considerations. A glaring example of seeming cultural opposition to a value espoused by many cultures is that of the valorisation of treachery and deceit on the part of the Sawi tribe living in West Papua, Indonesia. When missionaries brought the message of Christianity, they regarded Judas Iscariot as a fine example of defeating an enemy by deception. In this instance, it can be said that what caused the Sawi to glorify trickery was not so much a fundamental commitment to dishonesty as a principle of life, but rather a desire to express their commitment to protecting their loved ones and their community by outgunning their opponents who may be bent on pursuing their destruction. Consequently, the Sawi could be said to be driven by an in-group loyalty which determines to whom they can display honesty and integrity. Love and honesty are still expressed; however, in view of practical circumstances, there are limitations and boundaries circumscribing their expression. A. Boyd, 'Judas Iscariot: A Cultural Hero?', *The Boyds*, 1 August 2011, http://pngboyd.blogspot.com/2011/08/judas-iscariot-cultural-hero.html.

bodies, though blended in some way with the natural without losing its primarily spiritual nature, in this way inheriting the kingdom of God, which belongs only to spiritual beings.[68] In this process, angels in being chosen to be human are given an opportunity they did not possess previously, to form families and kinship among one another as human beings, so as to conceptually and experientially understand the inherent and relational nature of the trinitarian divine persons. On their own, angels are merely servants and messengers of God without any particular relationship to one another.[69] Other reasons God caused some angels to be incarnated as human beings are to fit them for service in the world by giving them bodies attuned to the physical world in the hope that they might have opportunity to master such service and, in the resurrection, when they shall regain their angelic and spiritual bodies, attuned as these are to the spiritual domain, come to serve both physical and spiritual worlds, and in order that they might learn and be an example of humility; it is the same with spirits which have a vocation to become sentient animals.[70]

This theory concerning the origin of human beings makes sense in light of Scripture's common reference to both Christians and angels as sons or children of God[71] as well as the depiction in Genesis chapter six of sons of God, possibly angels, coming together with the daughters of men, suggesting some fundamental affinity between angels and human beings. It explains why in Matthew 22:30 the Lord revealed that, at the resurrection, people will be similar to angels, similar because they have an angelic origin, not identical because they will have memories of having once been human.

It is necessary to postulate such a provenance for human beings rather than suppose that God directly at some point in time created human souls and human persons out of nothing, because to accord such an immense

---

68. 1 Corinthians 15:50.
69. Hebrews 1:14.
70. It is not the case that angels enjoy by default more peaceful and happier lives than human beings, so that the question might be posed as to why God does not authorise more people, particularly those who are undergoing tremendous affliction, to regain their angelic forms earlier. As a matter of fact, just as angels are given greater power, they also face greater challenges, primarily in the area of having to guard God's people against all their enemies.
71. I.e. Job 1:6, 2:1 and John 1:12.

degree of direct power to God is to leave unexplained the central aporia of theodicy concerning the reality of injustice and innocent suffering.

On these terms, the gift of the human body, and the appointment of God for a sentient essence to dwell within a human body and *eo ipso* constitute a human being, is a privilege and vocation for the sentient essence in question to be human.

If the real determinant of an angelic, animal or human nature is the nature of the spiritual or physical body of the entity in question, then, given that God unlike anything else is essence and complete without an additional, specific form or body, without, therefore, a specific God overlay or body, a divine essence or identity of any one of the three divine persons is able to take on humanity by assuming a human body without undermining its own divine nature.[72] That which, therefore, makes the one divine Christ also human is the fact that he inhabits a human body as a sentient soul with the authority, role, character and identity of God. It is also the reason he is male rather than female or non-gendered. When God the Son became incarnate, no other change than embodiment was involved, unlike human beings when they transition from being angelic entities to human persons, in the process of which they necessarily relinquish their angelic powers.

At this juncture, the question presents itself as to how powerful God is in Godself, apart from the mighty angels through whom God works. Not at all mighty is the response, for God being God has the dignity and place of being the monarch whom angels serve, and God does not need to serve Godself through acts of power.[73] An analogy in this regard can be found in the differences in physical strength and capacities between *homo sapiens sapiens* and their many other relatives in the animal kingdom who are far superior in might and physical competencies; it is the human being who excels in rationality and morality, rather than animals, and who employs animals in their service rather than the reverse.[74] This is how it can be that good Christians with the Holy Spirit indwelling them

---

72. On these terms, the visions of God in the Scriptures, apart from the Incarnation, are to be ascribed to the perceptions of God's forms produced in the minds of the recipients of those visions, or which God actually momentarily assumed.

73. Christ's inabilities, such as to do miracles when people in Nazareth had little faith (Matthew 13:53-58, Mark 6:1-6,) reveal the Father's inabilities, as when the angels of the Father choose to disobey the Father's orders.

74. Augustine, *Civ.*, VIII.15.

could be subject to tragedy of the worst possible kinds. God in them had no power to intervene. Well then, it might be asked, why do we even bother worshipping God? Such a train of thought betrays a self-serving religious profession in which the person in question only submits to God out of a sense that God is able to make things happen for them in the manner they desire. Yet this is nothing but a myopic view of Christian spirituality. We do not worship God merely and simply because God is able to bless us, but because of God's standing in our lives as Christians and what we can learn of God in terms of moral values.

The incarnation of Christ does not in any way disrupt the perichoretic constitution of the Trinity, even in regard to the constitution of the personhood of the incarnate Son. The Father and Spirit continue to offer their wisdom, agency of action and affect to the Son, while the Son offers the Son's will, which is in no way mitigated through the Incarnation.

Christ never ceases to centre his personhood on the faculties of wisdom of the Father and the agency of action and affect of the Holy Spirit. For all that Christ is eminently knowledgeable (through sharing the wisdom of the Father but without having direct access to the Father's thoughts apart from the Father's willing decision to share these thoughts) and present in many places (through sharing the agency of action of the Holy Spirit), he remains authentically human. At the Incarnation, the Word and Son assumed a human body with its frailties in its primary form while continuing to dwell, discarnate, in the primary forms of the Father and Holy Spirit in a secondary mode; the Father and Holy Spirit, in turn, dwell secondarily in Christ's incarnate person. Christ's human body and existence constitutes an addition of which St Athanasius spoke.

The value of the incarnation of Christ is how it reveals the experience of the triune persons. Scripture shows the way in which Christ is capable of being filled with the Father who advances Christ's mission through illumination of the Father's own plans and activity[75] and with the Spirit in the Spirit's commissioning of Christ,[76] whether it be on their own accord or at his behest.[77] This shows that, within the trinitarian life, mutual communication and impartation are the order of the day, with the Father communicating the Father's wisdom, the Son that Son's will, and the Holy Spirit the Spirit's action and affect in building up the life of each member of the Godhead.

75. John 5:19-23.
76. I.e. Luke 4:18-19.
77. Matthew 3:16-17, Matthew 14:23, Luke 6:12, Luke 22:41-42, John 5:19-23.

While Christ is said to have increased in wisdom and height as a boy, this was only a phenomenal observation on the part of people around the child. In fact, Christ possessed all the abilities he possessed prior to his incarnation from the day of his birth, but kept these things in his heart and revealed them in age-appropriate ways over a long period of time. The Father prepared the human body of the Son by instructing angels to create the material principle.[78] The Incarnation itself consists of a supernatural act leading to a modified creation in which the presence of a sperm is simulated in Mary's body so as to form a human body, while the function which leads to the formation of a human person is suppressed; namely, through the fact that, in the case of Jesus, no angel was dispatched to be incarnated in a human body.[79]

Due to the perichoretic constitution of the triune God which lays itself open to human scrutiny through the incarnation of the Son, it is possible to apprehend the instrumental powers and moral nature of God.

In accordance with all that has been said above, the consciousness of Christ as divine and his consciousness as human are one and the same. There is but one unified consciousness as held by Christ, and not two, contrary to the opinion of Lonergan.[80]

Such a view of ontological Christology, coupled with the idea that human souls are eternally posited by the Divine Nature, avoids the difficulty of a traditional conception which is hard-pressed to explain how it is that an authentically human Christ could at the same time have an essential aspect of himself being eternal, that is, his very soul, if human souls are not to be considered as eternal in themselves. It is conceivable, on the other hand, that a human person, that is, Christ, has the identity, character, role and authority of God, because these psychological, moral and social-political attributes which together constitute Christ's divinity do not impinge on Christ's humanity, which has regard mainly to his physical, human embodiment, with all the consequences that existing in such a manner entails, and is fully comparable to actual human beings, defined in terms of having an essence or identity originating, like the Word, at the beginning of all things in the Divine Nature, but with the difference that the Word, along with the Father and Spirit, is the proper owner of the Divine Nature. There is no loss of individual

---

78. See Hebrews 10:5.
79. Consequently, in Hebrews 10:5, the speaker, Christ, reports that God had 'prepared [a body] for [him]'.
80. Lonergan, *Const. Chr.*, 6.1, §84, pp. 190-94; 6.4, §96-99, pp. 242-49.

divine attributes through the Incarnation, since, with regard to the Word's physical location, this remains single, now humanly embodied, the Word's prior practical omnipresence, as well as omniscience and omnipotence, being due to the reports and delegation of angels and not some intrinsic quality of the Word's.

Chapter 7

Doctrines: Theodicy

Influenced as it is by Greek philosophy, the classical conception of God as a deity which sets everything in motion without itself being affected by any other entity, all of which is first posited by God, lends itself to a significant moral dilemma. Along with the subsidiary notions of God as all-knowing or omniscient and 'everywhere-present' or omnipresent, coupled with the biblical notion of the divine essence as love itself, the notion of God's omnipotence confronts the theologian with seemingly irreconcilable difficulties.

The Christian thinker has to address the question of how, if God knows everything, including any evil that is being perpetrated, is in fact everywhere, including at the places where evil is being perpetrated, is capable of attaining God's will, including terminating or removing any evil that is being perpetrated, and strongly desires to overcome that evil, because benevolent, good and loving, nevertheless, evil can continue to be rampant in the human experience, mocking faith, besmirching purity, paralysing emotions, corrupting minds, obscuring hope and destroying lives.

Definition

Theodicy may be defined as the attempt to make theological sense of the love and justice of a powerful God in allowing evil to run its course in the world.

Place in a Systematic Theology

Theodicy stands at the very heart of the Christian belief in a God defined by love. While sub-Christian and sub-biblical conceptions of

God as anything other than loving and just allow for the power God commands to be understood as being withheld because of just that deficit in love or justice, the biblical idea of God does not permit such an evasion or modification. To the extent that the justice and love of God cannot be maintained in the face of evil and injustice, the entire Christian theological edifice is called into question as an articulation of the nature and purposes of a loving and good God for humanity and the world.

Existing Conceptions: Strengths and Weaknesses

There are a few major types of theodicy, revolving either around God's nature and purposes,[1] the nature and design of humanity,[2] the interactions between human nature and its environment, or God's manipulation of human action through God's perfect knowledge of the choices people will make under all possible circumstances and shaping of the very circumstances that constitute the precondition for divinely preferred, particular human actions,[3] and the interactions between God and the world.[4]

In what has been christened a 'classical Calvinistic' doctrine of God, based on the thought of St Augustine of Hippo, St Anselm of Canterbury, St Thomas Aquinas and, of course, John Calvin, there are a number of pivotal themes encompassing an election – a 'chosen loving' (Aquinas) – in which God in God's inscrutable and incomprehensible purpose decides, apart from the future deeds or even faith of an individual, which particular individuals will be predestined for eternal life through salvation in the Lord Jesus Christ in such a way that they do not merit the salvation they receive, and which to perdition, through a form of divine permission of a human choice of a course of evil (Anselm), yet in such a way that that destiny is also their sinful and wilful choice. Apart from election and predestination, there is foreknowledge on the part of God, which designates God's knowledge of God's own choice of individuals as pertains to salvation or reprobation.

Along with these ends of salvation and perdition, as controlled by God, there are also the means by which salvation is brought to bear

---

1. The Calvinist doctrine of the secret divine decree governing all events in the universe.
2. The Arminian doctrine of human free will abused.
3. The Molinist doctrine of God's middle knowledge of counterfactuals, that is, events that could well happen but will ultimately not take place in view of God's election of other possibilities.
4. Open theism.

on individual persons, involving an unmerited and irresistible grace bestowed on these persons by God through which those predestined for salvation are brought to salvation through a divine calling followed by justification and preserved from slipping away from their divinely ordained destiny, in spite of their personal resistance, opposition or wilfulness.

Sometimes, such divine grace is presented as the unconditional ground for salvation in which human virtue is completely ignored, as in the construal of John Calvin. On other occasions, grace constitutes the possibility for the sure actualisation of the meritorious character and deeds of individuals destined for salvation, whereby grace enables the individuals to live meritoriously and virtuously, even ensuring that they do so, for which cause God in God's foreknowledge predestines these individuals to everlasting and heavenly glory.[5] In any event, glory is not

---

5. Hence, in Augustine's theodicy, it is important for him to highlight the justice in God's inclusion of good persons in the punishment of the wicked at the sack of Rome in 410. During that catastrophic event, many Christians lost their property and some were even tortured because they were not believed when they said they had no hidden wealth. Augustine attributes these misfortunes to God's desire to correct the ways in which believers had been complicit in evil by failing to speak up or correct people around them involved in wrongdoing out of fear of reprisal, or of loss of reputation and opportunity for advancement and worldly gain, or had opted to be attached to their material possessions rather than holding them loosely, or God's wish to prove the purity of their love for God and the perseverance of their trust in God, as in the case of Job. As for chaste Christian women who were ravaged during the invasion, Augustine justifies this occurrence with reference to a pride which some of these women may have taken or will come to take in their chastity, envy in those of others, or the need for these women to be shown that chastity lies not in the physical body alone (a woman does not have control over what is done to her body) but in the unfaltering, godly will. Augustine, *Civ.*, I.9-10, 28. Augustine also addresses the question of why territorial rule is given to both good and wicked alike – it is in order that it might be clear to the righteous that this is a meagre and contemptible gift incommensurable to that of salvation and eternal life by the grace of God through Jesus Christ (*Civ.*, IV.33); as to the reason godly persons do not always obtain worldly benefits, this is in order to increase a desire for the eternal benefits of the afterlife, and the innocent (such as babies) suffer, to induce a desire for eternal happiness (*Civ.*, XXII.22). Concerning the prosperity and extent of the Roman state, Augustine attributes this, along with the inclusion of the divinely favoured Jewish commonwealth

conferred on individuals purely by what they choose to do, apart from any connection with God's grace, in relation to the revelation of God's will for their lives. Furthermore, salvation, which includes perseverance in faith, is such that it is not possible to know beforehand who is saved and who is not, but only retrospectively.[6]

According to Augustine, not only in the matter of salvation and perdition is God's omnipotent will involved, but even in all movements of the free human will, including the things about which people would pray or whether a specific individual would voluntarily commit sin, let alone other, less rational wills. In this regard, God foreknows all things because God determines all things.[7]

The advantage of a Calvinistic doctrine of a secret divine decree is that it upholds the classical instrumental attributes of God as to God's limitless power and comprehensive scope of knowledge and presence, which it is easy to perceive as being consistent with – and a development of – the scriptural testimony, given the ancient Near Eastern worldview from which it emerges and the emphasis of this worldview on divine sovereignty.[8]

---

within it, to the merits of certain illustrious Roman individuals as well as the weal of the Christian community, by affording it sacrificial and selfless patriotic moral exemplars. Even so, God makes sure to discipline an unruly people by setting deceitful rulers above them (*Civ.*, V.15-19). As a matter of fact, God grants temporal rule such as to the Assyrians, Persians, and Romans. Indeed, God even goes so far as to determine the length and outcome of wars. Augustine is convinced that God bestowed a long rule on Constantine the Great to ward off the possible charge that God only gives earthly power to the impious and permits other Roman emperors like Gratian and Jovian to suffer misfortune to debunk the idea that an emperor will certainly attain worldly success through conversion. He also believed that the miraculous deliverance from Radagaisus, king of the Goths, and Theodosius' victory over Eugenius were to be attributed to divine favour (*Civ.*, V.21-26). On the whole, the Doctor of Grace, who believes God can never be charged with any degree of injustice, is of the view that temporal blessings are conferred on the non-elect by way of a distraction or consolation for the fact that they will not be eternally enriched, and that the elect suffer temporal afflictions in order that they might either be chastened for their sins or prodded toward virtue. Augustine, *Civ.*, XX.2.

6. Helm, 'Classical Calvinist Doctrine of God', pp. 5-28.

7. Augustine, *Civ.*, V.8-11.

8. However, this is not a sovereignty of direct control but one of direct responsibility. In an ancient Near Eastern setting, monarchs assumed

Even so, a Calvinistic notion of a secret divine decree is often lacking in its ability to vindicate the goodness and love of God. Despite the protestations of classical Calvinist theologians to the effect that God is not arbitrary in selecting some individuals for salvation and others for perdition, because God's secret will is 'incomprehensible' and 'inscrutable', and that human beings are in no position to assess the morality of God's choices and decisions, the fact remains that, whatever the theological justification, in experiential terms, the suggestions of the Calvinistic doctrine of God in relation to God's sovereignty and meticulous control over all human affairs will come across as cold and unfeeling to the victim of grievous suffering and heinous injustice.

Classical Calvinists appear to believe that God's glory is somehow vindicated through the predetermined selection of certain human beings for reprobation, as well as for gratuitous suffering, thus granting suffering, evil and what appears to the Calvinist to be ignorance at least some necessary instrumental role in accomplishing God's purposes for the world. These, presumably, demonstrate God's justice in punishing the descendants of Adam for Adam's disobedience and what is believed to be their latent or actualised sinfulness.[9]

It is challenging to move from such a worldview, in which all that transpires in the world and the way these things transpire are secretly endorsed by God as fulfilling God's purposes for the world, to a sufficiently robust ethic which encourages proactive and positive human action to overcome the causes of human suffering and disorder, including global poverty, disease, crime, as well as evangelism to those who do not yet have a Christian profession.

This is because involvement in these causes begs the question of the Calvinist: can we be involved in these causes in the first place? If so, how do we know when God is amenable to our involvement rather than desiring to preserve an existing state of affairs for divine self-glorification? Will we be offending against the majesty of God by seeking to eliminate all these causes of human suffering and disorder, or even just to preach the Gospel? Should people seek only to eliminate some of these evils, to evangelise only some of the time? Or, is it not appropriate for human beings to worry about such divine concerns,

responsibility for all that their representatives did, whether or not it was commanded by the ruler. Boyd, *Is God to Blame?*, pp. 90, 188.

9. Cf. J. Sanders, 'Responses to Paul Helm: Response by John Sanders', in B.A. Ware (ed.), *Perspectives on the Doctrine of God: Four Views* (Nashville, TN: Broadman & Holman, 2008), pp. 63-64.

since we should simply trust that God has God's means of ensuring that, regardless of how much we try to change the world, core structures of suffering, evil or perhaps ignorance (in this construal), which God requires for the accomplishment of God's ends, will always remain?

In a modified Calvinist permutation, which retains a strict view of God's sovereignty, the recourse is to a conception of human freedom in terms of a 'freedom of inclination'[10] in which a person's freedom consists in the degree to which they are able to pursue courses of action in accordance with their desire without being baulked or pressured to do otherwise.

Bruce Ware constructs a modified Calvinist conception of divine sovereignty as compatible with human freedom by drawing from the insights of Luis de Molina, a sixteenth-century Spanish Jesuit who argued that God possesses three types of knowledge: a natural knowledge of all the possibilities; within these possibilities, a free knowledge of those that will become actual in the universe as it has been shaped; and, finally, within natural knowledge but apart from free knowledge, a middle knowledge of what is known as counterfactuals, or states of affairs which do not and will not obtain in the universe as it has been constructed.[11]

In Ware's theory, the choice that an individual finally makes is tied to the nature of the person as expressed in his moral fibre and morally indifferent idiosyncrasies as this nature interacts with the circumstances presented to the person, resulting in the individual making the choice that he most deeply desires or strongly prefers. As such, with an accurate understanding of the distinctive nature of a person and a comprehensive knowledge pertaining to the orchestration of events and situations, it becomes possible to devise circumstances that would lead a person to act in one certain manner rather than another.

God uses God's knowledge of the nature and character of each individual, coupled with God's creativity in being able to visualise and fashion specific situations which would lead people to act in a manner that is consistent with God's purposes, to situate people in places, times and experiences such that the confluence of factors would work together to bring about God's intended outcomes for communities, nations and the world at large.

---

10. A conception of Jonathan Edwards, an eighteenth-century Puritan theologian and philosopher.
11. B.A. Ware, 'Responses to Paul Helm: Response by Bruce A. Ware', in B.A. Ware (ed.), *Perspectives on the Doctrine of God: Four Views* (Nashville, TN: Broadman & Holman, 2008), p. 74.

In practical terms, one can imagine God orchestrating the right conditions for particular, elected persons to be especially eager to embrace God's salvific grace through the right degree of humbling and encouragement, one after another, appealing to their most deeply held convictions and strongest preferences in presenting to them the Gospel.

In this way, God orchestrates not just the good that people do, but even the evil, as well as all amoral actions. As God does this, God is 'directly-causatively' responsible for all the good that occurs, because God brings about all this good as an ultimate end, while only 'indirectly-permissively' responsible for all the evil in the world, and this because God brings about all this evil not as an ultimate end but merely as an instrument by which to accomplish God's ultimate ends.[12]

The strength of a compatibilist view of divine providence is that it renders a logically coherent and plausible account of divine sovereignty working hand in glove with human free will. It shares its weakness with a Calvinistic conception: that is, it is unable to say in what sense the biblical God whose essence is love should think it fit to rule that only a limited number of persons are to be saved whilst the rest may be rejected, contrary to what Scripture itself predicates of the comprehensiveness of the scope of God's election – namely, for all to repent and therefore be saved.[13]

While it is true that every person who freely chooses to do an evil deed is solely responsible for his misdeeds, any party who contributes to the context in which that sinful decision is made or the way in which it is carried out has a part to play in acting to reduce the harmfulness of a potential misdeed. Therefore, while an abusive father cannot be made responsible for his son's crimes, for instance, he has a role to play in lowering the possibility or stakes of his son's misdeeds by committing to being a better parent.

Consequently, instead of being so abusive to his son that the latter finds himself in a constant struggle between being an abusive person himself or barely restraining his aggression, the father should refrain from abuse of the child, which is wrong in any case, so that the only two or more choices among which the son will have to choose will be less damaging, injurious or even fatal. The same state of affairs obtains with God, who, as far as a determinist or compatibilist conception of divine providence is concerned, we can say actually has a role to play in reducing the chances

---

12. Ware, 'A Modified Calvinist Doctrine of God', pp. 76-120.
13. 2 Peter 3:9.

or intensity of sinful behaviour, rather than setting people up so that, if they make a sinful choice, it will lead to grievous harm.

Whereas a classical and modified Calvinist viewpoint asserts a specific election of individual persons, an Arminian and open theist perspective argues for a general election of humankind in a corporate sense.

Within an Arminian or classical, free will theistic model of God, the appeal is to a construal of human free will as libertarian in nature, that is, of human individuals having the ability to choose otherwise than circumstances may appear to dictate. According to Roger Olson, the Jewish theological mainstream and all the Greek Church Fathers avowed libertarian free will, in common with the scriptural intimation of such a conception of freedom of choice in its depiction of God as summoning people to decide in favour of morality and piety.

A free will theistic conception of divine providence and human free will, while non-determinist in its outlook, is not contingent on a denial of classical divine attributes such as omnipotence and omniscience. Even though human free will is libertarian in character, God remains in possession of sure knowledge of future events; Arminians believe that divine omniscience is a scriptural notion. Even so, God retains the power to create and manipulate reality in any non-contradictory manner, yet nevertheless refrains from so doing in the majority of cases in order to uphold God's decision to grant human beings the capacity to make unrestricted and voluntary choices as conditioned and limited by specific situations.

Theologians such as Olson propound it to be beyond challenging and reasonably logical to accord to God determinist capability over compatibilist free human decisions and actions, without implying that God is the originator of sin and evil, and has motives and a character which are less than good. In the Arminian understanding, rather than determining human actions, God extends prevenient grace – whether through the human conscience, natural human insight or preaching of the Gospel – whereby the individual receives the ability to make good moral choices and to comprehend and believe the claims of the *kerygma* (the proclamation of the Good News) regarding God's nature, the mission of Christ, and the necessity for faith in Christ for salvation. Furthermore, God foreknows which individuals would respond in faith to God's overtures and so elects these ahead of time, whom God would subsequently grant the gift of prevenient grace.[14] Although all are

---

14. Sanders, 'Responses to Paul Helm', pp. 60-61; R.E. Olson, 'Responses to Bruce A. Ware: Response by Roger E. Olson', in B.A. Ware (ed.),

'antecedently' willed by God not to perish, when they reject a moral life, they are 'consequently' willed to perish.[15]

Arminians reject three of the five points of Calvinism, retaining only total depravity and the perseverance of the saints, and affirming, against Calvinists, the idea of a conditional election, unlimited atonement and resistible grace. In both an Arminian and open theistic view, there is no guarantee that a person will be saved rather than rejected, since the decision governing whether an individual receives or rejects God's salvation lies solely in the person's volitional capacity.[16]

The Arminian or free will theist conception of theodicy is enlightening in that it indicates a pole which tends to be ignored in compatibilist construals: that of human freedom as self-determined in some sense. It is essential to opt for a middle course between libertarian and compatibilist free will, on the one hand, acknowledging the role that circumstances play in interacting with our moral character and individual preferences, while, on the other, admitting of the possibility that a person might choose to act out of character, simply as an expression of individuality, to satisfy suppressed desires, or attain self-centred goals in a situation where these are felt to be threatened.

The shortcomings of the Arminian position are that it gives too much credit to human self-determination in the decision for salvation and eternal life, and that it fails to accord sufficient weight to fixity of human character and habituality of human conduct, which is to a considerable degree an accurate indicator of human actions. There will be individuals who choose to exercise their veto against the suggestion of circumstances out of a wish to assert themselves or in pursuit of selfish desires, but there will also be many who simply choose to act according to character and preference. It is simply not necessary to play off a libertarian understanding of human free will against a compatibilist one.

An Arminian view, of which Molinism and congruism are part, can be linked with a modified Calvinist view, also known as compatibilism, in that, similar to Calvinism, all have to do with God's choosing of some to be saved rather than others. However, the mechanism by which this happens differs between Calvinism, on the one hand, and modified Calvinism and Arminianism, on the other.

Perspectives on the Doctrine of God: Four Views (Nashville, TN: Broadman & Holman, 2008), p. 134.
15. Olson, 'Responses to Bruce A. Ware', p. 132.
16. Olson, 'The Classical Free Will Theist Model of God', pp. 148-72.

In Calvinism the emphasis falls squarely on God's completely determinative disposal of all human affairs, not just influencing but directing events and setting determinative parameters within each human person. In contrast, in both modified Calvinism and Arminianism, the human person and human affairs are a given whose particulars or responses to specific circumstances cannot be adjusted. In modified Calvinism, God seeks to determine or influence the responses of human persons whom God has selected for salvation through a foreknowledge of the individual, of the ways he would act under different circumstances. This determination of the salvific response of the human person is insurmountable and irresistible, that is, the individual is guaranteed to respond in this way. The reason for this is that God either has a natural knowledge of all possible responses on the part of each elected individual to the salvific offer based on the situations the individual encounters, and opts for the possible universe with the specific circumstances that will produce a forthcoming response of the individual to the offer of salvation (Molinism), predetermines those circumstances (modified Calvinism or compatibilism) or confers on them some form of special grace which serves to draw them in their specific situations toward salvation (congruism).[17]

As for open theism, this doctrine defends the moral attribute of God as relational in God's loving nature. God remains omnipotent and omniscient, as in previous permutations of the conception of God. However, in being omnipotent, God chooses not to exercise intervention or veto power except in rare cases so as to permit natural laws and laws of cause-and-effect governing human action to operate uninterrupted.

In being omniscient, God is neither the direct cause of God's omniscience, through sovereignly and meticulously decreeing any and every event that occurs, nor a being which possesses what is called 'simple foreknowledge', whereby God knows every event that will actually happen without determining their occurrence (free will theism)

Instead, God is 'dynamically' omniscient; that is, God is completely cognisant of every past and present event, and of certain future events – namely, those which God determines or brings about – but not of those other future events which are constituted by free human action, conceived in a libertarian sense, simply because, as far as open theists are concerned, these future events, along with events that God has ordained to take place in the future, have not yet happened and assumed the form of reality.

---

17. Helm, 'Classical Calvinist Doctrine of God', pp. 34-47.

222 Experience, Culture and Religion in Systematic Theology

Open theists such as John Sanders believe that such a doctrine of God best does justice to scriptural attestations to God's change of mind,[18] God's ability to relate in time with human beings and be influenced by their decisions and actions including prayer,[19] and collaborate with them in their being witnesses to God's work of reconciliation and redemption, and to the fact that God is not at all responsible for evil, and events do not always turn out as expected by God.[20] On these terms, the apostasy of a once genuine Christian believer is possible.

The virtue of open theism reposes in its alacrity to acknowledge the authentic character of the relationality of God as attested in the Bible. Along with Arminians, open theists are clear that, once divine predetermination is introduced to the mix, it becomes very difficult to defend the sincerity of God's responses and reactions as inferred in Scripture, including God's surprise and emotional outpourings of grief and despair, since God already knows everything that will happen from the beginning. It is also trying to explain on a determinist principle of divine providence how it is that certain divine prophecies can go unfulfilled, such as the predictions that Nebuchadnezzar would level Tyre and later Egypt.

Be that as it may, open theism, like Arminianism, seems to be oblivious to the need to give parity of weight to both the very significant possibility of people choosing to act according to their character and preferences as well as their ability to decide against circumstances – although proponents such as Sanders do incorporate both the idea of people being able to choose against their circumstances as well as the fact of their having a certain moral character which permits some degree of predictability of behaviour.[21]

---

18. For example, in relation to the human wickedness which prompted the great flood, the fate of the Israelites after the golden calf incident and its connection to Moses' intercession for Israel, the anointment of King Saul, King Hezekiah's time of death.
19. For example, Moses' intercession for Israel during the golden calf incident, King Hezekiah's pleading with God not to let him die prematurely, the fate of the Assyrians during the mission of Jonah.
20. For example, God's expectations for Israel's return and surprise that it had not yielded good grapes, the prophecies of the destruction of Tyre and Egypt by Nebuchadnezzar; Sanders, 'Divine Providence and the Openness of God', pp. 196-240.
21. J. Sanders, 'Responses to Bruce A. Ware: Response by John Sanders', in B.A. Ware (ed.), *Perspectives on the Doctrine of God: Four Views* (Nashville, TN: Broadman & Holman, 2008), pp. 143-44.

Perhaps a compatibilist perspective gives too much credence to the predictive power of moral character and personal preference and too little to self-determination and self-expression, while an Arminian approach which privileges a notion of simple foreknowledge may also be ultimately rootless in that it attempts to noetically control something, that is, human decision and action, which can only be controlled by the human being himself.[22]

To use an example, suppose God foreknows that a person, Samuel, would eat an apple pie at a fast-food joint at a certain time on a certain day. This foreknowledge is by definition always correct as a knowledge of all events that will actually happen, down to the minutest detail. Yet, its efficacy is contingent on God's foreknowledge of all events, including whether Samuel would eat an apple pie on that day, being held in confidence from the actors involved in the situation, for, imagine if Samuel were somehow to get wind of that knowledge and, mischievously, or defiantly, decides to depart from the script by having, instead, a chocolate pie. Would not God's infallible, or 'exhaustive definite' simple foreknowledge then have been proven wrong?

The simple foreknowledge theory does not work simply because human individuals are ultimately determinant of their own choices, except on the assumption that it is somehow utterly impossible to access God's foreknowledge. In preference to such a convoluted and inelegant model, it may be better to postulate, with open theists, that the future is to a significant extent open insofar as human choices are concerned.

To be sure, there is some degree of predictability of human behaviour on the basis of sure knowledge of a person's moral character, his personal preferences, the circumstances surrounding him at the point in question, and the way in which he is likely to respond to these circumstances in light of his character and preferences.

Nonetheless, there remains a certain measure of unpredictability inasmuch as the individual may choose to express his individuality by deviating from his typical response or pursue selfish ambitions by over-reaching himself and coveting that which does not belong to him, as Lucifer had done in an age, and with a character and individual preferences, devoid of sin. As can be clearly observed, such a qualification is necessary to account for the entry into the world of sin. At the opposite end, just as the individual retains the freedom, in spite of his settled

---

22. J. Sanders, 'Responses to Roger E. Olson: Response by John Sanders', in ibid., p. 185.

nature, to sin, so does he retain the freedom for love and good acts.[23] For God, freedom is a technical possibility, though not one that is ever fully actualised because God only freely makes choices of love out of a nature that is good, and this, indeed, is an archetype for the ultimate shape of human morality.

This inference very much agrees with the perspective presented and endorsed by Isaak Dorner's conceptualisation, in trinitarian terms, of the nexus and unity[24] between the ethical being[25] and ethical free act[26] of God.[27] Dorner strikes a clear pathway between the unsatisfactory alternatives and counterpoints posed by the schools of St Thomas Aquinas and John Duns Scotus. Whereas Aquinas conceived of the answer to Plato's question of whether goodness is good just because God wills it, and not because of any inherent goodness in goodness, or God wills the good because it is already good, quite apart from what God wills, in favour of the second possibility, Duns Scotus concluded that the first option is correct.

Applied to God's moral being, is God good because God decides what is good (Duns Scotus) or does God will goodness simply because God is already good in God's nature (Aquinas)? It is clear that to subordinate goodness under God as a matter for God to arbitrarily decide is inadequate, while there is no better solution in holding that goodness is purely a question of God's unchangeable and immutable essence; that is, to espouse goodness as apart from God, either beside or even above God. Instead, God should be identified with goodness and the good. Either way, this goodness is expressed both in terms of nature and freedom.[28]

---

23. Cf. Ezekiel chapter eighteen.
24. The Holy Spirit as expressing this mode of God's ethical being.
25. The Father as expressing this mode of God's ethical being.
26. The Son as expressing this mode of God's ethical being.
27. Dorner, *DI*, art. 3, pp. 167-75, esp. footnote 30.
28. Dorner in his attempted reconstruction of the Christian doctrine of divine immutability in *DI*, art. 3, pp. 131-80, considers his view of God's ethical nature and freedom as the solution to a theological impasse reached by a classical doctrine of divine immutability, in which a conception of God as static eternity leads finally either to a form of pantheism in which God is to be identified with the divisible world (with the divisible nature of the world to be regarded as an illusion), giving rise to acosmism, or to deism, whereby God sets the parameters for the world to operate independently of God, leading to atheism. He avers his viewpoint to be intellectually superior in that it moves beyond a static immutability of God, which considers only the necessary nature of God, into a 'living

Proposition: Advantages and Prolepses

Having surveyed four major systems of theodicy in Christian theology, namely, a classical Calvinist, modified Calvinist, Arminian and open theistic perspective, we see an attempt to make sense of God's sovereignty as attested in the Scriptures, and observations about human character and preferences, as well as the freedom vested in individual persons to act against the direction in which circumstances might be leading them out of either self-expressive wish, or selfishness.

There remains a sense in which in any explanation of how God is sovereign, God's love is not yet fully vindicated, not even in a free theistic system, considering that even in that construal, God is, in fact, capable of preventing evil and gratuitous suffering but elects in many tragic cases against that option simply because of a desire to preserve the laws of nature and human conduct. It is also necessary to delve into the anatomy and causes of the formation of human nature and preferences, especially as these pertain to a question of morality.

The emphasis of a cultural system should not be permitted to overwhelm the theological enterprise in an unbalanced way. I have in mind, particularly, the doctrine of divine sovereignty, which flowered during the Protestant Reformation of the sixteenth century, notably through the theologies of John Calvin and his self-proclaimed successors, the Calvinists. I use the word 'overwhelm' because, while a theory of God as being the Lord or King is indeed a traditional doctrine with scriptural warrant, this should not be turned into an almost mechanistic, speculative theory about how God ultimately pulls the strings behind every event in the universe.

If we subscribe to such a notion, it becomes very difficult to wrap our minds around the fact of unjust suffering in light of the central Christian conviction of God as loving, indeed, as love in itself, personified, epitomised. In place of absolutist doctrine, we should pioneer a relative, modern theological approach which takes a meta-level and overarching view of how different doctrines interact. The irrefragable presence of unjustified and gratuitous suffering and human brutality, as we see happening in the long course of human history wherever wars and crimes take place, demands that we relativise the doctrine of divine sovereignty, soften our stance and try our level best to relate this doctrine with other doctrines. It is possible to revise theological sovereignty and articulate a

---

immutability' (p. 175), in which the freedom of God is also taken into account.

theology of God's claim over the kingdom of God's believers which leaves room for a divine non-presence, non-activity and even non-capacity in situations of gross injustice.

With regard to the connection between divine immanence and the presence of evil, the Divine Nature and the World of Entities exist as complements and counterparts to one another, the Divine Nature as the presupposition of the being and of the formal possibility of the activity,[29] fulfilment,[30] morality,[31] self-understanding and world-understanding[32] of the World of Entities and all its parts, as well as the source of its good moral, psychological, and scientific vision and inspiration.[33] The activity

---

29. This includes the ability to experience physical sensation, to feel, think, speak and to act.

30. This includes the ability to form goals of committed action or interaction in accordance with one's intrinsic and primeval pre-human encounter with God.

31. This includes the ability to attain a harmony of disposition, attitude and ethical character with God in accordance with one's intrinsic and primeval pre-human encounter with the same.

32. By this is meant the mental structures of logic, analysis, critique and construction that characterise all human rational thinking and enable perception, an ordered accumulation of a plexus of knowledge, recognition of things seen as in the category of the generally known, an ability to detect contradiction in faulty theories of knowledge and the world, and a capacity to exercise brilliance in the manipulation of things toward some higher end of human or worldly wellbeing.

33. Cf. Dorner, *DI*, art. 3, pp. 177-78, 181, which expounds the way in which God creates all things out of love and in order to impart God's ethical self to the world, not as things completely external to God, or which God is compelled intellectually or emotionally to create, but which God chooses out of God's free decision of love so to do; *GDT*, s.v. 'Islam' (J.D. Woodberry, p. 429): 'Humans, [Al-Maturidi] said, possess an innate moral sense and have prophets as guides. God creates the root of acts, but human freedom makes them good or evil.' See also *GDT*, s.v. 'Hinduism' (M.T. Cherian, p. 391): 'Hinduism teaches that God, being the creator, greater than time and eternity, is unnamable and unseen. Therefore, human beings are unable to apprehend his essence and so use the help of sounds, names, pictures and images.' To the extent that quantum theory evinces that nature at the atomic and sub-atomic scales behaves randomly, such scientific insight lends credence to the notion that a structural substratum, in itself inscrutable, underlies all of reality as a structural-determining source of being by which just the particular souls and spiritual bodies are posited which exist, and not others, or the same in other ways, in just as random a fashion as its positing of the exact position

of the Divine Nature in guiding human religiosity or the philosophical inclination is facilitated by the presence of what John Calvin called *sensus divinitatis* and what modern science holds to be an evolutionary trait, a predisposition toward religious behaviour that promotes social cohesion in human communities, believed to have been in existence since 50,000 years ago, beginning, in the case of the Oaxaca Valley of Mexico, with communal religious dances among hunter-gatherers (*c.* 7,000 BC), progressing to ancestral-cult shrines among corn-based agricultural communities (*c.* 1,500 BC) and then elaborate, cosmologically-shaped temples by the end of the first century BC.[34]

All things, apart from the Divine Nature, are posited rather than directly created by a divine act, with the difference that the Trinity, angels and nature spirits are directly posited by the Divine Nature, while all other things, that is, material elements and the material embodiment of living things such as human beings and animals, are created by the Trinity through the power of angels using processes of evolution. As such, the Divine Nature pervades the entire universe as an invisible, fundamental, simple, not fully comprehensible, immaterial, spiritual essence.

The Trinity as the foremost complement and counterpart of the Divine Nature is this Nature's obedient servant, acknowledging the Divine Nature's role as the presupposition of the Trinity's being and of the formal possibility of its activity, fulfilment, morality, self-understanding and world-understanding, and completely yielding to the Divine Nature as the source of its good moral, psychological and scientific vision and inspiration. As such, the Trinity serves as the moral, psychological and rational archetype for all its fellow entities of a moral, psychological and rational nature in the World of Entities, whether it be angels or human beings.

Apart from the Trinity, the other entities of a moral, psychological and rational nature in the World of Entities may or may not have come to a recognition of the Divine Nature's role as the presupposition of their being and of the formal possibility of their activity, fulfilment, morality,

---

of particles on a quantum scale, such as electrons which move randomly and indeterminately in orbital clouds. See 'Superposition', *The Quantum Atlas*, accessed December 29, 2022, https://quantumatlas.umd.edu/entry /superposition.

34. N. Wade, 'The Evolution of the God Gene', *The New York Times*, 14 November 2009, https://www.nytimes.com/2009/11/15/weekinreview/12wade .html.

self-understanding and world-understanding, and as the source of their good moral, psychological and scientific vision and inspiration.

They may or may not revere and worship the Trinity as their moral, psychological, and rational archetype. They may yield neither to the Divine Nature nor to the Trinity because they falsely suppose that another nature underlies, defines and inspires their moral, psychological and rational being, and that another kind of god exemplifies their morality, psychology and rationality. Instead, they allow a culture or an individual psychological dysfunction to tell them what their true Nature is, and Cultural Exemplar to exemplify their morality or a psychological dysfunction to guide their morality. This history of rebellion and dysfunction began, as narrated in the saga of Adam and Eve, when angels or people, lifting up their hearts, desired and arrogated to themselves the place of the Divine Nature, to decide what should or should not be, ontologically, phenomenally, psychologically or morally.

The Trinity does not have absolute control over the thoughts, desires and actions of angelic and human beings because the Trinity as a moral, psychological and rational archetype for other entities of a moral, psychological and rational nature possesses but limited power and ability to safeguard and promote its moral, psychological and rational kingdom. This is because the Trinity possesses no direct ability to act in the world and relies on angelic representatives to do so. As a matter of fact, such physically or spiritually manipulative force reposes in the angels as the hands of God rather than the Trinity itself.

In light of the Trinity's reliance on its angelic agents to mediate its will in the form of interventions, help is not always available at the most pressing time. Indeed, Scripture speaks of the Spirit as capable of being grieved by the wrongful attitudes and actions of believers, rather than somehow having the ability to transform their minds and conduct. The sovereignty and power of the Trinity lie primarily in its communication of the truth about the Divine Nature, which it emulates, and how it yields to the Divine Nature as source of its good moral, psychological and scientific vision and inspiration to do the same.

At times, the Trinity sees fit to intervene directly and spectacularly in the affairs of the universe, such as the blessings of the people of Israel and the curses against Israel in rebellion and against Israel's enemies. All these actions of divine intervention are mediated through the hand of angels.

There is a need to discern a certain 'one-offism' in biblical theology in which God acts directly and supernaturally even in violation and disruption of the order of nature or ethics solely to shore up faith in

God's ability to achieve God's promised ends, whether by revealing God's might and power, vindicating God's laws or testing God's people. As concrete and specific examples: God demanded of Abraham the sacrifice of his beloved and miraculously promised son, Isaac, in a transgression of the ethical order, as Kierkegaard realised; God, for specific purposes, chooses to seal the mouth, eyes or ears of a person so that they are born with a disability (yet only with a small number of people and for a set period of time, perhaps, as we see in the case of Zechariah in Luke chapter one in which the priest was rendered mute because of his unbelief regarding the miraculous birth of his son, John the Baptist); or God brings disaster[35] in a violation of the natural order.

We aver that God does not afflict those with physical disabilities with their burdens, given that Jesus' personal mandate to set people free from their bondages as the representative of the Father, whom James says is not of ambiguous morality, plainly contradicts such a religious claim or theological belief. There is also a related idea of a specificity and the qualified nature of scriptural reference to matters including God's orchestration of events in history, such that God's ability to predestine is limited to specific events of salvific centrality, such as the Cross, and does not extend to all events in history or justify the erection of a watertight theory of divine predestination.[36]

In the aforementioned way, all things in the World of Entities are meant to be permeated completely by the Divine Nature in the former's recognition of the latter's foundational and inspirational role in the former's being, phenomenology, psychology and morality, through the further inspiration of the Trinity as the moral, psychological and rational archetype for moral, psychological and rational beings in the World of Entities.[37] Insofar as these entities do so, they constitute a reflection of the Divine Nature. Consequently, all moral, psychological and rational beings in the World of Entities are tethered to the Divine Nature through a fundamental desire to seek the good as found in that Nature.

---

35. This is akin to what Isaiah says God does in Isaiah 45:7 and the Scriptures attest in regard to God's bringing of calamities upon Pharaoh, Joseph, David, Uzzah, as well as Moses' near-death encounter in Exodus 4:24-26.

36. Barth applies such a principle to the teachings of Jesus about the need for his disciples to leave their families in pursuit of the goals of the kingdom of God. See Barth, *KD* III.4, §54.2 (*CD* III.4, §54.2, pp. 261-63).

37. Boff, *Trinity and Society*, pp. 135-36, and Acts 17:28.

This desire comes from the Divine Nature as the source of good moral, psychological and scientific vision and inspiration, and in every human and angelic individual exists in the very depths and at the bottom of the soul, unable to be completely effaced by any distortion owing to culture, compulsive evil or psychological disorder. Any human or angelic individual is able to hear and hearken to the voice of the Divine Nature speaking within the depths of their being, suggesting good thoughts, desires and actions. Yet, in order that this voice might be greatly strengthened, the Trinity, as chief servant of the Divine Nature, stirringly models a perfect moral, psychological and rational conduct based on the recognition of the Divine Nature as the presupposition of the being and of the formal possibility of the activity, fulfilment, morality, self-understanding and world-understanding of the World of Entities, and an utter, absolute and unreserved yielding to the Nature as the source of its good moral, psychological and rational vision and inspiration.

As the presupposition of the being and of the formal possibility of the activity, fulfilment, morality, self-understanding and world-understanding of the World of Entities, the Divine Nature is omnipresent, constituting every conceivable and actual space within the universe and the complex of universes as the possibility of all being and well-being, so that the nature occupies no space.[38] As the source of the good moral, psychological and scientific vision and inspiration of the moral, psychological and rational beings within the World of Entities, the Divine Nature subtly, invisibly and intangibly moves all moral, psychological and rational beings toward their good moral, psychological and rational purpose, speaking endlessly in the darkest and deepest depths of the human and angelic soul in what may well be called the conscience.

This Nature communicates with all moral, psychological and rational beings not in the second person, or even the first person, but the zeroth person. A person that converses with another usually does so in the second person, employing the use of 'you' in reference to the fellow interlocutor. One does not usually refer to another person in the first person, except, possibly, when one is quoting that person. The case differs for a spirit,

---

38. The being of the all-pervasive Divine Nature differs from that of all other things in that the former, being inclusive, affords space in such a way as to admit another entity in the exact, same location, whereas, in the case of all other things, their being is exclusive, that is, occupying space in such a way as to admit no other entity in the exact, same location, except for that which already constitutes the thing in question.

which to the extent that it has access to the thoughts of a person, could hypothetically be imagined to engage in a tactic of confusion and plant thoughts in a person's mind which might masquerade as their own.

As an example, a spirit in a person's mind might express itself thus, 'I am an unworthy person', when the person did not, in fact, think that thought, therefore leading that person to suppose that he indeed thought himself unworthy. The devil and the devil's agents have no such access to a person's mind as to be capable of entering it and disguising themselves as the person's own source of thoughts; at the very most, they can speak directly to a person's mind, often attempting to sow confusion and doubt, as happened in the case of Jesus during the course of his temptations by the devil, who sought to give the Son of God cause to question his self-identity.

The devil and the devil's agents may frequently decide to curse God without the use of speaker-referential pronouns in a person's mind, and this will tend to lead the person in question to wonder whether those voices arise from himself, inducing religious guilt. They may also issue a command for a person to act in some criminal way to harm another person, and this might lead the person, suffering from such psychosis, to believe that he has been instructed by God to execute a murder or some other harmful action.

In a famous incident in the Bible (Genesis 22:1-18) much discussed throughout modern history, Abraham heard the voice of God commanding him to sacrifice his son, Isaac.[39] Although there is no substantive difference between such a voice and another voice, from the devil, say, enjoining harm on other people, the critical distinction lies in how, behind the voice and behind the instruction, there are spirits of very different intent, one attempting to bring about action so as to harm, and another ostensibly attempting to bring about harm as well, but with the actual aim of testing and establishing a person's faith in God's goodness in spite of circumstances suggesting the contrary.

It may not always be easy to distinguish one from the other, and so we have reason to believe that Abraham had a very special and unrepeatable justification for trusting that the voice that commanded him to harm his son was indeed the voice of God rather than of the devil or the devil's agents. Perhaps God had God's presence permeate Abraham's entire soul and being with a powerful and abiding inner peace and serenity,

---

39. A notable instance being the discussion by the Danish philosopher Søren Kierkegaard (1813-55), writing as 'Johannes de Silentio', in his *Frygt og Bæven* (*Fear and Trembling*).

a sangfroid as it were, a feat the devil could never pull off, such that no peradventure was left as to the source and origin of the voice, because God is a God of peace[40] whereas Satan creates confusion and dissension.[41]

While the Holy Spirit has full access to a person's mind and is notionally capable of speaking in the mind of a person in that person's own mental and inaudible voice, the Spirit resorts to no such subterfuge, but elects to affirm, reveal the neediness of,[42] give revelation to and comfort a person regarding God's untainted goodness and glorious purposes and the importance of right thought and conduct as promoting authentic and just communion with God and among people and the rest of the existent universe,[43] all in the second person. The Spirit is also able to communicate via prophetic vision as the devil and the devil's agents are able to impart a premonition of evil.

When it comes to the Divine Nature, the bounds of description are burst as the Nature imperceptibly and ineffably moves a person to compose his own good thoughts without actually speaking in such a way as to even be mentally perceived in the mind. Consequently, it is not simply a case of the Nature saying to a person, 'Why don't you think this way or do this thing?', but rather, the Nature silently moves a person, and he thinks to himself, in his own voice, 'I have wronged him', is prompted to feel love and kind affection towards another, and acts to express those inner feelings.

The Divine Nature operates at the level of deep sense and intuition, suggesting and proposing to people and angels what they ought to do so far as intent is concerned, but, in effect, in terms of form, method and medium, motivating the inner dynamics of their souls such that they themselves take ownership of the suggestion and proposition, without, in most cases, ever detecting the involvement and action of the Divine Nature.

---

40. 1 Corinthians 14:33, Hebrews 13:20-21.

41. Matthew 13:24-30, James 3:13-18.

42. Cf. Barth, *KD* III.4, §53.3 (*CD* III.4, §53.3, p. 114).

43. Cf. Karl Barth's conception of humanity in terms of a threefold order of decreasing importance in which the former element determines the succeeding one: (i) the triune communitarian nature of God, which determines, (ii) the design of human beings as being in a covenant relationship with God, which, in turn, determines, (iii) the essence of the human being as being in relationship with one another, 'humanity as fellow-humanity'. Barth, *KD* III.4, §54.1 (*CD* III.4, §54.1, pp. 116-17).

The Divine Nature works at a subconscious and subliminal level, imparting its loving, trusting and good disposition toward God, self, humanity and the world, a sense of the moral, psychological and scientific truth about God, humanity and the world, *mutatis mutandis*, in a manner similar to how a source of heat transfers its heat to an object.

In turn, the human person articulates these feelings and sentiments in the form of loving and good words and actions, profound reflections about himself and others, and accurate understanding of the world.

This is what it means to say of the Divine Nature that it speaks to moral, psychological and rational beings and makes suggestion to them in the zeroth person, creating longing, desire and affection for the Divine Nature itself as the source of the good moral, psychological and scientific vision and inspiration for all moral beings, for the Trinity, for other members of their community and for the rest of the existent order at large.[44] As a person seeks God, it is this Divine Nature which fills him with the grounds for good, loving and insightful thoughts. It remains for people to allow these thoughts and feelings to take root in their minds and hearts.

As the moral, psychological and rational archetype for all moral beings in service of the Divine Nature as its chief servant, acknowledging the Divine Nature's role as the presupposition of the Trinity's being and of the formal possibility of its activity, fulfilment, morality, self-understanding and world-understanding, and completely yielding to the Divine Nature as the source of its good moral, psychological and rational vision and inspiration, the Trinity is present directly in heaven, though the Holy Spirit is directly present in every believer, and relies on its angelic representatives and messengers to accomplish its earthly interventions in its complete yielding to the Divine Nature as source of its good moral, psychological and scientific vision and inspiration, thereby stirring human and angelic hearts to do the same.[45]

Thence, divine help does not always avail in a time of desperate need on earth, for the Trinity relies on its angelic representatives to carry out its

---

44. Cf. Augustine, *Conf.*, XIII.i.1, iv.5, for a statement of longing for the divine as arising from a divine source towards the latter as source of good.
45. The divine council temporarily shrinks with the departure of the Son for earth but returns to full strength when he ascends to heaven after his resurrection. The Holy Spirit begins the Spirit's concentrated activity on earth upon the ascension, filling every person who calls on the name of Christ.

interventions, including its communications, as in the case of Daniel.[46] The angelic mediation of divine activity supplies the efficient cause for the delay of God's response, not because God willingly chooses to put God's children to grief, but because God relies on fallible angels to do God's work on earth. Aside from angelic mediation, God also resorts to a human mediation in the work of preaching and ministry.

What is the relationship between theodicy and redemption? That is, to what extent was God successful in redeeming humankind? Moreover, what is the specific role of God's redemptive activity as a response to a question of the efficacy of God's work among people in the midst of the prevalence of sin and evil? The work of redemption is closely connected to the question of the power of God, of how a powerful God could manifest weakness at the Cross, and why God would do so.

At the most crucial point in his life as the Lord sought the face of the Father just prior to his arrest, he forbore an appeal for angelic military support from heaven, and this was only because he wanted to put an end to the threat of the devil for good. Therefore, subsequently at his trial, he was silent in front of his accusers.[47] All along, the devil had held the reins of human destiny in holding the 'power of death' and through the human 'fear of death [subjecting them] to lifelong slavery'.[48]

This devilish thrall operated through the guilt of condemnation that arises from an inability to adhere perfectly or sincerely to the laws of God, sometimes out of wilfulness, but more often out of a compulsive evil cooperating with psychological disorder, which in biblical times was not well understood, and fairly or unfairly constituted a barrier to one's relationship with God within the community. It was not possible for the sacrificial system which relied on animals to cleanse the conscience because the intensity and frequency of disobedient thought and action were exceedingly great, and the burden of guilt and condemnation was crippling and debilitating for authentic persons such as St Paul, who spoke

---

46. Daniel 10:1-14; an indwelling Holy Spirit relies on angels even in the event of communication to believers, because any divine-human communication entails establishing a link between God and the human interlocutor by which thoughts and feelings can be transmitted and producing the physical signals, in a form receivable by the human brain, by which these thoughts and feelings can and will be transmitted.

47. L. Morris, *The Gospel According to Matthew*, Pillar New Testament Commentary (Grand Rapids, MI: Eerdmans, 1992), p. 683.

48. Hebrews 2:14-15, ESV.

of a principle of disobedience within his mind and heart that subjected him to the death of condemnation.[49]

It is not untrue to say, as Romans 5:12 appears to suggest, that this principle emerged in the course of Adam's disobedience and befell all humanity from his time because of the psychologically inadequate practices of childrearing concomitant with Adam's desire to usurp the role of the Divine Nature. Covetousness was possible but not at all inevitable because of the natural, comprehensive superiority of God to humankind. Adam was capable of committing an original sin against God because he, along with Eve, were the first human beings, and did not have the benefit of precedents in disobedience to warn him against its consequences; as for the people who came after him, even though they had Adam as a precedent of how not to behave, yet they would have been negatively affected by the way they were brought up by him or their parents as children, and would for that reason have grown up with a psychological disorder and the influence of a compulsive evil of some sort.

During biblical times, the deep-seated and negative psychological impact of the principle of disobedience operating in every person would have been cushioned, first, by the provision of an animal sacrifice through which the Israelites and then the Jews could obtain the assurance of the forgiveness by God of their sins. However, its noble intent and purpose notwithstanding, the blood of bulls and goats was not capable of truly supporting the conscience of the psychologically disordered individual.

Into this situation, Jesus plunged himself, having in his previous existence as the spiritual Son ventured with the rest of the divine council an answer, in which he would allow the brunt of the devil's attacks to destroy his physical life and thereafter be resurrected through the command of the Father by the hand of mighty angelic intermediaries so as to complete the picture formed by earlier and later prophecies as to the victory of a descendant of Eve over the serpent, a symbol of the devil,[50] and the atoning death of Christ,[51] in an offer of hope to those who would embrace this olive branch being held out by God as an effective and sustainable way of coping and dealing with an often guilty

49. Romans 7:7-23.
50. Genesis 3:15.
51. Isaiah 52:13-53:12.

conscience, because Christ offers the promise of divine forgiveness to all who confess their sins.[52]

It is not unconscionable to suggest that the angels were the intermediaries through whom the Lord himself was resurrected, seeing that angels have such immense power as to be able to wipe out whole armies.[53] During the rule of King Hezekiah, it is recorded that the angel of Yahweh, the Trinity, killed 185,000 Assyrian soldiers encamped outside Jerusalem,[54] while, in the days of David, an angel of pestilence single-handedly took the lives of 70,000 men.[55] Even though the angels constitute the instrumentality of divine action in the world, the authority undergirding those actions rests with the Trinity, particularly the Father, so that Jesus was fully justified in remarking that the Father works in the world, raising the dead and giving life to them.

As for Jesus himself, by virtue of his physical body he is able to act in a physical manner; yet, when he says that he has the power to raise the dead, this, along with any other miracle for that matter, is an activity beyond human ability and, thus, what he really means is that through the angels, vested with his authority, he is able to raise the dead by their power, as he did in the case of Lazarus, and perform other miracles.[56]

Necessarily, the non-incarnate members of the Trinity are capable of directly communicating among themselves and with other entities, as in the case of the Father in giving commands to the Father's angels, and that of the Holy Spirit who speaks to the believers in their hearts, although, if it is a matter of the Trinity communicating with other entities excluding angels and spirits, it is always through angelic mediation. Through the atoning act of sacrifice of Christ on the Cross, the divine council through

---

52. 1 John 1:9; as Karl Barth rightly underscores, forgiveness from God is not automatic or permanent, and has to be appealed to again in each instance. Cf. Barth, *KD* III.4, §53.3 (*CD* III.4, §53.3, p. 105). The Lord's prayer reminds us of the same material fact.

53. Christ was resurrected by the Father's authority (Acts 2:32), in which angels were charged to restore bodily life to him. Just as Christ voluntarily gave up his life for execution by the Roman authorities, not having acted to deprive himself of physical life, so Christ readily receives again his life from the Father through the angels, not having acted to revitalise himself (John 10:17-18), *contra* Augustine's reading of this subject in *Civ.* XVI.41.

54. 2 Kings 19:35.

55. 2 Samuel 24:15-16.

56. Cf. John 5:19-23.

Christ dealt with the advances of the devil and his army and brought the devil to judgement.[57]

Some may opine that such a theology gives a free pass to selfish individuals to do as they wish in their lives, continue hurting people and assume no personal responsibility for their misdeeds. It is vital in this regard to distinguish clearly between the care and provision of the Trinity for the guilty conscience, that it may not crush the individual, and the need to repent and perhaps even make amends. Those who misuse and exploit God's provision for guilt-ridden consciences are oblivious of the purposes of God for their own lives and perversely imagine that God is either pleased with whatever they do or uninterested in it.

Therefore, the dilemma in question is not an issue of the validity of the provision for the consolation and salving of the guilty conscience *per se*, but one of having the right understanding of and relationship with God. Guilt can be a positive driving force behind behavioural and attitudinal change, and there will be special circumstances that call for an ecclesiastical or communal condemnation of a sinner, such as in the case of a Corinthian church member who was alleged to have been sleeping with his mother,[58] but even this is only temporary and calculated at evoking repentant feelings.[59] Again, these are special circumstances demanded by what are felt to be special sins. If there is no such necessity, a believer should always depend on God's forgiveness through Christ.

The advantages of a theodicy which reconceptualises the Christian doctrine of creation in terms of a Divine Nature as a basis (origin, fount) for all existence, the Trinity as its chief agent, angels as the functionaries of the Trinity in morality, self-understanding and world-understanding, and human beings as secondary functionaries in the making in a ministry and service to the rest of the universe rest in its ability: (i) to make sense of the mighty acts of God in Scripture, through the finite scope of action on the part of angels, without having to commit itself to an inelegant and crass doctrine of divine omnipotence; (ii) to make sense of scriptural attestation variously to an omnipresence and situation of God; (iii) to make sense of scriptural witness to God as having a very comprehensive knowledge of the affairs of the world, again through angels, without having to commit to an inelegant theory of divine omniscience, in such a way that the divine goodness and love is not endangered but vindicated.

---

57. John 12:31, Colossians 2:13-15.
58. First Corinthians chapter five.
59. Cf. 1 Corinthians 5:5 and 2 Corinthians 2:5-11.

In what material ways does this construal of the divine immanence differ from existing doctrine? A major distinction between the current formulation and a classical doctrine lies in its reinterpretation of the original creative act of God. Instead of conceiving of God in the beginning creating all things non-self-sufficient and contingent by a fiat command, bringing about the totality of creation from complete nothingness in a doctrine of *creatio ex nihilo*, or from pre-existing matter previously made, in which case *creatio ex nihilo* would still obtain but with a second stage of creation in which God shapes out of shapeless matter an orderly totality, a cosmos, in the understanding here propounded, the non-physical handiwork of God is reconceived as a complement of a Divine Nature, with the Trinity itself being included alongside this totality as an order of the World of Entities, so that all non-physical things in the World of Entities exist through being posited by the nature rather than the act of the Divine Nature. Consequently, we may say of the Divine Nature that it is the presupposition of the being of the World of Entities and its individual constituents.

On these terms, creation means quite simply that our origin is in the Divine Nature and not that God directly created us, only the material principles of the universe, including our physical bodies, and this through the angels, with Godself having begun at some point through the position of the Divine Nature, before which there could be nothing in what we can call, 'the horizon of all possibility'.[60] Formulating the doctrine of the origin of all things in this way judiciously avoids unanswerable questions as to what God was engaged in before the creation of the world, and for what duration of time, and why any specific response is given to those questions rather than others. Instead of involving oneself in that philosophical-theological dilemma, it may be more elegant to depict all entities, the World of Entities, as having one beginning, one existence and still continuing that same existence.

There is no particular need to situate this beginning of all things anywhere in time, subsequent to a period of time during which God as

---

60. On these terms, the divine invitation in Genesis 1 to jointly create the various components of the world including humankind can be construed as addressed to angels as well as the other members of the triune godhead, as opposed to indicating a plural of majesty; the plural form of the name for God, *Elohim*, can be taken as validating the doctrine of a perichoretic constitution in which all of the godhead is contained in each divine person as mutually and fully enveloping one another and yet each person is able to address the others as distinct subjectivities.

creator and artificer may be thought to have been inactive in relation to the original creative act, but simply to intimate that there must have been a beginning of the totality of all things in the World of Entities by the very nature of those same things as spatio-temporal. The Trinity itself has a beginning in this timeline, but not by means of having been created in any way. That the Trinity has always existed in time rather than also, properly, or exclusively, in eternity marks a development as well from traditional doctrinal paths. Even though God did not directly create the non-material part of the universe, yet the Divine Nature and the Trinity are rhapsodically pleased with the established fact of the existence of all things.[61]

Of what does the writer of Genesis speak when he depicts God as having created humankind in God's image if indeed God did not create human souls but these are posited by the Divine Nature? Even if the human soul is posited, this is still an event that only transpires as a result of what God is as the Divine Nature. The universe of souls being posited experiences a beginning; the Divine Nature is an unchanging principle – as the Trinity is paradigm – of what is good, producing all that makes for existence and perfection without ever being in any need of what it produces. This Divine Nature does not experience a beginning, though it generates many inceptions, even one for the personal and interpersonal history of the Trinity. Just as the Divine Nature posits the human soul, the angels by the authority of the Trinity create the physical bodies into which these souls are poured, having put off their former angelic forms. The human person, soul and body, image God in that we each have the seeds of divine love and the means to practise it and eradicate obstacles that prevent its incarnation.

Why is it felt necessary to move away from a logically viable conception of God, as an eternal being dwelling in an eternal realm, in which God as Trinity lives in unperturbed bliss and, at the same time, eternally and unchangeably, holds a decree of creation out of which emerges, and which gives justification and basis to, a whole other realm and province of life? Why move away from the conception of a world bounded by space and carried along in time, a world into which the eternal triune God pours Godself to translate Godself into another realm of existence, in a somewhat different mode of existence, without diluting or altering in any way God's mode of existence in the eternal realm, in which there is no before or after in regard to whether God's eternal being or the creative decree, and therefore creation itself, came first, because simultaneous?

---

61. Consequently, the first creation story consistently relates God's happy approval of the being of all things.

One prime reason for this is that it seems incongruous to discourse of God as vested with glorious majesty and attendant power and yet incapable of preventing any particular act of evil from occurring within such a God's realm. If God indeed engendered all creatures by a direct act of creation, there is nothing stopping the same God from manipulating the forms of existence of these creatures in such a way as to bring about a fruitful and profitable result for one and all.

Instead of this, the strong presence of evil and injustice obliges us to recognise the relative nature of God as an active being, holding some power, yes, in the form of angelic helpers, yet not such as to always be availing, because the angelic assistance itself is finite and liable to change, but generally situated within the very same dimension of existence as the entities with which God is engaged in what often seems like a mortal struggle.[62] This is not to suggest a dualism of any sort, given that the activity of the devil and the devil's minions presupposes the primacy of the Trinity and the angels of the Trinity against which that activity constitutes rebellion, a primacy that stretches beyond the order of authority and importance, in that this very Trinity is most properly associated with the omnipresent, immanent, all-pervasive and all-suffusing Divine Nature itself and the Divine Nature with the Trinity. Even so, there is a feature of our doctrine which is reminiscent of classical theology insofar as it testifies to the creation but by angels of the material principles of the universe.

Yet, there are greater logical difficulties entailed in a traditional doctrine of creation. First of all, if indeed God created all things through an eternal decree which came into effect only at some point during God's eternal existence, since God has always existed both simultaneously with the

---

62. On these terms, to take just one example from the Bible, God brought about such an event as the Flood by means of God's angels, acting subserviently with respect to a divine command. Could such a destructive event again be ordered and carried out? It could technically be so. However, the effectiveness of this ordinance will be dependent not only on the obedience of the angels so instructed but on whether any or sufficient numbers of them as are necessary to bring about such a tremendous effect are presently available rather than engaged in myriad tasks around the universe, as well as the justification for God's commanding something of the magnitude of the great flood, one which has generally ceased to exist since the eras during which it was needful for God to have powerful deeds performed in order to establish divine authority among humankind, both among the Israelites and their descendants, as well as the Gentiles, for good or for evil.

universe and even before the universe and the universe did not always exist, then is this not to introduce the idea of succession into God's eternal being, in which there is a milestone constituted by the appearance of the universe, thus rendering eternity successive, changing and therefore less than eternal? Granted our proposition raises other questions such as how it could be that everything, including God, began at some point chronologically, and what could have given rise to all those things when they came about. Also, if we recur to the notion of a Divine Nature, which posits all things that came into being at first, we find the inquirer seeking understanding regarding what brought about this Divine Nature and determined its particular all-determining nature. This, however, is an unanswerable question, insofar as to any response that may be proffered, another similar one can be proposed about the further or more ultimate cause antecedent to and bringing about this Divine Nature. In the end, therefore, the best solution that can be articulated has to involve some theory that all things, including divinity, begin at some chronological juncture, and some valid apprehension of the nature of this divine being, whose legitimacy reposes in the fact that it explains and anchors morality and existence, among other things.

Second, such a notion satisfies the condition for Christian theology, highlighted by Augustine of Hippo, of being able to secure the eternal lordship of God through the constant presence of subordinate creatures, without necessarily having to affirm some notion of cosmic eternity.[63] This is because in my theory, there is no idea of a chronological infinity, while the ontological distinction of God is safeguarded by an account of God as the ultimately positing factor and fount of all being, existence, and intellectual, psychological, moral and physical perfection.

Another differential feature between the present doctrine of the divine immanence and classical is the manner in which a quite separate element, that is, the Divine Nature, as presupposition of the being and of the possibility of the activity, fulfilment, morality, self-understanding and world-understanding of the World of Entities, and the source of its good moral, psychological and scientific vision and inspiration, is placed before the Trinity.

The Trinity is understood as the first complement of the Divine Nature and perfect and chief servant which fully recognises the role of the Divine Nature in constituting and maintaining ontology, phenomenology, psychology and morality among entities, and yielding so completely to the Divine Nature as source of the good moral, psychological and

---

63. Augustine, *Civ.*, XII.15.

scientific vision and inspiration of the World of Entities that it becomes the moral, psychological and rational archetype for human and angelic being. In contrast, in the traditional doctrine, the Trinity itself and monolithically is the ultimate being.

This bifurcation is thought necessary in order to permit the construction of an equitable doctrine of God's immanence amid gratuitous evil without relinquishing the attribute of the divine as all-pervasive and omnipresent principle of being. An incidental benefit is that the Trinity in this way is rendered as a moral exemplar, the original and first true believer, for the human and angelic being, not simply by being what it is but instead through its meritorious action.

Whereas the human conscience in many cases is appropriated to the human person in question as a sort of individual property, in this instance, the voice of morality which speaks from the depths of a person's soul is located not within the person but in an all-encompassing Divine Nature, which provides the source for the good moral vision and inspiration of all things in the World of Entities.

Furthermore, the positing of a structural Divine Nature distinct from an entitative Trinity permits us to comprehend the historical conditioning of the biblical writings, which do not quite advance beyond the social norms of their particular periods, including slavery and sexism, or the relatively primitive cosmologies, as related to the fact that the Trinity itself began at the horizon of all possibility, and seeks to understand the sociological, scientific, medical, psychological, moral and religious wisdom of the Divine Nature, which by nature only discloses such wisdom according to an evolutionary sequence. This incidentally accommodates the need of entities for progression. The Trinity is able to comprehend this wisdom only progressively but in a such a way that the Trinity is able to spearhead advances in all these areas as a chief interpreter of the Divine Nature.

The next, and possibly most crucial, point of contrast between a pre-existing view of the divine immanence and our current conception is the thought that the Trinity does not hold complete control over the world for the reason that it does not possess physically or spiritually manipulative force, which is the property only of the angels as the hands of God.[64]

---

64. Such a doctrine can, in effect, be built up by recourse to Augustine's construction of the realm of earthly people, as opposed to heavenly people, as defined by the rule of bad angels, in *Civ.*, XVI.17.

As such, it was possible for the Trinity's plans to be thwarted, because its angelic messengers and agents can be hampered by other errant, angelic forces. This happened in the Book of Daniel when the angel Gabriel was hindered by an angelic force, a prince of Persia, from more quickly reaching Daniel to relay the fact that God had heard his prayer.

Christ having been reconstituted as a human being and thereby made vulnerable to temptation, because now the Son of God had been relegated to being somewhere in the middle of a hierarchy of a material human society, it became necessary for the rest of the Trinity to mediate their assistance to him through the angels as well, as we see happening after the period of temptation by the devil, at Gethsemane, and at Calvary.

Why is it important to transfer the locus of the execution of power from the Trinity to the angels? This is in order to account for the ubiquitous presence of evil and gratuitous suffering in the world: that is, misdeeds committed by people for reasons of selfishness or out of blindness or ignorance, engendering suffering that afflicts the innocent.

If this is the case, what is the place of prayer in the life of the non-Christian and the Christian? Among non-Christians, there are two main categories: the non-Christian person, who is not particularly looking to adopt the Christian religion as his own; and the non-Christian person, who is seeking to become a Christian. For the first group, the non-seeking non-Christian, prayer is to be encouraged in time of distress to find support from the Christian God, if the person so wishes. The unseen process that occurs when such a request is made of God is that angels hear and mediate the request to the Trinity in heaven. This leads to a decision being made by the divine council to offer some form of support, and the same or other angels are dispatched to perform the task. For the second group, the seeking non-Christian, in addition to appealing to prayer as a means of spiritual support, the teaching of the Lord can be underscored in which he urges those who desire the Spirit of God to earnestly ask God for the gift. As they ask for this gift, the angels bring the request to the divine council in heaven, a decision is made, and the Spirit is sent into the heart of the new believers.

As for those who are Christians, prayer plays a critical role in allaying fear and anxiety due to circumstances and needs. With the Christian, it is not necessary for an angel to bear the message to the divine council in heaven, for the Holy Spirit is in the heart of the believer; moreover, the Holy Spirit, while indwelling believers on earth, nevertheless, maintains a presence in heaven. For this reason, the Spirit is able, though only through angelic mediation, to directly minister comfort and a sense of solace to the Christian, to assure him that God is for him and not against him. At the same time, being both on earth in the heart of the believer and in heaven among the rest of the divine council, the Spirit is able to convey the needs and requests of the believer to the council, and the relevant angels dispatched to attend to those needs.

Because God the Father already knows all the needs of believers through God the Holy Spirit, there is no actual need for the believer to make those needs known to God and, as soon as a need arises, the divine council has already set out to attend to those needs through angelic intermediaries. However, the believer is not prevented from bringing those needs and requests to God in prayer, because there will be occasions when what is asked for is not necessarily good for the believer in question, so that coming to prayer affords the Spirit an opportunity to reason with the believer about his request, and also because when the believer lays himself bare before God in supplication and humility, the Spirit is able to do a work of reassurance in the believer's heart.[65]

It has to be emphasised that, even if the angels are dispatched from heaven to assist in some situation of need, there will always be either a possibility of the help being ineffectual, because the powers of angels are limited, greatly extended across the entire world, counteracted significantly by the presence of angelic rebels under the leadership of the devil, or even recruited by the devil. The devil is 'the ruler of this world',[66] 'the god of this world',[67] or 'the prince of the power of the air, the spirit that is now at work in the sons of disobedience',[68] and commands a considerable and immense host of demons comprising rulers, authorities, cosmic powers 'over this present darkness', 'spiritual forces of evil in the heavenly places'.[69] Ostensibly, the power of God as leader of an angelic host is almost effectively countered by that of the devil also as leader of an angelic host, flung into the world after having been defeated in heaven.

As a matter of fact, there are strong indications in the Gospel of John in particular that the crucifixion of the Lord itself was a ploy of the devil, who 'put it into the heart of Judas Iscariot, Simon's son, to betray [Jesus]',[70] 'entered into him'[71] and marshalled the devil's spiritual forces

---

65. Karl Barth leaves no doubt concerning God's readiness to grant the believer's wishes. Barth, *KD* III.4, §53.3 (*CD* III.4, §53.3, pp. 106-7).

66. John 14:30, ESV.

67. 2 Corinthians 4:4, ESV.

68. Ephesians 2:2, ESV.

69. Ephesians 6:12, ESV.

70. John 13:2, ESV.

71. John 13:27, ESV.

against the powers of the angels of God.[72] Thus, at a critical moment, the Lord had to remark that, if he so wished he could have had recourse to twelve legions of angels from the Father, suggesting that he was there and then faced with a spiritual army of equivalent might, or at least something approximating to that, so that, if he desired it, liberation could come only through the dispatch of forces of this strength – if the evil spiritual army with which the Lord was confronted was of little number and strength, why would there be any need to request, in particular, twelve legions of angels? The crowds with which Jesus was confronted in Gethsemane were not of such great prowess as to require such a large force.

The angels as heralds from God and instruments of creative and destructive power are constricted, whether by number or obedience, in their ability to fulfil requests to God made in prayer on the part of believers. Hence, while they may be able to bring a good or love-oriented, encouraging or inspiring thought to a person, as the Holy Spirit is able to do with believers, or to destroy the person utterly, they are not capable of subtly manipulating a person's emotions or directly affecting his decision-making capacity so as, say, to cause a Human Resources manager and hiring committee to approve a job application and candidacy. Although this is so, God may influence them with positive thoughts and feelings which, in turn, drive behaviour, such as inspiring decision makers to be more charitable, helping them to appreciate the suitability of a job candidate, or suggesting to them the importance of attending to some need of the candidate. However, these sentiments can be refused or rejected by choice, and ultimately the main deciding factors would be secular and practical factors such as the current job market and the extent to which the skills, experience and qualifications of the individual may be a good fit for the role, rather than religious or spiritual elements. While it is necessary for the believer to make his requests known to God in supplication, God already knows the heart of the believer and, whether or not God is able to effect the desired answer to prayer, God is, nonetheless, capable of extending to the supplicant a knowledge of circumstances which may influence the possibility of attaining a desired outcome.

Personal tragedy need not be attributed to God, since the source of tragedy can easily be distinguished from the effect of the same. The devil and the devil's agents, or some natural cause, brings it about that some tragic circumstance obtains, yet God and God's agents are capable of encouraging the victim of the calamity to learn or gain something from

---

72. John 14:30.

the tragedy, which the tragedy itself does not automatically or naturally impart, or the intelligent and malicious sources of the same, if any.[73]

Conclusion

Why do we essay to move away from a notion of a direct creative act of God? The idea of a creative act in relation to an eternal God is an oxymoron. God never acted to create the world. If that were the case, there would be a time before which God created the world, yet according to Augustine, God dwells in an unmoving eternal present.[74] Barth would add that, out of that eternal present of God, the movements and progression of time in the history of the world find their basis and form, and this may be because all of time is represented in a single unchanging moment in God's eternity.[75] However, God is also dynamically present in history.[76]

Therefore, God in history is part of the simultaneous representation of history in divine eternity, which is accompanied by the eternal presence of God. This eternal presence of God apart from time summed up in eternity is a prerequisite for time and therefore time in eternity, since, without God conceived apart from time, it is impossible to account for the existence of creation through an act of God. The divine decrees of election and creation precede creation itself and therefore even eternity as the summation of all time, and this accounts for the divine presence which is concomitant with time summed up in eternity.

Thus, in history God is still able to have created, but what occurred prior to creation and what caused God to create at the point God did rather than any other? In fact, the idea of an act of creation is repugnant to Christian theology, since according to Augustine time did not exist before the creation of the world but was created along with the world.[77] If there was no time before creation, there was no possibility of God creating the universe through an act situated in a progression with a before and after as necessitated by a doctrine of a non-eternity of the universe. Whatever exists must be based on some firmer foundation, and this I have called the Divine Nature. Equally obnoxious is the idea of an

---

73. Cf. Augustine, *Civ.*, XIII.7.
74. Augustine, *Conf.*, XI.xiii.16, XI.xi.13, IX.iv.10-11, XIII.ix.10, XIII. xvi.19.
75. Barth, *KD* III.1, §41.1, (*CD* III.1, §41.1, pp. 67-68).
76. Barth, *KD* III.4, §53.3 (*CD* III.4, §53.3, pp. 108-9).
77. Augustine, *Conf.*, XI.xiii.15.

eternal God with time prior to creation.[78] For time came into existence with the history of the world. God has no time in eternity. God's time begins, continues and ends in the history of the universe. Time is an essential element in God as a concrete and particular being, rather than abstract essence which does not exist in a concrete sense.[79]

In support of the idea of God as being in time, Scripture depicts God as being 'in the beginning',[80] rather than in a domain separate from time. If God were timeless, Scripture would describe God as being beyond time and not merely before time.[81]

It is normal for a person afflicted with grievous suffering to wonder where God is in all their troubles, blame God for not coming through for them or doubt God's pure love. Yet, God is in all our sorrows. God may well be the only one who fully understands the agony we go through and which those who wrong us refuse to admit, the only one who hears our voiceless screams and cries with us. As Hagar discovered, God is one who witnesses, who sees us in our pain and suffering, and is concerned about us.[82]

---

78. Augustine, *Conf.*, XI.xiii.15.
79. Lonergan, *Const. Chr.*, 4.4, §72, pp. 146-47.
80. John 1:1.
81. Psalm 90:2; John 8:58, Revelation 1:8, 4:8; W. Grudem, *Systematic Theology: An Introduction to Biblical Doctrine* (Leicester: InterVarsity Press, 1994), 11.3a, p. 169.
82. Genesis 16:13.

Chapter 8

Doctrines: Sin and Salvation

Christianity as a religion is preoccupied with the fact that people are morally flawed beings. Indeed, the central component of the message of the Gospel, which crystallises the mandate, mission, ministry and teaching of the Lord Jesus Christ, namely, divine forgiveness through atonement, presupposes the reality of sin in humankind and presents itself as a solution to this tragic and painful predicament.

Definition

Original sin as a doctrine posits the fundamental moral corruption of humankind. This flawed state did not exist in the beginning, but was acquired from the time of the disobedience of Adam and Eve, the progenitors of humankind, in relation to the divine commandment issued to them in the garden of Eden against consuming a fruit from the tree of the knowledge of good and evil.

Understood in this manner, original sin came to define the moral-spiritual state of Adam and Eve after the act of disobedience, and so tainted their being that all their descendants, that is, the rest of humanity, could not escape the corruption which sets in from the time of birth and plagues human individuals throughout their lifetimes. The sinful nature of humanity ensures that sin does not remain latent but is expressed in thoughts and actions.

Place in a Systematic Theology

If the doctrines of God, the Trinity, and anthropology constitute the ontological core of Christian theology, and the doctrines of Christology and pneumatology the epistemological core, the doctrine of original sin forms the existential centre of Christian theology. It attempts to explain the universal human experience of a struggle between a noble and ignoble self and of evil and injustice in the world.

Existing Conceptions: Strengths and Weaknesses

St Augustine of Hippo: The Doctrine of Original Sin

The theologian whose name is most closely affiliated with this doctrine is the fourth-century Algerian Church Father, Augustine of Hippo, whose theological and philosophical works laid the foundation for Western philosophy.[1]

St Augustine developed the idea that, when the first human being, Adam, broke the command he was given from God not to eat the fruit of the tree of the knowledge of good and evil, his action served to drag all his descendants, that is, the entire human race, into the state of moral degradation into which he had been precipitated and set in motion a process which corrupted human nature, to the point that in our natural selves, we do not have any desire to do what is right but continuously entertain evil intentions and thoughts and carry out evil deeds.

Augustine called this moral corruption of human nature, original sin, and he believed that it was transmitted from Adam to all humanity by sexual intercourse in the process of procreation. With this corrupt nature and the resulting wicked deeds come the guilt and culpability which God assigns to fallen human nature. In light of original and actual sin, it is necessary for God to send God's Son Jesus Christ to redeem us through his sacrificial and propitiatory death on a cross.

Theologians like Maurice Wiles are of the view that St Augustine misinterpreted a key prooftext used to support his theory of original sin.[2] This verse, Romans 5:12 (ESV), reads: 'Therefore, just as sin came into the world through one man, and death through sin, and so death spread to all men because all sinned' – Augustine has 'in whom' in place of 'because' so that it seems as though all people sinned in Adam's sin, in which the actions of the first human being and their consequences

---

1. In Augustine's view, sin constitutes a privation of goodness, an example of which is served by angels who of their own volition elected to abjure the cause of servitude to and worship of God, choosing rather to elevate themselves above God (*Civ.*, XII, 6, 9).

2. M. Wiles, *The Making of Christian Doctrine: A Study in the Principles of Early Doctrinal Development* (Cambridge: Cambridge University Press, 1967), pp. 55-56.

are in some way ascribed to the rest of humanity during what was a probationary period in the garden of Eden.

Augustine adduces Hebrews 7:9-10 in support of his theory. These verses suggest that Levi, the progenitor of the ritual-ceremonial class in biblical Israel, already existed during the time of his great grandfather in his reproductive organs, in what is known as a view concerning the natural headship of Adam.

Reformed Theologians: The Regeneration of the Human Heart

Is salvation of grace alone or is it partly of human effort? A pious desire to give God all the credit has led theologians from early to modern history to devise a system whereby from start to finish the human being is rendered completely dependent on and forever indebted to the divine power of providence and redemption. Humankind is degraded into a quintessential sinner while God is elevated to being an all-powerful and wonder-working deity capable of translating even the meanest, most contemptible and most repulsive transgressor into the purest saint.

At their most extreme, these notions have given rise to a theory that not only did God have something to do with the fall of humankind but indeed that God directly orchestrated the human fall into the depths and abyss of depravity, with all its tragic and unspeakably painful ramifications, and that God only ever intended to save a select few by a secret decree bordering on, if not actually reflecting, arbitrary personal preference.

A doctrine of the necessity of a supernaturally regenerated heart for salvation is to be jettisoned because the scriptural foundations are not strong.[3] Recourse is typically had to passages which appear to attest to a divine working in a human heart to transform it and render it suppliant to

---

3. In this section, we consulted pertinent chapters in David Dickson's commentary on the Westminster Confession of Faith, to understand and engage the scriptural support for different aspects of the doctrine of regeneration, touching on Holy Scripture, God's eternal decree, free will, effectual calling, saving faith and good works. See D. Dickson, *Truth's Victory Over Error: A Commentary on the Westminster Confession of Faith*, ed. J.R. de Witt, trans. G. Sinclair (1684) (Edinburgh: Banner of Truth, 2007).

God's commands,[4] God's protective assistance to guard a person in their faith,[5] God's resurrection of the spiritually dead to life in faith,[6] the apparent inability of a believer to commit sin,[7] indications of God's marking out believers from non-believers,[8] God's revelation of God's will and purposes to chosen ones,[9] God's opening of blind spiritual eyes,[10] the devil's blinding of non-believers,[11] non-believers as being devoid of any hope,[12] salvation as being of Christ alone,[13] a 'golden chain' of redemption,[14] a hardening of hearts,[15] a divine plan for salvation,[16] God as having done and as continuing to do a work in human hearts,[17] God's appointment to eternal life or setting apart of those who believe.[18]

In attempting to identify cues from Scripture for theological construction, one has to always take care not to commit a fallacy of thinking that just because a specific individual experienced powerful divine help through faith in the Christian God, this establishes a principle of expecting such help in any circumstances and legitimises a doctrine of God's ever-availing, powerful assistance. Experience amply bears out that faith in the Christian God does not always lead to encouraging outcomes, and this not necessarily because of any deficient capacity to believe in the Christian God on the part of the believer in question. Some will be able to receive God's help in their time of need, and others will fail to receive the same help, for the reason of God's limitation, and not because of a lack of readiness on God's part to grant a person a capacity to receive God's salvation.

In fact, a doctrine of God's goodness obliges a theologian to believe and teach that God will not intentionally withhold God's grace from anyone

---

4. E.g. Ezekiel 11:19-20.
5. E.g. 1 Peter 1:5.
6. E.g. Ephesians 2:1, 5.
7. E.g. 1 John 3:9.
8. E.g. John 13:18; 2 Thessalonians 2:13-14; 2 Timothy 2:19; Titus 1:1; Jude 1:4-5.
9. E.g. Matthew 11:25-27, 13:11-12.
10. E.g. Acts 26:18.
11. E.g. 2 Corinthians 4:3.
12. E.g. Ephesians 2:1-5, 11-12.
13. E.g. Acts 4:12.
14. Romans 8:30.
15. E.g. Romans 11:7.
16. E.g., Acts 15:18; Romans 11:33; Ephesians 1:10-11.
17. E.g. 2 Corinthians 3:3, 6; Philippians 2:13; Hebrews 12:2.
18. E.g. John 17:6; Acts 13:48.

just in order to prove that God is sovereign. As such, all the passages about disbelief and blindness on the part of unbelievers in the Bible[19] are to be taken not so much as definitive and unchangeable pronouncements on people's spiritual destinies but rather as an admonition and invitation to the same individuals to take a long, hard look at themselves and take stock of their spiritual and psychological lives, to consider the possible influence of a principle of compulsive evil conspiring with psychological disorder, socio-cultural bias, and even religious misconceptions on their reluctance or even outright opposition to accepting the message of Christ, without giving the slightest suggestion that people of other faith groups are not entitled to their respective religions.

John is not wrong to write in 1 John 3:9 that no true believer will consciously choose to live a life of sin, and this is true, because, even if Christians are not immune to wrongdoing, yet no believer will deliberately act with the explicit intent of causing harm to others or disobeying God. In writing those words, John probably had in view believers who were hating each other in their hearts, and urged them, by way of a gentle reminder, to see that brotherly and sisterly love is very much a mandate of the Christian God for all believers, instead of laying down a rigid rule that anyone who nursed such hatred could not actually be a bona fide believer. Christian believers need to be recalled to the original ethical vision to which they have committed themselves every now and then, when they go astray.

Acts 26:18 and similar passages need not be read as shoring up a doctrine of regeneration. Although Acts 26:18 testifies to the way in which God opens the eyes of the spiritually blind, this remark has to be located in the context of a commission by the risen Christ of St Paul to preach the Gospel to those who have not heard it. Moreover, even though it is indubitable that, as Scripture declares, God is active in revealing God's message of salvation to people,[20] people are saved through Christ[21] and, even, only through Christ,[22] and everlasting judgement is being prepared for those who do not know God or obey the Gospel,[23] this salvation consists in an offer of divine absolution and promise of divine assistance in moral living rather than a mechanistic process whereby God in secret

---

19. E.g. Matthew 13:11-12.
20. E.g. Matthew 11:27; John 6:44.
21. E.g. John 3:16; Acts 16:31.
22. E.g. Acts 4:12.
23. E.g. 2 Thessalonians 1:8-9.

pulls strings to manipulate and ultimately cause a person to do God's bidding perfectly.

Salvation need not be construed in religiously exclusive terms given that it is the same God that works in different religious traditions, revealing different and equally valid aspects of the Godhead and the divine purpose for humanity. The threats of divine and final judgement are only issued to those who practise great wickedness such as persecuting believers and who, on that account, lose their status as a people predestined for salvation.[24]

If the Christian message is sometimes cast in exclusive terms, as in Ephesians 2:1-5, 11-12, this is only because it is indeed the case that the Christian faith has the power to save those who genuinely embrace it, without downplaying the legitimate elements of other religious traditions. Where Scripture speaks of a blinding of unbelievers by the devil,[25] this is to be interpreted as a general remark on the spiritual state of those who, in choosing to persecute believers, disobey the moral teachings not just of the Gospel but any major religious faith. It is not an exact description of the inability of non-Christians to come to the Christian faith for, if that were the case, there would be no need to preach the Gospel, a matter of which St Paul speaks extensively in the same epistle.

In line with the 'golden chain', in David Dickson's usage, of Romans 8:30, all are predestined, that is, earmarked in advance for a certain purpose, but not all are capable of being successfully confirmed in that initial purpose and called to responsibility.[26] The proof of this reposes in the statement of Jesus to the effect that this calling of God's is effected through the miraculous acts of Jesus performed on the authority and decree of the Father, and this calling is made to all, yet not all believe, but only those who will become part of Christ's flock,[27] thus showing that God does not restrict God's call to only those God had selected out of many others, because all of humanity is known and earmarked in advance for a certain purpose, that of imaging Christ the Son of God and firstborn of creation.[28]

---

24. Cf. Revelation 20:7-15; such judgement will be orchestrated by those angels that have remained obedient to God.
25. E.g. 2 Corinthians 4:3.
26. Cf. 2 Thessalonians 2:13-14; Titus 1:1; *NTDNTW*, s.v. *'proorizō'* (trans-literated), p. 1092.
27. John 10:25-29; cf. Matthew 13:11-12.
28. Romans 8:29.

Ephesians 1:4 suggests that all human souls pre-exist with God in heaven prior to their incarnation at the point of birth. These pre-existent souls may have been angels before their earthly birth. At the point of conception, by the authority of God, these spiritual beings transform themselves into human beings by attaching to a biological framework, in the process giving up their angelic forms and memories with them but retaining their innocence. Human beings evidently predate their earthly existence because it is impossible for God to have chosen – and, in the case of Romans 8:29, also, known – something which had not as yet come into existence but only existed in ideal form.[29]

All souls have been selected in Christ antecedent to the emergence of the world to be set apart and follow a path of morality, whether or not they ultimately receive incarnation as human beings. There are more angels than human beings can possibly procreate. Not just human beings, but other sentient entities such as animals derive their life principle from a previous existence as spirits not amounting to angels. Like the Trinity, angels found themselves to exist at the beginning of time on the basis of being directly posited by the Divine Nature. Non-sentient objects arise purely through material creation and evolution; for sentient beings, while the bodily form may have arisen from material evolution, the vital principle is constituted by pre-existent spiritual beings.

Such an apprehension of the origin of human souls imparts radically new meaning to the doctrine of Christ as a second and new Adam, in that like Christ, all human beings that came to be underwent a bodily transformation tantamount to a full incarnation. The difference between Christ and other human beings is that in the case of Christ, the physical body was specially crafted by the Father working through the Spirit by the agency of angels to produce a body which possesses the biological principle of Mary but not of Joseph and yet not physically deficient just because it lacks a human paternal genetic contribution. In this way, the Bible is able to speak of Christ as the 'firstborn' among many siblings.[30] Apropos Christ being spoken of as the 'firstborn' of all creation,[31] this is to be understood in the sense that Christ represents and constitutes the first renewed element of a renewed universe, the cornerstone of that cosmic renewal.[32]

---

29. *Pace* A.T. Lincoln, *Ephesians*, WBC 42 (Waco, TX: Word, 1990), pp. 22-24.
30. Romans 8:29.
31. Colossians 1:15.
32. Cf. Colossians 1:18.

The golden chain of Romans 8:30, therefore, simply lays out the process by which a believer receives the full blessings of God, highlighting that God is intimately involved at every stage and progresses past predestination as the person in question allows God to do this. It does not suggest a watertight process in which every individual without exception who is predestined progresses on to glorification, thereby implying that God only has in mind a small number of people in God's plan of salvation, intentionally leaving out many others, who are condemned to a life and destiny without God, all in order to make some theological point which will really only benefit that select few. This more nuanced and ornate interpretation is reasonable, considering that the passage following (Romans 8:31-39) goes on to expatiate on a divine love which overcomes all odds, indicating that the golden chain is really a gentle invitation to all hearers and readers to embrace the wonderful destiny held out by God, if they have not already done so, and to hold on tightly to it, if they have.

In John 17:6, the meaning is that those who came to believe in Jesus are obviously among those who were given to him by the Father in the beginning (predestined, selected beforehand to fulfil a particular purpose), since the Father gave all people to the Son, and, even if some dropped out eventually, the fact remains that those who have stuck with him were originally selected by the Father. As for Acts 13:48, the reason it is said that those who believed were appointed to eternal life is that, as they placed their faith in Christ, the Father made such an appointment.

In accord with scriptures such as 2 Corinthians 3:3, 6, Ephesians 1:17-19, Philippians 2:13 and Hebrews 12:2, God does strengthen the believer in faith, wisdom, knowledge and hope, yet this is not to imply that God does everything for the believer. As a matter of fact, with regard to the literary context of Ephesians 1:17-19, the initiative in this building of faith rests not in God but the epistle writer, who prays for God to enrich the faith of the believers at Ephesus and encourages them to do the same for themselves and others. In the case of Philippians 2:13, the believers are urged to express their faith and salvation in the knowledge that God is working alongside them in all their endeavours of faith, constantly encouraging them to desire and act according to God's good will. It is therefore not a statement about how God causes the believer to act in ways that he would not normally act if left to his own devices; if that were the case, it would be unnecessary to use the method of exhortation to entreat the believers to act in a certain way, seeing that everything is done by God.

Although Romans 11:7 discusses a hardening of the hearts of unbelieving members of Israel, this has to be situated in the literary milieu of a reference to the tyrannical political system under the rule of Ahab and Jezebel, during which Jezebel murdered the prophets of God (vv. 2-3). It was these intractable and violent persons from whom God withdrew God's assistance in spirituality, in a manner reminiscent of what God did in the case of Pharaoh;[33] the passage does not suggest that God knowingly made it difficult for Israelites who had done no wrong whatsoever to seek God.

Even if verses such as Ephesians 1:10-11 appear to indicate a divine plan for salvation, the context strongly suggests that this is a reference not to God as the ultimate author of all events, good as well as evil, but that God does all that God does in accordance with the plan to bring salvation through the cross of Christ (vv. 4-9); in the cases of Romans 11:33 and Acts 15:18, the plan of God there referred to is the general plan for the faith and redemption of Israel on the basis of the Cross.

Works of the law do not serve to justify one or declare them innocent in God's court of law, but only God's free offer of grace through the Cross of Christ as an atoning act; this is because people are imperfect and even sinful, and will at some point require an instrument by which to be reconciled with God.[34]

It is true that God chooses, helps and protects those who come to faith in God, but these things are not spoken in order to exclude anyone, but, on the contrary, invite all to experience and embrace the fullness of life in Christ. It is true that God is able to turn a wretched life around, but this is not to be used against other believers, who may not have experienced such desperation, to foment self-doubt as to the authenticity of their own faith because of their lack of such experiences, or against non-believers, who may not have embraced Christianity because they are members of other faiths, to imply that they are somehow dead in sin, having not experienced a supernatural regeneration of their hearts by God, and for that reason alone, unable to be Christians at the time in question.

Perhaps by far the most important support against a doctrine of original sin as it has been conventionally understood are the original literary contexts of the citations by St Paul in Romans 3:10-12, a passage typically adduced to evidence the scriptural foundation of the doctrine of original sin, the relevant quotation in which reads in the ESV: 'None is

---

33. Romans 9:11-18. Vv 12-13 show that God loved Jacob for not rejecting service.
34. Romans 3:10-31.

righteous, no, not one; no one understands; no one seeks for God. All have turned aside; together they have become worthless; no one does good, not even one.' As Augustine of Hippo rightly observes, Psalm 14:3-4 and Psalm 53:3-4, from which the quotation in Romans 3:12 is sourced, designate the religiously and morally wayward, valueless and evil behaviour not so much of all people in general and universally, but rather, in a comment both on inward disposition and outward conduct, only of the people who have turned against God, typified in the generations of Cain, who trust in their own strength and seek their own glory, 'the earthly city', instead of looking to God's grace and pursuing God's glory, 'the city of God'.[35] This is evident in the fact that the verses following those which are cited by Paul, that is, Psalm 14:4 and Psalm 53:4, make it clear that the psalmist speaks of a people belonging to God who are oppressed by evildoers, implying a limited scope of meaning for the preceding three verses, Psalm 14:1-3 and Psalm 53:1-3, both of which are cited and paraphrased in Romans 3:10-11 in a manner that seems to suggest some universally binding, comprehensive, and thoroughgoing influence of human sinfulness. As such, it is not tenable to appeal to Romans 3:10-12 as a prooftext for a doctrine of original sin.

Scripture passages attesting to a regenerative work on the part of God should, therefore, be read as hopeful messages pertaining to the potential benefit a Christian faith and relationship with the Christian God could bring to an individual even in the midst of great personal distress, and not dogmatic deliverances concerning how Christians are somehow luckier than the rest of the human community because their faith reveals that God handpicked them, and without such arbitrary selection on God's part, no one could ever really be Christian.

While the religious zeal underlying ideas of original sin and the necessity of a supernatural regeneration of the heart of the believer is laudable, such ideas tend to obfuscate the nuances of human reality and ignore socio-psychological factors. Original sin is to be reconceived in psycho-dynamic terms where the roots of sinful disposition are situated in the presence of a compulsive evil, ushered into the life of an individual through that individual's failure to challenge and reject thought and emotional patterns suggested by parental neglect, abuse by various actors during childhood, or negative influence.[36]

---

35. Augustine, *Civ.*, XVI.10.
36. Karl Barth concedes the real possibility of malicious spiritual activity coming upon the lives of people as children through their parents. Barth, *KD* III.4, §54.3 (*CD* III.4, §54.3, p. 284).

Proposition: Advantages and Prolepses

There is evidence that the classical theological experience of a bondage or slavery to sinful passions is a manifestation and sign of a compulsive evil conspiring with a psychological disorder.

St Augustine of Hippo, who wrote about having such a wearying and troubling state of mind, may have suffered from compulsive sexual behaviour and binge-eating disorder owing to traumatic events in childhood, leading him to conclude that his bondage to fornication and food consumption, in the form of uncontrollable, spontaneous and non-volitional thoughts, feelings and desires which seemed to lead very naturally and inevitably to volitional thoughts, feelings, desires, intentions, resolves and actions, was a telltale sign of his sinfulness on a personal level and evidence of a universal plague of original sin on the level of humanity.

Augustine's autobiography affords a clearer glimpse of the mental processes that might have taken place in his psyche. He writes in his *Confessiones* of a pubertal sexual desire which arose from a deficit in physical affection and intimacy[37] and continued into adulthood.[38] He was traumatised as a child by the harsh and terrifying corporal punishment he received at the hands of his teachers for not being sufficiently diligent in his studies. Augustine remembers that adults, including his own parents, relished in his shame and compares the way these adults treated him to the use of torture.[39]

Augustine's sexual indulgence was characterised by a confusion of sexual passion with genuine affection,[40] as well as an irresistible inward force which drew him uncontrollably to sexual behaviour. He uses imagery of being arrested, tormented by being dragged through sharp stones, drowned in an eddy, held in manacles, given no sleep, being thrown around, thrown out, spread-eagled, caused to evaporate,[41] subject to a potent push or pull and utter subjugation,[42] placed in a field of towering thorns,[43] deceived, stamped upon, restrained,[44] boiled in a

---

37. Augustine, *Conf.*, II.ii.2.
38. Ibid., VI.xv.25, VII.xvii.23, VIII.v.10, VIII.xi.26.
39. Ibid., I.ix.14-15.
40. Ibid., II.ii.2.
41. Ibid.
42. Ibid., II.ii.4.
43. Ibid., II.iii.6.
44. Ibid., II.iii.8.

pot, having an irresistible urge to scratch a boil, experiencing privation[45] and burned by hot tar.[46] These constitute rather clear signs of a form of compulsive sexual disorder in a spiritually inclined individual.

Augustine was of the belief that his sexual impulses were ordered, manipulated and controlled by an unseen, malignant spiritual force.[47] Because of these experiences, he was certain that God had put Godself far from him, even going as far as to designate the operations of this evil power within his sexual life as sinfulness.[48] It is likely that Augustine never overcame the fear or trauma of his compulsive sexual behaviour.[49] As a matter of fact, the Church Father painfully describes his life at the point of writing as a mixture of life and death.[50] We know for a fact that physical abuse is a risk factor for compulsive sexual behaviour and that a negative self-image contributes to the development of binge-eating disorder.[51]

Martin Luther, the sixteenth-century Protestant reformer, probably suffered from a version of religious obsessive-compulsive disorder (OCD) or scrupulosity, obsessed as he was with observing religious regulations to the letter for fear of offending God, whom he perceived to be a demanding father, and receiving divine judgement. Such an image of God may have arisen in connection with Luther's own difficult experience with his draconian parents, whose strictness caused him to enter the monastery.[52]

---

45. Ibid., III.i.1.
46. Ibid., III.ii.3.
47. Ibid., II.iii.8.
48. Ibid., II.i.1, II.ii.2, II.iii.8.
49. Ibid., X.xxx.41.
50. Ibid., I.vi.7.
51. Mayo Clinic Staff, 'Compulsive Sexual Behaviour: Symptoms & Causes', Mayo Clinic for Medical Education and Research, 7 February 2020, https://www.mayoclinic.org/diseases-conditions/compulsive-sexual-behavior/symptoms-causes/syc-20360434; Mayo Clinic Staff, 'Binge-eating disorder: Symptoms & causes', Mayo Foundation for Medical Education and Research, 5 May 2018, https://www.mayoclinic.org/diseases-conditions/binge-eating-disorder/symptoms-causes/syc-20353627.
52. B. Stolt, 'Martin Luther on God as a Father', *Lutheran Quarterly* 8, no. 4 (1994), p. 388. A 2010 study showed a 'significant' link between an authoritarian parenting style, characterised by pedantry and rules-based conformity, and symptoms of and beliefs associated with obsessive-compulsive disorder; D.M. Whitford, 'Martin Luther (1483-1546)'," *International Encyclopedia of Philosophy*, accessed 27 April 2022, https://

While God's laws constitute an invaluable guide to internal and external morality, there is no warrant for viewing them as severe threats promising grave penalties which may be meted out at any time.

To be sure, God's laws serve to point the believer to the moral perfection God desires in each person, yet God also accommodates the frailty of humanity, providing a means of divine forgiveness pledged at the Cross to those with a contrite heart and commitment to do differently, giving people time to attend to their disordered emotions, and showing empathy in regard to the limited scope of a believer's contribution to the work of the Church and bettering of humanity.

Nevertheless, these nuances were easily lost on the disturbed mind of Luther, who mounted a relentless and brutal crusade against his transgressions, the latent, non-volitional, spontaneous and uncontrollable thoughts, feelings and desires which ostensibly so naturally and inevitably progress to become volitional thoughts, feelings, desires, intents, resolves and actions, until he found a way to resolve the affliction or *Anfectung* of his spiritual insecurities, through a doctrine of an imputation of God's righteousness in Christ to the believer. As an Augustinian monk, Luther followed in the footsteps of the great bishop of Hippo and wrote a detailed treatise and defence of a bondage of the will.

Centuries before either of these theologians, St Paul expressed his struggle against his sinful flesh in a poignant section of his epistle to the Roman Church;[53] Paul clearly suffered from post-traumatic stress disorder (PTSD) because of his horrifying experience in Asia Minor, especially Lystra, where he was stoned and left for dead,[54] and may have experienced any number of the common symptoms of PTSD, which include self-destructive behaviour, irritability, angry outbursts, aggressive behaviour and overwhelming guilt or shame, of which aggressiveness may have accentuated a latent cupidity of some sort.[55] Paul wrongly internalised the non-volitional, spontaneous and uncontrollable thoughts, feelings and desires and in this way ceded himself to the tyranny of volitional

iep.utm.edu/luther; K.R. Timpano *et al.*, 'Parenting and Obsessive Compulsive Symptoms: Implications of Authoritarian Parenting', *Journal of Cognitive Psychotherapy* 24, no. 3 (2010), pp. 151-64; Villines, 'Religious OCD: Separating Shame from Spirituality'.

53. Romans 7:7-25.
54. Acts 14:19; 2 Corinthians 1:8-10.
55. Mayo Clinic Staff, 'Post-Traumatic Stress Disorder (PTSD): Symptoms & Causes', Mayo Foundation for Medical Education and Research, 6 July 2018, https://www.mayoclinic.org/diseases-conditions/post-traumatic-stress-disorder/symptoms-causes/syc-20355967.

thoughts, feelings, desires, intents, resolves and actions resulting from a failure to uproot the weeds in his spiritual-psychological garden or tame an inner beast.

It is not the morality of this behaviour that is at issue here. Depending on the context, fornication, eating disorders, a failure to observe one particular commandment at a careless moment, self-destructive or aggressive behaviour or excessive guilt may or may not be sins and, even if sins, not very serious transgressions.[56] Nonetheless, the real issue in hand is the possibility, definitely actualised in the cases of Augustine, Luther and Paul, of an internalisation of and identification with the provisionally uncontrollable feelings, desires and thoughts associated with such mental health conditions as binge-eating disorder, compulsive sexual behaviour, religious OCD and PTSD and a failure to interfere through renunciation and psychological examination with the pathway between non-volitional thoughts, feelings and desires and volitional thoughts, feelings, desires, intents, resolves and actions.

The conditions for depression, suicidal thought, anxiety disorder, post-traumatic stress disorder and aggressive behaviour and any number of psychological disorders associated with these states of mind are laid for many through traumatic events transpiring during childhood.[57] The description of the psychological state of humanity right from the time of Adam and Eve clearly illustrates dysfunctionality.

Life after the disobedience of the primal couple, characterised by a distrust of God's pure motives and a betrayal of God's good intentions for humankind, would be marked by personal shame and insecurity,[58] distrust of and estrangement from God, accusation and resentment,[59] disunity within the family, domination (by the husband of the wife, in the case of the first couple but, in general terms, by one partner of the

---

56. There are psychological disorders which cooperate with clearly immoral behaviour, such as psychopathy.
57. S. Baracz, "How Childhood Trauma Changes Our Mental Health into Adulthood", *Psychlopaedia*, Australian Psychological Society, 13 January 2018, https://psychlopaedia.org/health/republished/how-childhood -trauma-changes-our-hormones-and-thus-our-mental-health-into- adulthood.
58. Genesis 3:8-11.
59. Genesis 3:12-13.

other),[60] the painful and arduous toil of work, economic hardship and the fear of an impending mortality.[61]

These constitute a fertile soil for the budding of the weeds of a very intractable jealousy, rage, simmering hatred and murder.[62] We are told curtly by Scripture that, after Cain murdered Abel and left, Adam fathered another son, Seth, and this son was 'fathered … in [Adam's] own likeness, after his image' rather than God's,[63] suggesting that the issues that dogged the family were handed down in some manner to Seth and through him, to his descendants, and the lineage, not just of the physical body and bloodline but of the struggle with God, self, others and the world, was continued down through human history.

It is likely that, among other things, in the catalogue of sins in Romans 1:29-32, St Paul had in mind the disobedience of Adam and Eve in describing a turn by humanity away from the Creator to idols, including images of 'creeping things',[64] an allusion to the serpent which enticed the couple in the garden of Eden. This led to all manner of sexual impurity as well as myriad sins which encompass the spectrum of wrongdoings committed by human beings.

Classical theology has by and large been rather fixated on the spiritual dimensions of the moral decline of humanity since the days of Eden. The emphasis is placed upon the cosmic victory which the devil temporarily won over humankind for a succession of many centuries, as in the patristic doctrine of *Christus Victor*, the debt of fealty which humankind has owed God the feudal king *par excellence* since Adam, as in St Anselm's theory of a substitutionary atonement, or the need for humankind to suffer the forensic penalty for their transgressions, as in Calvin's doctrine of penal substitutionary atonement. Moral influence theory tries to buck the trend by focussing instead on the poor example set by the first Adam which led humankind into all manner of sin and rebellion.[65]

---

60. Genesis 3:16; the domination of the woman is revealed in earlier culture in the guise of a conceptualisation of the female as occupying the role of being ruled and that of the male as occupying the role of ruling. Cf. Augustine, *Civ.*, XIV.22.
61. Genesis 3:17-19.
62. Genesis 4:1-8.
63. Genesis 5:3, ESV.
64. Romans 1:23, ESV.
65. For a succinct exposition of each of the major theories of the atonement, see J. Stott, *The Cross of Christ* (Downers Grove, IL: InterVarsity, 1986).

In fact, however, the psychological nature of human sin has generally been given short shrift. To adopt an approach to human sin that takes account of emotional development during the formative years of a human person is by no means to neglect either the traditional theological concern with the universality, pervasiveness and perdurance of sin as enshrined in the classical Augustinian theory of original sin, nor the need for people to turn to God in search of a moral solution.

These facets are preserved in some way, through specific modifications of the classical doctrine. One of these adjustments lies in how, instead of locating the transmission of human sin in physical generation, reproduction and procreation, as Augustine did, the mode of transmission is shifted to the tumult and assaults experienced in the emotional and psychological life of a child, through neglect or abuse linked to domination and past experience of abuse, begetting further domination and abuse in the life of the child and opening the floodgates to all manner of sin and evil, sexual, psychological, physical or material.[66] This is only because every act of domination, abuse or neglect carries with it a subtle and often imperceptible psychological message and challenge to its victims – whether to accept it inwardly without murmur or protest and thereby be bullied into fearful submission or to become like the bully out of a desire for self-preservation, or to reject it consciously and firmly.

These dysfunctional experiences facilitate a compulsive evil, in which people tacitly come to approve of sinful behaviour through failing to discern the error of the wrongful way they have been treated or being led and allowing themselves to be inwardly persuaded that that way is somehow right. People allow this to happen because they may not have been personally taught as children that those ways are actually wrong. Consequently, they come to be guided by a wicked, corrupt and insidious spiritual principle working in the undercurrent of their lives. The effect of such guidance is that the person is actually quite unaware that what he is doing is wrong,[67] incapable of appreciating the fact or degree of the harm he is perpetrating against another person, unable to master his thoughts, feelings and desires and directly and externally control his behaviour and held in the grip of lifelong condemnation before God.

There is only one way for a person to leave his life of sin: through coming to see the error of his ways through the stirring of the conscience by the Divine Nature, choosing to renounce wicked feelings and thoughts

---

66. Cf. Augustine, *Civ.*, XIV.15-16.
67. Cf. John 9:39-41.

as and when they occur, and embracing the forgiveness of God toward himself as a sinner.

In no way does this theory of sin invalidate the pervasiveness of sin through the generations of humankind, for the disordered emotional formation of a person is a significant risk factor in bringing about or contributing to the dysfunction of later generations, thus ensuring that humanity is held in the death grip of sin. The cardinal difference, therefore, between a conception of original sin and my theory of sin is that human sinfulness is not biological in nature or its manner of transmission, but psychological and spiritual, with a deleterious impact on relationships.

However, one must avoid the impression that repentance is completely in the hands of God, who decides who repents and when they repent. In fact, moral renewal is cued by the Divine Nature, which is present in all human beings, who are then responsible to act on that prompting.[68] The various religions only differ in the form in which that law is presented, and not the substance of that law. Nonetheless, it remains necessary to hear of divine forgiveness for the sinner, whether through Christianity or another religion, in order for the sinner to be able to actually move into a state of moral recovery.

Another modification to the traditional theological proposition reposes in the way in which, if psychological factors are so salient in the transmission of sin, then the science and academic disciplines of psychology and psychiatry are strongly vindicated. Then it becomes important to consider the insights of child psychiatry and psychology as well as the counterparts for teenagers and adults. Counselling and therapy are no longer a luxury or option for those with better endowments of finances or time, but a crucial go-to for the holistic and even moral wellbeing of the individual.

Even then, the role of God as Saviour is not thereby diminished, for the Christian faith remains a guide for human morality, in pursuit of which the individual consults a counsellor or therapist in a bid to attain a better, clearer, more comprehensive and profound understanding of himself, in the hope of addressing whatever undiagnosed disorders a person might suffer from. As fount, source and giver of all truth, God leads a person even into a clearer state of self-awareness and enables researchers to make inroads in psychology and psychiatry.

It is imperative to recognise the link between psychology and morality, though not all actions that arise from psychological disorders will necessarily be regarded as sin, simply because religious morality has

---

68. Cf. Romans 2:12-16.

a proclivity for reductionism and simplistic explanation. A religious community detached from psychological insights will easily fall prey to the misconception that all it takes for a person to lead a moral life is a good dose of biblical understanding, sincere faith and resolute willpower. This is usually accompanied by the belief that psychological therapy does not exist for the typical person but only those whom society considers to be severely disturbed.

Nothing, of course, could be further from the truth. Modern psychology considers any psychological condition that impedes a person's normal functioning, causes personal distress and is maladaptive to be a psychological disorder, but this, as one will see, is not necessarily sufficient to encourage people to seek the help they may need. Cultural stigmas attach to the idea of seeing a 'shrink' or psychologist and people are accustomed to conceal or ignore facts they know about themselves for which they might benefit from a visit to the therapist's. A culture which fixates over personal success and a show not just of physical but also emotional wellbeing is not likely to make it easy for individuals who need guidance and medicine to open up to a mental health professional.

However, to return to a key idea, morality should not be conceived exclusively in terms of volitional choices and decisions a person is able to make through preference and willpower. Psychological disorders cannot be tackled by determination and religious faith alone. Granted, determination is an important element even in therapy, yet one is seriously mistaken in the conviction that negative thoughts and feelings or compulsive behaviour can easily be prayed, wished or driven away by sheer mental and physical effort.

Oftentimes there will be emotional driving forces behind these negative thoughts, feelings and compulsive behaviour, and these driving forces will have roots in the formative years of a person's emotional development. To the extent that that is true, it will not be sufficient simply to resort to religion or personal determination. A simplistic theory of how powerful emotional driving forces may be resolved constituted a blind spot for well-known theologians such as St Paul, St Augustine and Martin Luther, as we have seen.[69] The study of the human mind was not well developed in their times; as people living in a modern age, we are able to avail of psychological therapy and counselling.

Sin cannot be excused on the premise that it involves a psychological disorder. While strong emotional forces may be involved, which may appear to compel a person to act in a certain way, even a sinful one which

---

69. *Supra.*

causes harm to self or others, there is always an element of choice even for the disordered individual, who can decide how to respond to his unhealthy and unwholesome urges, especially when they seem to guide a person toward harmful behaviour. It may not be easy or possible to fully embrace all who have hurt or had a part in hurting an individual, or who remind him of these persons, and an individual may therefore react in a manner less than ideally social towards all of them, yet a concession can be made towards people who give in on occasion to such behaviour. Obviously, such a person can also avail of the opportunity to commit himself to psychological therapy.[70]

Just as a person may not justify his sinful actions even in cases of psychological disorder, one need not succumb to the temptation to be overwhelmed by guilt for his enduring pattern of negative thoughts, feelings and compulsive behaviour. These are factors with deep psychological roots and the primary aim is to attain such a clear and accurate self-understanding in relation to possible causes of these emotional impulses and catalysts that a person becomes capable of exercising some level of control over them. This attempt to achieve greater self-awareness need not be confined to a professional therapeutic setting, yet should surely include it, if possible, but may also be practised daily, through methods of self-introspection. Ideally, a short space of time is set aside for prayer or self-reflection, if need be, in order that mistakes which are completely preventable are not repeated.

All sinful thought and behaviour should be confessed before God, if a person is religious, or acknowledged as wrong in one's heart if one happens not to believe in any deity. The importance of this inner decision and commitment cannot be overemphasised. One should not suppose that God would not need to hear a confession of a sin, in which a person not only takes ownership for his actions but also acknowledges its wrongful or imperfect nature, given that God is already well aware of everything that happens in the heart of a believer, or that it is needless to confess to oneself something that one obviously already knows. It matters that a person acknowledges his own sin in the secret place of the heart because it alters the state of mental acceptance of that thought, feeling or action. For many, there will have been the wrong or imperfect kind of thoughts, feelings and actions nurtured from the days of childhood which one would need to radically disavow. Confession is necessary to

---

70. In modern, developed societies, help is often to hand for those who will seek it, even if one may be financially needy.

deprive compulsive evil of its inner power through a conscious rejection of that force.

The act of confession is empowered by the presence of a self-awareness which penetrates external behaviour to arrive at the root of a personal dissatisfaction which may have a tendency to break out into sinful reaction.

A case in point may be a person who has come to a recognition that the reason he has been desperately impatient over his lack of success in his efforts to launch a career in a desired field is that he has come to attach his sense of self-worth to outcomes of professional success and the approval of others, due quite possibly to having uncritically and unthinkingly accepted the unfavourable comparisons made by his parents at a young age. In this circumstance, he might tell himself, 'You are desperately impatient over your perceived lack of professional success because you have come to tie your sense of self-worth to these outcomes of professional success and the approval of others, and this is due to the fact that your parents compared you to your siblings when you were very young. Those comparisons no longer matter and nobody now is comparing you to anyone else; therefore, you can stop tying your sense of self-worth to these outcomes of professional success and the approval of others, and you can stop being desperately impatient over your perceived lack of success in your efforts to launch a career in your desired field of work.'

In another example, a person who is easily provoked by selfish and rude driving conduct may be feeling this way because of an acute sense that he is not being treated fairly, and this, in turn, only because he may have been bullied, abused or exploited as a young child and keenly experienced a sense of injustice, to which he is very alive years later because any act of unjust treatment reminds him of a past traumatic episode of injustice. In this case, he could say to himself, 'You are so easily provoked by selfish and rude driving behaviour because of a sense that you are not being treated fairly, and this is only because you were abused as a child and have a strong memory of having been unjustly treated, and these incidents of rude driving conduct remind you of past traumatic episodes of being treated unfairly. But those drivers aren't the people who abused you, so you can allow yourself not to be so badly affected when you encounter people driving recklessly or inconsiderately.' More importantly, in choosing to extend forgiveness – or at the very least a sincere and unbegrudging forbearance mediated by an acceptance rooted in the apprehension that certain, indeed, many, factors are beyond one's control and there is no real need to allow the actions of others to emotionally perturb one and threaten to make of a self-possessed person an anti-social individual characterised by excessive reactions – to the perpetrators of abuse, a person is able to move toward a resolution of emotional triggers.

Another person might be accustomed to imagining the worst possible outcome only because he has been shaped by a past traumatic experience of having had his school grades compared by his parents with those of his siblings and left feeling less than worthy and intelligent. As the source of a child's affirmation, parents, who fail to nurture the child in joyful anticipation of the good things that might result from its efforts, and the horrific experience of rejection, set the child up for fear when it feels its mettle to be tested, long after its parents have ceased to express dissatisfaction at academic performance. At these times, the very same individual could address himself in the following salutary manner: 'You are imagining the worst that could happen, and you know in your rational mind that what you imagine to be the reasons for your perceived rejection may not necessarily be the actual reasons for a non-response relating to professional recognition, which need not imply rejection, or an outright rejection, and even if a bad outcome does result, it does not necessarily mean that you are without value. And you think this way simply because you were compared by your parents when you were very young to your siblings, told that you did not do as well as them, and given the impression that you were simply not good enough. That traumatic moment of parental rejection has followed you all these years. But you are not worthless, useless, or unintelligent. You did your best then, and you are gifted in your own ways. You do not have to continue to feel unworthy.'

An individual may find it difficult to admit a mistake, but only because as a child he felt a compulsion from people in authority to perform well or face severe punishment, which may come either in the form of social disapproval or direct corporal punishment. In this instance, self-awareness will go a long way towards enabling this individual to move towards psychological wholeness and wellbeing. A person may be carried away whenever people pay attention to him simply because he felt rejected when he was very young. A similar cognitive-emotional strategy can be employed.

Yet another instance involves a person, who once adopted a cross-gender self-identification and has since officially detransitioned.[71] This

---

71. This example comes from the experience of a detransitioner and is in no way intended to invalidate the internal sense of gender many transgender people experience at variance with their assigned sex. For more on the

man finds his personal envy stoked whenever he descries a beautiful young woman, because he was rejected as a boy and child by his parents, who seemed to love his attractive, older sister far more than him, and subjected to what was interpreted as physical affection in the form of being raped, emotionally abused and treated as a girl by two men at an early age, leading to the unquestioned assumption that he would have been better loved were he born female and beautiful. This creates the conditions for frequent, powerful and lasting surges of grief over how his physical appearance does not conform to these images.[72] It has been

---

phenomenon of detransitioning, in which a person who once made a gender transition and then at some subsequent point decided to identify with his/her birth gender, mostly due to difficulties in social adaptation but, in a few cases, also because of physical complications, as well as a shift in gender identity, in many instances, only temporarily, but in a smaller number of cases, also over the longer term. S. Davies, S. McIntyre and C. Rypma, 'Detransition Rates in a National UK Gender Identity Clinic', in *3rd Biennial EPATH Conference 'Inside Matters: On Law, Ethics and Religion'* (European Professional Association for Transgender Health, 2019), p. 118.

72. In the case of this man, lewdness and femininity having become linked with acceptance through his early exposure to gender rejection and abusive sexual intimacy, involving bondage, sexual self-stimulation revolving around personal fantasies of living the life of a young and attractive woman in bondage has become an ersatz to temporarily fill an endless emotional void opened up by a desolating feeling of parental-social rejection, self-alienation and complete isolation. Such self-sexual satisfaction is always only momentary because sexual pleasure never lasts by dint of its reliance on the excitation of sexual organs with the pleasure it brings, all of which reaches an end with the sexual climax, which, in turn, generates an inferior but nevertheless real sense of relief, returning him to a mental state of stability and sensibility, as happens at the end of a trigger or aggressive and triumphant tussling with an emotionally perceived world of bullies and abusers. Certain images provoke a stronger reaction, stemming from the extent to which the features of these women are desired by others, as indicated by mass media, and as proposed by René Girard's theory of mimesis. P. Miller, 'How to Gain an Audience and Lose Your Soul', *TGC*, 12 December 2022, https://www.thegospelcoalition.org/article/gain-audience-lose-soul. The pathway to self-acceptance for such an individual is a function of an admiration of what is often seen as the most primally attractive quality of the other sex, which is, in turn, dependent on the male (and even female) subjective appreciation of feminine pulchritude. To the extent that the individual in question is able to come to terms with the subjective nature of such nearly

helpful, in the sense of tackling the roots of self-rejection and loneliness, for this man to say to himself, 'You are envious about these young and beautiful women and desire to be just like them, but cannot be because you were born in a male body. You feel this way because you perceive that they are well-loved and powerfully accepted. This reminds you of the way your parents and the abusers treated you, the former party favouring a beautiful, young girl over you, the latter taking you for a girl and forcing you to dress like one under emotionally abusive conditions, all this suggesting subliminally to you that you would not have been rejected, that you would have been accepted if only you were a beautiful woman. However, you do not need to allow the past actions of your parents and the abusers to continue to affect your self-acceptance today. You are no longer the hapless child who was mistreated, and you do not have to accept the suggestions of your parents or the adults who abused you. In the past, you may have needed the acceptance of your parents, and, to a certain extent, even adults thrive on the acceptance of their parents. But you are already capable of functioning as a self-contained, self-reliant person who is able to break free from the thrall of social approval. You can be strong and your own person now, in emotional terms. You do not need anyone to tell you what gender you ought to be or how you ought to look so that you can be loved or accepted. You are no less worthy as a male, and society does not think any less of you as a male. You can tell yourself on a daily basis that you are worthy, loved and accepted in your own skin.'[73] Crippling loneliness experienced during childhood being the source of this individual's distress and the true impetus behind attempts to contain it, by unconsciously seeking to win self-acceptance based on an understanding shaped by parental rejection, first, through striving for achievement and, subsequently, a gender transition, full healing for him will come through such self-realisation and re-imagining his childhood as graced by the emotional care he knows he needs and can give to his younger self by travelling back in time, as it were.[74]

---

intrinsic appeal, apprehending its chiefly biological-procreative function and transcending its sway, he will find his soul liberated for the first time from fixation upon receiving acceptance through fulfilling perceived requirements of feminine attractiveness.

73. This individual knows that his love for feminine beauty is linked to the social acceptance it secures; the proof of this lies in how he is not obsessively attracted to things that are beautiful in themselves but other than feminine.

74. This might help with a lack of assertiveness, linked as loneliness is to a sense of rejection.

The same person also struggles with an issue of patience, because when he was abused and held in bondage by a babysitter, he did not reject the notion that what the latter did was utterly wrong, and recognise that it was not right for him to be treated the way he was. Thence, the man imbibed the false understanding that, just as he could be mistreated and oppressed by being controlled by another person, so he could mistreat and oppress another person by controlling them, and finds it challenging to wait patiently for a response in a situation where a desirable outcome is not guaranteed, a circumstance which makes him feel especially vulnerable.[75] Again, it would benefit this person to rebut the wrong thinking he had come to accept regarding how he and therefore other people ought to be treated.[76]

An individual might be afflicted with an addiction to viewing scenes of distressed women in situations of bondage by way of a post-traumatic play, a psychological process by which a traumatic incident is re-enacted through repetitive actions involving some element of reminiscence in the desperate hope for succour that did not obtain; this can be satisfied by telling oneself that the trauma is over, and that the soul can finally repose.[77]

Both a confession and apology are requisite of the sinner, the apology differing from the confession in that the confession is primarily an acknowledgement of personal responsibility for an action agreed by all parties concerned to be wrong or imperfect, while the apology is fundamentally an expression of personal sorrow and regret for an action agreed by all parties concerned to be wrong.

---

75. This dovetails with the theory that people with a history of abuse perpetrate the same kind of abuse simply because their view of the world as dangerous and insecure compels them to behave in this aggressive way in the supposition that other people or the circumstances of life are beastly things to be tamed.

76. In all the above examples, while the thought pattern may not necessarily be sinful, it is certainly unexamined, or not recently enough introspected. Even so, they have a propensity to engender secondary effects and consequences which may be unconscionable or even outright wrong, and it is important to consider and discuss these thought patterns if only for that reason under the heading of a confession of sin, or, better yet, a self-confession leading to a removal of an inner mental state fertile and explosive for the emergence of sinful thoughts and behaviours.

77. L.C. Terr, '"Forbidden Games": Post-Traumatic Child's Play', *Journal of the American Academy of Child & Adolescent Psychiatry* 20, no. 4 (September 1981), pp. 741-60.

The confession as well as the apology constitute an imperative and radical insistence that wrongdoing or imperfection emanates from freedom and not nature, and that, no matter the number of factors that conspire to incline a person to a misdeed, the crucial decision to act on a negative or harmful thought, however much it may beg to be enacted, is finally at the disposal only of the individual and not circumstances. A person may feel utter misery in consequence of past neglect, abuse or trauma, and yet it is not his place to take out his unhappiness on others. Moreover, the decision whether to allow the principle of compulsive evil to continue to inhabit the human heart is in the hands of the individual in whom the Divine Nature, who is in one and all, earnestly and continuously pleads with the individual to renounce his sinful patterns of emotions, thoughts and actions.[78]

Clarity – the knowledge concerning which feelings, thoughts, desires, attitudes, intents, resolves and behaviour are right or ideal and which ones wrong or imperfect, and the reasons these feelings and desires arise – and concession – the self-acceptance of the wrongness or imperfection or rightness or ideal quality of specific feelings, thoughts, desires, attitudes and behaviour – are imperative to dealing with compulsive evil, without which the latter becomes uncontrollable, bringing about a situation where the offender is resigned continuously to hurt self and other. As attested in Daniel, compulsive evil has the potency to create monsters of human beings[79] but, for all its seemingly irresistible power, it can be arrested by means of clarity and concession.

That first step of ownership covered, there are two other key steps, involving, second, the act of commitment not to allow oneself to continue pursuing that wrong course of action, and, third, an act of decision to seek help for those issues, if necessary, from God, or from a therapist.

In addition, except in cases of flagrant or utterly reprehensible because inhumane behaviour, nobody should arrogate to themselves the authority and right to condemn another person for their moral failures. In no event should a person think to despise a person for their psychological disorders. This is neither right nor helpful. The battleground of ethical success or failure does not subsist in external behaviour, or even confessed feelings or thoughts. These merely represent markers or guideposts indicating the psychological wellbeing of an individual.

---

78. This is comparable to the necessity of lovingly guiding one's own soul from egocentrism to ego-loss in Sikh philosophy. See Mandair, *Sikhism: A Guide for the Perplexed*, pp. 131-55.
79. Daniel 4:16, 33.

Just as an affluent person is ill-advised to look down upon a less well-off individual because each person has equal worth regardless of the number of status symbols each may own, or the amount of assets each controls, similarly, it is shallow to boast of one's emotional health, as though it were something that differentiates one from other people as somehow morally superior to them. What truly matters is not the number of possessions a person presently controls, whether physical or psychological, but rather that person's stewardship of the resources he has at his disposal.

As such, a person is judged by the extent to which he has been responsible to God, himself and the world. Moreover, we are truly responsible to these players, not necessarily because we owe them a great debt, but simply because human beings flourish when they assume their rightful moral roles in relation to God, themselves, one another and the world around them, roles which prescribe love, compassion, empathy, respect, generosity, faithfulness, purity, holiness, trust, understanding, appreciation, peacefulness and patience.

Most crucially, one should never give up on oneself. Augustine's exhortations in his *Confessiones* as to how one ought to treat one's enemies or those of whom one disapproves may be instructive in this regard. Augustine learned of the dishonourable and deceitful manner in which students of rhetoric at Rome conducted themselves, defrauding their teachers of the fees they deserved by banding together and collectively transferring to another tutor. Nonetheless, he chose not to allow his detestation of their behaviour to prevent him from exerting himself toward their correction.[80]

Even so, he explains in a later passage, concerning the hatred he has toward the enemies of God, that it is not the usual strong revulsion that engenders fury and verbal and possibly physical aggression and violence, but, on the contrary, a pious desire for God to bring an end to their self-absorption and raise them to a new mode of existence in which they are wholly concerned about God's purposes.[81] Again, he admonishes love for the cherished human soul with a view to urging a love for the Lord above all things, which recognises the fact that God is affectionate toward human souls in holding them together in their being.[82]

What this means is that, even should one fail oneself whether through recurrent negative or harmful thoughts, feelings or even actual misdeeds,

---

80. Augustine, *Conf.*, V.xii.22.
81. Ibid., XII.xiv.17; *Civ.*, XXI.24.
82. Augustine, *Conf.*, IV.xii.18.

one should still continue to show mercy and compassion to oneself, whether or not one feels there is hope. In the same way, one ought always to forgive others for their misdeeds, without failing to deploy vigilance in further relations with such persons, if such relations are necessary, and trusting that processes are in place to deter and contain crime.

In addition to psychological disorders with a moral element, there are also ideological sins, in which the prevailing values of a culture are simply accepted without question.[83] It will be the rare individual who attains clarity enough to be able to challenge these widely held norms and, as a result, suffer terrible consequences for daring to go against the grain in regard to the things that a society or community holds dear. To an external party, such ideologies may be incomprehensible, yet one does well to bear in mind the affinity with psychological disorder and emotional dysfunction, where a child grows up in an environment which propagates the wrong or lopsided values, assimilates them and becomes an instrument for their manifestation and perpetuation.

Individual psychology and culture work hand in glove. Psychology in this regard entails a disorder of individuals in a family or kinship grouping which shapes a familial or kinship culture in which certain prevailing streams of thought, prejudices, moralities and modes of thinking are given moral sanction, never objectively understood or analysed, always influencing thought, feeling and behaviour at an imperceptibly deep level. These processes are replicated on a larger scale at a communal or cultural level, producing sensibilities and prejudices which largely determine a national or communal response to stimuli.

There are two specific historical instances of a cultural brainwashing worth mentioning in the particular context of a discussion concerning original sin reconceived as psychological-spiritual-cultural sin: the biblical narrative of the conspiracy to bring about the death or execution of Jesus; and the large-scale cooperation between the German Evangelical Church and the Nazi regime.

The main factors which drove the group response on the part of religious leaders and other factions to tackle the emergence of Jesus as an existential threat comprised a religious fanaticism on the part of some

---

83. Augustine of Hippo reveals the extent to which sociality can be a salient factor in the transmission of sinful behaviour, if not also attitudes, in his discussion of how Eve persuaded Adam to sin as she did by eating the fruit of a forbidden tree, Aaron felt compelled by the wishes of the Israelites to construct a golden calf and King Solomon became an idolator because of his love for his foreign wives (*Civ.*, XIV.11).

of the Pharisees, a Jewish sect devoted to detailed observance of the Mosaic law, who imagined that their religious views were indisputable, and the obsession with power, wealth and professional stability, on the part of the religious authorities as a whole, represented in the theocratic legislative-judicial-executive body that was the Sanhedrin.

The Pharisees sought to obey God in every area of life in which the scribes or interpreters of the law of God had derived minute regulations, and they believed the numerous rules they kept were an expression of their faith in God and a means by which to maintain the sanctity of the Jewish religion and culture.[84] Some were, therefore, shocked to encounter a teacher in their midst who taught that these laws, such as fasting,[85] proper washing of hands prior to eating[86] and strict Sabbath-keeping,[87] were no longer important and, to their further chagrin, repeatedly exposed the inadequacy of their authoritative teachings and their hypocrisy, and also assumed the position of God in absolving people of sins.

With the advent of the ministry of Jesus, these religious men worried not just that their livelihoods were directly threatened but that the whole Jewish way of life which had served their communities so well was under attack. The Pharisees responded the way any religious group would which was facing an internal challenge with the potential to split and wreck the community. Jesus redefined the laws of Moses; furthermore, there were rumours that he was proclaiming himself to be a prophet, and not just a prophet, but a Christ and even a Son of God, that is, God in the flesh. To all intents and purposes, then, it appeared to some, because they could not accept Jesus' teaching and ministry, that something akin to a charismatic cult leader had arisen to seduce the hearts and faiths of the Jewish people. They were understandably alarmed.

On another dimension, however, this happened only because the Pharisees as a religious group were not receptive to the novel and innovative religious ideas Jesus brought. They were confident that they were right about religious matters, and looked with contempt on anybody who did not outwardly conform to their version and vision of religious faith.[88] They were most unwilling to accommodate startlingly new – to them but, in effect, essential – religious insight, and overly quick to

---

84. J.R. Edwards, *The Gospel According to Mark*, PNTC (Grand Rapids, MI: Eerdmans, 2002), p. 88.
85. Mark 2:18-22.
86. Mark 7:1-23.
87. Cf. Mark 2:23-28; 3:1-6.
88. Luke 18:9-14.

conclude that those who did not agree with their teaching or conform to their religious system were heretics.

The advent of Jesus was a revolutionary period for Judaism, a great opportunity, and as in any historical transitional period, the threat of instability and ruination drove many people to act irrationally even as others properly received the enlightenment that they were afforded. We have to bear in mind that the coming of Jesus was an unrepeatable event of tremendous social and personal significance. Moreover, if it were to recur today, very few would be able to stand the test of faith.

As for the Sanhedrin, they monitored the rapidly developing religious scene with deep concern, fearing that the widespread popularity of Jesus because of the miracles he had been able to perform, would quickly degenerate into political chaos and incur the terrible wrath of the Roman authorities, swift as they had been to put down rebellion. These religious and political leaders were fearful for their own professional stability and potential threats to their wealth and standing.[89] They would not have been persuaded concerning the authenticity of Jesus' miracles, thinking these to have been the work of some demonic force.

These were some of the key considerations which governed the decision of the Jewish religious leaders to conspire to put Jesus to death. They feared that the success Jesus was experiencing in building a community of followers would directly impinge on their way of life, including their ambitions, hopes and dreams. They did not realise that obeying the will of God entailed, in their time, humility in seeking to learn from a seemingly innovative teacher and receiving him as a divine being, as well as the acceptance of the possibility of a loss of status, wealth and power. It is because such cultural bias arises from ignorance and a blindness to issues of significant concern that, as Jesus hung on the cross, he prayed for the Father to forgive those who crucified him for their ignorance.

There were other forces involved in the Christian-Nazi cooperation before and during the Second World War. Among these were a reaction against the political, economic and social implications of the Weimar Republic and communism, public anger against the international community for what was perceived to be an unfair attempt to bring closure to the First World War, in which the Germans were forced to make weighty reparations, European anti-Semitism colluding with a

---

89. D.A. Carson, *The Gospel According to John*, PNTC (Grand Rapids, MI: Eerdmans, 1991), pp. 420-21.

traditional interpretation of the Bible and the rise of nationalism.[90] In short, the emotional forces at work were resentment, ambition, fear, racial prejudice and biblical literalism. German Christians were, therefore, by and large not able to embrace humility and forgiveness on a national scale as the will of God for them in this instance.

Social forces will always be active in any community and society, not just in cases of extreme historical significance such as the crucifixion of the Son of God or the Christian cooperation with the Nazi regime in Germany. In any modern society, there may be issues of consumerism with which people might have to deal, in which personal identity and worth may be tied to the degree of success, often narrowly defined by external standards, attained in terms of one's professional career, family, personal assets, personal image, influence and symbols of status and respectability which may vary from culture to culture. There will also be latent racism or discrimination simmering under the surface, against minority groups. In addition, there will be issues of national, ethnic or religious pride and ambition which afflict a community from time to time.

For these reasons, a person should always take it upon himself to question and critique prevailing socio-cultural modes of thought, their philosophies of life and *modi vivendi*, subject these to a probing cultural critique, renounce these modes of thought and venture to move away from them, considering the cost of disobedience in relation to culturally accepted, endorsed and sanctioned modes of thinking.

The key to liberation from both psychologically and socially dysfunctional thought patterns is to embrace a sense of detachment and contentment rooted in a consciousness of God's recognition of the inherent worth of an individual, which does not care for any external or internal trappings or gains because the love of God is all-sufficient. This is an effective way to tackle greed, which manifests as a need to satisfy an unbearable and false feeling of lack.

This is a good place cursorily to discuss the doctrine of heaven and hell.

In the Christian faith, the theme of immortality figures prominently both at the beginning as well as at the end of the narrative of the history of salvation. In the inception, it was offered then withdrawn

---

90. United States Holocaust Memorial Museum, 'The German Churches and the Nazi State', *Holocaust Encyclopedia*, accessed 8 October 2022, https://encyclopedia.ushmm.org/content/en/article/the-german-churches -and-the-nazi-state.

from humanity in the persons of the first couple because of the changed situation of disobedience, so as to prevent humanity from becoming immortalised in their sin-infected mortality. Rather than baptising and blessing humanity in its morally decrepit condition, God elected to lead humankind via a way of consciousness of its sinfulness, repentance and faith in the divine pardon through Christ.

In this way, as Jesus taught in the parable of the sheep and goats, those who are penitent and renounce their complicity with compulsive evil and therefore their sinful ways are appointed to be among the saints in a blessed immortality, while those who refuse to heed the prompting of the Divine Nature are also assigned a permanent place, but with those who have chosen the way of the accursed. This is how God preserves the righteous from evil and suffering, by grouping them together with like-minded souls, and sequestering the wicked in another location. By the age of immortality, the number of human persons would have been fixed, and there will be no more marriage and procreation;[91] in place of marriage, there might be some other form of mutual interpersonal commitment of varying degrees of intimacy.

To what extent is God able to guarantee the positive destinies of human beings? Because people have the freedom to act otherwise than circumstances seem to lead, resulting in the ever-present possibility of individuals seeking to overreach themselves and covet what does not belong to them, regardless of how much the truth is preached, God does not have perfect control over the spiritual responses of people. God only has the loyalty of those who choose sincerity over self-centred desire.[92]

What is the final state of the human being? Augustine of Hippo affords some insight into this in his remarks on the nature of the existence of the good and undefiled angels, towards whose community a redeemed humankind ever moves, these blessed creatures experiencing everlasting and most delightful repose and complete effortlessness in all that they put their unblemished and untrammeled minds to being acquainted with and all the succour they wish to render to us.[93]

While the second law of thermodynamics may describe the processes of the universe as tending towards disorder in a physical sense, this is indicative also of the history of human structures, orders, communities, societies and civilisations, none of which have been known to be immune

---

91. Matthew 22:30; Luke 20:35.
92. Cf. Olson, 'The Classical Free Will Theist Model of God', p. 171; and Sanders, 'Divine Providence and the Openness of God', pp. 198, 205-7.
93. Augustine, *Civ.*, XI.31, XIX.27.

to the vicissitudes of dissolution. This, however, as Jesus apprises us, is only because no body of people has ever been reputed to be fully and continually submitted to the moral laws of God and divine truth.[94] To the extent that these groupings and societies keep God's laws, they will endure.

Conclusion

God gave God's Son as an atoning sacrifice for deliverance from the power of sin, not by withholding God's power to remove the moral corruption of human nature, but by withholding God's power to rescue Jesus from the clutches of evildoers who were seeking to put him to death on false charges, with Jesus' full consent. This was in order to provide a clear and definite means by which any person could be assured of God's forgiveness for any past wrongs if only this is penitently sought.

The logic is that, whatever might cause a person to believe that God may hold a grudge against them, the same person is able to recognise that any punishment God might wish to mete out or any score God might wish to settle with this person has already been fully settled at the Cross, on which the unblemished and innocent Son of God died for sinners, payment more than enough for any individual sin, no matter the gravity, and all the sins committed by an individual over his or her lifetime, regardless of their number and gravity.

---

94. Matthew 7:24-27.

....

Selected Bibliography

Ainsworth, T., 'Form vs. Matter', *The Stanford Encyclopedia of Philosophy* (Summer 2020), https://plato.stanford.edu/archives/sum2020/entries/form -matter

Anderson, J.N., 'Why Did God Allow the Fall?' *The Gospel Coalition*, 27 June 2017, https://www.thegospelcoalition.org/article/why-did-god-allow -the-fall

Angelici, R., Introduction and Commentary, Richard of Saint-Victor, *On the Trinity: English Translation and Commentary*, trans. R. Angelici (Eugene, OR: Cascade, 2011), pp. 3-61

Anglicans Online, 'The Chalcedon Formula', 23 May 2017, http:// anglicansonline.org/basics/chalcedon.html

Aquinas, Thomas, *Summa contra gentiles*
  Critical edition:
  Sancti Thomae Aquinatis, Doctoris Angelici, Opera Omnia, Leonine Edition 13-15 (Rome: Ex Typographia Polyglotta S.C. de Propaganda Fide, 1882-)
  Translation:
  Summa Contra Gentiles, trans. A.C. Pegis, J.F. Anderson, V.J. Bourke, and C.J. O'Neil, 4 vols (London: University of Notre Dame Press, 1975)
  ———, *Summa Theologiae*
  Critical edition:
  Sancti Thomae Aquinatis, Doctoris Angelici, Opera Omnia, Leonine Edition 4-12 (Rome: Ex Typographia Polyglotta S.C. de Propaganda Fide, 1882-)
  Translations:
  Summa Theologiae, ed. T. Gilby et al. (Dominicans from English-speaking provinces of the order) 61 vols. (London: Blackfriars, c. 1964-81) *Summa Theologiae: A Concise Translation*, ed. T. McDermott (Allen, TX: Christian Classics, 1989)

Athanasius of Alexandria, *Orationes contra Arianos*
  Critical edition:
  Werke: Band I/Teil 1: Die Dogmatischen Schriften: Lfg 3: Orationes I et II contra Arianos, K. Metzler, D.U. Hansen and K. Savvidis (eds), Vol. 1-2 (Berlin, Boston: De Gruyter, 2016)

Werke: Band I/Teil 1: Die Dogmatischen Schriften: Lfg 3: Oratio III contra Arianos, K. Savvidis and K. Metzler (eds), Vol. 3 (Berlin, Boston: De Gruyter, 2015)

Translation:

Against the Arians, trans. J.H. Newman and A. Robertson, *St. Athanasius: Select Works and Letters*, in P. Schaff and H. Wace (eds), A Select Library of Nicene and Post-Nicene Fathers of the Christian Church, Second Series, vol. 4 (New York, NY: Christian Literature, 1892)

Augustine of Hippo, *Confessiones*

Critical edition:

Sancti Augustini Confessionum libri XIII, ed. L. Verheijen, Corpus Christianorum, Series Latina, XXVII (Turnhout: Brepols, 1981) (Available online)

Translation:

Confessions, trans. H. Chadwick, Oxford World's Classics (Oxford: Oxford University Press, 1992)

————, *De civitate Dei*

Critical edition:

De civitate, ed. B. Dombart and A. Kalb, Corpus Christianorum, Series Latina, XLVII-XLVIII (Turnhout: Brepols, 2014)

Translation:

The City of God, trans. M. Dods (New York: Modern Library, 1993)

————, *De diversis quaestionibus octoginta tribus*

Critical edition:

De diversis quaestionibus octoginta tribus. De octo Dulcitii quaestionibus, ed. A. Mutzenbecher, Corpus Christianorum Series Latina, XLIV A (Turnhout: Brepols, 1975)

Translation:

Responses to Miscellaneous Questions, trans. B. Ramsey, 2nd edn, The Works of Saint Augustine: A Translation for the 21st Century, Pt I, Vol. 12 (Hyde Park, NY: New City, 2008)

————, *De Trinitate*

Critical edition:

De Trinitate libri XV, ed. W.J. Mountain and F. Glorie, Corpus Christianorum Series Latina, L (Turnhout: Brepols, 1968)

Translation:

The Trinity, trans. E. Hill, 2nd edn, The Works of Saint Augustine: A Translation for the 21st Century, Pt I, Vol. 5 (Hyde Park, NY: New City, 1990)

————, *De vera religione*

Critical edition:

De doctrina christiana. De vera religione, ed. K.D. Daur and J. Martin, Corpus Christianorum Series Latina, XXXII (Turnhout: Brepols, 1962)

Translation:
"True Religion", trans. E. Hill, in *On Christian Belief*, The Works of Saint Augustine: A Translation for the 21st Century, Pt I, Vol. 8 (Hyde Park, NY: New City, 2005), 29-104

Aune, D.E., *Revelation 1-5*, Word Biblical Commentary 52A (Dallas, TX: Word, 1997)

Ayres, L., *Nicaea and Its Legacy: An Approach to Fourth-Century Trinitarian Theology* (Oxford: Oxford University Press, 2004)

Baaren, T.P. van, the Editors of Encyclopaedia Britannica, 'Monotheism in world religions', *Britannica*, Encyclopaedia Britannica, accessed 25 May 2022, https://www.britannica.com/topic/monotheism/Monotheism -in-world-religions

The Bahá'í Faith, 'What Bahá'ís Believe: Revelation', *The Official Website of the Worldwide Bahá'í Community*, accessed 18 May 2022, https://www .bahai.org/beliefs/god-his-creation/revelation

——, 'What Bahá'ís Believe: The Coming of Age of Humanity', *The Official Website of the Worldwide Bahá'í Community*, accessed 18 May 2022, https://www.bahai.org/beliefs/god-his-creation/revelation/coming-age -humanity

Baracz, S., 'How Childhood Trauma Changes Our Mental Health into Adulthood', *Psychlopaedia*, Australian Psychological Society, 13 January 2018, https://psychlopaedia.org/health/republished/how -childhood-trauma-changes-our-hormones-and-thus-our-mental -health-into-adulthood

Barclay, W., *The Mind of Jesus* (New York: HarperCollins, 1976)

Barth, K., *Die Kirchliche Dogmatik*, 13 part-vols (1932-67)
Translation:
Church Dogmatics, ed. T.F. Torrance and G.W. Bromiley, trans. T.H.L. Parker, W.B. Johnston, H. Knight *et al.*, 13 part-vols (Edinburgh: T&T Clark, 1936-69)

Basil of Caesarea, *De spiritu sancto*
Critical edition:
The Ascetica, Contra Eunomium 1-3, Ad Amphilochium de spiritu sancto, dubia et spuria, with Supplements to Volumes I-II, ed. P.J. Fedwick, Corpus Christianorum Bibliotheca Basiliana Universalis 3 (Turnout: Brepols, 1997)
Translation:
On the Holy Spirit, trans. S. Hildebrand (Yonkers, NY: St Vladimir's Seminary Press, 2011)

Beale, G.K., *The Book of Revelation*, New International Greek Testament Commentary (Grand Rapids, MI: Eerdmans, 1999)

Bernhardt, R., 'Trinity as a Framework for a Theology of Religions', *Svensk Teologisk Kvartalskrift* 90, no. 2 (2014), pp. 52-62

Boff, L., *Trinity and Society*, trans. P. Burns (Eugene, OR: Wipf & Stock, 2005)

Bowker, J., *The Message and the Book: Sacred Texts of the World's Religions* (London: Atlantic Books, 2011)

Boyd, A., 'Judas Iscariot: A Cultural Hero?' *The Boyds*, 1 August 2011, http://pngboyd.blogspot.com/2011/08/judas-iscariot-cultural-hero.html

Boyd, G., *Is God to Blame? Beyond Pat Answers to the Problem of Suffering* (Downers Grove, IL: InterVarsity Press, 2003)

Bradshaw, D., 'Plato in the Cappadocian Fathers', in R.C. Fowler (ed.), *Plato in the Third Sophistic*, Millennium Studies 50 (Berlin: De Gruyter, 2014), pp. 193-210

Brown, D., 'Trinitarian Personhood and Individuality', in R.J. Feenstra and C. Plantinga Jr (eds), *Trinity, Incarnation, and Atonement: Philosophical and Theological Essays* (Notre Dame, IN: University of Notre Dame Press, 1989), pp. 48-78

——, *The Divine Trinity* (Eugene, OR: Wipf & Stock, 2011)

Brownson, J.V., *Bible, Gender, Sexuality: Reframing the Church's Debate on Same-Sex Relations* (Grand Rapids, MI: Eerdmans, 2013)

Calvin, J., *Institutio Christianae religionis.*
Critical edition:
Institutio Christianae religionis, Ioannis Calvini Opera Selecta, Vols III-V, ed. P. Barth and G. Niesel (Munich: Chr. Kaiser, 1926-1952)
Translation:
Institutes of the Christian Religion, ed. J.T. McNeill, trans. F.L. Battles, 2 vols, The Library of Christian Classics (Louisville, KY: Westminster John Knox, 2006)

Carson, D.A., *The Gospel According to John*, The Pillar New Testament Commentary (Grand Rapids, MI: Eerdmans, 1991)

Castelo, D., 'Qualified Impassibility', in R.J. Matz and A.C. Thornhill (eds), *Divine Impassibility: Four Views of God's Emotions and Suffering* (Downers Grove, IL: IVP Academic, 2019), pp. 53-74

Cherian, M.T., 'Hinduism', in W.A. Dyrness and V.-M. Kärkkäinen (eds), *Global Dictionary of Theology* (Downers Grove, IL: InterVarsity, 2008), pp. 386-96

Cherry, K., 'The Story of Genie Wiley', *Verywell Mind*, Dotdash Meredith, last modified 7 February 2022, https://www.verywellmind.com/genie-the-story-of-the-wild-child-2795241

Chia, R., 'Question 11: What about Those Who Have Never Heard about Jesus? Are They Going to Hell?' in R. Chen (ed.), *Honest Questions, Honest Answers: 20 Tough Questions on Issues of Life & Eternity* (Singapore: St Andrew's Cathedral, 2011), pp. 52-55

Child Family Community Australia, 'Effects of Child Abuse and Neglect for Adult Survivors', The Australian Institute of Family Studies, January 2014, https://aifs.gov.au/resources/policy-and-practice-papers/effects-child-abuse-and-neglect-adult-survivors

Chua, E.Z.-K./Chua, Z.-K., *'God-ness', 'God-ity', and God: A Historical Study and Synthesis of the Christian Doctrine of the Divine Being*, 2nd edn (New Orleans: LA: University Press of the South, 2022)

———, 'How Is Jesus One Person with Two Natures? Heresies and the Mainstream "Chalcedonian" Position', *The Courier* (January 2019), pp. 36-38, https://cathedral.org.sg/uploads/bulletin_files/courier _jan_2019_web.pdf

———, 'Jung Young Lee's Biblical-Cultural Trinity: A Systematic Theology from East Asia, PhD diss., University of Otago, 2021

Collver III, A.B., 'Who Is Man?: Image and Likeness in Irenaeus', *Concordia Student Journal* 22, no. 1 (Epiphany 1999), pp. 27-36

Colwell, J.E., 'Time and Eternity', in S.B. Ferguson, D.F. Wright, and J.I. Packer (eds), *New Dictionary of Theology* (Downers Grove, IL: IVP Academic, 1988), pp. 688-89

Copan, P., *Is God a Moral Monster? Making Sense of the Old Testament God* (Grand Rapids, MI: Baker, 2011)

Corduan, W., *Pocket Guide to World Religions* (Downers Grove, IL: InterVarsity, 2005)

Cross, F.L., and E.A. Livingstone (eds), *The Oxford Dictionary of the Christian Church*, 3rd edn (Oxford: Oxford University Press, 1997)

Cuncic, A., 'What Does It Mean to Be "Triggered": Types of Triggering Events and Coping Strategies', *Verywell Mind*, Dotdash Meredith, updated 10 March 2022, https://www.verywellmind.com/what-does-it-mean-to-be -triggered-4175432

Davies, S., S. McIntyre and C. Rypma, 'Detransition Rates in a National UK Gender Identity Clinic', in *3rd Biennial EPATH Conference, 'Inside Matters: On Law, Ethics and Religion'* (European Professional Association for Transgender Health, 2019), p. 118

D'Costa, G., *The Meeting of Religions and the Trinity*, Faith Meets Faith (Maryknoll, NY: Orbis, 2000)

———, *Theology and Religious Pluralism: The Challenge of Other Religions*, Signposts in Theology (Oxford: Basil Blackwell, 1986)

Denny, F.M., *An Introduction to Islam*, 4th edn (Boston: Prentice Hall, 2011)

Dickson, D., *Praelectiones in confessionem fidei*, lectures, University of Edinburgh, 1650s
  Translation:
  Truth's Victory Over Error: A Commentary on the Westminster Confession of Faith, ed. J.R. de Witt (1684) (Edinburgh: Banner of Truth, 2007)

Dillard, R.B., and T. Longman III, *An Introduction to the Old Testament*, 2nd edn (Grand Rapids, MI: Zondervan, 2007)

Dolezal, J.E., 'Strong Impassibility', in R.J. Matz and A.C. Thornhill (eds), *Divine Impassibility: Four Views of God's Emotions and Suffering* (Downers Grove, IL: IVP Academic, 2019), 13-37

Doniger, W., *On Hinduism* (Oxford: Oxford University Press, 2014)

Dorner, I.A., 'Über die richtige Fassung des dogmatischen Begriffs der Unveränderlichkeit Gottes, mit besonderer Beziehung auf das gegenseitige Verhältniss zwischen Gottes übergeschichlichem und geschichtlichem Leben', in *Jahrbücher für deutsche Theologie* I/2 (1856), pp. 361ff.; II/3 (1857), pp. 440ff.; III/4 (1858), pp. 479ff (Gotha and Stuttgart: Besser)

Translation:
Divine Immutability: A Critical Reconsideration, trans. R.R. Williams and C. Welch, Fortress Texts in Modern Theology (Minneapolis, MN: Fortress, 1994)

Duggan, L.G., 'Indulgence', *Britannica*, Encyclopaedia Britannica, last updated 25 February 2023, https://www.britannica.com/topic/indulgence

Dunn, J.D.G., *Did the First Christians Worship Jesus?: The New Testament Evidence* (Louisville, KY: Westminster John Knox, 2010)

Dupuis, J., *Toward a Christian Theology of Religious Pluralism* (Maryknoll, NY: Orbis, 1997)

Dyrness, W.A., and V.-M. Kärkkäinen, Introduction to *Global Dictionary of Theology*, ed. W.A. Dyrness and V.-M. Kärkkäinen (Downers Grove, IL: InterVarsity, 2008), pp. vii-xiv

Edwards, J.R., *The Gospel According to Mark*, The Pillar New Testament Commentary (Grand Rapids, MI: Eerdmans, 2002)

Erickson, M.J., *Christian Theology*, 3rd edn (Grand Rapids, MI: Baker Academic, 2013)

Esslemont, J.E., *Bahá'u'lláh and the New Era: An Introduction to the Bahá'í Faith* (Wilmette, IL: Bahá'í Publishing, 2006)

Evans, C.A., *Mark 8:27-16:20*, Word Biblical Commentary 34B (Nashville, TN: Thomas Nelson, 2001)

Fairbairn, D., 'The Chalcedonian Definition: Christ's Two Natures', *Credo Magazine* 11, no. 2 (12 July 2021), https://credomag.com/article/the-chalcedonian-definition

Felman, A., 'What to Know about Compulsive Sexual Behaviour', *Medical News Today*, Healthline Media, 8 October 2019, https://www.medicalnewstoday.com/articles/182473#treatment

Ferguson, E., 'Irenaeus', in S.B. Ferguson, D.F. Wright and J.I. Packer (eds), *New Dictionary of Theology* (Downers Grove, IL: IVP Academic, 1988), pp. 340-42

Fohr, S., *Jainism: A Guide for the Perplexed* (London: Bloomsbury, 2015)

Ganssle, G.E., (ed.), *God and Time: Four Views* (Downers Grove, IL: InterVarsity Press, 2001)

Gentz, J., *Understanding Chinese Religions* (Edinburgh: Dunedin Academic, 2013)

Gingrich, F.W., and F.W. Danker (eds), *Shorter Lexicon of the Greek New Testament*, 2nd edn (Chicago: University of Chicago Press, 1983)

Goh, W.S.-C., 'Doctrines: An Interplay between Experience and Scripture', *Roman Catholic Archdiocese of Singapore*, 19 May 2022, https://www.catholic.sg/19-may-2022-thursday-5th-week-of-easter

Gregory of Nyssa, *Ad Ablabium* (*Quod non sint tres dei*)
   Critical edition:
   'Ad Ablabium, Quod non sint tres dei', Gregorii Nysseni Opera Vol. 3, Pt 1, ed. F. Müller, (Leiden: Brill, 1958)

Translation:
On *'Not Three Gods'*, to *Ablabius*, trans. H.A. Wilson, in P. Schaff and H. Wace (eds), *A Select Library of Nicene and Post-Nicene Fathers of the Christian Church*, Second Series, vol. 5, (New York: The Christian Literature Company, 1893), pp. 331-36

Grudem, W., *Systematic Theology: An Introduction to Biblical Doctrine* (Leicester: Inter-Varsity Press, 1994)

Gustafson, H., 'Is Transreligious Theology Unavoidable in Interreligious Theology and Dialogue?' *Open Theology* 2, no. 1 (2016), pp. 248-60

Hardacre, H., *Shinto: A History* (Oxford: Oxford University Press, 2016)

Harnack, A., *What is Christianity? Sixteen Lectures Delivered in the University of Berlin during the Winter-term, 1899-1900*, trans. T.B. Saunders (San Diego, CA: The Book Tree, 2006)

Hart, T.A., *The Dictionary of Historical Theology* (Grand Rapids, MI: Wm B. Eerdmans, 2000)

Hedges, P., *Controversies in Interreligious Dialogue and the Theology of Religions*, Controversies in Contextual Theology (London: SCM, 2010)

Heim, S.M., *The Depth of the Riches: A Trinitarian Theology of Religious Ends* (Grand Rapids, MI: Eerdmans, 2001)

Helm, P., 'Classical Calvinist Doctrine of God', in B.A. Ware (ed.), *Perspectives on the Doctrine of God: Four Views* (Nashville, TN: Broadman & Holman, 2008), pp. 5-52

———, 'Responses to Bruce A. Ware: Response by Paul Helm', in B.A. Ware (ed.), *Perspectives on the Doctrine of God: Four Views* (Nashville, TN: Broadman & Holman, 2008), pp. 121-29

Hick, J., Review of S.M. Heim, *The Depth of the Riches: A Trinitarian Theology of Religious Ends* (Grand Rapids, MI: Eerdmans, 2001), *Reviews in Religion and Theology* 8, no. 4 (September 2001)

Holder, R., 'Karl Barth and the Legitimacy of Natural Theology', *Themelios* 26, no. 3 (Summer 2001), pp. 22-37

Holladay, W.L., *A Concise Hebrew and Aramaic Lexicon of the Old Testament* (Leiden: Brill, 2000)

Hoover, J., 'Islamic Monotheism and the Trinity', *The Conrad Grebel Review* 27, no. 1 (Winter 2009), pp. 57-82

Hudson, M., 'Battle of Milvian Bridge', *Britannica*, Encyclopaedia Britannica, 12 February 2021, https://www.britannica.com/topic/Battle-of-the -Milvian-Bridge

Hunsinger, G., *How to Read Karl Barth: The Shape of His Theology* (Oxford: Oxford University Press, 1991)

Hurtado, L.W., *One God, One Lord: Early Christian Devotion and Ancient Jewish Monotheism* (London: SCM, 1988)

Inwagen, P. van, and D. Howard-Snyder, 'Trinity', in E. Craig (ed.), *Routledge Encyclopedia of Philosophy Online* (London: Routledge, 1998) https://doi .org/10.4324/9780415249126-K105-1

Jackson, A.V.W., 'Zoroastrianism and the Resemblances between It and Christianity', *The Biblical World* 27, no. 5 (May 1906), pp. 335-43, https://www.jstor.org/stable/3140852

Johansen, T.K., Review of S. Broadie, *Nature and Divinity in Plato's Timaeus* (Cambridge: Cambridge University Press, 2012), *Notre Dame Philosophical Reviews*, University of Notre Dame, August 2012, https://ndpr.nd.edu/reviews/nature-and-divinity-in-plato-s-timaeus

Johnson, N.D., and M. Koyama, 'The State, Toleration, and Religious Freedom', GMU Working Paper in Economics No. 18-18 (George Mason University, 30 May 2018)

Johnson, R., and A. Cureton, 'Kant's Moral Philosophy', *The Stanford Encyclopedia of Philosophy* (Spring 2022), https://plato.stanford.edu/archives/spr2022/entries/kant-moral

Karamanolis, G., 'The Platonism of Eusebius of Caesarea', in R.C. Fowler (ed.), *Plato in the Third Sophistic*, Millennium Studies 50 (Berlin: De Gruyter, 2014), pp. 171-92

Keehn, G., 'Does the Theory of Recollection Preclude Learning? A New Dimension to Platonic Nativism', *Philosophy of Education* (2014), pp. 158-65

Kelly, J.F., *The Ecumenical Councils of the Catholic Church: A History* (Collegeville, MN: Liturgical, 2009)

Kelly, J.N.D., *Early Christian Doctrines*, rev. edn (San Francisco: Harper & Row, 1978)

Kenny, A.J.P., 'Aristotle: The unmoved mover', *Britannica*, Encyclopaedia Britannica, accessed 13 July 2022, https://www.britannica.com/biography/Aristotle/The-unmoved-mover

Kim, H.Y., *A Theology of Dao* (Maryknoll, NY: Orbis Books, 2017)

Komjathy, L., *The Daoist Tradition: An Introduction* (London: Bloomsbury, 2013)

LaCugna, C.M., *God For Us: The Trinity and Christian Life* (New York: HarperCollins, 1992)

Latourette, K.S., *A History of Christianity: Vol. 1: Beginnings to 1500* (Peabody, MA: Prince, 1997)

Lee, H.-L., 'National Day Rally 2009', Prime Minister's Office Singapore, 16 August 2009, https://www.pmo.gov.sg/Newsroom/prime-minister-lee-hsien-loongs-national-day-rally-2009-speech-english

Lee, J.Y., *Cosmic Religion* (New York: Philosophical Library, 1973)

———, *The Theology of Change: A Christian Concept of God in an Eastern Perspective* (Maryknoll, NY: Orbis, 1979)

———, *The Trinity in Asian Perspective* (Nashville, TN: Abingdon, 1996)

Lincoln, A.T., *Ephesians*, Word Biblical Commentary 42 (Waco, TX: Word, 1990)

Loke, A.T.-E., *A Kryptic Model of the Incarnation*, Ashgate New Critical Thinking in Religion, Theology and Biblical Studies (Farnham: Ashgate, 2014)

Lonergan, B., *De constitutione Christi ontologica et psychologica* (Rome: Pontifical Gregorian University, 1956)
Latin text with translation:
The Ontological and Psychological Constitution of Christ: Volume 7, trans. M.G. Shields (Toronto: University of Toronto Press, 2005)
Luther, M., *De servo arbitrio*
Critical edition:
D. Martin Luthers Werke XVIII, Kritische Gesamtausgabe, ed. A. Freitag (Weimar: Böhlau, 1883-), pp. 597ff.
Translation:
The Bondage of the Will, trans. J.I. Packer and O.R. Johnston (Grand Rapids, MI: Revell, 1990)
MacDonald, S., 'The Divine Nature: Being and Goodness', in D.V. Meconi and E. Stump (eds), *The Cambridge Companion to Augustine*, 2nd edn (Cambridge: Cambridge University Press, 2014), pp. 22-26
Madole, J.W., S.L. Johnson, and C.S. Carver, 'A Model of Aggressive Behavior: Early Adversity, Impulsivity, and Response Inhibition', *Journal of Aggression, Maltreatment & Trauma* 29, no. 5 (2020), pp. 594-610
Mandair, A.-P.S., *Sikhism: A Guide for the Perplexed* (London: Bloomsbury, 2013)
Matthews, J.F., and D.M. Nicol, 'Constantine I', *Britannica*, Encyclopaedia Britannica, 26 July 1999, https://www.britannica.com/biography/Constantine-I-Roman-emperor
Mayo Clinic Staff, 'Binge-Eating Disorder: Diagnosis & Treatment', Mayo Foundation for Medical Education and Research, 5 May 2018, https://www.mayoclinic.org/diseases-conditions/binge-eating-disorder/diagnosis-treatment/drc-20353633
———, 'Binge-Eating Disorder: Symptoms & Causes', Mayo Foundation for Medical Education and Research, 5 May 2018, https://www.mayoclinic.org/diseases-conditions/binge-eating-disorder/symptoms-causes/syc-20353627
———, 'Compulsive Sexual Behaviour: Symptoms & Causes', Mayo Clinic for Medical Education and Research, 7 February 2020, https://www.mayoclinic.org/diseases-conditions/compulsive-sexual-behavior/symptoms-causes/syc-20360434
———, 'Post-Traumatic Stress Disorder (PTSD): Symptoms & Causes', Mayo Foundation for Medical Education and Research, 6 July 2018, https://www.mayoclinic.org/diseases-conditions/post-traumatic-stress-disorder/symptoms-causes/syc-20355967
McDonald, H.D., 'Nestorius', in S.B. Ferguson, D.F. Wright and J.I. Packer (eds), *New Dictionary of Theology* (Downers Grove, IL: IVP Academic, 1988), pp. 457-58
Merton, T., Introduction to Augustine, *The City of God*, trans. Marcus Dods (New York, NY: Random House, 1993), pp. xi-xvii

Miller, P., 'How to Gain an Audience and Lose Your Soul', *The Gospel Coalition*, 12 December 2022, https://www.thegospelcoalition.org/article /gain-audience-lose-soul

Moltmann, J., *Der gekreuzigte Gott: Das Kreuz Christi als Grund und Kritik christlicher Theologie* (Munich: Chr. Kaiser, 1972)

Translation:

The Crucified God: The Cross of Christ as the Foundation and Criticism of Christian Theology, trans. R.A. Wilson and J. Bowden (New York: Harper & Row, 1974)

———, *Trinität und Reich Gottes: zur Gotteslehre* (Munich: Chr. Kaiser, 1980)

Translation:

The Trinity and the Kingdom: The Doctrine of God, trans. M. Kohl (Minneapolis, MN: Fortress, 1993)

Mong, A.I.-R., 'In Many and Diverse Ways: Examining Jacques Dupuis' Theology of Religious Pluralism', *Dialogue & Alliance* 25, no. 2 (2011), pp. 71-85, https://www.upf.org/resources/speeches-and-articles/4092 -a-mong-ih-ren-in-many-and-diverse-ways-examining-jacques-dupuis -theology-of-religious-pluralism

Morris, L., *The Gospel According to Matthew*, The Pillar New Testament Commentary (Grand Rapids, MI: Eerdmans, 1992)

Mozley, J.K., *The Impassibility of God: A Survey of Christian Thought* (Cambridge: Cambridge University Press, 1926)

Muck, T.C., 'Buddhism', in W.A. Dyrness and V.-M. Kärkkäinen (eds), *Global Dictionary of Theology* (Downers Grove, IL: InterVarsity, 2008, pp. 121-25

Murphy, B., 'The Development of Doctrine', *Simply Catholic*, accessed 22 July 2022, https://www.simplycatholic.com/the-development-of-doctrine

Newman, J.H., *An Essay on the Development of Christian Doctrine* (London: James Toovey, 1845)

NHS, 'Treatment – Post-Traumatic Stress Disorder', last reviewed 13 May 2022, https://www.nhs.uk/mental-health/conditions/post-traumatic -stress-disorder-ptsd/treatment

Nostra Aetate: Declaration on the Relation of the Church to Non-Christian Religions, The Holy See, 28 October 1965, https://www.vatican.va/archive /hist_councils/ii_vatican_council/documents/vat-ii_decl_19651028 _nostra-aetate_en.html

Novotney, A., 'The Risks of Social Isolation', *Monitor on Psychology* 50, no. 5 (March 2020), https://www.apa.org/monitor/2019/05/ce-corner-isolation .html

Oei, A.W., 'The Impassible God Who "Cried"', *Themelios* 41, no. 2 (2016), pp. 238-47

Oliver, J.D., *Buddhism: An Introduction to the Buddha's Life, Teachings, and Practices*, The Essential Wisdom Library (New York: St. Martin's Essentials, 2019)

Olson, R.E., 'Responses to Bruce A. Ware: Response by Roger E. Olson', in
B.A. Ware (ed.), *Perspectives on the Doctrine of God: Four Views* (Nashville,
TN: Broadman & Holman, 2008), pp. 129-36
———, 'The Classical Free Will Theist Model of God', in B.A. Ware (ed.),
Perspectives on the Doctrine of God: Four Views (Nashville, TN: Broadman &
Holman, 2008), pp. 148-72
———, *The Journey of Modern Theology: From Reconstruction to Deconstruction*
(Downers Grove, IL: IVP Academic, 2013)
Oord, T.J., 'Strong Passibility', in R. J. Matz and A. C. Thornhill (eds), *Divine
Impassibility: Four Views of God's Emotions and Suffering* (Downers Grove,
IL: IVP Academic, 2019), pp. 129-51
Outler, A.C., 'The Wesleyan Quadrilateral in Wesley', *Wesleyan Theological
Journal* 20, no. 1 (Spring 1985), pp. 7-18, https://wtsociety.com/files/wt
s_journal/1985-wtj-20-1.pdf.
Packer, J.I., 'God', in S. B. Ferguson, D. F. Wright, and J. I. Packer (eds), *New
Dictionary of Theology* (Downers Grove, IL: IVP Academic, 1988),
pp. 274-77
Pannenberg, W., *Systematische Theologie*, 3 vols (Göttingen: Vandenhoeck &
Ruprecht, 1988-93)
Translation:
Systematic Theology, trans. G.W. Bromiley, 3 vols (Grand Rapids, MI:
Eerdmans, 1991-98)
Park, A., *The Genesis Genealogies: God's Administration in the History of
Redemption* (Book 1) (Singapore: Periplus, 2009)
Patheos, 'What Is the Creation Story in Hinduism?' *Patheos Library of
World Faiths & Religions*, accessed 25 May 2022, https://www.patheos
.com/library/answers-to-frequently-asked-religion-questions/what-is-the
-creation-story-in-hinduism
Patton, J., 'Including the Exclusivists in Interfaith', *The Review of Faith &
International Affairs* 16, no. 3 (2018), pp. 23-33
Peckham, J.C., 'Qualified Passibility', in R. J. Matz and A. C. Thornhill (eds),
Divine Impassibility: Four Views of God's Emotions and Suffering (Downers
Grove, IL: IVP Academic, 2019), pp. 87-113
Pelikan, J., *The Christian Tradition: A History of the Development of Doctrine*,
5 vols (Chicago: University of Chicago Press, 1971-89)
Plato, *Timaeus*
Critical edition:
Timaeus, inter alia, Platonis Opera, IV, ed. J. Burnet (Oxford: Clarendon,
1902)
Translation:
Timaeus and Critias, trans. R. Waterfield (Oxford: Oxford University
Press, 2008)
Porvaznik, P., *et al.*, 'The Facts and Stats on "33,000 Denominations": The
20,000, 30,000 numbers and David Barrett's statistics, Part II', *Evangelical*

Catholic Apologetics, 28 August 2007. https://freerepublic.com/focus/
f-religion/1956752/posts#Independents
Potgieter, P.C., 'Calvin and Other Religions', *Acta Theologica* 24, issue 1
(2004), pp. 148-49, http://hdl.handle.net/11660/7188
Pratt, D., 'Exclusivism and Exclusivity: A Contemporary Theological
Challenge,' *Pacifica* 20, no. 3 (October 2007), pp. 291-306.
———, 'Fundamentalism, Exclusivism and Religious Extremism', in
D. Cheetham, D. Pratt and D. Thomas (eds), *Understanding Interreligious
Relations* (Oxford: Oxford University Press, 2013), pp. 241-61
———, 'Religious Identity and the Denial of Alterity: Plurality and the
Problem of Exclusivism', in P.D. Bubbio and P.A. Quadrio (eds),
The Relation of Philosophy to Religion Today (Newcastle-upon-Tyne:
Cambridge Scholars Publishing, 2011), pp. 201-15
Prince, J., *Destined to Reign: The Secret to Effortless Success, Wholeness and
Victorious Living* (Tulsa, OK: Harrison, 2007)
———, 'Receive Two Gifts to Reign Over Addictions' (Pt 1/3), accessed
8 June 2022, https://blog.josephprince.com/two-gifts-to-reign-over
-addictions
The Quantum Atlas, 'Superposition', *The Quantum Atlas*, accessed 29
December 2022, https://quantumatlas.umd.edu/entry/superposition
Raina, K., 'How Did Sati Get Abolished In India?' *Feminism in India*, 29
October 2018, https://feminisminindia.com/2018/10/29/sati-history-india
Rea, M.C., 'Polytheism and Christian Belief', *Journal of Theological Studies* 57,
no. 1 (April 2006), pp. 133-48
Richard of Saint-Victor, *De Trinitate*
  Critical edition:
  *Ricardus, Prior S. Victoris Parisiensis, De Trinitate: Texte critique avec
  introduction, notes et tables*, ed. J. Ribaillier, Textes philosophiques du
  Moyen Age 6 (Paris: J. Vrin, 1958)
  Translation:
  On the Trinity: English Translation and Commentary, trans. R. Angelici
  (Eugene, OR: Cascade, 2011)
Römer, T., *The Invention of God*, trans. R. Geuss (Cambridge, MA: Harvard
University Press, 2015)
Rose, J., *Zoroastrianism: An Introduction* (London: Bloomsbury, 2012)
Samartha, S.J., *Between Two Cultures: Ecumenical Ministry in a Pluralist
World* (Geneva: WCC, 1997)
———, *One Christ, Many Religions: Toward a Revised Christology* (Maryknoll,
NY: Orbis, 1994)
Sanders, J., 'Divine Providence and the Openness of God', in B.A. Ware (ed.),
Perspectives on the Doctrine of God: Four Views (Nashville, TN: Broadman &
Holman, 2008), pp. 196-240
———, 'Historical Considerations', in C. Pinnock, R. Rice, J. Sanders, W.
Hasker and D. Basinger, *The Openness of God: A Biblical Challenge to the
Traditional Understanding of God* (Downers Grove, IL: InterVarsity, 1994),
pp. 59-100

——, 'Responses to Bruce A. Ware: Response by John Sanders', in B.A. Ware (ed.), *Perspectives on the Doctrine of God: Four Views* (Nashville, TN: Broadman & Holman, 2008), pp. 137-47

——, 'Responses to Paul Helm: Response by John Sanders', in B.A. Ware (ed.), *Perspectives on the Doctrine of God: Four Views* (Nashville, TN: Broadman & Holman, 2008), pp. 58-70

——, 'Responses to Roger E. Olson: Response by John Sanders', in B.A. Ware (ed.), *Perspectives on the Doctrine of God: Four Views* (Nashville, TN: Broadman & Holman, 2008), pp. 179-89

Smith, M., 'Japanese Mythology: Cosmogony', Canadian Studies Center, Michigan State University, 29 August 2019, https://canadianstudies.isp .msu.edu/news_article/22292

Solomon, L.D., 'A Meditation on God's Omnipotence that Has Been Called into Question by the Holocaust and the Threat against Israel', *Midstream* (Summer 2012), pp. 33-35, *Gale General OneFile*, accessed 12 October 2020, https://link.gale.com/apps/doc/A310867317/ITOF?u=otago &sid=ITOF&xid=62e0951c

Stahl, W.A., 'Christendom: One Thing the Reformation Did Not Change', *Impetus* (Winter/Spring 2017), Luther College, University of Regina, https://www.luthercollege.edu/university/academics/impetus /winterspring-2017/christendom-one-thing-the-reformation-did-not -change

Stark, R., *Discovering God: The Origins of the Great Religions and the Evolution of Belief* (New York, NY: HarperOne, 2007)

Stolt, B., 'Martin Luther on God as a Father', *Lutheran Quarterly* 8 (1994), pp. 384-95, ATLA Serials, https://gudribassakums.files.wordpress. com/2012/10/1994-luther-on-god-stolt.pdf

Stott, J., *The Cross of Christ* (Downers Grove, IL: InterVarsity, 1986)

Swaab, D.F., 'Sexual Differentiation of the Brain and Behavior', *Best Practice & Research Clinical Endocrinology & Metabolism* 21, no. 3 (September 2007), pp. 431-44

Terr, L.C., '"Forbidden Games": Post-Traumatic Child's Play', *Journal of the American Academy of Child & Adolescent Psychiatry* 20, no. 4 (September 1981), pp. 741-60

Thatamanil, J.J., *Circling the Elephant: A Comparative Theology of Religious Diversity*, Comparative Theology: Thinking Across Traditions (New York: Fordham University Press, 2020)

Timpano, K.R., M.E. Keough, B. Mahaffey, N.B. Schmidt and J. Abramowitz, 'Parenting and Obsessive Compulsive Symptoms: Implications of Authoritarian Parenting', *Journal of Cognitive Psychotherapy* 24, no. 3 (2010), pp. 151-64

Tornau, C., 'Saint Augustine', *The Stanford Encyclopedia of Philosophy* (Winter 2019), https://plato.stanford.edu/archives/win2019/entries /augustine

United States Holocaust Memorial Museum, 'The German Churches and the Nazi State', *Holocaust Encyclopaedia*, accessed 8 October 2022, https://

encyclopedia.ushmm.org/content/en/article/the-german-churches-and
-the-nazi-state

University of Memphis, 'Amun, Mut, and Khonsu', accessed 1 June 2022,
https://www.memphis.edu/hypostyle/meaning_function/mut-khonsu.php

Verbrugge, V.D., (ed.), *The NIV Theological Dictionary of New Testament
Words* (Grand Rapids, MI: Zondervan, 2000)

Versaldi, G., and A.V. Zani, '"Male and Female He Created Them": Towards
a Path of Dialogue on the Question of Gender Theory in Education,'
Congregation for Catholic Education, Vatican City, 2019, http://www
.educatio.va/content/dam/cec/Documenti/19_0997_INGLESE.pdf

Villines, Z., 'Religious OCD: Separating Shame from Spirituality',
GoodTherapy, 2 November 2018, https://www.goodtherapy.org/blog
/religious-ocd-separating-shame-from-spirituality-1102184

Volf, M., *Allah: A Christian Response* (New York, NY: HarperOne, 2011)

Vos, A., 'Aristotelianism', in S. B. Ferguson, D. F. Wright, and J. I. Packer
(eds), *New Dictionary of Theology* (Downers Grove, IL: IVP Academic,
1988), pp. 43-45

Wade, N., 'The Evolution of the God Gene', *The New York Times*, 14
November 2009, https://www.nytimes.com/2009/11/15/weekinreview/12wade
.html

Walters, K., *Atheism: A Guide for the Perplexed* (London: Bloomsbury, 2010)

Ward, G., *How the Light Gets in: Ethical Life I* (Oxford: Oxford University
Press, 2016)

Ware, B.A., 'A Modified Calvinist Doctrine of God', in B.A. Ware (ed.),
Perspectives on the Doctrine of God: Four Views (Nashville, TN: Broadman &
Holman, 2008), pp. 76-120

———, 'Responses to Paul Helm: Response by Bruce A. Ware', in B.A. Ware (ed.),
Perspectives on the Doctrine of God: Four Views (Nashville, TN: Broadman &
Holman, 2008), pp. 70-75

Warfield, B.B., 'Introductory Essay on Augustin and the Pelagian Controversy',
in P. Schaff (ed.), *A Select Library of the Nicene and Post-Nicene Fathers of the
Christian Church* (Grand Rapids, MI: Eerdmans, 1956), pp. xiii-lxxi

Watts, J.D.W., *Isaiah 1-33*, Word Biblical Commentary 24 (Nashville, TN:
Thomas Nelson, 2005)

———, *Isaiah 34-66*, rev. edn, Word Biblical Commentary 25 (Grand Rapids,
MI: Zondervan, 2005)

Wax, T., '"Christ and Culture": An Overview of a Christian Classic', *The
Gospel Coalition*, 25 February 2015, https://www.thegospelcoalition.org
/blogs/trevin-wax/christ-and-culture-an-overview-of-a-christian-classic

WebMD Editorial Contributors, 'Signs of Low Self-Esteem', *WebMD*, last
reviewed 16 December 2022, https://www.webmd.com/mental-health
/signs-low-self-esteem

Welby, J., 'The Big Idea: Is a World without Violent Conflict Really Possible?'
The Guardian, 6 June 2022, https://www.theguardian.com/books/2022
/jun/06/the-big-idea-is-a-world-without-violent-conflict-really-possible

The Westminster Confession of Faith, The Westminster Assembly, 1647, Free Presbyterian Church of Scotland, accessed 28 March 2023, https://www.fpchurch.org.uk/about-us/important-documents/the-westminster-confession-of-faith

Whitaker, J., '"The Story of God"': A Buddhist Perspective on Creation', *Patheos*, 20 April 2016, https://www.patheos.com/blogs/americanbuddhist/2016/04/the-story-of-god-a-buddhist-perspective-on-creation.html

Whitford, D.M., 'Martin Luther (1483-1546)', *Internet Encyclopedia of Philosophy*, accessed 27 April 2022, https://iep.utm.edu/luther

Wiles, M., *The Making of Christian Doctrine: A Study in the Principles of Early Doctrinal Development* (Cambridge: Cambridge University Press, 1967)

Williams, M., 'Gnosticism', *Britannica*, Encyclopaedia Britannica, 20 July 1998, https://www.britannica.com/topic/gnosticism

Woodberry, J.D., 'Islam', in W. A. Dyrness and V.-M. Kärkkäinen (eds), *Global Dictionary of Theology* (Downers Grove, IL: InterVarsity, 2008), pp. 425-31

Wright, D.F., 'Theology', in S.B. Ferguson, D.F. Wright, and J.I. Packer (eds), *New Dictionary of Theology* (Downers Grove, IL: IVP Academic, 1988), pp. 680-81

Wright, N.T., *Evil and the Justice of God* (Downers Grove, IL: IVP, 2006)

Yong, A., *Beyond the Impasse: Toward a Pneumatological Theology of Religions* (Grand Rapids, MI: Baker Academic, 2003)

——, *The Spirit Poured Out on All Flesh: Pentecostalism and the Possibility of Global Theology* (Grand Rapids, MI: Baker Academic, 2005)

Subject Index

Scripture Index

Old Testament

New Testament